Knock 'em Dead helps you find jobs *and* turn the interviews into job offers

"I just wanted to say thank you! After reading your book and following its precepts, I got my dream job within two months! (And I've been searching for almost a year!)"

—J. B. D.

"I landed a job that was over double the salary of my previous job, on the same day as I interviewed, which is very, very rare in a state job. *Knock 'em Dead* really says it all. I was able to negotiate to the absolute top end of the starting pay [because] of my resume, cover letter, and interview, and the chapter on salary negotiations. Your book was extremely helpful in presenting the best part of me."

—S. J., KANSAS

"The interviews nowadays are much tougher than they were four or five years ago. I am so thankful that I had heard about you! I heard of your book right after I bombed out on three interviews. I read and studied it. The first interview that I went on after doing this ended up in a job being offered to me! The interviewer told me that I was the best interviewee she'd seen! Thanks a million for writing your book."

—K. P., HOUSTON, TX

"Your book changed my life!! It really did. It shaped the way that I went about getting back into the workforce and the way that I see myself and what I bring to a company. Thank you!"

—R., LITTLETON, CO

"One of my most-admired authors in the career advice space. Martin always challenges me to think about career development issues in new and innovative ways."

—THE *WALL STREET JOURNAL'S* ALEXANDRA LEVIT ON HER *WATER COOLER WISDOM* BLOG

Knock 'em Dead helps people from everywhere get great jobs anywhere

"I'm a graduating senior from Johnson & Wales University. I read your book, *Knock 'em Dead*, which has helped me score many offers in just the past weeks."

—D. T., HONG KONG–BOUND

"I have used the UK version of *Knock 'em Dead* to successfully improve my career prospects. This is the best job-hunting book on the market bar none; keep up the good work."

—PAUL BREMNER, LONDON, UK

"WOOOOOOOOHOOOOOOOOO!!!!!
It worked!! I got the job!!!!!!!!!!!!!!!!!!!!!!!!!!!!!!!!!!!
I luv u Martin!"

—A., EDMONTON, CANADA

Knock 'em Dead works for career changers

"[After leaving the Army] I bought all three of your books, *Knock 'em Dead Resumes, Cover Letters*, and *The Ultimate Job Search Guide*. I read each book cover to cover. I followed each step in your books and I got an entry-level job of my dreams. I was prepared because of your books. Thanks!"

—K. G.

Knock 'em Dead is inspirational

"I've been a reader of the KED books for quite some time. You've made a difference in my life and saying 'Thank you' doesn't begin to express my gratitude."
—T. S.

"You helped me get a job a couple years ago; now I've just accepted a new job. Thank you again for everything you do and all the people you help; I've read your books so many times you feel like a friend. You've been an inspiration to me again and I could not take this job in good conscience without acknowledging your contributions. Take care and God Bless."
—T. F., Houston, TX

Knock 'em Dead is motivational

"*Knock 'em Dead: The Ultimate Job Search Guide* inspired me. I have turned my job search into multiple interviews and offers in just a couple of months. The motivation and positive energy will steer you to stay focused on getting the best job offer! Thank you, Martin!"
—E. R., New York, NY

"*KED* has been a rock in turbulent emotional waters. It is amazing to see the changes that have occurred so far, I can't wait to see what comes next."
—R. L.

Knock 'em Dead helps professionals at all ages and stages of their careers

"I wanted to let you know that I've just landed a National Account Manager job. I can't thank you enough; your help and support in my job search was invaluable."
—K. S., IN

"I just got a new job and $16K raise using your approaches at my venerable age. Number of years employed: thirty-four."
—S. S., Little Rock, AR

More praise from Knock 'em Dead users

"My husband has been wondering why I'm laughing out loud reading a book on job search. Your book is not only imparting valuable advice: It is a very refreshing read, sprinkled with humor."
—M. W., Toronto, Canada

"My recommendation to job seekers everywhere: buy it, read it, and use it. It works. Using the techniques in it has led to three initial interviews within the first week of putting it into action. I just wanted to thank you for your excellent book."
—J. R., San Antonio, TX

KnOCK 'em DEaD

THE ULTIMATE JOB SEARCH GUIDE 2017

MARTIN YATE, CPC
New York Times bestseller

Adams Media

New York   London   Toronto   Sydney   New Delhi

To your successful job search

ACKNOWLEDGMENTS

Knock 'em Dead is now in its third decade of publication and has become a staple of job searchers around the world. My thanks to Peter Archer, the finest editor I have had in thirty years; Jane Hauptman for her accurate and conscientious copyediting; Bethany Carland-Adams for her PR efforts; and Angela Yate for her consistent contributions to this and all *Knock 'em Dead* books.

Adams Media
An Imprint of Simon & Schuster, Inc.
57 Littlefield Street
Avon, Massachusetts 02322

For information about special discounts for bulk purchases, please contact Simon & Schuster Special Sales at 1-866-506-1949 or business@simonandschuster.com.

The Simon & Schuster Speakers Bureau can bring authors to your live event. For more information or to book an event contact the Simon & Schuster Speakers Bureau at 1-866-248-3049 or visit our website at www.simonspeakers.com.

Manufactured in the United States of America

10 9 8 7 6 5 4 3 2

Library of Congress Cataloging-in-Publication Data has been applied for.

ISBN 978-1-4405-9601-8
ISBN 978-1-4405-0155-8 (ebook)

CONTENTS

Part II Get the Word Out . . . 133

Job search is all about getting into conversations with the people who can hire you as quickly and as often as you can. Powerful networking techniques to *quadruple* your hit ratio on every job posting.

CHAPTER 7: Making Contact . . . 134

Study the best strategies for making contact with employers, from emailing resumes to making calls. Here's how to introduce yourself to employers, get past gatekeepers, and handle initial interview questions and objections to your candidacy. Effective tactics for getting *useable leads from every* conversation you have.

CHAPTER 8: Ace the Telephone Interview . . . 158

Telephone interviews are a common screening device. How to prepare for the scheduled telephone interview and to be ready for the unexpected call. **Headhunter tactics** for turning the telephone interview into a face-to-face meeting.

CHAPTER 9: Dress for Job Interview Success . . . 167

You never get a second chance to make a first impression at a job interview; so unless you dress the part, don't expect an offer. Here are men's and women's **guidelines for correct professional dress**.

CHAPTER 10: Body Language . . . 180

Learn the **seven techniques for body language success** during a job interview. Learn to employ positive body language messaging that can help your entire career.

CHAPTER 11: The Curtain Rises on the Job Interview . . . 189

First impressions are the strongest. Here are **twenty small preparations** you can make before you walk into the interviewer's office that will help calm your nerves and psych you up for a successful interview.

Part III Great Answers to Tough Interview Questions . . . 193

Hundreds of tough job interview questions, what's behind them, and how to develop **powerful, honest answers**.

CHAPTER 12: The Five Secrets of the Hire . . . 196

Knowing how an interviewer thinks is a critical element of the job search that is frequently overlooked. Here are the five secrets of the hire, showing you how to get **inside the hiring authority's head**. Master them now and they will serve you throughout your career.

CHAPTER 13: Why Interviewers Do the Things They Do . . . 203
Learn the questioning techniques an interviewer uses to find out whether you will fit into the department and the company, whether you are a **team player**, and if you are going to be a management headache.

CHAPTER 14: How to Knock 'em Dead: Great Answers to Tough Interview Questions . . . 215
The greatest fear is fear of the unknown. Learn about the toughest questions an interviewer can throw at you: **what's behind the question**, what they are looking for in an answer, and how you can give an honest and winning answer without sounding like a snake-oil salesman.

CHAPTER 15: Questions of Manageability and Team Spirit . . . 234
Learn the right way to answer questions an interviewer asks to find out **whether you will fit into the company and department**, and, most important, whether you are a good person to work with, and will fit into the team.

CHAPTER 16: How to Handle Stress and Illegal Questions . . . 248
Your worst nightmare can come true at a stress interview, but once you learn that these questions are just **amplified versions of much simpler ones**, you'll remain cool and calm. Also: a vital discussion on handling illegal interview questions, what mock meetings, role-playing, and in-basket tests are looking for, and how to handle them.

CHAPTER 17: Answering Unanswerable Questions . . . 265
For jobs that require **high analytical skills** there are some baffling questions—but they all have answers.

CHAPTER 18: Welcome to the Real World . . . 274
For the **entry-level candidate**, some special interview questions specifically tailored to discover your business potential when real-world experience is lacking.

CHAPTER 19: Strange Venues for Job Interviews . . . 282
Learn the tips that will help you master job interviews in noisy, distracting hotel lobbies, in restaurants, at poolside, and in other **unusual settings**. Includes an essential review of table manners you'll remember for the rest of your career.

CHAPTER 20: How to Ace the Psychological Tests . . . 287
We are all professional schizophrenics! Approaching psych tests casually can be hazardous to your professional health. How to prepare for them, what's behind the questions, and techniques for answering correctly in the heat of the moment.

CHAPTER 21: The Graceful Exit . . . 298
All the critical dos and don'ts to ensure that the **lasting impression** you leave is the right one.

Part IV Finishing Touches . . . 301
Steps you can take to keep your impression fresh in the interviewer's mind.

CHAPTER 22: How to Fight Age Discrimination in Your Job Search . . . 303
Learn to fight against silent discrimination with the **hard-won street smarts** that come with age, experience, and understanding.

CHAPTER 23: The Stealth Job Search . . . 320
How to conduct a **confidential job search** while you're still employed.

CHAPTER 24: Out of Sight Can Mean Out of Mind . . . 335
The seven steps that keep you **fresh in the interviewer's mind** and encourage the continuation of your candidacy.

CHAPTER 25: Negotiating the Job Offer . . . 343
The job offers finally begin to arrive, and you're never going to have this much leverage with this employer again. Learn the essentials of salary and benefits negotiations: handling good job offers and poor job offers, negotiating future salary, and how to evaluate the salary and the job offer. **Fifty great questions** you can ask to make sure the job offer is one you want to accept; and essential information on reference checking, job offer letters, employment agreements, relocation, and stock options.

CHAPTER 26: Snatching Victory from the Jaws of Defeat . . . 365
Rejection? Impossible! Then again, you won't be right for every job. Here are some techniques that help you to **create opportunity** in the face of rejection.

CHAPTER 27: Multiple Job Interviews, Multiple Job Offers . . . 369
Relying on one interview at a time can only lead to anxiety, so you must **create and foster an ever-growing network** of interviews and, consequently, job offers. Implement the *Knock 'em Dead* job search plan and you will be able to both generate multiple job interviews and turn them into job offers. This is not hype; it really happens when you get onboard with the plan.

CHAPTER 28: Clouds on the Horizon . . . 371
You never want to be caught in a **layoff**, job hunting with 500 of your colleagues; this is how you stay ahead of **disruptions to your career** and economic stability.

WHY *KNOCK 'EM DEAD?*

You didn't come to this book because everything is good in your professional life. You came because these are times of upheaval, crisis, and change. Managing a successful career isn't easy, so I'm not going to waste your time.

You are somewhere in the middle of a half-century work life, in which, statistically speaking, you are likely to change jobs about every four years (not always by choice) and have three or more distinct careers.

Add an awareness that recessions causing widespread job loss rear their ugly heads every seven to ten years (I have worked in career management through five of them in the past thirty-five years), and you can see that smart career management strategies and a firm grasp of practical job search tactics are critical to your survival and happiness. *In the context of your whole work life, career management and job search skills are the most important skills you can ever develop, bar none.*

All the advice you've been given about careers—get an education, choose a career, settle down and do a good a job; patience and loyalty to the company will be rewarded with job security and life success—all the promised rewards of running straight and true have proved themselves a crock.

We live in a global economy where voracious political and corporate greed has turned your life into a disposable commodity to be used and discarded. It is time for a radical shift in your career management strategy. You need to move from hapless employee at the whim of financial currents beyond your control to enlightened professional who puts the pathway to personal success in its proper context.

What's this context? Those job changes coming round every four years or so add up to twelve or more over fifty years, with perhaps three of them involving the greater challenges concerned with career change. *This means professional change is constant; professional change is a given.* You need to recognize that your career is not a fixed thing that came as a gift with the purchase of your college diploma. Instead, it's a critical aspect of your life, and it needs management. Face this and you can begin to change your situation, today and forever.

It's Time for Enlightened Self-Interest

Enlightened self-interest means placing *your* financial survival front and center in your life. I want you to start to think of yourself not as a person looking for a job, but as a company, a financial entity that must maintain a steady cash flow over half a century. Start to think of yourself as MeInc., a corporation that must always plan and act in its own best interests; in doing so, you will begin to see this job search and the management of your career in a new light.

As a corporation, MeInc. has products and services that are constantly under development. These are the bundle of skills that define the *professional you* and are positioned and sold to your targeted customer base: those employers who hire people like you.

The success of MeInc. depends on how well you run your company, which means that just like every successful company in the world, you must have ongoing initiatives for:

- *R & D*: Your identification and development of products and services that will appeal to your customers. This translates to skill building in response to market trends; it also relates to

11

your development of job search, interview, and career management skills.

- *Strategic Planning*: The development of effective career management strategies that make you more visible and more desirable for the times when you must look for work, and strategies you pursue when employed to make your job more secure and to encourage professional growth with that company, as you continue with strategies that build your credibility and visibility within your company and profession.
- *Marketing and PR*: The establishment of personal credibility for the services you deliver, and the positioning of these services so that your professional credibility becomes visible to an ever-widening circle of potential customers.
- *Sales*: A state-of-the-art sales program to sell your products and services, including resume, job search, and interviewing tactics.

Now, this may or may not be your first job search, and it almost certainly won't be your last, but it can be the last one that you begin in confusion. This can be the last time you have no clear idea of your options or how best to pursue them.

In these pages you will learn how to achieve your goal of a successful and happy professional life as I show you the best ways to find job openings, effectively turn them into interviews, and transform not one but sometimes many of those interviews into job offers.

This intelligent approach to job search will not only help you land jobs but will also show you how to achieve greater success *within* each of those jobs. This book has been updated and expanded every year for more than twenty-five years, always reflecting the changing needs of the job hunter in changing times. People who used this book all those years ago tell me they still use it today. They tell me it is why they are VPs at *Fortune* 500 companies or why they own their own companies and how it changed both their sense of self and their life for the better.

This is not because *Knock 'em Dead* or any of my fourteen career books is some motivational quick fix. Instead, what this book gives you is an infinitely flexible, completely down-to-earth plan of attack for your job search, which also happens to make sense as a blueprint for a successful professional life. That just happens to be something no one else has really thought through the way I have, but then I've been at it as my chosen mission for more than thirty years. This is what I think about every day of my life: no hidden religious or political agendas, just me talking to you, using all my insights about work and careers to help you get out of a tough spot in your life and into a better place for the future, so you understand how it works and how to play the game.

No one ever thought to give it to you straight. I will because I understand, and I care about your well-being. Change and the unexpected are constants in professional life today, and I have an intelligent approach to dealing with these issues. Follow the job search advice in these pages, and you will make that next step up the professional ladder. Follow the strategic career management advice in these pages and you will be in far greater control of your destiny.

I update this *Knock 'em Dead* book every year because too much of what I find online and in bookstores lacks real insight into vitally important issues: your financial survival and success.

Thirty-two years and millions of copies later, *Knock 'em Dead* has become a time-tested and proven commodity both here in America and in many countries around the world. If you want to make sense of your career, I have a carefully coordinated approach for making this job search and your professional life a success, and I'm here to help.

Sincerely,
—**Martin Yate, CPC**

PART I
THE WELL-STOCKED BRIEFCASE

THIS SECTION WILL show you how to discover, define, and package your skills, and to put together a comprehensive plan of attack that uses all the most effective job search techniques.

ONCE UPON A TIME, long ago, there lived a man who spent his days watching life go by. He lived in a town ravaged by bears, and one of his dreams was that if he could shoot bears, he could travel the world as a bear slayer. Every day he sat on his porch and waited for a bear to go by. After weeks of watching and waiting, he thought he might go looking for bears.

He didn't know much about them, except that they were out there somewhere. Full of hope, he loaded his single-shot musket and set out. Arriving at the edge of the forest, he raised his rusty old flintlock, and fired blindly into the trees. Then, disappointed at hitting nothing he could eat, he slouched back to sit on the porch.

Because our hero couldn't tell dreams from reality, he went hunting unprepared and earned exactly what he deserved: nothing. The moral is: When you go bear, or job-hunting, get a grip on reality, and don't go off halfcocked.

Out there in the forest of the professional world are countless opportunities. Even in times of severe economic downturn—remember they are cyclical and likely to come by every seven to ten years throughout your career—there are always jobs out there. Yes, they are harder to find, and yes, the competition is tougher, but someone is going to find those jobs and land those job offers. It can be you.

All companies have two things in common: They are in business to make money; and things go wrong, so they hire problem solvers to fix them. This is an important life lesson. Think about your present job: You were hired to cope with certain problems within your area of expertise, to *anticipate* and *prevent* them from arising, and where they cannot be prevented, to *solve* them. At some elemental level, *everyone, in every profession and at every level, is paid to be a problem solver.* There are three lessons you should take away from this:

Lesson One: Companies are in business to make money; they have loyalty only to the bottom line. They make money by sales and by being efficient and saving time. If they save time, they save money and have more time to make more money; we call this productivity.

Lesson Two: Companies and MeInc. are exactly alike. You both want to make as much money as possible in as short a time as possible: think efficient *systems and procedures*, and *multitasking* (time management and organization). Think of focus and goal, not task and activity.

Lesson Three: There are buyers' markets (advantage: employer) and there are sellers' markets (advantage: employee). Job offers put you in a seller's market and give you the whip hand.

Lesson One tells you the three things every company is interested in. Lesson Two teaches you to recognize that MeInc. has the same goals as any company. Lesson Three reminds you that anyone with any sense wants to be in a seller's market.

If you look for jobs one at a time, you put yourself in a buyer's market; if you implement my advice in *Knock 'em Dead*, you can generate multiple job offers (even in a tough economy) and put yourself in a seller's market. This means making sure MeInc. is ready with a properly packaged product and integrated sales process.

In this first part of the book you will:

- Learn to evaluate market needs and package your professional skills for those needs.
- Discover how to identify *every* company in your target location that could be in need of your services.
- Get connected to the most influential people in your profession so that you'll have personal introductions at many prospective companies.
- Implement an integrated job search plan of attack.

While I will cover each of these areas in sequence, I recommend that you mix and match the activities. In other words, when working on your resume starts to drive you nuts, switch to researching your target market, or building your professional networks. An hour of one activity followed by an hour of another will keep your mind fresh and your program balanced.

CHAPTER 1
THE REALITIES OF A JOB SEARCH

JOB SEARCH ISN'T nanotechnology; you'll find a common-sense logic in everything I show you and wonder why you didn't see it before. You can get your job search moving onto a new trajectory this week, and reap the rewards for the rest of your career. You can do this.

Everyone feels crappy when they are looking for a job—you aren't the only one—but while there used to be a stigma about looking for a job, times have changed. Job change is an integral part of modern life. It comes around about every four years, making change and job search a constant factor for everyone.

Because everyone understands this, once you organize and follow the plan of attack, you will find many, many people are ready to give you a helping hand if they can.

We live and work in a time of immense change. When you were born, there still existed a world in which hard work, dedication, and sacrifice led to long-term job security and a steady, predictable climb up the ladder of success. The world you now work in is entirely different: Companies still expect hard work, dedication, and sacrifice, but their only loyalty is to the profit imperative. You are expendable.

Different times require different strategies; you need a new mindset for today's job search and for your long-term career success. The job security and professional growth our parents were raised to expect as the norm is a thing of the past. Here are the realities you're facing, expressed in numbers:

50—4—3—7—10
A **50**-year work life
Job change about every **4** years
3 or more distinct careers
Economic downturns every **7–10** years

KNOCK 'EM DEAD TIP
Changing careers at the same time as you change jobs adds another level of complexity to the process because you are leaving behind many of the skills that usually help you land that new job. If a career change is part of your job search—for example, if you are changing from a career in finance to one in education—go to Career Management Issues on the *Knock 'em Dead* website, *www.knockemdead.com*.

Read the additional commentary you find on those pages and then come back to this page and proceed.

Integrate my job search advice into the long-term career management plan I outline in these pages and you need never again be caught flat-footed, urgently needing a job to put food on the table.

Along the way, we'll discuss many long-term career management initiatives that are also essential parts of your job search plan of attack. For example, you'll learn about credibility, visibility, and professional branding. These are all issues that can have great impact on your job search and even greater impact on your long-term career management initiatives.

Not surprisingly, the process starts with your resume. The resume creation process helps you focus on the job you want and package your skills effectively. It's the first step in turning your dreams into realities, and as you'll see, the resume techniques you'll learn in Chapter 3 to help you land a new job can also be leveraged to get you promotions on that job; but first things first.

How Business Works

Companies exist to make money for the owners, as quickly, efficiently, and reliably as possible. They make money by selling a product or service, and they prosper by becoming better and more efficient at it. When a company saves time, it saves money, and then has more time to make more money; this is called productivity.

If a company can make money without employees, it will do so, because that means more money for the owners. Unfortunately for the owners, a company requires a complex machinery to deliver those products and services that bring in revenue. You can think of any and every job as a small but important cog in this complex moneymaking machine, and every cog has to be oiled and maintained; this costs money. If the company can redesign its machinery to do without that cog (automation) or can find a cheaper cog (outsourcing that job to Mumbai), of course it is going to do so.

There are two reasons jobs exist. First, as I've said, every job is a small but important cog in the corporation's complex moneymaking machine: It exists to help the company make money. Second, the company hasn't been able to automate that job out of existence because in your area of technical expertise, problems arise.

Consequently, the company hires someone who has the *technical skills* to solve the problems that typically occur within an area of specific expertise. The company hopes to hire someone who knows the territory well enough to predict and prevent many of these problems from arising in the first place.

It doesn't matter what your job title is, you are always hired to be a problem solver with a specific area of expertise. Think about the nuts and bolts of any job you've held: At its heart, that job is chiefly concerned with the *anticipation, identification, prevention, and solution of problems*. This enables the company to make money for its owners, as quickly, efficiently, and reliably as possible.

These aren't the only factors that are critical to your success and that all jobs have in common. In the next chapter you'll learn about a specific set of *transferable skills and professional values* that all employers are anxious to find in candidates, whom they then hire and promote just as quickly as they can find them.

GET A FREE RESUME REVIEW FROM MARTIN YATE!
Go to the website of the store where you bought the book, write an honest review, and send the link with your resume to *MartinYate@KnockEmDead.com*.

ER 2

THE TRANSFERABLE SKILLS AND PROFESSIONAL VALUES THAT GUARANTEE A SUCCESSFUL JOB SEARCH AND CAREER

UNDERSTAND WHAT YOUR customers want to buy.

There are certain keywords you see in almost every job posting that relate to skills: *communication, multitasking, teamwork, creativity, critical thinking, leadership, determination, productivity, motivation,* and a few more we'll discuss shortly. These words represent a secret language that few job hunters ever show they understand. The ones who do "get it" are also the ones who get the job offers.

That is because, as discussed in the previous chapter, these keywords and phrases represent the skills that enable you to do your job well, whatever that job may be. They are known as *transferable skills and professional values* because no matter what the job, the profession, or the elevation of that job, these skills and values make the difference between success and failure.

The Professional Everyone Wants to Work With

Over the years, I've read a lot of books about finding jobs, winning promotions, and managing your career. One theme that runs through many of them is just plain harmful: the advice to "be yourself." Wrong. Remember that first day on your first job, when you went to get your first cup of coffee? You found the coffee machine, and there, stuck on the wall behind it, was a handwritten sign reading:

> YOUR MOTHER DOESN'T WORK HERE
> PICK UP AFTER YOURSELF

You thought, "Pick up after myself? Gee, guess I've got to develop a new way of doing things." And so you started to observe and emulate the more successful professionals around you. You weren't born this way. You developed new skills and ways of conducting yourself, in effect creating a *professional persona* that enabled you to survive in the professional world.

There is a specific set of *transferable skills and professional values* that underlie survival and professional success: skills and values employers all over the world in every industry and profession are anxious to find in candidates from the entry level to the boardroom. Why this isn't taught in schools and in the university programs that cost a small fortune is unfathomable, because these skills and values are the foundation of every successful career. They break down into these groups:

1. **The Technical Skills of Your Current Profession.** These are the technical competencies that give you the ability to do your job—those skills needed for a task and the know-how to use them productively and efficiently. These *technical skills* are mandatory if you want to land a job within your profession. *Technical skills*, while transferable, vary from profession to profession, so many of your current *technical skills* will only be transferable within your current profession.

2. **Transferable Skills That Apply in All Professions.** This set of skills underlies your ability to execute the *technical skills* of your job effectively, whatever that job might be. They are the foundation of all the professional success you will experience in this and any other career (including dream and entrepreneurial careers) that you may pursue over the years.

3. **Professional Values.** These are a set of beliefs that enable all professionals to make the many judgment calls required during the working day to ensure that the best interests of the department and the employer are always promoted. They complement the *transferable skills* and together form a firm foundation for a successful professional life.

A Review of Transferable Skills and Professional Values

As you read through the following breakdown of each *transferable skill* and *professional value*, consider your own varying strengths and weaknesses. You may, for example, read about *communication*, and think, "Yes, I can see how *communication skills* are important in all jobs and at all levels of the promotional ladder, and, hallelujah, I have good *communication skills*." Take time to recall examples of your *communication skills* and the role they play in the success of your work.

You might also read about *multitasking skills* and realize that you need to improve in that area. Whenever you identify a *transferable skill* that needs work, you have found a *professional development project*: improving that skill. Your attention to those areas will repay you for the rest of your working life, no matter how you make a living.

Here are the *transferable skills and professional values* that will speed the conclusion of this job search and your long-term professional success. You'll find that you already have some of them to a greater or lesser degree, and if you are committed to making a success of your life, you'll commit to further development of all of them.

Transferable Skills	Professional Values
Technical	*Motivation and Energy*
Communication	*Commitment and Reliability*
Critical Thinking	*Determination*
Multitasking	*Pride and Integrity*
Teamwork	*Productivity and Economy*
Creativity	*Systems and Procedures*
Leadership	

Transferable Skills

There is a body of skills that transcend industry lines. These skills will not only enhance your employability in your current profession, but will ease your transition should you ever change your career—something that the statistics say you will do three or more times over the span of your work life.

Employers are always on the lookout for employees who, in addition to the must-haves of the job, possess the *written communication skills* to create a PR piece or a training manual; who know how to structure and format a proposal; who are able to stand up and make presentations; or who know how to research, analyze, and assimilate hard-to-access data.

Some of the *transferable technical skills* sought across a wide spectrum of jobs include:

- Selling skills: Even in non-sales jobs, the art of persuasive communication is always appreciated, because no matter what the job, you are always selling something to someone.
- Project management skills
- Six Sigma skills
- Lean Management skills
- Quantitative analysis skills
- Theory development and conceptual thinking skills
- Counseling and mentoring skills
- Customer Resource Management (CRM) skills
- Research skills
- Social networking skills

There are also *technology skills* that have application within all professions in our technology-driven world. It is pretty much a given that you need to be computer literate to hold down any job today, as just about every job expects competency with Microsoft Word and email. Similarly, proficiency in Excel and PowerPoint is becoming a skill it is risky not to possess.

Any employer is going to welcome a staff member who knows his way around spreadsheets and databases, who can update a web page, or who is knowledgeable in CRM.

Some of the *technology skills* that enhance employability on non-technological jobs include:

- Database management
- Spreadsheet creation
- Word processing
- Building and designing of presentations
- Email and social media communication

Eventually, more and more of these skills will become specific requirements of the jobs of the future. Until then, possession of these skills will add a special sauce to your candidacy for any job.

All the *transferable skills* are interconnected—for example, good *verbal skills* require both *listening* and *critical thinking skills* to accurately process incoming information; these enable you to present your outgoing verbal messaging persuasively in light of the interests and sophistication of your audience so that it is understood and accepted. Develop effective skills in all seven of the subsets that together comprise the *transferable skills* and you'll gain enormous control over what you can achieve, how you are perceived, and what happens in your life.

Technical

The *technical skills* of your job are the foundation of success within your current profession; without them you won't even land a job, much less keep it for long or win a promotion. They speak to your *ability* to do the job, those essential skills necessary for the day-to-day execution of your duties. These *technical skills* vary from profession to profession and do not refer to anything technical *as such* or to technology.

However, it is a given that one of the *technical skills* essential to every job is technological competence. You must be proficient in all the technology and Internet-based applications relevant to your work. Even when you are not working in a technology field, strong *technology skills* will enhance your stability and help you leverage professional growth.

Some of your *technology skills* will only be relevant within your current profession, while others (Word, Excel, and PowerPoint, to name the obvious) will be transferable across all industry and professional lines. Staying current with the essential *technical* and *technology skills* of your chosen career path is the keystone of your professional stability and growth.

When people are referred to as "professionals," it means they possess the appropriate *technical* and *technology skills* necessary for success in their profession and have interwoven them with the other major *transferable skills*. Staying current with the essential *technical* and *technology skills* of your chosen career path through ongoing professional education is going to be an integral part of your growth and stability. That's why the education section toward the end of your resume can be an important tool in developing your *professional brand*: It speaks to your technical competence and your commitment, exemplified by your continuing pursuit of professional skills.

Technology constantly changes the nature of our jobs and the ways in which they are executed. As a result, if you want to stay employable, you need to stay current with the skills most prized in your professional world.

Communication

Without *communication*, you live in silence and isolation. With *communication*, you make things happen in your life.

As George Bernard Shaw said, "The greatest problem in communication is the illusion that it has been accomplished." Every professional job today requires *communication skills*; promotions and professional success are impossible without them. Good verbal *communication skills* enable you to accurately process incoming information and also to present outgoing information persuasively and appropriately to your audience and message, so that it is understood and accepted.

But *communication* embraces much more than listening and speaking. When the professional world talks about *communication skills*, it is referring to four primary skills and four supportive skills.

The primary *communication skills* are:

- Verbal skills—what you say and how you say it.
- Listening skills—listening to understand, rather than just waiting your turn to talk.
- Writing skills—clear written communication, essential for success in any professional career. It creates a lasting impression of who you are.
- Technological communication skills—your ability to evaluate the protocols, strengths, and weaknesses of alternative communication media, and then choose the medium appropriate to your audience and message.

The four supportive *communication skills* are subtler, but, nevertheless, they impact every interaction you have with others. They are:

- Grooming and dress—they tell others who you are and how you feel about yourself.
- Social graces—these are demonstrated by how you behave around others. If your table manners are sketchy, odds are you'll never sit at the CEO's table or represent your organization at the higher levels.
- Body language—this displays how you're feeling deep inside, a form of communication mankind learned before speech. For truly effective communication, what your mouth says must be in harmony with what your body says.
- Emotional IQ—your emotional self-awareness, your maturity in dealing with others in the full range of human interaction.

Develop effective *communication skills* in all these areas and you'll gain enormous control over what you can achieve, how you are perceived, and what happens in your life.

You can check out resources for developing each of these skills at *www.knockemdead.com*.

Critical Thinking

You know to come in from the rain, right? Then you know *critical thinking* impacts everything you do in life.

Life and the world of work are full of opportunity, and every one of those opportunities is peppered with problems. With *critical thinking skills*, you can turn those opportunities into achievement, earnings, and fulfillment. This is the professional-world application of all those problem-solving skills you've been developing since grade school: a systematic approach to uncovering all the issues related to a particular challenge that will lead to its solution.

Critical thinking, analytical, or problem-solving skills allow the successful professional to logically think through and clearly define a challenge and its desired solutions and then evaluate and implement the best solution for that challenge from all available options.

You examine the problem and ask the critical questions:

- What's the problem?
- Who is it a problem for?
- Why is it a problem?
- What is causing this problem?
- What are the options for a solution?
- What problems might a given solution create?
- What is the most suitable solution?

You look through the factors affecting each possible solution and decide which solutions to keep and which to disregard. You look at the solution as a whole and use your judgment as to whether to use it or not. Once you have decided on a course of action, you plan out the steps, the timing, and the resources to make it happen:

- How long will it take to implement this solution?
- How much will it cost?
- What resources will I need?
- Can I get these resources?
- Will the solution really resolve the problem to everyone's benefit?
- Will this solution cause its own problems?

Einstein said that if he had one hour to save the world, he would spend fifty-five minutes defining the problem. It's a thought worth remembering, because a properly defined problem always leads to a better solution, and 50 percent of the success of any project is in the prep. *Critical thinking* is an integral part of preparation.

Multitasking (Time Management and Organization)

This is one of the most desirable skills of the new era. According to numerous studies, however, the *multitasking* demands of modern professional life are causing massive frustration and meltdowns for professionals everywhere. The problem is *not multitasking*, the problem is the assumption that *multitasking* means being reactive to *all* incoming stimuli and therefore jumping around from one task to another as the emergency of the moment dictates. Such a definition of *multitasking* would of course leave you feeling that wild horses were attached to your extremities and tearing you limb from limb.

Few people understand what *multitasking* abilities are built on: sound *time management* and *organizational skills.* Here are the basics.

Establish Priorities

Multitasking is based on three things:

1. Being organized
2. Establishing priorities
3. Managing your time

Plan, Do, Review Cycle

At the end of every day, review what you've accomplished:

- What happened: A.M. and P.M.?
- What went well? Do more of it.
- What went wrong? How do I fix it?
- What projects do I need to move forward tomorrow?
- Rank each project. A = Must be completed tomorrow. B = Good to be completed tomorrow. C = If there is spare time from A and B priorities.
- Make a prioritized To Do list.
- Stick to it.

Executing the **Plan, Do, Review Cycle** at the end of every day keeps you informed about what you have achieved, and lets you know that you have invested your time in the most important activities today and will tomorrow, so you feel better, sleep better, and come in tomorrow focused and ready to rock.

Teamwork

If you become a successful leader one day, it will be due to the fact that you were a great *team player* first; that's the way it works. The professional world revolves around the complex challenges of making money, and such challenges require teams of people to provide ongoing solutions. This, in turn, demands that you work efficiently and respectfully with others who have totally different responsibilities, backgrounds, objectives, and areas of expertise.

Teamwork asks that a commitment to the team and its success come first. This means you take on a task because it needs to be done, not because it makes you look good. The payback, of course, is that management always recognizes and appreciates a *team player*.

As a *team player* you:

- Always cooperate
- Always make decisions based on team goals
- Always keep team members informed
- Always keep commitments
- Always share credit, never share blame

Teamwork skills are especially important if you intend to be a leader, because all successful leaders need to first understand the critical dynamics of *teamwork*. It is only by being a *team player* that you will understand the subtleties of what makes a team pull together and function productively as a unit, and how to recognize and encourage those who display a team spirit; so if you intend to be a leader, learn to be a *team player*.

The Complex Transferable Skills

Each of the *transferable skills* helps you become successful in whatever career you pursue because they help you do whatever you do well. At the same time, *transferable skills* rarely exist in a vacuum. Each interacts with one or more of the others as a given situation demands: For example, *communication skills* include listening skills, listening implies the goal of understanding, and understanding requires the use of your *critical thinking skills*.

There are seven *transferable skills*, and the sixth and seventh, *creativity* and *leadership*, are called *complex transferable skills* because they can only come into being when a fully integrated combination of each and every one of the other *transferable skills* is brought into play.

Creativity

Your *creativity* comes from the frame of reference you have for your work, profession, and industry. This wide frame of reference enables you to see the *patterns* that lie behind challenges, and so connect the dots and come up with solutions. Others might have missed those solutions because they were mired in details and didn't have that holistic frame of reference that enabled them to step back and view the issue in its larger context.

There's a big difference between *creativity* and just having ideas. Ideas are like headaches: We all get them once in a while, and like headaches, they disappear as mysteriously as they arrived. *Creativity*, on the other hand, is the ability to develop those ideas with the strategic and tactical know-how that brings them to life. Someone is seen as creative when his ideas produce tangible results. *Creativity* also demands that you harness other *transferable skills* to bring those ideas to life. *Creativity* springs from:

- Your *critical thinking skills*, applied within an area of *technical expertise* (an area in which your *technical skills* give you a frame of reference for what works and what doesn't).
- Your *multitasking skills*, which in combination with your *critical thinking* and *technical skills* allow you to break your challenge down into specific steps and determine which approach is best.

- Your *communication skills*, which allow you to explain your approach persuasively to your target audience.
- Your *teamwork* and *leadership skills*, which enable you to enlist others and bring the idea to fruition.

Here are five rules for building *creativity skills*:

1. Whatever you do in life, engage in it fully. Commit to developing competence in everything you do, because the wider your frame of reference for the world around you, the higher octane fuel you have to propel your ideas to acceptance and reality.
2. Learn something new every day. Treat the pursuit of knowledge as a way of life. Absorb as much as you can about everything. Information exercises your brain and fills your mind with the ever-widening frame of reference that allows you to make creative connections where others won't see them.
3. Catch ideas as they occur. Note them in your smartphone or on a scrap of paper. Anything will do, as long as you capture the idea.
4. Welcome restrictions in your world. They encourage *creativity*—ask any successful writer, artist, musician, or business leader. Restrictions in time, money, or resources are all negative in their initial impact, but they become the realities under which you must operate. Consequently, the professional defines those restrictions very carefully and then proceeds with the work under these new guidelines. From a production point of view (and *creativity* is all about giving abstract ideas some concrete form), restrictions make you think harder about the essentials and building blocks of your task. When you can take complex ideas and reduce them to their elemental parts, you have a real understanding of that task. Similarly, restrictions increase the need for simplicity in design, function, and expression, and simplicity leads to elegance no matter the project at hand. Restrictions are part of life; you can whine or suck it up and get on with the job.
5. Don't spend your life glued to Facebook or TV. You need to live life, not watch it go by out of the corner of your eye. If you do watch television, try to learn something or motivate yourself with science, history, or biography programming. If you surf the Internet, do it with purpose.

Building *creativity skills* enables you to bring your dreams to life, and the development of each of these interconnected *transferable skills* will help you do just that.

Leadership

"A leader has two important characteristics; first, he is going somewhere; second, he is able to persuade other people to go with him." The guy who said this, Maximilien Robespierre, was a principal figure in the French Revolution and literally changed the world. As you develop *teamwork skills*, notice how you are willing to follow true leaders, but don't fall in line with people who don't respect you and who don't have your best interests at heart. When others believe in your competence, and believe you have everyone's success as your goal, they will follow you; you accept responsibility, but "we" get the credit. When your actions inspire others to think more, learn more, do more, and become more, you are on your way to becoming a leader. This will ultimately be recognized and rewarded with promotion into and up the ranks of management.

Leadership is the most complex of all the *transferable skills* that you will develop to make a success of your professional work life. It is a combination and outgrowth of all the other *transferable skills*:

- Your job as a leader is to make your team function, so your *teamwork skills* give you the smarts to pull your team together as a cohesive unit.
- Your *technical* expertise, *critical thinking*, and *creativity skills* help you correctly define the challenges your team faces and give you the wisdom to guide them toward solutions.
- Your *communication skills* enable your team to buy into your directives and goals. There's nothing more demoralizing than a leader who can't clearly articulate why you're doing what you're doing.
- Your *creativity* comes from the wide frame of reference you have for your work and the profession and industry in which you work, enabling you to come up with solutions that others might not have seen.
- Your *multitasking* (time management and organization) *skills* enable you to create a practical blueprint for success, and they help your team to take ownership of the task and deliver the expected results on time.

Leadership is a combination and outgrowth of all the *transferable skills* plus the clear presence of all the *professional values* we are about to discuss. Leaders aren't born; they are self-made. And just like anything else, it takes hard work.

Professional Values

Motivation and Energy

Employers realize that a *motivated* professional will do a better job on every assignment. *Motivation* expresses itself in a commitment to the job and the profession, an eagerness to learn and grow professionally, and a willingness to take the rough with the smooth in pursuit of meaningful goals.

Motivation is invariably expressed by the *energy* you demonstrate in your work. You always give that extra effort to get the job done and get it done right.

Commitment and Reliability

This means dedication to your profession, and the empowerment that comes from knowing how your part contributes to the whole. The *committed* professional is willing to do whatever it takes to get a job done, whenever and for however long is necessary, even if that includes duties that might not appear in a job description and that might be perceived by less enlightened colleagues as beneath them.

Commitment is also a demonstration of enlightened self-interest. The more you are engaged in your career, the more likely you are to join the inner circles that exist in every department and company, enhancing opportunities for advancement. At the same time, this dedication will repay you with better job security and improved professional horizons.

Your *commitment* expresses itself in your *reliability*. Showing up is half the battle; the other half is your performance on the job. This requires following up on your actions—not relying on anyone else to ensure the job is done and done well—and it also speaks to your *reliability* as a *team player* committed to the greater good of the team.

Determination

Your *determination* speaks of a resilient professional who doesn't get worn down or back off when a problem or situation gets tough. It's a value that marks you as someone who chooses to be part of the solution rather than standing idly by and being part of the problem.

The *determined* professional has decided to make a difference with his presence every day, because it is the *right* thing to do.

The *determined* professional is willing to do whatever it takes to get a job done, even if that includes duties that might not appear in his or her job description.

Pride and Integrity

If a job's worth doing, it's worth doing right. That's what *pride* in your work really means: attention to detail and a *commitment* to doing your very best. This, in turn, means paying attention to details and to time and cost constraints.

Integrity means taking responsibility for your actions, both good and bad, and it also means treating others, within and outside of the company, with respect at all times and in all situations. With *pride* in yourself as a professional with *integrity*, your actions will always be in the ethical best interests of the company, and your decisions will never be based on whim or personal preference.

Productivity and Economy

Always work toward enhanced *productivity* through efficiencies of time, resources, money, and effort. Most problems have two solutions, and the expensive one isn't always the best.

Remember the word "frugal"? It doesn't mean miserliness. It means making the most of what you've got, using everything with the greatest efficiency. Companies that know how to be frugal with their resources will prosper in good times and bad, and if you know how to be frugal, you'll do the same. Ideas of efficiency and *economy* engage the *creative* mind in ways that others would not consider.

Systems and Procedures

This is a natural outgrowth of all the other *transferable skills and professional values.* Your *commitment* to your profession in all these ways gives you an appreciation of the need for *systems and procedures* and their implementation only after careful thought. You understand and always follow the chain of command. You don't implement your own "improved" procedures or encourage others to do so. If ways of doing things don't make sense or are interfering with *economy and productivity,* you work through the system to get them changed.

How Transferable Skills and Professional Values Impact Your Job Search

Development of *transferable skills and professional values* will be repaid with job offers, better job security, and improved professional horizons. When you are seen to embody these *transferable skills and professional values* in your work and in the ways you interact with the people of your professional world, you will become known and respected as a consummate professional, and this can dramatically differentiate your candidacy.

That you have these admirable traits is one thing; that *I* know you have them, well, that's another matter. You need to:

- Develop these skills and values.
- Make them a living dimension of your *professional brand.*
- Understand how each enables you to do every aspect of your job just that little bit better.
- Reference them subtly in your resume and other written communications.
- Reference them appropriately in your meetings with employers as the underlying skills that enable you to do your work well.

Examples of your application of these skills or the impact of these values on your work can be used in your resume, cover letters, and as illustrative answers to questions in interviews. But most important, when these skills become a part of you, they will bring greater success to everything you do.

GET A FREE RESUME REVIEW FROM MARTIN YATE!
Go to the website of the store where you bought the book, write an honest review,
and send the link with your resume to *MartinYate@KnockEmDead.com.*

CHAPTER 3
HOW TO BUILD A KILLER RESUME

AND FIX A resume that isn't working.

Your resume is the most financially important document you will ever own. When it works, the doors of opportunity open for you. When it doesn't work, you don't either, so writing that resume is a job that deserves your full attention. Your resume establishes an achievable goal for your search, opens the doors of opportunity for interviews, prepares you for the questions interviewers will ask, and acts as a powerful ambassador at decision time.

A good resume is not simply a recitation of all the things you have done in your work life. In fact, if your resume just lists all the things you happen to think are important, it will likely sit unread in countless resume databases.

The growth of technology in our world has had a major influence over how resumes have evolved. Used to be that someone would review your resume almost as soon as it was delivered. Today, resumes no longer go straight to a recruiter or manager's desk; instead, they usually go into a resume database. Some of those databases contain over 50 million resumes. So you can see that for a human being to review your resume, it must first be discoverable in an ocean of other resumes by a recruiter tapping in search terms, just like you do on Google.

The Discoverable Resume

When recruiters are searching for talent in resume databases (or social networking sites) they invariably do so with a specific Job Description (JD) in mind. This is important, because job postings invariably reflect the exact wording of the Job Descriptions they come from. This means you can identify the words and phrases your target companies use when they are looking for someone like you.

If you and I want to hire an accountant, here's how the process works. First, we need to identify the job title, so we type "accountant" into the dialogue box and specify a location. Next we click on the keyword options (words that describe the hard skills of the job), and up pops a list of words that have been frequently found in job postings for similar job titles. Finally, we add keywords of our own that do not appear in the offered keyword options.

The software then scours the database and builds a list of all the resumes that contain *any* of those descriptors or keywords. It then weights the list. Those resumes with the most frequent use *and* greatest total number of keywords rise to the top of the list. Mentioning keywords in a Professional Skills/Core Competency section at the front of your resume, and then repeating them within the context of the jobs in which they were used, will *increase* your ranking in recruiters' database searches.

This is the *first* keyword test your resume *must* pass: Because *recruiters very rarely go beyond the top twenty resumes in a database search*, not enough relevant keywords means that no human will review it.

The *second* keyword test your resume *must* pass comes when your resume gets in front of recruiters' eyes. The first scan takes no more than six seconds according to a recent study by TheLadders.com. No immediately accessible and relevant keywords/phrases means no second read.

The second read is a little more careful. The reviewers are looking *only* to see if the resume reflects the skills and competencies required for the job they are trying to fill. Recruiters and HR typically plow through enough resumes to create a "long list" of six to eight candidates.

There will be screening interviews with the recruiters and eventually your resume will land in front of the manager who actually has the authority to hire you. *Managers hate reading resumes*—they just want to hire someone and get back to work.

In fact, no one likes to read resumes; try reading six of them in a row and feel your brain melting into a gelatinous goop. Bear this in mind, because you can learn to use this to your advantage.

Research on what percentage of submitted resumes actually generate job interviews varies from 47 percent down to 4.3 percent. Whatever the actual facts are is irrelevant; what's important to recognize is that *most resumes don't work*. You can see that a resume that crams in everything you have ever done, without any real focus, is doomed to stumble at these initial hurdles. And no interview means no job offer. In a world without job security, where the statistics say that through a fifty-year career you will likely have to change jobs about every four years, you need to learn how to build a resume that works.

Get Inside the Employer's Head

The first lessons in the professional world are invariably: The customer is always right, listen to the customer, learn the customer's needs, and sell to those needs. And yet we seem to forget this first step when it comes to writing a resume. Before writing your resume, you need to get inside the heads of your target employers and understand exactly how they think about, prioritize, and express their needs for the job you need to land. I have devised a tool that will do this and deliver:

- A template for the story your resume *must* tell to be successful
- An objective tool against which to evaluate your resume's likely performance
- An understanding of where the focus will be at interviews
- A good idea of the questions that will be heading your way and why
- Relevant examples with which to illustrate your answers
- A behavioral profile for getting hired and for professional success throughout your career
- A behavioral profile for not getting hired and for ongoing professional failure

Start with Simple Common Sense

Your resume will always be most effective when it begins with a clear focus on, and understanding of, a specific target job. Once you have this focus, you can look backward into your work history for those experiences that best position you for the target job. This will enable you to tailor a killer resume.

The big question is: How do you do this? The answer is what I call the Target Job Deconstruction process.

Target Job Deconstruction (TJD)

Step One: Decide on a Primary Target Job

Focus on a specific and realistic target job, one in which you can succeed based on the skills you possess today. Some people think you change jobs to get a promotion, but this is largely incorrect, especially in a tight job market. *People get hired based on their credentials, not their potential.* Most people don't get promotions to the next step up the professional ladder when they change jobs, because that would mean coming onboard as an unknown quantity in a job they've never done.

Typically, most professionals accept a position similar to the one they have now, but one that offers opportunity for growth once they have proven themselves. The most common exception is an employee already doing that higher-level job but without the title recognition. Also, sometimes you can combine experience and credentials from a number of jobs into a new configuration. This is always more likely to happen when the economy is on the upswing. In down economies, there are just too many thoroughly qualified candidates for an employer to warrant the risk, because with every hire the hiring manager's performance comes under scrutiny.

So of all the jobs you can do—and we can all do more than one—decide on the one that will be *the easiest sell for you and the easiest buy for the employer.* This will be:

- A job you can do and that you can justify on paper
- A job you can convince skilled interviewers that you can do
- A job in which you can succeed

Let's look at "a job in which you can succeed." Seventy percent of the requested skills/ experience will usually get you in the running for the selection cycle in any economy. In your search for jobs, don't throw out opportunities because one line in the job description speaks of skills you lack. If you meet the 70 percent guideline you are a good candidate. Less than this and you may need to reconsider your target job or anticipate a longer job search to reach your goals.

If you have more than five years of experience, there are probably a couple of jobs you can do. More than fifteen years' experience and there could be half a dozen jobs in which you can succeed. Carefully evaluate and rank these jobs based on their availability, remuneration, fulfillment, and potential for growth or shrinkage. This way you will target a "primary job" based on practicality and common sense. If you ultimately decide you want to go after that White Water Rafting Guide job because you once owned a canoe . . . well, at least you'll be doing it with your eyes open, knowing that you won't have most of the required skills, and that your search will take considerably longer.

This does not mean you cannot pursue any of those other jobs for which you have the desire or some of the qualifications. However, be sensible, create your primary resume with a single "primary target" job in mind, and make that job one you can nail!

Targeted Resumes for Different Jobs

The one-size-fits-all resume covering all the skills you possess for all the jobs you can do doesn't work anymore; you have to have a resume focused on a single target job. This means that you have to tailor individual resumes for each of the different jobs you want to pursue, but fortunately, this isn't nearly as hard as it sounds. Once you have created a *primary* resume to your job search, you can quite easily customize it for any of those other jobs you are interested in. There is usually considerable overlap in the deliverables of the different jobs for which we are qualified, so you can take that primary resume, make a copy, retitle it, and make the necessary changes to give the secondary resume a specific focus. To determine what changes to make, go through the TJD process for each additional job-targeted resume and you will quickly maximize the impact potential of each one; you won't have to start from scratch, and you'll have customized resumes for each opportunity.

Step Two: Collect Job Postings

Collect a half-dozen job postings for your chosen primary target job; if you want to save some time, try one of the job aggregators, or spiders (so-called because they *crawl* the web looking for suitable jobs based on your search criteria) listed, each of which will search thousands of job sites for you. Some are free, and some are for a fee, but they all work similarly. The homepage has a couple of dialogue boxes: one for a job title and one for a geographic area. If you cannot find half a dozen jobs in your target location, just try another major metro area: For the purpose of TJD it doesn't matter where the jobs are located:

- *www.indeed.com*
- *www.simplyhired.com*
- *www.jobbankusa.com*
- *www.jobster.com*

Put them in a folder on your desktop and also print them out. From the collected Job Descriptions we will carefully define exactly the way employers think about, prioritize, and express their needs when they consider that particular job. The result will be a template that describes your target job *the way employers themselves think about, prioritize, and describe it.*

Step Three: Look at Your Job from the Other Side of the Desk

This is where you deconstruct your collection of JDs so that you understand exactly how employers *think about, prioritize, and describe the deliverables of your job.*

1. Start a new MSWord document, and name it "Primary TJD" or something similar.
2. Under the subhead "Target Job Titles," cut and paste all the variations on the job title you are pursuing from your collection of job postings.
3. Add a second subhead entitled: "Experience/Responsibilities/Skills/Deliverables/Etc."

Review your collection of job postings and find one requirement that is common to all six; of these six, choose the most complete description of that particular experience/responsibility/ skill/deliverable, paste it under the second subhead, and put the number 6 in front of it to signify that it is common to all six job postings. Underneath this, list additional keywords used in the other five job postings to describe this same requirement.

For this step you may find it easier to work with the printed copies, since your kitchen counter is bigger than your computer screen ;-).

Repeat these steps for any other requirements that are common to all six of your collected job postings, placing the number 6 alongside each one.

4. Repeat this process with requirements that are common to five of the six job postings, then four of the six postings . . . and so on down the line.

At the end of this first part of the TJD process you will be able to read the document and say to yourself, *"When employers are looking for _____ , these are the job titles they use; this is the order in which these needs are prioritized; these are the skills, experiences, deliverables, and professional behaviors they look for; and these are the words with which they describe the deliverables of the job."*

As you read through your TJD document, the story your resume needs to tell will be laid out before you, and some of those promises I made a few paragraphs back will begin to sound a lot less like smoke and mirrors.

Step Four: Identify What's Missing

Add to your TJD any additional skills/experiences you believe are relevant to this job. There are plenty of Job Descriptions that don't tell the whole story. In some companies, even publicly traded multinationals, the Job Descriptions can be maddeningly vague because the company hasn't paid close enough attention to the hard skills of the job. Furthermore, in many companies, Job Descriptions won't go into all the nuts and bolts of a particular job, because they all have to be approved by the Legal Department before they see the light of day. This is part of an overall corporate cost-containment policy designed to protect against the release of JDs that might aid individual or class-action lawsuits brought by disgruntled employees. How can I be sure of this? I used to be a director of human resources in Silicon Valley. I've overseen this process.

If you know a specific skill is mandatory for this job, feel free to add it at the bottom of your list. Job postings can also be vague or poorly thought through, which is why you collect a number of them and add responsibilities that you know belong.

KNOCK 'EM DEAD TIP

If you are new to the professional world and cannot bring personal awareness of a job's needs to the TJD process, you might want to do a little additional research to ensure that your resume has the proper focus.

For further insight into a specific target job, visit the Occupational Outlook Handbook pages at *www.bls.gov/ooh*, which give detailed analyses of hundreds of jobs. After that, talk to people who are actually doing the work and have them deconstruct the job for you along the lines discussed. Check the section on networking for ways to identify and reach out to the right people.

Step Five: Problem Solving

At their most elemental level, all jobs are the same—they all focus on *problem identification, prevention, and solution*; this is what we all get paid for, no matter what we do for a living.

Go back to your TJD and start with the first requirement. Think about and note the problems you will typically need to *identify, prevent, and/or solve* in the course of a normal work day as you deliver on this requirement of the job; then list specific examples, big and small, of your successful *identification, prevention, and/or solution to the problems*. Quantify your results when possible.

Repeat this with each of the TJD's other requirements by identifying the problems inherent in that particular responsibility. Some examples may appear in your resume as significant professional achievements, while others will provide you with the ammunition to answer all those interview questions that begin, "Tell me about a time when . . ."

Step Six: Achievements

Make a list of your greatest solo professional achievements from each of the jobs you have held, quantifying the results where you can, to demonstrate the value of your work. Add to this list with examples of team achievements to which you contributed.

Once you have made this list, come up with a couple of examples of projects that went wrong and couldn't be fixed; you need these to illustrate your answers to questions that might well be asked about projects that went wrong. Ideally, you want examples that are in the past, where the *going wrong* was less than catastrophic and where other people were involved, so you weren't solely responsible. In every example you must be able to illustrate what you learned from the experience.

Interviewers are fond of asking you questions about the following:

- Things that didn't work out well (but did in the end)
- Things that didn't work out well ever, and what you learned
- Unpopular decisions you have had to make
- How you developed new processes (because existing ones didn't work or weren't efficient)
- How you improved something that was already working well
- How you fixed something that was broken

Being ready with appropriate answers for tough questions in these areas takes some thought. Now, as you do the TJD and as you gather information about your experience in the coming resume questionnaire, is a good time to think about examples to use in answer to these questions.

Come back to these examples as you are preparing for an interview. This may seem like a lot of work, but the better prepared you are, the more job offers you will land and the better companies you will land those job offers with.

Step Seven: A Behavioral Profile for Success

Interviewers always have an image of the person they want to hire (and the person they don't). This is not about height, weight, and hair color; it's a composite behavioral profile of the best people they've known in the job. It's what hiring managers want to find and will hire when they see.

Have you ever thought about the behavioral profile that defines success in your area of expertise and then measured yourself against it? Doing so can help you define the professional you want to be and the persona you want to show to the professional world. Not understanding how your behavior can help or hinder your success usually means that you are unwittingly sabotaging future potential.

Work your way through each of the responsibilities itemized in your TJD one by one, profiling the *best* person you ever saw doing that aspect of the job and what made her stand out. Describe how she went about the work, skills hard and soft, interaction with others, general attitude and demeanor, and anything else that sticks out in your mind about that person, and you'll get something like: *Carole Jenkins, superior communication skills, always asking questions and listening, a fine analytical mind, great professional appearance, and a nice person to work with; she'd do anything for anyone.* Do this for each one of the job's deliverables and you will have a detailed behavioral profile of the person all employers want to hire and everyone wants as a colleague: *You will have a behavioral profile that will help you land job offers and, just as important, a behavioral profile for professional success.*

Step Eight: A Behavioral Profile for Failure

Now think of the *worst* person you have ever seen for each of the requirements and what made that individual stand out in such a negative way. Describe the performance, professional behaviors, interaction with others, and general attitude and demeanor of that person and you'll get something like: *Jack Dornitz, insecure, critical, passive-aggressive, no social graces.* You are describing the person that all employers want to avoid and no one wants to work with; and *you will have a behavioral profile for long periods of unemployment and professional suicide.* Then compare yourself against this profile and see if there is anything you need to change or work on.

Step Nine: Transferable Skills and Professional Values

The final step of the TJD is to review each of the skills/responsibilities/deliverables of the job one last time to identify which of the *transferable skills and professional values* help you execute your responsibilities in each of the target job's requirements.

Once you complete and review your TJD, you will have a clear idea of the way employers think about, prioritize, and express their needs for this job; you'll know what they'll need to ask about at interviews and, beyond the hard skills, exactly the person they will hire. Yes, it will take time and it would be easy to cut corners or just skip it, but this is your career and this is your life: Make the choice that is right for your long-term success and happiness.

The more immediate result will be to give you a template for the story your resume has to tell and an objective tool with which to evaluate your work. And when you apply what you learn from the TJD exercise to your professional life, it will increase your job security as it opens doors to the inner circles that exist in every department and company.

Promotions, Ongoing Employability, and Career Strategy

Professional success has traditionally been defined by occupation, job title, and prestige of employer, because financial rewards have similarly been determined by occupation, job title, and employer: Better companies and higher titles lead to greater earnings and greater social prestige.

Part One: The Story

This idea has been the norm for the past five or six generations, since the industrialization of our country, and has become an integral part of traditional (and largely irrelevant) career management lore. Passed on from parent and teacher to child, conventional career management wisdom says:

1. You can go anywhere you want in life as long as you base your pursuits on a firm educational footing. (NB: If you live in America, for many people this means getting deep into debt.)
2. Be prepared to start at the bottom and work your way up.
3. Do whatever is required of you without complaint; sacrifice your energy and your time for the benefit of your employer.
4. Hang on with ten fingers and ten toes—and if you lose one, then hang on with nine, because you will be rewarded with gradually increasing responsibilities, earnings, and titles.
5. You will be rewarded with long-term employment and a steady career with an employer who makes sacrifices on your behalf equal to your own.

Part Two: The Facts
1. With exceptions as rare as hens' teeth, employers make no sacrifices on your behalf.
2. With all that hard work and sacrifice, you get to keep that job just as long as it takes the employer to find someone cheaper (here or abroad) or automate your job out of existence entirely.

Part Three: The Big Lie

Our political and business leaders have told us for twenty years that, yes, we are losing jobs, but, "They're those dirty old jobs that you don't want anyway. What you want is one of those shiny new jobs that globalization is making possible.

"All you have to do is go back to school for retraining (getting deeper into debt) and then start at the bottom, and work hard, make sacrifices, hold on with ten fingers and ten toes . . ." You know how this story ends.

In short, you are being sold a pack of lies again. It is not that any one person is setting out to tell you lies, but cumulatively this is what the advice amounts to.

Part Four: The Truth

1. All jobs are under threat all the time from the inexorable march of automation and the globalization of work it makes possible.
2. No job today is secure from the impact of technology-driven change.
3. The better you become at your work and the more you earn as a result, the more you increase the probability that with some new software development, there's a cheaper alternative that can be found to replace you.
4. The better you become (which is something you strive to do because that is where the rewards have always been), the higher you climb.
5. Climbing ever higher on the ladder of professional success has traditionally meant security, but now with the globalization of manpower and age and wage discrimination, many people are beginning to recognize that the higher you climb, the fewer alternatives are open to you and the bigger the target on your back for all the people coming up behind you and snapping at your heels.

What Keeps You Marketable?

You can't rely on hard work and loyalty to deliver a successful career, because behind the scenes your employer, and every employer, is constantly looking to contain costs by automating and outsourcing work.

Consequently, you have to take a more active role in managing your career. Now, while this section is primarily focused on creating a resume to get you a new job, these same tactics can be applied to pursuing a promotion on that job and maintaining your desirability as an employee in the event of the unforeseen (but not unforeseeable!) occurring.

In fact, the TJD process we discussed should play a twice-yearly role in your ongoing career guidance strategy, both for maintaining employability and for pursuing professional growth.

Maintain Employability

To keep yourself employable, you must stay in tune with the new skills that employers are seeking when they hire people like you.

Twice a year, collect half a dozen job postings for the job you have now and the job you would likely pursue in the event of an unexpected layoff. Review these job postings for the skills employers are seeking. You should consider adding any skill you do not have to your professional skill development program. If the skill is relevant to your work, employers will often support you in acquiring it.

Pursue Professional Growth

You can also use the TJD approach to climbing the ladder of professional success. Many people mistakenly assume that promotions come with time, hard work, and loyalty. Promotions do indeed take time and hard work, but are based more on the presence of the necessary skills than oafish loyalty.

So if you have plans to climb the professional success ladder, it is common sense to identify the skills and experience needed to take that next step up the ladder, then set about acquiring those skills and that experience.

Resume Building

Once you have a clearly defined target job, you can look back into your work history and pull out the experiences that best reflect your ability to do this job. The following questionnaire will help you assemble all the data you will need for a productive resume.

You can find an electronic version of this questionnaire at *www.knockemdead.com* on the resume advice pages. The electronic document will expand to fit your needs.

Resume Questionnaire

You can find an MSWord version of this and all other documents used in resume development at *www.knockemdead.com*.

In answering the questions, don't worry about grammar or perfect expression (that comes later), but do take the time to think about the issues. Be descriptive—don't just say you were a manager: Say that you were a manager with fifty-five direct reports in Decatur and a further fifteen in Mumbai. Be specific whenever possible. Mention full budgetary responsibility (with dollar amount) plus selection, development, discipline, and termination responsibilities. Wherever you can, illustrate with real-world examples, and quantify those examples in terms of money earned or saved, time saved, and productivity improved. Round these examples down, rather than up. Always identify your role as a team member when appropriate. This makes your claims more believable.

Contact Information

Name
Address
Email
Home telephone (*recommend alternate #*)
Cell
Current job title
Variations on this job title
Operational area (*sales, finance, R & D, IT, supply chain, etc.*)
Industry/market sectors (*technology, pharma, financial services, etc.*)

Education and Skills

Postsecondary education (*You might not use all this but do collect it.*)
Degree
Concentration
Graduation date
Major
Minor
GPA
GPA major
GPA minor
Ranking
Honors, scholarships
Special accomplishments

International studies
Degree
Concentration
Graduation date
Major
Minor
GPA
GPA major
GPA minor
Ranking
Honors, scholarships
Special accomplishments

Professional Education (*Ongoing professional education signals commitment to success.*)

Course name
Completion date
Duration
Certification
Sponsoring organization

Professional Credentials Not Covered Elsewhere

Professional memberships and affiliations (*American Management Association, American Marketing Association, etc.*)

Organization
Leadership role

> **KNOCK 'EM DEAD TIP**
> Active membership in a professional association is a key tool for career resilience and success.

Technological Skills (*List all that apply to you.*)

No one gets ahead today without technological competence. Capture your fluency here, and update regularly. That alphabet soup of technology just might help your resume's performance in database searches.

Corporate Accomplishments (*You can also include here your work on projects that resulted in copyright and patents, so long as you make clear your real contribution.*)

Awards and recognition
Public speaking/presentations
Profession-related publications
Patents and copyrights

Global Experience, Cultural Diversity Awareness

In a global economy, any exposure here is relevant, and it doesn't have to be professional in nature. That you were an Army brat and grew up in ten different countries can be a big plus. Just name the countries, not the circumstances.

Foreign Languages

Community, Civic Involvement (*List all organizations and any special projects/activities/leadership roles.*)

Other Activities

This should include all the activities with which you fill your out-of-work hours. Your resume may include those activities that can say something positive about the *professional you*. For example, in sales and marketing just about all group activities show a desirable mindset. Bridge might argue strong analytical skills, and the senior executive who still plays competitive lacrosse and runs marathons is crazy not to let the world know.

Valuable Profession-Related Skills Developed Outside of Your Professional Work

Military Service

Rank
Discharge
Promotions
Decorations
Honors

Professional Development Courses

Achievements

What professional capabilities/skills do you feel have most contributed to your professional success?

What professional behaviors (analytical or *communication skills*, for example) do you feel have most contributed to your professional success?

Employment History

(To ensure a proper focus, I strongly advise that you complete your TJD exercises before looking back at your work history.)

Current position	Standing (division, public, private)
Company	Industry/market sector
Employment dates	What does your company do?
Location	

EXAMPLE:

Squanto Corporation, Inc., Orlando, FL

1997 to present

$500 million company

One of the largest resort and vacation sales/development companies in the United States.

In rapid growth through international expansion, strategic M & A, industry roll-up, and IPO.

What were you hired to do?

EXAMPLE:

Worldwide Director of Operations, Entertainment Imaging, 1998–2006

Selected to re-engineer and revitalize this $65 million business unit with accountability for thirty-two direct reports in four cities across the United States. Established strategic vision and developed operational infrastructure. Managed Supply Chain, Logistics/Distribution, Forecasting, System Integration, Project Management, Contracts Administration, and Third-Party Site Operations.

Or, more simply:

EXAMPLE:

DryRoc, Inc., Indianapolis, IN, 2004–present
Production Director
Drove production for world's largest wallboard plant, with 258 employees working in multiple shifts.

Your Title

Title you report to
Department/unit
Leadership or membership of executive teams, project teams, or committees
Responsibilities/deliverables
Quotes, praise, and endorsements from management
How do you hope a professional colleague would describe your most desirable professional qualities?
Having taken a first pass at the responsibilities/deliverables area, take a few moments to review your TJD. Identify the ways in which your department or unit is expected to contribute to the bottom line (making or saving money, improving *productivity*, and so on).

EXAMPLE:

Internal auditor: to contain costs by audits to ensure adherence to company policies and financial reporting procedures.

The PSRV Process

All jobs revolve around *problem identification, prevention, and solution*.
At some level every job exists for four major reasons:

1. To *identify* potential problems and prevent them
2. To *identify* and *solve* the problems that arise daily as an integral part of the job
3. To *identify, prevent, or solve* the major problems that occur in every business on a regular basis
4. To identify opportunities for contributing to the bottom line

Develop examples of problem identification and opportunity initiatives, both small and large, for every job title you have held. The more you come up with the better, because they will add weight and reality to your resume and show that you think with employers' needs in mind, which will boost your resume's punch. All examples are valuable; those most relevant to your target job are most valuable.

To help you bring out the information that will be most useful to you in your resume and in interview situations, you can apply the PSRV process (you might know this as STAR—same process, different acronym):

- Identify a **P**roblem.
- Envision your **S**olution, including strategy and tactics.
- Take note of the **R**esult of your actions.
- Understand the **V**alue of this to the company (usually in earnings or productivity enhancements).

Now describe four typical or notable problems with which you have been involved on your last (or current) job. Analyze each in terms of PSRV and include the following information:

Company

Employment dates	Your title
Location	Department/unit
Standing (division, public, private)	*Leadership* or membership of executive
Industry sector	teams, project teams, or committees
What does the company do?	Responsibilities/deliverables
What were you hired to do?	Quotes, praise, and endorsements from
Title you report to	management

Repeat for Other Employers

Putting It All Together

The TJD process gave you a clear idea of the way employers think about, prioritize, and express their needs for this job; as such, it provided a template for the story your resume has to tell and an objective tool with which to evaluate your work. Next you filled out the questionnaire, which helped you gather all the raw data that you will shape to match the employer priorities uncovered by the TJD. Because all jobs at their heart are about *problem identification and solution,* you went through your work history using the PSRV process to help identify examples of problems you have surmounted. This helps you figure out what exactly it is you've been doing for forty hours a week all these years, how it contributes to the company's bottom line, and how to pack this information into trenchant, high-impact sound bites for your resume. Now it's time to decide on a resume format that fits your work history.

Three Standard Resume Formats

There are three standard types of resume:

1. Chronological: The most frequently used format. Use it when your work history is stable and your professional growth is consistent within a profession. The chronological format is exactly what it sounds like: It follows your work history backward from the current job, listing companies, dates, and responsibilities.
2. Functional: A functional resume concentrates on the skills and responsibilities that you bring to the target job, and it de-emphasizes when, where, and how you got that experience. It is useful when changing careers, returning to the workplace or the profession after an absence, or when current responsibilities don't relate to the job you want. It is written with the most relevant experience to the job you're seeking placed first and de-emphasizes jobs, employment dates, and job titles by placing them toward the end.
3. Combination: A combination of chronological and functional resumes. Use this format if you have a steady work history with demonstrated growth and if you are continuing your progression within an industry or profession. It often starts with a brief performance profile, then lists job-specific skills relevant to the objective, and segues into a chronological format that lists how, where, and when these skills were acquired.

Check your resume against these six resume rules:

Rule One: Always have a target job title.
Place a target job title at the top of your resume, right after your contact information. This will help your visibility in database searches and will give human eyes an immediate focus. Use the most common job title for your target job title; because different employers use different titles for the same job, you want to use a title specific enough to put you in the running, but vague enough not to rule you out. One way you can make a job title "specifically vague" is to

add the term "specialist" (Computer Specialist, Administration Specialist) or "management" (Operations Management, Financial Management).

John-Taylor Thomas, 4857 Jefferson Street, Arlington, Virginia 22205
646.555.6785 Marcompro@gmail.com

CORPORATE COMMUNICATIONS MANAGEMENT

Performance Profile

Strategic communications professional with . . .

Rule Two: Always have a Performance Profile or Career Summary.

Following your target job title, give a summary of your capabilities as they relate to the demands of the target job. You can title this section Career Summary or Performance Profile.

I suggest you stay away from Job Objective or Career Objective for two very good reasons:

1. Your needs will not help your ranking in the database searches.
2. At this stage no recruiter has the slightest interest in what you want.

If you do need to state a specific job objective—for example, if you are at the start of your career and have absolutely no experience—follow the advice in the following paragraphs for what you should put here.

I like the new term Performance Profile for this important section of your resume because it captures the essence of the *professional you* as it relates to your TJD, and until everyone and their dog starts using the phrase it subtly positions you as a "performer" and separates you from other applicants.

No more than five lines of unbroken text, this section can be followed by a second similar paragraph or short list of bullets. Your intent is to capture your ability to do the target job. For what to put in this section, refer back to your TJD exercise and rewrite the major priorities as your Performance Profile. This will help your resume's database visibility and will create immediate resonance when read by the recruiter. Always note any bilingual skills here, since we live in a global economy.

CORPORATE COMMUNICATIONS MANAGEMENT

Performance Profile

Strategic communications professional with nine years' experience developing effective, high-impact, and cost-efficient media outreach plans for consumer, business, and policy audiences in media, entertainment, and technology practice areas. Experienced in managing corporate and crisis communications. Goal and deadline oriented with five years' experience managing internal and external communications team members. Adept at working with multiple teams and stakeholders.

If you are starting your career and have no relevant experience, that's okay—your chief competitors will be in the same boat. You can tilt the game in your favor by starting your objective with "The opportunity to" and then, referring back to your TJD exercise, rewriting the target job's major priorities as your job objective. This will make a big difference in your resume's productivity.

Rule Three: Always have a Core Competencies section if the list of your core skills creates a block of type longer than five lines.

Large blocks of text are less likely to be read by human eyes, especially if those eyes are older (which the hiring manager's probably are) or tired (which the hiring manager's definitely are). Depending on your skills, you may even consider a separate Technology Competencies section. This helps database visibility because it guarantees you are using the words employers use. You can repeat many of them again in the body of your resume in the context of each job in which you used them, further increasing your visibility. For the human eyes that see your resume, each word or phrase acts as a headline for a topic to be addressed at the interview and increases the odds of that interview happening.

You can also use keywords in these sections that won't fit in the body of your resume; this will result in better performance with the database spiders and bots. Here's an example of a Core Competencies section followed by a Technology Competencies section.

—CORE COMPETENCIES—

Strategic Planning ~ Full-Cycle Project Management ~ Technical & Application Standards ~ IT Governance Process ~ Technical Vision & Leadership ~ Architecture Roadmaps ~ Technical Specifications & Project Design Best Practices ~ Teambuilding & Leadership ~ Standards & Process Development

TECHNOLOGY COMPETENCIES	
Hardware	Sun Servers; HP-UX; AIX; p-Series; Windows Server
Operating Systems	Sun Solaris; AIX; HP-UX; Linux; z/OS; OS/400
Languages	C / C++; COBOL; Visual Basic; Java; Unix Korn Shell Scripting; Perl; Assembler; SQL*Plus; RPG
Databases	Oracle; DB2; SQL Server; Microsoft Access; Informix Visio; HP Service
Applications	MQSeries; Tuxedo; CICS; Microsoft Project, Word, Excel, Outlook, PowerPoint, Sharepoint, and Visio; HP Service Desk; Provision; Telelogic Doors; Change Synergy; Rational System Architect; Rational System Developer; Visual Studio; CA Clarity; LiveLink
Other	Cobit 4.1

Rule Four: Never put salary on a resume.

It does not belong there. If salary information is requested for a specific opening, put it in your cover letter and don't tie yourself to a specific figure: Give a range. If you are earning too little or too much, you could rule yourself out before getting your foot in the door. For the same reason, do not mention your desired salary. For details on developing a realistic salary range, see Chapter 25, "Negotiating the Job Offer."

Rule Five: Keep your resume focused.

The standard for resume length used to be one page for every ten years of experience, and never more than two pages. However, as jobs have gotten more complex, they require more explanation. The length of your resume is less important than its relevance to the target job. If the first page of your resume is tightly focused and contains a target job title, Performance Profile, Core Competency, and perhaps Career Highlight section, you will have the reader's attention. If the first page makes the right argument, the rest of your resume will be read carefully. A longer resume also means that much more space for selling your skills with relevant keywords and more opportunities to establish your *professional brand*. No recruiter or hiring manager, reaching the bottom of the second page of your resume, thinking you are a great candidate, and seeing that there is a third page will throw the resume down in disgust shouting, "OMG he was so good but a third page means I could never interview him." The two-page rule is a hangover from an earlier age. Don't get hung up on it. However, you should still make every effort to maintain focus and an "if in doubt, cut it out" editing approach.

Rule Six: Emphasize your achievements.

Make your achievements, problem-solving skills, and *professional brand* the focus of your resume.

Resume Appearance and Applicant Tracking Systems

Your goal is always to save your resume from getting lost in the big databases, but inevitably this is going to happen. Many commercial resume databases and about half of all companies use some form of Applicant Tracking System (ATS), which helps organize, store, and access the sometimes millions of resumes in those databases. Understanding a little about how ATS works can help your resume gain maximum visibility in the databases.

An ATS typically asks you to supply the same initial information. This information is subsequently used as an initial screening tool by recruiters. The requested information generally includes:

1. *Address*, to determine commutable distance
2. *Career level* (student, entry, experienced, manager, executive). Note that as you grow older there is considerable social pressure in the professional classes to be seen as an executive. But when it comes to resumes, classifying yourself that way will put you into a category with fewer opportunities and fierce competition. If you are on the borderline or could be classified as either a manager or an executive, go for the category that will have the greater number of opportunities.
3. *Education level* (high school, vocational, degrees, certifications)
4. *Occupational area*
5. *Industry/industry sector*

If there are multiple-choice options offered in any of these initial questions, make use of them. You may also be asked about language proficiency, salary level, and employment status. It is preferable to define yourself as employed, even by consulting or temping if necessary.

Resume Formatting

Twenty-seven years ago ATS came into being to help recruiters find resumes in their growing databases. In the early days, the ATS programs had problems dealing with italics, lines, boxes, bolding, some kinds of bullets, the tables that give resume layouts a precise, snappy look, and some fonts, among other shortcomings.

We have come a long way in twenty-seven years, and just as you are not using the software you used in the mid 1980s (if you were alive and working then), neither are corporations.

The colleagues I trust on these issues don't think formatting affects discoverability as much as it did years ago. Personally, I don't think the precise formatting that comes with the use of grids and tables matters at all.

For example, last year, I wrote a resume for an EMEA marketing guy living in Vienna, Austria. His resume was built with grids and tables, and after uploading it to twenty-five databases, he got interviews with all seven of his top target companies within two weeks—and this despite the fact that you can *usually* count on the rest of the world to trail the United States when it comes to technology. The formatting had no negative impact whatsoever, and common sense tells me that while corporations tend to keep up-to-date with new software releases, even when they don't, they certainly are not using twenty-seven-year-old software.

You can achieve the same look without formatting with grids and tables if you are feeling wary; it just takes longer. The decision is up to you.

When you have a choice to either copy and paste your resume section by section or upload the whole document, always choose the upload option, because it gives you more control over what human eyes will eventually see.

Neat Tricks and Quick Saves

1. When you submit a resume, how you saved it becomes part of your messaging. "Resume .doc" says nothing; you'll find saves like "Sales Manager/ABC Corp.doc" much more effective.

2. Sometimes recruiters use Windows Search or Apple's Spotlight to find documents. Knowing can give you an edge. In Microsoft Word, under the *File* menu, choose *Summary Info* and insert keywords and terms with semicolons between them in the keyword file. On a Macintosh, the *File* menu can help you find this same capability under *Summaries*.

3. Older versions of ATS cannot read header and footer information, so never put contact information there.

4. ATS doesn't like surprises. You will have greater success with your resume when you use standard business fonts like Times, Arial, Georgia, Impact, Courier, Lucinda, Palatino (MAC), Tahoma, and Verdana.

5. If you have bulleted lists in your resume, stick to bullets and stay away from arrows, dingbats, and check marks, because some systems won't be able to recognize them.

6. Use section headings like the ones in the following template, such as Performance Profile, Professional Skills, Experience, and Education. They don't affect ATS performance and they help the reader.

Resume Template

Name
Mailing address (if appropriate) • Telephone & cell phone • Email address

---

Professional Target Job Title
This helps database visibility and tells people what they will be reading.

Performance Profile / Career Summary
No more than five lines of unbroken text, perhaps followed by a second similar paragraph or short list of bullet points. The idea is to capture your ability to do the target job. What goes in here? Take the most common requirements from your TJD exercise Step Three and rewrite them as your performance profile. (For more on this, see the Competitive Difference Questionnaire on the *Knock 'em Dead* website.) This will help your resume's database visibility and will immediately resonate with the recruiter. Always note bilingual skills, since we live in a global economy.

Core Competencies (Professional Skills and Skill Prioritization)
Specific and detailed. This is the bulleted list of keywords that you identified in Step Three of the TJD. It can be as long as you like. This list gives the reader an immediate focus ("Oh, she can talk about this and this"), and each word can be repeated in the context of the job to which it applied. Some of your keywords can be written in two or more ways; for example, a recruiter might use "Profit and Loss" responsibilities or "P & L," and you have no way of knowing which. The solution is to use one variation in your Professional Skills/Core Competencies section, and the other within the context of the jobs where you used them.

    Your professional skills are most readily accessible when they appear in three or four columns. This section contains a list of your important professional skills and so needs to be near the top of your resume, for the following reasons:

1. Coming after a Target Job Title and a Performance Summary that focuses on the skills you bring to the target job, skills reflect employer priorities. With accurate prioritization, you help both the discoverability of your resume and its impact with knowledgeable readers.
2. The ATS programs that recruiters use to search resume databases in turn use algorithms that reward relevant words near the top of a document as a means of judging that document's relevance to the recruiters' search terms. This means your professional skills need to be relevant to the target job and appear near the top of your resume. I have been suggesting this for years—perhaps because I have been using ATS since 1987, when it first came on the scene, and have an understanding of how it works.
3. A recent study showed that once a resume has been pulled from a resume database, recruiters spend an average of six seconds on a first-time scan of that resume. This means your qualifications have to jump out, and you achieve this by using a Target Job Title, followed by a Performance Summary that reflects employer priorities and a Professional Skills section that supports all the above claims of professional competency with a list of your relevant skills. This gives a recruiter plenty of time to see your abilities in that first six-second scan.

    However there is another issue at play when it comes to the Professional Skills section of your resume. Ultimately it will be read by someone who really knows this job—knows what's a "must have" and what's a "nice to have."

    The easiest way to explain this is with an example: A couple of years back I did a resume for a dental assistant. She gave me a list of all the important technical skills of her job. I put these into three columns for visual accessibility, and when I did so, something terrible jumped out at me: Her list started with "Teeth whitening" and ended with "Four-handed dentistry." What was so terrible about this? After all, all the skills were there . . .

Yes, they were, but in the West we read from left to right and top to bottom, and common sense says that the most important skills for a job should come before the less important skills. I immediately switched these phrases so that "Four-handed dentistry" came first and "Teeth whitening" came last.

Bear this story in mind when you are creating your own Professional Skills section: By prioritizing your skills, you are subtly telling the man or woman who will ultimately hire you that you have a firm grasp of the relative importance of all the necessary professional skills of your work, and that adds to the clear focus and power of the opening first half page of your resume. This shows that:

- You can do the job
- Your skills list backs up your statements of ability
- You understand the relevant importance of the component parts of your job

The result is that within the first half page of your resume you have gone a long way toward making the short list of candidates who will be brought in for an interview.

Technical Competencies
An optional category, depending on your needs.

Professional Experience
Company name and location
Job title and employment dates
(Repeat this format as many times as necessary.)

Education
This may come at the front of the resume if these credentials are critical or especially relevant to the Target Job description, or highlight your greatest strength.

Licenses / Professional Accreditations
As with Education, this may come at the front of the resume if these credentials are critical or especially relevant to the Target Job description, or highlight your greatest strength.

Ongoing Professional Education

Professional Organizations / Affiliations

Publications / Patents / Speaking Languages

Military Service

Extracurricular Interests
If—and only if—they relate to the job.

References Available on Request
Employers *assume* that your references are available. Only end your resume with this if there is no better use of the space. Never list references on your resume.

An excellent final test for your revamped resume is to first reread your TJD and then read your resume from front to back. If it clearly echoes your TJD, then you are likely to have a productive resume. If it doesn't, you'll be able to tell easily where your content needs fine-tuning.

Sample Resume

Jane Swift, 9 Central Avenue, Quincy, MA 02169. (617) 555-1212 jswift@careerbrain.com

SUMMARY: Ten years of increasing responsibilities in the employment services industry. Concentration in the high-technology markets.

EXPERIENCE: Howard Systems International, Inc.
2004–Present

Management Consulting Firm
Personnel Manager

Responsible for recruiting and managing consulting staff of five. Set up office and organized the recruitment, selection, and hiring of consultants. Recruited all levels of MIS staff from financial to manufacturing markets.

Additional responsibilities:
- Coordinated with outside advertising agencies.
- Developed PR with industry periodicals—placement with over twenty magazines and newsletters.
- Developed effective referral programs—referrals increased 32 percent.

EXPERIENCE: Technical Aid Corporation
1996–2004

National Consulting Firm. MICRO/TEMPS Division

Division Manager	2001–2004
Area Manager	1998–2001
Branch Manager	1996–1998

As Division Manager, opened additional West Coast offices. Staffed and trained all offices with appropriate personnel. Created and implemented all divisional operational policies responsible for P & L. Sales increased to $20 million dollars, from $0 in 1990.

Additional responsibilities:
- Achieved and maintained 30 percent annual growth over seven-year period.
- Maintained sales staff turnover at 14 percent.

As Area Manager, opened additional offices, hired staff, set up office policies, and trained sales and recruiting personnel.

Additional responsibilities:
- Supervised offices in two states.
- Developed business relationships with accounts—75 percent of clients were regular customers.
- Client base increased 28 percent per year.
- Generated over $200,000 worth of free trade-journal publicity.

As Branch Manager, hired to establish the new MICRO/TEMPS operation. Recruited and managed consultants. Hired internal staff. Sold service to clients.

EDUCATION: Boston University
B.S. Public Relations, 1995.

KNOCK 'EM DEAD TIP

Once you are on that new job, keep a low profile for three to six months while you learn the culture of the company, get up to speed with all your job's deliverables, and determine who is in the inner and outer circles of your department and why. Acquire allies by your commitment to doing a good job and by your behavior with the group that will most support your career goals. Quietly identify the next step up the promotional ladder at this or any other company, and then start working toward it. Promotions don't come as a reward for loyalty and tenure; they come as a result of capabilities.

Identify that next job, collect six to twelve job postings for it, and complete a TJD on the position. Then do a gap analysis: Identify the gaps between what you can do and what the next job requires. These gaps become your *professional development program*.

Resume writing is a major topic all on its own, so you can find more help:

- On the resume advice pages at *www.knockemdead.com*
- In the latest edition of *Knock 'em Dead Resumes*
- With a professionally written resume from the credentialed resume writers at *www .knockemdead.com*

Integrating a Professional Brand Into Your Resume

Your *professional brand* should be communicated throughout your resume, but especially with opening and closing brand statements. The first place you begin to establish a *professional brand* is with your Target Job Title (TJT), where you consciously decide on the job that best allows you to package your skill sets and create a *professional brand*.

Target Job Title and Brand Statement

Your TJT and subsequent brand statement give the reader a focus for what this resume is about and what to expect. The brand statement is a short phrase following the TJT that defines what you will bring to this job. It says, in effect, "These are the benefits my presence on your payroll will bring to your team and your company." Put this statement after your TJT and you have a succinct brand statement, or, if you prefer, "value proposition."

Notice the following brand statements focus on the benefits brought to the job, but do not take up space identifying the specifics of how this was done.

Professional brand statements often start with an action verb: "Poised to," "Delivers," "Dedicated to," "Bringing," "Positioned to," and "Building."

Pharmaceutical Sales Management Professional

Poised to outperform in pharmaceutical software sales. Repeating records of achievement with major pharmaceutical companies.

Senior Operations / Plant Management Professional

Dedicated to continuous improvement ~ Lean Six Sigma ~ Start-up & turnaround operations ~ Mergers & change management ~ Process & productivity optimization ~ Logistics & supply chain

Bank Collections Management

Equipped to continue excellence in loss mitigation / collections / recovery management.

Mechanical / Design / Structural Engineer

Delivering high volume of complex structural and design projects for global companies in manufacturing / construction / power generation.

Account Management / Client Communications Manager

Reliably achieving performance improvement and compliance within financial services industry.

Marketing Communications

Consistently delivering successful strategic marketing, media relations, and special events.

Administrative / Office Support Professional

Ready, willing, and competent: detail-oriented problem solver, consistently forges effective working relationships with all publics.

Senior Engineering Executive

Bringing sound technical skills, strong business acumen, and real management skill to technical projects and personnel in fast-paced environment.

Edit for Consistent Brand Messaging

Review the body copy of your resume to see that the messaging supports the *professional brand* you have defined. Refer to the list of action verbs for words that you can add to a statement and further clarify your brand. Make sure your branding is front and center in the following sections of your resume:

- Performance Profile
- Performance/Career Highlights
- Professional Experience

Closing Brand Statement

You will occasionally see a resume closed with a third-party endorsement:

I've never worked with a more ethical and conscientious auditor.

—Petra Tompkins, Controller.

This endorsement can act as a closing brand statement: a bold statement clarifying the value proposition of the product (that's you, that's the brand). It's a great way to end a resume. If you have just the right kind of supportable quote, use it, but suitable quotes aren't always as readily available as we would like.

However, you can achieve an equally powerful effect with a final comment of your own, a comment that relates to your *professional brand* and is written in the first person to make it conversational and different from the voice of the rest of your resume. Most resumes are written in the third person, allowing you to talk about yourself with a semblance of objectivity. Moving into the first person for a final comment at the resume's end acts both as an exclamation point and a matching "bookend" for the brand statement at the beginning. For example:

> *I believe that leadership by example and conscientious performance management underlie my department's consistent customer satisfaction ratings.*

You Must Have a True and Truthful Brand

You have to be able to deliver on the brand you create. It must be based on your possession of the *technical skills* of your profession, plus those *transferable skills and professional values* that you take with you from job to job.

It is all too easy to overpromise, and while the employer might initially be attracted by the pizzazz of your resume, whether or not you live up to the value proposition determines the length and quality of the relationship. If a box of cereal doesn't live up to the brand's hype you simply don't buy it again. The same logic applies to your career, but the stakes are higher: Sell yourself into the wrong job with exaggerations or outright lies and it is likely to cost you that job, plus the possibility of collateral career damage that can follow you for years.

Your Cover Letter

Conversations have to happen before any hiring decision is made, which means that *getting into conversations with the people who can hire you* is the prime focus of every smart job search.

1. Because the majority of resumes typically end up in resume databases, where cover letters often can't help you, learning to use the more personal approaches where a cover letter can make a difference will greatly impact the productivity of your search. When you identify hiring managers by name (advice on how to do this coming up), you can avoid the resume databases altogether, and when you have a name, your cover letter is a very effective marketing tool.
2. Many resume banks and corporate websites have a place where you can upload or paste a cover letter along with your resume, and employers look more favorably on candidates who take the extra step.

In a professional world where *communication skills* are a must for any job, your cover letter introduces you, puts your resume in context, and demonstrates your *writing skills*. In fact, from your first contact with an employer to the day you start that new job, there are a number of opportunities to use letters/emails to advance your candidacy. There are different types of cover letters for different situations: follow-up letters after telephone and face-to-face interviews, resurrection, negotiation, acceptance, rejection, and resignation letters, to name but a few. It's a bigger topic than can be handled here, and for proper coverage you should get the latest edition of *Knock 'em Dead Cover Letters*, with over 125 examples covering all these categories and more; you can also find job search letter templates at *www.knockemdead.com*. Meanwhile, here is a very effective form of cover letter:

The Executive Briefing

I developed this type of cover letter many years ago, and it continues to get rave reviews from users. You can use its striking format to clearly link skills to employer needs or to quickly customize an application when your resume doesn't tell the complete story.

An executive briefing enables you to customize your resume quickly to any specific job, and is especially helpful on the other side of the desk—for overworked recruiters, hiring managers, HR professionals, or administrative assistants, who may not understand all the requirements of a specific job function. It is a powerful focusing tool for any harried resume reader. Furthermore, the executive briefing allows you to update and customize a more general resume with lightning speed without derailing the rest of your day's mission or missing out on an opportunity.

Like many great ideas, the executive briefing is beautiful in its simplicity. It is a cover letter on your standard letterhead/email with the company's requirements for the job opening listed on the left side and your skills—matching point by point the company's needs—on the right. It looks like this:

EXECUTIVE BRIEFING
From: A1coordpro@earthlink.net
Subject: Assessment Coordinator
Date: February 28th, 2010 11:18:39 PM EST
To: jobs@pepsi.com

Dear HR Staff,
Your advertisement on the *New York Times* website on February 27, 2014, for an **Assessment Coordinator** seems to perfectly match my background and experience. As the International Brand Coordinator for Kahlúa, I coordinated meetings, prepared presentations and materials, organized a major offsite conference, and supervised an assistant. I believe that I am an excellent candidate for this position, as I have illustrated:

YOUR REQUIREMENTS	MY QUALIFICATIONS
Highly motivated and diplomatic.	Successfully managed project teams involving different flexible, quality-driven professional business units. The defined end results were achieved on every project.
Exceptional organizational skills and attention to detail.	Planned the development and launch of the Kahlúa Heritage Edition bottle series. My former manager enjoyed leaving the details and follow-through to me. Coverdale project management training.
College degree and six years of experience.	B.A. from Vassar College (2002). 6+ years' relevant business experience in productive, professional environments.
Computer literacy.	Extensive knowledge of Windows and Macintosh applications.

I'm interested in this position because it fits well with my new career focus in the human resources field. Currently, I am enrolled in NYU's adult career planning and development certificate program, and am working at Lee Hecht Harrison.

My resume, pasted below and attached in MSWord, will provide more information on my strengths and career achievements. If after reviewing my material you believe that there is a match, please call me. Thank you for your consideration.

Sincere regards,

Jane Swift

An executive briefing sent with a resume provides a comprehensive picture of a thorough professional, plus a personalized, fast, and easy-to-read synopsis that details exactly how you can help with current needs. Using the executive briefing as a cover letter for your resume will greatly increase the chance that your query will be picked out of the pile in the Human Resources department and hand carried to the appropriate manager.

The use of an executive briefing is obviously not appropriate when the requirements of a specific job are unavailable.

Branding Your Competitive Difference

One of the buzzwords you often hear in job search is "branding." The word is overused and tends to make people think in terms of surface over substance, but understood properly, branding is about establishing a reputation for your *technical* and *transferable skills and professional values*, and creating a consistent way of messaging that reputation.

To discover what sets you apart from others and will help you build a worthy reputation and viable brand over the years, download the *Competitive Difference Questionnaire* from the downloads page at *www.knockemdead.com*. The questionnaire will help you distill what sets you apart from others in your field to the point where you will have a single, condensed sentence expressing your greatest professional strengths and so give substance to your professional reputation and evolving brand.

We have covered a lot of territory in discussing how to put together a killer resume, because *your resume is the most financially important document you will ever own.* Furthermore, the processes through which you develop a compelling resume (TJD, questionnaire, and PSRV) are also crucial in defining the *professional persona* you present to the world; this is almost as important as having a resume that tells a compelling story. Additionally, the process has prepared you for just about all the questions you are likely to be asked at an interview; this will become apparent when you start learning about how to turn job interviews into job offers.

CHAPTER 4

NETWORKING AND THE SUCCESSFUL JOB SEARCH

GETTING INTO CONVERSATIONS with the people who can actually offer you a job is the only way you are going to get hired. The faster and more frequently you get into these conversations, the sooner your job search will be over. In the following four chapters you will develop new skills in how to use networking to get names, titles, contact information, and get into conversations with the people who will ultimately hire you.

Use intelligent networking strategies in an organized plan of attack for your job search and you can quadruple the number of interviews you get; more job interview experience helps you learn how to turn interviews into offers—a critical skill that's a great weakness for most people. In these chapters you will learn skills with the most effective interview-generating tactics and supercharge your results by learning how to build strong relevant networks and then leveraging them to generate a consistent stream of interviews.

Networking and Professional Survival

Networking is natural to younger professionals, while for many senior workers it is a function that was never deemed that important. If networking is part of your DNA you are going to learn how to do it with a focus that will increase your professional stability and growth over the years. If networking is something relatively new in your universe you will learn the same effective tactics, but first you have to do a headset-reset: You were trained to think that networking wasn't necessary, that if you worked hard, were loyal, and made sacrifices, you would be rewarded with long-term employment. Those days are gone; no company offers this carrot any longer. We all must accept that job change and even career change are not once-in-a-lifetime events but occur with regularity. Consequently, loyalty to our colleagues will help us through the rough patches of a professional career far better than blind loyalty to a corporation that does not return our good faith.

Nothing Happens Without Conversation

Nothing happens, no one gets a job interview, and no one gets a job offer without conversations happening. This fact should form the basis of your job search strategy every day:

"Today my primary goal is to get into communication with the people who can hire me as fast and frequently as I can."

The most effective way to get into direct conversations with those people who hold the job titles that will hire you is to build strong profession-relevant networks. This means requires becoming better connected to your professional community so that you can find and reach out to the people in a position to hire you, or who will know the people who can hire you, while simultaneously making it easier for recruiters and headhunters to track you down.

When you connect with your professional community, you get to know, and become known by, all the most dedicated and best-connected professionals in your target geography (where you live and commute). Depending on your needs and the seniority of your position, this may perhaps happen across the entire span of your profession.

There are four types of networks that can be helpful to the success of your job search:

1. Social networks
2. Professional associations
3. Alumni networks
4. Community networks

We will address each of these networks in turn, and discuss how best to leverage your involvement with them.

Social Networks

For corporate recruiters and headhunters, social networking sites are honey pots, offering millions of qualified candidates. For you, social networks provide a reliable pathway to millions of jobs through the people connected to them. Social networking competency is a must for any effective job search plan of attack today. It allows you to reach out to friends, colleagues, and specific categories of as-yet-unknown professional colleagues who might have the perfect lead or introduction.

The better connected you are to your profession, the greater your odds of locating opportunities in the hidden job market. The connections you make can lead to referrals and introductions to recruiters and hiring managers, and in many instances, you'll be able to bypass the resume banks (always a good thing, even though a *Knock 'em Dead* resume is designed to be *discoverable* in resume database searches). You can search a social networking site's database by job title, company name, zip code, or any keywords of your choice. The database will pull up the profiles of people who match your requirements and allow you to initiate contact directly, through your common membership in groups or through the chain of people who connect you.

For example, a soldier cycling out of the military sought my help in her search for a new civilian career. I took her to *www.linkedin.com*, the premier professional networking site (about which, more to follow). First, to find other individuals with a similar background, I plugged the word *army* into the dialogue box and hit enter. The result was more than 4,000 profiles of people who shared her military experience. (That was eight years ago; the same search today produces more than 1,768,000 profiles.) We then tried a search using the phrase *information technology* (reflecting her desired career change) and got 39,000 profiles (today it is 360,000). While both these potential networks would have relevance to her job search, it got even better when we combined the keywords *information technology* and *army*. This pulled up 908 profiles (today over 250,000) of people who shared her life experience and who had, in about half of these results, already made the same transition into her desired profession.

This shows how fast social networking is growing and how important it can be in building productive relationships with a wide range of people, all of whom can be helpful to your job search.

Networking and Confidential Job Search

When you are employed and engaged in a confidential job search, a properly constructed social media profile will make you *discoverable*. Because a social networking site is not a resume database, you do it without an "I'm for sale" sign. Additionally, if you are cycling out of one profession and into another, you can use social networking sites to build a network of people who do the target job in your chosen profession and, whenever possible, people who have made a similar transition—and who can therefore offer you useful advice on making that transition yourself. If you are involved in a job search or a career change, go to the *Knock 'em Dead* website. We have lots of advice and services to help you through the difficult time of transition.

Which Social Networks Are Right for You?

You'll find networking sites that cater to an almost limitless array of special interests. There are thousands of these social networks, and the list is growing every day (see Wikipedia entries for a complete list of sites). For the most effective network-integrated job search, you should have a presence on the top four: LinkedIn, Facebook, Twitter, and Google+. Let's look at each of these in turn.

LinkedIn: The Center of Professional Networking

By far the most important networking site for professionals is LinkedIn. Use it correctly and it could well help you land your next job and sustain your future professional growth. While the following discussion is focused on how best to leverage your presence on LinkedIn, most social networking sites function in very similar ways, and many topics we discuss in connection to LinkedIn will apply to the other networking sites we discuss later.

When you first join a networking site, or finally decide to make something of that terrible profile you currently have, your goals are twofold: You want to be discoverable by recruiters, and you want to develop professional connections that can help you with job search and with other issues that relate to career management. With LinkedIn, as with any social networking site, there are certain steps to take that help you get the most out of your social networking experience:

- Register and create a profile: This gives you a presence so that others can find and connect with you.
- Connect with everyone you know or have worked with in the past.
- Expand your network by joining special-interest groups that are relevant to your profession, and connect with members whose acquaintance could prove mutually beneficial; more on the specifics of whom to connect with shortly.
- Join job search groups for mutual support and tactics. There are many groups; one of them is the *Knock 'em Dead Secrets & Strategies* group: It's a friendly, vibrant group that exists to help you with job search and career management issues.
- Link with me personally, which will immediately increase your reach by thousands; I also randomly give books to my connections.
- Engage in social networking activities that will increase your visibility and attract others to you.

All this begins with creating a profile.

How to Create a Killer LinkedIn Profile

There are now well over 420 million LinkedIn users (about half of them in North America) and the site is growing daily, so building a profile that helps you stand out from the crowd will pay real dividends. It is also increasingly common for recruiters and hiring managers to check out your social media profile(s) once they have seen your resume. The profile you create will give you greater visibility with search engines and enable recruiters and others to find you from outside LinkedIn.

Headshot

Your headshot appears at the top left of your LinkedIn profile, and it's the first thing recruiters (or anyone else) who visits your profile, or merely discovers it in a list of search results, sees. Additionally, upward of 90 percent of Human Resources pros say they check out social media profiles, especially LinkedIn and Facebook, before inviting a candidate in for an interview. As the face you show to the world, your headshot is the face of your brand.

We all make judgments based on visual first impressions; with search results, a profile with a headshot will get many more clicks than a profile without one, and the people who come to your profile will form an opinion based on your headshot before they read anything you have written. How professional and accessible your headshot makes you look will also color the impressions of anyone who then reads your profile.

This means the wrong headshot could hurt your chances of making the cut. Five out of every ten social media profile headshots make me want to laugh, cry, or lose my lunch. I see headshots that are too close (you want to minimize wrinkles or acne), too distant (I need to see your face), too sexy, too casual, that show you grinning like a congenital imbecile or scowling like a mass murderer. These problem headshots show a lack of appreciation for how important this first impression really is.

We all have different personas at work and at play, so a killer headshot for your Match.com profile could be the kiss of death for your LinkedIn profile. Your social media profile gives the reader visual clues about who you are and what your self-image is. Your appearance and facial expression provide the clues, and these are communicated through your headshot. It will happen whether you want it to or not, so the only smart choice is to make sure your headshot presents a confident professional. If you're seen as both professional (which implies competence) and friendly, you will encourage acceptance of the claims made within your profile, whereas a too casual or too sexy shot will call your judgment of professional issues into question.

You can probably get a friend/lover/partner to shoot a bunch of photos of you against a plain background, and it will come out as an acceptable candid shot. Since we all need these shots in our professional lives, find a competent headshot photography partner.

KNOCK 'EM DEAD TIP
Can you get away with a DIY headshot? As long as you look professional, the headshot doesn't have to be done by a professional, but headshots aren't snapshots, and you should dress for yours as you would for a job interview.

The beauty of a digital camera is that you can take as many shots as you want, pick the best one, and maybe even do some basic cleanups. Shoot straight on and then experiment with distance. Once you've settled on a distance (between four and eight feet for many cameras), experiment with angles to see which is most flattering; adjust the lighting to get the most complimentary result.

You need the best headshot you can generate for immediate use, but bear in mind that summer is the best time to upgrade your social media headshots: You look happier and more relaxed because it's summer, and for paler skins any kind of tan makes you look healthier and more attractive. For more, see the blogs on the importance of headshots.

Your Headline

After your headshot, the next thing recruiters notice is your headline. This headline should say who you are and what you do. It is important to give recruiters focus, and this is one of the areas the search engine rates as important in establishing your profile's ranking in searches. This headline is limited to a 120-character thumbnail description about you and works as a brief biography of the person behind the headshot. You have just these 120 characters to say who you are, so your headline should include your Target Job Title and the keywords that capture your most critical skills. You increase the odds of these working well by doing searches on LinkedIn for your own target job title and looking at how the people who show up on the first few pages of results build a winning headline. Use this insight to adapt what you have to offer to synchronize with your findings.

Your headline should use words likely to be used in searches made by recruiters and will include job titles, critical skills, credentials, and/or experience. Never have "looking for opportunity" or anything remotely similar as your headline, as no one uses words like these for a database search, plus it shows how out of touch you are with modern communications media.

Summary

You have a huge amount of space in this section, and, consequently, your summary can grow over time as you develop the rest of your profile.

To begin with, you need to give recruiters the right information to make you *discoverable*. Your LinkedIn profile (as on other social networking sites) provides more space than your tightly focused, job-targeted resume, and you need to take full advantage of this. Start by adding those five or so lines from your *primary* resume's Performance Profile, because this is the condensed version of the critical skills and experience that employers seek when looking to hire someone with your title. You should see *Knock 'em Dead Resumes* for complete details on resume writing; the phrase *primary resume* relates to the need for each resume to have a specific focus. Add to this any additional information from the Performance Profiles of any additional resumes you might have created. Real estate was at a premium in your resume, so sentences were often truncated; now you can restore them to full sentences.

Use any remaining available space to show critically important skill sets in action. Wherever possible, repeat the keywords your TJD work told you are most important for increasing your discoverability in searches.

Work Experience

The experience section of your profile begins with your work experience. Again, you can cut and paste the entry from your resume first, then add to this with additional information that you feel is relevant.

Review your entries to see if there is additional experience you would like to add. You have plenty of space here, so as long as your headline and entries for each job start with the most important information as determined by your TJD—making your profile more discoverable and a more tempting read for recruiters—you can continue to add additional supporting information you deem important.

The inclusion of keywords in each job's headline and in the details of that work experience helps make you more visible. This helps recruiters see your claims of professional competency in context and will dramatically increase the frequency of keyword usage. Do this with each job and your discoverability will steadily rise in the results of recruiters' searches.

Skills

Adding skills to your LinkedIn profile has the same benefits as adding them to your resume: They make your profile more visible in database searches and your skills more readily accessible to readers. The number of endorsements you get for your skills increases your visibility. Now while you can add a list of up to fifty skills in the *professional skills* area of your profile and make it possible for others to add skills I DON'T RECOMMEND IT! Listing fewer skills can mean more endorsements for each skill, and more endorsements help your discoverability.

Limit the skills to those you've determined are important to your resume (when you did the Target Job Deconstruction exercise). Fewer options mean more likelihood that the volume of endorsements for those skills will increase at a faster rate. Turn off the option on your *Settings* page that allows friends and colleagues to add skills as this will only dilute the impact by having a slew of not very important skills that have been endorsed by one or two people—you do not want to underwhelm your readers.

The best way to get these endorsements is to give them to others and then, if someone doesn't reciprocate in a day or two, to ask her to do so: "Hi Carole, I endorsed your profile for half a dozen skills the other day and wonder if you can do the same for me when you have a moment. Thanks." The more endorsements you have for your skills, the more *discoverable* you become to recruiters. As your networks grow, they'll certainly include others who are in transition, and mutual skill endorsements can help you both.

Education

Start with your highest educational level and work backward. While your educational attainments will usually stop with postsecondary education in your resume, with a LinkedIn profile you might want to consider listing high school as well: This increases your networking opportunities.

Certifications

Add all your professional certifications; they demonstrate that either your employers, or you personally, have seen fit to invest in your ongoing professional education. They also speak to money that a new employer doesn't have to invest. Additionally, they can be used by recruiters as search terms, making you more discoverable.

Associations and Awards

Include membership in any associations or societies, as these are also search terms a recruiter might use, on the assumption that people who belong to professional associations are, by definition, likely to be more committed to—and therefore more up-to-date with—the *technical skills* of their profession.

Reading List

Be sure your list includes profession-oriented materials, because the target audiences you want to impress are recruiters and hiring managers.

Recommendations

LinkedIn doesn't recognize your profile as complete until you have three recommendations, and the more you have, the more *discoverable* your profile will become. This is in your best interests too, as recommendations from colleagues, coworkers, and past managers give your profile depth and increase your appeal to recruiters. The easiest way to get recommendations is to do them for your colleagues and then ask them to reciprocate. LinkedIn will send a recommendation you write to the recipient and ask him (a) if he would like to upload it, and (b) if he would like to reciprocate. Nevertheless, if the recipient doesn't reciprocate within a couple of days, send a personal request: You don't need to tell someone he *owes* you a reference in return for yours, just that you'd appreciate it.

Link a Resume to Your Profile

Uploading your resume to your LI profile is useful because a resume is still the most succinct vehicle for sharing your professional skills, and recruiters will use it for their records and to review with hiring managers. Your resume in turn should have a hyperlink to your LinkedIn profile (beneath your hyperlinked email address). LinkedIn now offers a badge that you paste onto resumes and emails, etc., so that HR or the hiring manager can click through and gather more insight into your potential candidacy.

Always define the professional face you show to the world with your resume and be absolutely certain that every aspect, especially dates and employers, of the LI profile matches the information on your resume—discrepancies encourage red flags about your candidacy.

Privacy and Saving Your Work

Every time you change a sentence on your LinkedIn profile and log out, LinkedIn will automatically send a change of status to your network, unless you specify otherwise. As it will take you at least a week or two and many changes to get your profile right, you don't want your contacts notified every few minutes. To avoid this, go to *Settings* from the drop-down menu under your name on the top right of your homepage; once the page loads, look for *Privacy Controls*.

As with all things computer related, if you don't back up your work, somewhere along the line you are going to lose it. My recommendation is to create your profile in a Microsoft Word document *and to back up that document*. Then, when you have a complete (and grammatically correct) social media profile in Microsoft Word, it's ready to be uploaded to this and other social networking sites you might join (after a slight tweaking to create unique content for each of those sites).

Search Engine Optimization (SEO) and You

At this point you have a profile ready to be optimized for maximum discoverability by search engines. LinkedIn, like all social networking sites, has specific and, annoyingly, ever-changing advice for Search Engine Optimization (SEO), so you should always check the "Help" pages to ensure that you are current. Despite this constantly changing advice, a couple of SEO-worthy actions have remained consistent.

Your headline (coming next to the headshot at the top of your profile) should include your target job title and as many priority skills as space permits. The special skills you list should be those terms you think a recruiter would be most likely to use, based on your findings in the TJD exercise.

Your target job title and these relevant skills are attractive to a search engine, and using them increases your discoverability. So, working through your professional history, for each new job, always fill in the job title and then test how many skills, relevant to your target job, can be added before you run out of space.

Making Connections

LinkedIn does not consider your profile complete until you have at least fifty connections. Therefore you should immediately reach out to anyone with whom you have connections from present or past employers, college or high school, neighbors and friends, and people you have gotten to know through either professional association or local community. Then start connecting with anyone who is working or who has worked with the same employers.

The Webmail Import Feature

An easy way to discover almost everyone you know who is already on LinkedIn is to use the webmail import feature. This will compare the webmail addresses in your email program with members and tell you of people you're likely to know.

Once you have reached out to connect with all current and past colleagues, professional acquaintances, and coworkers, it is time to start expanding the depth and breadth of your network to people you don't know, but who, by virtue of their titles and where they work, you feel might be beneficial to your professional future.

Beware the 800-Pound LinkedIn Elephant

LinkedIn started out saying that you should only connect with people you already know, and it has never changed its stance, so unless they backpedal between my writing and your reading, you may well see this advice when you first join. However, the site's users have dramatically changed the way that the site is used. It is now common practice and completely allowable to connect with people you don't know and have never met. Using LinkedIn groups is one of the most effective ways to do this.

LinkedIn Groups

LinkedIn only permits you to reach out to someone directly if you know each other or if you have a shared interest, and being a member of the same group counts as that shared interest. LinkedIn has thousands of special-interest groups where you can find exactly the people most likely to shape your future for the better. Group membership allows you to reach out and establish relationships with a very significant cross-section of your professional community. You are allowed to join up to fifty groups and can change the groups you belong to whenever you want. Joining groups that attract people from your profession should be a primary goal.

To connect with people within these groups, you can "like" someone's comment on one of the discussions (she will be notified and flattered) or even add your own comments. Subsequently, anyone you have complimented in this way can then be approached for a connection in the following thirty-six hours—long enough not to look needy and soon enough that you'll still be remembered. If the people you want to connect with are group members but not active on the discussion groups, you can also simply approach them for a connection based on your common interests as expressed by your shared membership in that particular group. Once you belong to a group you will have access to a list of the other members.

Who Makes the Most Valuable Connections?

Almost anyone in your industry or immediate area can be useful, regardless of title or experience, but the people of most interest, the people who, based on your professional goals, hold high-value job titles, are most valuable. They will fall into these categories:

1. People who hold job titles that are one, two, or three levels above your own, because these are the people most likely to be in a position to hire you, now and in the future.
2. Those with the same job title as you, and ideally within your target industry and target geographic location.
3. Those people one job title below yours, and ideally within your target industry and location.
4. Those job titles with whom you would interact on a regular basis at work. They will have different functions and might work in different departments, but they are close enough to potentially hear of opportunities.

People with these job titles are the people most likely to know about suitable opportunities, have the authority to hire you, or have the ability to make a referral or introduction to someone who does.

Advanced People Search

Apart from finding high-value job titles in groups, you can use the "advanced people search." You can enter a sequence of varying job titles and/or companies/industries/geographic areas and expect thousands of responses within seconds.

As people with a lot of connections are typically more active and involved with LinkedIn, go to "sort by" and look for "number of connections," then start by limiting your search to 500+ connections. Prepare a short and professional invitation, because this sector of the LI community is most likely to accept your request. You can subsequently work your way downward on the connectivity ladder. As you examine your search results in this exercise, you should also check the groups these people belong to, which will either show a bond of interest through common group membership, or alternatively make you aware of groups that might benefit you.

Once you have more than 100 connections, you want to become more focused on finding and connecting with the high-value job titles we discussed earlier. You should always continue to grow your connections, because the greater the number of your contacts, the more people you are able to reach and the wider the range of people to whom you become discoverable.

Pay It Forward

You can initiate relationships by asking for advice; many people will give you a few minutes of their time, but you will develop the best relationships by reaching out to others with help and advice, because when you offer good things, forging a relationship with you becomes important to the other person.

Making Posts

You can help your growing circle of colleagues who make up the different groups you belong to just by sharing useful information—with the added benefit that you simultaneously increase your credibility and visibility. We are all drowning in Internet-delivered information, and whatever your profession, it undoubtedly has its fair share of bloggers and curators (re-posters) of content.

One option is to identify half a dozen respected resources; for example, if you are sharing business issues, you can't go wrong linking to the *Harvard Business Review*, and the mere fact that you refer to them on a regular basis (as we do on the *Knock 'em Dead* blog) is seen as evidence that you are someone who keeps abreast of the important topics with reliable commentators. All you have to do is write a post that consists of a sentence or two that say why you think a particular article or topic is interesting, and then add a link to the source. In effect, you are making intelligent posts by curating the work of others.

People change jobs on average every four years, only sometimes by choice, and this means making occasional intelligent posts about career issues can also increase your visibility and credibility. You get points for perception but don't waste job search time writing the damn things.

An alternative is to use Google Alerts. With this option, you click on *Alerts* on Google.com and enter search terms that are of professional interest to you and others in your profession. Google will send you links to matching results. One word of caution: stay away from politics, religion, and sex; they will all damage your professional reputation. We'll discuss further tools for curating profession-relevant information over the coming chapters.

Other Ways to Leverage Your Connections

When you find an online job posting that seems like a good fit, you are usually faced with uploading your resume into a corporate or headhunter database . . . and then waiting and waiting for a response. However, your social networks can quite possibly deliver direct contact with the people who can hire you or the people who know the people who can hire you. On all of your social networking sites, you can find people who work at your "companies of interest" or have done so in the past. Search for them, using the company name in your keyword search, then look for job titles one, two, and three levels above your own; for titles at your rank and a level below it; and for job titles that interact with yours on a regular basis.

Once you have identified profiles of desirable titleholders, you can approach them to connect. You can do this based on your common professional interests or shared group membership, or with an email stating your professional interests. Check out *Knock 'em Dead Job Search Letter Templates* for sample social networking letters.

Other LinkedIn Resources

LinkedIn, like most social networking sites, offers an array of tools for your professional networking activities:

- Job postings from employers and headhunters
- Reminders of when to nurture your relationships with a follow-up call or email
- Thousands of special-interest groups
- Links to job sites
- Offline social events to network in person

LinkedIn Is Just the Start

LinkedIn is just one of hundreds of social networking sites, and you'll find that most follow the same general format and request the same topics of information. We will move on now to examine the other three major social networking sites: Facebook, Twitter, and Google+. Because much of the profile information you'll be requested to provide will mirror what you needed to create your LinkedIn profile, we will focus on the variations that make these other sites different.

Facebook

Many people are leery of using Facebook as a serious professional networking platform. However, if you do—and you should—you need to keep your profile professional in word and tone.

Your Facebook Profile

Many of the sections of your Facebook profile correspond to similar ones already discussed in the previous section on LinkedIn, so we'll focus on those portions of the profile that are unique to Facebook.

On Facebook your profile appears under the heading *Timeline*. While it allows you to include all the professional information you'd expect on LinkedIn or Google+, Facebook focuses on your personal life by encouraging casual photos (which you should approach with professional caution), showing your recent activities (keep them professional), whom you recently connected with (like the other sites), whom and what you have recently liked, what you've been watching on Netflix or Hulu, and the music you've been listening to on Spotify. Like LinkedIn, you can show covers of books you've recently read (a good advertisement opportunity for your dedication to professional matters).

Now you can hide or highlight these and many more features, but talking about and sharing your tastes and the most personal information about yourself is strangely addictive. To help you keep yourself focused on the professional image you want to promote, keep this thought in mind: You are trying to get hired, not dated. In a couple of paragraphs, we'll discuss an app that helps you keep things professional.

Home Town

Recruiters search by skills and by geographic location (to avoid relocation costs), so you should provide the name of your current city of residence. In an age in which relocation is seen as a barrier to recruitment, I have known professionals in transition who are intent on moving from say, Phoenix to Nashville, listing Nashville as their current residence to overcome that barrier. I'm not recommending this, but people are doing it.

Clean Up Your Profile

If you grew up with social networking, there are probably details of your wilder times available online for the world to see. You need to do searches for yourself to discover exactly what is out there about you, and when you find something that is inappropriate for your professional image, go back and clean up your digital dirt.

I just returned from an appearance at a major convention for college career services and corporate campus recruiters. It was noted at the conference that upward of 80 percent of recruiters are using publicly available online data about short-list candidates as a screening tool. Twenty-five percent said they would reject a candidate based on this information. This means we all have to police the image we have online, so delete those once-amusing pictures of you projectile vomiting at a frat party.

Your mantra needs to be: Cause the least offense to the greatest majority of people. For professional networking purposes, you should leave out references to sexual, political, or religious issues, because whatever your POV is, it is guaranteed to offend someone who might otherwise offer you a great professional opportunity. Your profile can still represent the real you without causing offense in these areas. A neat app called Reppler will review your profiles, help you manage your online image across all social networks, and alert you to questionable content.

Privacy Settings

If you are determined to include content that common sense or Reppler finds questionable, make sure that your privacy settings are very strict. Set them to just "friends"; even "friends of friends" opens you up to danger. With the *friends only* setting, employers won't be able to see the details of your profile, your photos, or your personal status updates.

Restricting Access

On your Account page, choose *Edit Friends* from the drop-down menu, then *Create List*. For employers and recruiters, you can create a *High-Value Titles* or *Restricted* list and add them to that (when we come to Google+, we'll do something similar and put all your high-value management connections into their own Circle). Make sure that this Circle (on Facebook, your

High-Value Titles or *Restricted* list) receives only audience-appropriate posts from you. People on this list will only see posts you tag as "public."

Also, if you have connections with crazies who have no concern for their professional reputation or who post sexual, religious, or political comments or comments about employers or coworkers, you can deactivate your "wall" until you land that new job.

Becoming Discoverable

Facebook is one of the biggest websites in the world, and your profile is one of hundreds of millions. In effect, you are a single indistinguishable stalk of wheat in the vast prairie lands of America. This means that unless someone is looking for you in particular, recruiters' searches for your professional skill set will only find you when you do everything you can to make yourself *discoverable*, both with the profile you create and by the activities you engage in on Facebook.

First, your Facebook profile, along with your posts (clean up any questionable past comments), needs to complement the messaging you have on LinkedIn, Google+, and any other social networking sites. While the information you share and how you share it can vary, the messages you send and comment on should be compatible with your established *professional brand* and the messaging you use on all your social media sites.

"Liking" and "Following" Company Pages

About 80 percent of American companies, beyond local mom-and-pop operations, have a social media presence on one or more of the big four social recruiting sites. While eight out of ten use social media to recruit, a recent study of corporate recruiters found that 87 percent of those who used social media as a recruitment tool said that the best way to get on company radar is to "Like" the company's page.

If you take the time to identify desirable employers in your target job search area, you can then visit each of your social networking sites, search for that company's homepage, and "follow" them. If you choose to follow that company's page, their posts will show up in your newsfeed under their *list* heading.

This allows you to become much more visible to that company's recruiters by responding to comments and posting questions (non-self-serving) of your own. When company recruiters make posts, add a "like" to the post and, when appropriate, make an intelligent comment or ask a question; this will increase your visibility. Because social media is still new as a recruiting tool, recruiters are excited about it and want success stories. They pay attention to their social media company pages—and that certainly can't hurt your candidacy.

Any "games" you find on a company page are extremely likely to be tied to skills and aptitude testing, so if you play them, expect your involvement to be part of the recruitment process. Don't leave anything unfinished, and "play" like the serious professional you are. An interesting approach I've heard to gaming these disguised aptitude tests is to have a friend who would never be interested in this company permit you to log in under his name. This allows you to preview the test before taking it under your own name. Sneaky, I know, but isn't the company being equally sneaky by not being upfront about their intent? Remember the MeInc. philosophy? If so, you'll recognize that what is good for one company is good for another, and this activity falls under the heading of "competitive intelligence."

Facebook Communities

For like-minded people who may not initially know each other, LinkedIn has Groups, Facebook has Communities, and Google+ has Circles and Communities. These pages all work in similar ways and offer similar benefits. You add value to a Community when you "like" existing discussions, comment on them positively, or start your own discussions. When you do this, you also become more visible, and if your comments/discussions are carefully thought out, they can impress recruiters and professional colleagues, thus improving your credibility.

Useful Facebook Job Search Apps

By the time you read this, Facebook could have over 3 million jobs posted, and there are a growing number of apps that can be useful in your job search.

Graph Search

When you see an interesting opportunity, you can flag it and use Graph Search to find connections. For example, if you see a job with Bloomberg Media, you can ask it to search for "Bloomberg"; it will search all your connections for people who work or have worked there. You can also use Graph Search to find Facebook members who work at that company and view their public information (such as groups they are involved with). This can open the door to conversation and connection. This app also allows you to find companies and analyze the personal interests of its employees.

SimplyHired

SimplyHired is a job aggregator that cruises around 4,000 sites on your behalf. The neat wrinkle here is that when you sign in with your Facebook account, you can see jobs available at your friends' employers. Of course, these friends can give you introductions.

BeKnown

This is an easy way to search for jobs and apply without leaving your computer.

CareerFriend Facebook App

This app uses your Facebook friends' work information to find potential job opportunities within your network.

IngBoo

You can select advanced search options (keyword, location, etc.) on Monster, Simply Hired, CareerBuilder, and more.

LinkUp Facebook App

This is a good one. It allows companies to automatically publish jobs from their corporate websites onto their Facebook Fan pages. Headhunters use this tool too.

BranchOut

BranchOut, Facebook's app for professional networking, is designed to help you leverage your social networks for job search and professional development, and it's quite impressive. It currently has more than 800 million professional profiles, and it's growing every day. It's the largest networking service on Facebook. You can use it in a couple of valuable ways:

- To search for job postings
- To search for connections at these companies

When you create a brief professional profile on BranchOut, you become visible to the hordes of recruiters who search this enormous database every day.

Social Jobs

Social Jobs connects you to open positions where you live.

Facebook in Your Networking Strategy

I don't think Facebook is going to surpass LinkedIn as the number one professional networking site just yet. However, it is becoming more useful every day and should definitely be part of your networking plan of attack. With the tactics we've discussed and the growing list of tools built for the site, the odds of Facebook adding real value to your search are now steadily improving. Just remember that Facebook really is geared to the social side of life, and while it is developing assets focused on the professional side, you still have to be careful not to get wooed into making inappropriate comments.

Twitter

When Twitter first launched, it wasn't immediately clear how the service could be used effectively by job hunters or professionals looking for new career management tools. Gradually, though, useful applications evolved, and now the service has a real role in both job search and career management.

"Tweeting" is Twitter slang for making a post. Twitter allows a user to make tweets of 140 characters, including spaces and a hyperlink. You can't say much of weight in 140 characters.

Twitter is useful in a job search for tracking companies, recruiters, headhunters, and the activities of high-value job titles in your profession. You can, of course, also tweet to your heart's content, but using Twitter to *listen* to what your professional world is doing will lead you to companies, jobs, and recruiters of interest. Once you have created a profile and begun to identify the companies and high-value people to whom you want to become visible, intelligent tweeting activities can put you on the radar of high-value contacts in a way that showcases your *professional persona* as thoroughly engaged and committed—not necessarily by what you say but by the questions you ask and the worthy comments of others you pass along with your tweets.

Your Twitter Profile

Many of the sections required for your Twitter profile correspond to the components we discussed in your other social media profiles, so in our discussion of Twitter, we'll just look at those parts of the profile where Twitter adds new twists to the conversation.

Twitter Handle

When you sign up for Twitter, you have to select a "Twitter handle," which is the name you become known by when you tweet (express your own thoughts) or retweet (share the thoughts and information of others). The same considerations apply here as applied to your headline on LinkedIn and our discussions on appropriate email addresses; your presence is profession oriented, so your handle should speak to your job and your profession in some way. Checking out the Twitter handles of other people in your profession can also give you ideas for handles that support rather than hurt your brand.

Bio

Your bio should state your job title and capture the essence of your responsibilities and your work capabilities, and do so in an informal, "cut-to-the-chase" manner reflective of the Twitter approach to communication. If you accept the common-sense approach of the *Knock 'em Dead* career management philosophy, you will have completed a TJD on your target job (as we discussed in Chapter 3) as the first step in creating social media profiles that speak with a consistent voice about your *professional persona*. Read a few Twitter profiles and then, using your TJD information, edit your profile to match Twitter's informal style to the extent you can without sounding unprofessional.

It is acceptable to announce that you are in transition and looking for new opportunities; mostly this will be seen by the people with whom you have established connections, but with the right hashtags you will get the attention of a wider audience that was not previously aware of you.

Hashtags

The big problem with all social media is filtering out the white noise of irrelevant information. *Hashtags*—searchable terms used in tweets and identified by a preceding pound sign (for example: #jobsearch or #accountantjobs)—help the Twitter search engine categorize and find messages that follow a common theme.

You can use hashtag terms to find job opportunities and profession-relevant information. You can also use them in your tweets to share information with your own followers, as well as to attract new followers who have similar interests. They can help build your Twitter network with a relevant and distinct focus. You can use them anywhere in a tweet: at the beginning, middle, or end. You can increase your visibility with recruiters who are looking for people like you with hashtags like:

- #resume
- #profile, #linkedin, #google+, #facebook
- #accountant. Or whatever your job title may be. Recruiters will look for people by their job title, and using an appropriate hashtag helps them find you.
- # "A key skill." If you possess an in-demand skill, there's an excellent chance recruiters will be using that as a search term. Placing a hashtag in front of that word or phrase makes it, and you, more *discoverable*. For example: #MBA, #Leanmanagement, #datasourcing.

Some people recommend hashtags such as #unemployed or #needajob, but I feel these make you sound altogether hopeless. They're the online version of that poor homeless person's sign reading: "Will work for food." To find more useful hashtags for job seekers, google: "popular job search hashtags."

Twitter Job Leads

Companies and headhunters use Twitter to post jobs because it is a fast, cheap, and effective way to get the word out to a large audience. *You* will use it to:

- Learn about job opportunities
- Share the ones that aren't right for you as you retweet and mention them in your other social networking activities
- Retweet the more interesting announcements from companies in your profession

If you use the direct research and approach tactics I address in Chapter 6, by the time you start using Twitter you will have identified every company of interest and every headhunter who works within the target location of your job search. You can then find and follow them on Twitter. Once identified, you can get their tweets linked to your Twitter feed, so that their tweets come to you automatically for review at your convenience.

How to Become Visible to Recruiters

Recruiters tweet about specific job openings and, to a lesser degree, general information of interest to their target audience. Following a company on Twitter also gives you insight into its activities and culture, and these insights can help you tailor your communications with that company.

Recruiters will notice that you are a follower and that you "like" and retweet their posts. This will lead them to look at your tweets and profile; in other words, it increases your visibility and credibility.

By following companies and individual recruiters, you will hear about job openings. When they aren't relevant to your needs but might be helpful to your network, you should retweet them (as you should a recruiter's other profession-related tweets). This will raise your visibility with the company recruiters (to say nothing of strengthening your network).

Some of the common hashtags used by employers to make their employment needs more discoverable include:

#hiring	#jobpostings
#joblisting	#employment
#jobopening	#opportunity

You can use these hashtags as search terms, both on their own and followed by a job title and/or key skills.

Good Twitter Apps for Job Tracking

Apps that help you discover and track jobs can be a great timesaver. You should check out:

Jobmob.co.il	JobShouts
@linkedin_job	MicroJobs

All of these apps help you find job openings and you can find plenty more when on Twitter or by doing a Google search.

You Are What You Tweet

Next to informing you about job opportunities, your Twitter presence is best suited to helping increase your visibility and credibility by allowing you to share professionally relevant information and resources with a wider audience.

To become a source of interest to others who don't know you personally, the focus of your tweets has to be professional and relevant.

You can tweet fifty times a day if you want, but tweeting takes time, and many recruiters and others in your profession will wonder what you are doing for a living, or for your job search, if you spend all day tweeting.

Increase Ur Tweet Content

Twitter only allows tweets of 140 characters *including a link*, and this limitation requires you to be concise in everything you say; as of this writing Twitter is about to enable a new feature that allows longer tweets. As the purpose of any tweet is to drive the reader to more detailed information, try to think of your tweets as headlines. Many Twitter users feel that posing a headline as a question draws people to click on a link to discover the answer.

Your tweets need to demonstrate that you have strong *written communication skills* for the medium. Twitter has rules that are different from traditional communication, so when you can't get your tweet and hyperlink into the allowed 140 characters including spaces, start abbreviating. This link will give you some more good ideas about how to communicate effectively with 140-character-or-less tweets: *www.pardot.com/blog/8-ways-cram-tweets-140-characters-2/*.

How to Compress Long Hyperlinks

Hyperlinks can be very long, and your 140 character–limited tweets must also include the link you want readers to follow for more detailed information. Fortunately, there are tools called URL shorteners that compress your links, such as Bitly. You copy the original link into a dialogue box, and within seconds Bitly delivers a compressed version comprising just a few characters.

Think Before You Tweet

All professional jobs require good judgment and a positive attitude, so keep your tweets free of negativity, questionable comments, and absolutely stay away from politics or religion because, whatever your beliefs on these issues, you are guaranteed to annoy at least 50 percent of your audience.

Sources for Tweets and Retweets

Following experts prominent in your profession gives you content to retweet that adds to your credibility and puts you in good company. By consistently sharing intelligent commentary on your profession and its issues, you might not become an overnight industry expert, but you will be taken that much more seriously by those who could hire you. Here are some good sites for finding these experts:

- Twellow
- wthashtag.com
- Muck Rack
- Twiangulate
- Followerwonk

You Are Who You Retweet

The Internet has given us a world in which anyone can state that he is the world's greatest authority on whatever grabs his fancy, but that doesn't necessarily make it so. For example, *The Daily Muse*, a usually carefully researched publication, recently advised unemployed people that they could pick up a few bucks on the side by promoting themselves as coaches! Verify the credentials of the people you listen to and subsequently quote in your tweets and posts on other social networking sites, because to people you don't know, you are who you quote. You don't want to be caught quoting such instant experts—professionals can tell the difference.

Build Your Network

The bigger your network, the more likely you are to have an inside connection at companies you'd like to approach. Look for friends and colleagues, coworkers, former managers, college friends, and so on. Re-establishing connections with people you've known allows you to ask what they are doing and share what you are doing, and these contacts will in turn bring you within reach of new potential connections.

Connect with Recruiters and Headhunters

Recruiters live on social media sites, so you can find headhunters and corporate recruiters who work in your profession and target geography and add them as friends. With a *friend request*, always add a personal note explaining why you want to add her or him as a friend. Headhunters' and recruiters' lifeblood is connectivity, so most will accept. With that connection you have just gotten that much closer to starting a conversation that could lead to interviews and job offers.

Status Updates

With social networking, being helpful and paying it forward is important. Read your connections' updates regularly, "like" them, and whenever you can offer help, do so.

If you are in a job search, you should also add two or three search-related posts each week, generated from the resources we discussed earlier.

That may seem like overkill, but people are forgetful, and while you might write three status updates, that doesn't mean all your contacts read or see any of them. By updating your network with your job search updates, you stay in the forefront of their minds. Hootsuite saves you time and enables you to manage your social networks by posting comments across all your social networking sites at once.

Google+

Google+ is the least important of the four major social media platforms, but it is valuable once you have the top three set up, functioning, and under control. Google+ has a professional focus similar to LinkedIn but combines it with many of Facebook's attractions. Google+ also makes it easy to locate and connect with relevant and high-value professionals you don't know without requiring an introduction.

If you have a free gmail account, you automatically have a Google+ account—you just have to complete your profile and then become part of the Google+ networking community.

Your Google+ Profile

Many of the sections of your Google+ profile correspond to similar ones already discussed in the section on LinkedIn, so here we will only discuss features unique to Google+. However, your Google+ profile shouldn't be an exact replica of your LinkedIn profile. The Google search engine algorithms don't give you points for exact duplication. In fact, some authorities claim you will be penalized. Unfortunately, to stop people gaming their algorithms, Google isn't precise on how they track this issue.

However, Sergey Brin, one of Google's founders, when talking about blogs, suggested that as long as the first paragraph or two aren't identically worded, you should be all right. It's safe to assume this advice holds for other documents on Google+.

Phone

Do not use your employer's phone number, but rather use your landline at home or your cell phone number—as long as either of these is unknown to your employer. If both numbers are known, consider buying one of those cheap burner phones, which will give you a unique number and the ability to take messages. You can find more information on phones and confidentiality in Chapter 6.

Professional Experience

When transferring your work history from LinkedIn to Google+, watch out for dates and employer names. When moving between different social media profiles and your resume, the number of your jobs and employment dates can easily get jumbled. You must exercise extreme caution in ensuring that this does not happen, as such discrepancies can get your candidacy dismissed from consideration.

Other Profiles

Link to your other social networking profiles if they *don't* conflict with your central messaging and *do* add fresh but complementary views of you. From a practical perspective, if you create profiles on LinkedIn, Twitter, Facebook, and Google+, over time there *will* be inconsistencies. So whenever you update one profile, review it against the others for consistency.

"Contributor to" and "Links"

Offer links to any blogs, websites, articles, books, or patents you created or have contributed to. This helps people learn more about your knowledge and professionalism, and also helps with Google Authorship, which rewards creation of original content with increased visibility in search rankings.

Phone

Google+ also asks for a work phone. Do not use your employer's phone number, but rather your preferred contact number, probably your cell phone. The issue of supplying telephone numbers is a thorny one for women, who are more likely than men to be harassed by stalkers.

Birthday

This is no one's business unless you choose for it to be. No matter your age, supplying this information is likely to work against you at some point.

Gender

Your gender will probably be obvious from your name. Either way, it should be irrelevant to your professional activities and can only be used against you, if only by helping create a marketing profile.

Places Lived

Largely irrelevant unless it speaks to your cultural diversity or the geographic target location of your search. The first entry here should reflect where you live now. It's a big plus in a global economy if you have lived overseas or read or speak a foreign language, so you might try something like: "Iran, fluent Farsi. Singapore, basic Mandarin."

Relationship

Personally oriented subject headings in your profile such as this one are Google+'s attempt to be both LinkedIn (professionally oriented) and Facebook (socially oriented) by giving you control of who sees what on your profile. Your relationship status is entirely personal, and I would advise against filling this in, unless you know it to be beneficial to your professional image.

Bragging Rights

If you have interests that support your professionalism, use them. For example, games such as chess speak to your analytical skills, while distance running, swimming, and riding speak to both health and your determination and resilience. Use verifiable professional achievements or skills related to professional achievement, such as "Top regional sales last three years out of five" or "Member of Mensa and appeared on *Jeopardy!*"

Profile Discovery

When your profile is complete, leave it for twenty-four hours and then come back and read it with fresh eyes. You will almost certainly make some tweaks. Once everything is just as you want it, check it against your resume and other social media profiles to ensure compatibility. Once this is done, you can enable "profile discovery," which makes your profile public.

YOUR GOOGLE+ ADDRESS/URL

You'll have the opportunity to create a Google+ URL address. To create this URL, Google+ asks for your name or nickname, then your current Google+ ID. Rather than using your name or nickname, which only your familiars know, try something that speaks to your profession, captures the essence of your *professional brand*, and hopefully adds to your discoverability, like KillerSystemsAnalyst or TopAccountant. If these are taken (and they probably are), try adding your area code or zip code—TopAccountant516 or TopAccountant31405—or your town—TopAccountantCharleston.

Building Google+ Circles

LinkedIn has established *Groups* that you can join, whereas Google+ has *Communities* you can join and *Circles* you can create and populate with whomever you want. You can create as many Circles as you wish, using your own criteria for defining who goes into which Circle. You can add both people you know and people you don't know to your Circles.

Google+ gives you control of your profile and who gets to see what. You can drag and drop your contacts into the different Circles that you create, and thereby keep your employers and professional peers completely separate.

These contact Circles can be potential employers, contacts at target companies, or others who are helping you get a job. You can keep them in one group or separate them out and send them relevant updates on your current job search. Keeping high-value hiring titles separate is helpful in maintaining your professionalism and some control over what recruiters and potential hiring managers see about you.

Locating Contacts for Specific Circles

Let's say you're an accountant looking to create a Circle for high-value contacts—those people with job titles that imply the authority to hire you or who hold titles that imply professional contact with those potential hiring authorities. All you need to do is a search within the

Google+ site using "google.com google" followed by your choice of keywords. For example, an accountant might try searching:

google.com google Accounting Manager

google.com google Accounting Director

google.com google Finance Director

google.com google Controller

google.com google VP of Finance

Repeating "google.com google" in your search term may seem strange, but it's just the way to get the Google+ search engine to find what you want efficiently.

Once a search delivers results, you decide who to put in each particular Circle. For example, it would make sense to put all those contacts with titles one or more levels above your own into their own Circle so that you can customize your messages to be of interest to that Circle. Keeping employers away from professional colleagues is a good idea in a job search, because mingling the two could reveal to recruiters potential competitors for the job you want.

You can add contacts to your Circles without their authorization (unlike on LinkedIn) and/or a request that they "friend" you back (as on Facebook).

Follow High-Level Contacts

As you find the names that go with your targeted high-value job titles and add them to a Circle, you are getting that much closer to *getting into conversations with the people in a position to hire you*. So when you identify an especially interesting prospect, follow his posts and, as appropriate opportunities arise, comment on them, or repost with the person's name and a flattering comment. Most people remember flattering comments, especially when reminded of them. Consequently, when you reach out to this person for direct communication, you can make reference to the post you liked and commented on as an icebreaker.

Other Unique Google+ Features

Streams, Sparks, and Posts

- **Streams**—On your homepage you'll see your *Home Stream*. This tool collects and filters all the posts made by all the people in your different Circles. With the *All* filter selected, you can choose to see all these posts in either one long stream or by individual Circle. When you are engaged in a job search, reviewing the posts made by Circles that include recruiters and potential hiring managers should be a top priority, because these are the posts most likely to mention job openings, and can give you the most mileage when you like or comment on them, potentially building bridges of connection with the very people who can most influence your professional future.

- **Sparks**—The *Sparks* function allows you to track posts, videos, and other information on topics of interest. This can contribute to your ongoing education and/or alert you to valuable information that you can subsequently share with your Circles, identifying you as a committed and engaged professional who contributes to the common good. You can also use it to gather insights into any company with whom you've landed an interview.

  On your homepage you can find Sparks underneath Circles near the top of the page. Google+ has set up a number of Sparks categories from which you can choose.

- **Posts**—Making your posts public allows Google+ to index your expertise and supply it as a link in response to other people's queries on this topic, which makes you and your knowledge discoverable by a much wider audience. Just be aware, though, that if you post something and it's re-shared, your friends will be able to see the post even if the original was not shared with them. You can avoid this when you click the down arrow button in your post and choose "disable re-share."

Google+ Hangouts

The future is here. Hangouts are Google+'s version of group video chat (like Skype), and allow you to join in conversations with people in your field. These video chats are currently limited to ten people; however, they can broadcast to an unlimited number, so I can see it being used as a platform for industry experts to share their expertise with much larger audiences. Look for *Knock 'em Dead Hangouts* coming soon!

Google is a financial powerhouse with every intention of dominating the social networking scene, so you can expect ongoing enhancements to the networking capabilities of Google+.

Social Networks in Your Job Search

We have talked about LinkedIn, Facebook, Twitter, and Google+. There are many more networking sites that could be useful for your job search. However, you should be careful to focus your energies on a handful of sites, rather than dilute the impact of your social networking activities with a minimal presence on too many.

Any successful professional networking strategy also leverages a handful of additional online and offline networks too, and these are what we will turn to next.

CHAPTER 5
PROFESSIONAL, ALUMNI, AND COMMUNITY NETWORKS

ONE OF THE best things you can do for this job search and your long-term career success is connect with your professional community, both online and offline.

Professional associations have monthly meetings in all major metropolitan areas, plus regional and national get-togethers every year. The local meetings are of immediate interest, and, unless you work on a national level, membership in the local or state chapters of a national association will be quite sufficient for your needs—and cheaper, too.

Professional Associations

When you join a local chapter of a recognized national association and attend the local meetings, you get to know, and become known by, the most committed and best-connected people in your profession in your target marketplace. Your membership will help you stay attuned to the skill changes that are occurring in your profession, as associations offer ongoing training that makes you a more knowledgeable, and therefore a more desirable, employee. Of course, almost everything that is happening locally is also happening in the association's online groups.

The professional association is a new "old boy" network for the modern world. Your membership becomes a link to millions of colleagues, most of whom will gladly talk to you based on your connection through the association.

All industries and professions have multiple associations, any one of which could be valuable depending on your needs. For example, if you are in retail, you could join any of some thirty national associations and their fifty state associations. Together these associations represent employees of more than 1.5 million retail organizations, which in turn provide employment for more than 14 million people. Most other associations offer similarly impressive networking potential.

If you fit the profile of a special-interest or minority group, you will also find professional associations that cater to another dimension of the *professional you*. These include—but are by no means restricted to—associations for African Americans, Latinos, Asian Americans, professionals with disabilities, women, and multilingual professionals. If you can find a niche association that's a fit, it represents a whole new network for you; and besides, companies actively recruit identifiable minorities.

The Value of Volunteering

It is easier to get to know other association members than you might think. All professional association members are there, at least in part, to advance their careers through networking.

When you join an association, you'll benefit greatly from attending the meetings, because this is where you will meet other professionals in your field. But don't just attend the meetings; get involved. Associations are largely volunteer organizations and always need someone to set out chairs or hand out paperwork and name tags. The task itself doesn't matter, but your visible willingness to be an active participant most certainly does and will get you on a first-name basis with people you would probably never meet otherwise.

Given the nature of association membership, you don't have to go straight from introductions to asking for leads on jobs. In fact, it can be productive to have initial conversations in which you do not ask for leads or help in your job search, but where you make a contribution to the group.

Once you have the lay of the land, volunteer for one of the many committees that keep associations running. It's the best way to meet people and expand your sphere of influence, as you can reach out to others while you engage in your volunteer association activities. Committee involvement doesn't take much time, because volunteer associations invariably employ the "many hands make light work" approach. They are structured to function with the help of full-time professionals like you who have mortgages to pay and families to support.

There is a good argument that, from a networking point of view, the bigger the committee, the better. Membership and program committees are among the best to join. However, involvement in any committee will serve your needs, because being on one will enable you to reach out to those on other committees. If you join the conferences and events committee, you can initiate contact with just about anyone in your professional world: "Hi, Bill Parsons? I'm Becky Lemon with the conference committee of the local association. I'd like to invite you to a meeting we are having next week on . . ."

Don't join committees for which you lack the experience to be a productive member, unless you make it clear that the reason you want to become a part of that team is for professional development—if this is the case, expect to become the designated water carrier, at least initially.

If you volunteer and become active in an association, the people with whom you come in contact will begin to identify you as a *team player*. This perception can be instrumental in landing that new job and surging ahead in your career.

Association Databases and Directories

Access to the association database comes with your membership and delivers a superb networking resource for telephone and email networking campaigns. You can feel comfortable calling any other member on the phone and introducing yourself: "Hi, Belinda Carlyle? My name is Martin Yate. We haven't spoken before, but we are both members of the Teachers' Federation. I need some advice; can you spare a minute?"

Your mutual membership, and the commitment to your profession that it bespeaks, will guarantee you a few moments of anyone's time—a courtesy you should always return.

You can also use your association membership database to generate personal introductions for jobs you have heard about elsewhere. For example, you might have found an interesting job posting on *www.careerbuilder.com* or perhaps on a company website, with the request that you upload your resume; this is where your networking can pay big dividends. Apply just as requested on the website where you found the job, then return to your various membership databases and find people who work for, or have worked for, that company. A judicious call or two will frequently get you a personal referral and some inside information on the opening, and you have just *doubled your chances of landing that interview*. Once you have an interview scheduled, these same contacts can help you prepare for the interview with insider knowledge about the company, the department, the hiring manager, and the usual steps in their selection cycle.

Newsletters

Professional associations all have online newsletters, and many have a jobs section that appears on their website and is linked to the newsletter. Companies post job openings with professional associations because they know the applicants will be qualified. For this reason, you will often see job postings that don't appear anywhere else. In down economic times, a savvy corporate recruiter will use an association website to skim the cream of available talent while at the same time screening out the less committed.

You will also notice that association members write all the articles in the newsletters. Everyone likes to have their literary efforts appreciated, and telling a member you have read an article he's written gives you a great introduction to a networking call or letter.

KNOCK 'EM DEAD TIP

List professional associations at the end of your resume under a "Professional Affiliations" heading. This is guaranteed to get a second glance, as it signifies professional awareness. Employers and headhunters will sometimes use words like *association*, *club*, and *society* in their keyword searches, so association membership will also help get your resume pulled up from the databases for investigation by human eyes.

Alumni Associations

Almost every school, from Acme Welding to Wellesley College, has an alumni association, and being a member of your alma mater's can play a pivotal role in your professional life. Historically, alumni associations have existed primarily to raise money from alumni for the school, but in these changing times, they increasingly see career outreach as a cost-efficient way to stay in touch with alumni.

If you are an alumni member, you have access to the alumni association membership database, which puts you in touch with other graduates. Additionally, going to the meetings and occasionally volunteering for some tasks are activities that will ease you into collegial relationships with men and women on every rung of the corporate ladder—people who are in a position to boost your career.

Alumni associations all have online newsletters, and many include information about job openings. An increasing number even have semi-formalized job-hunting networks in which alumni are encouraged to pass on their companies' employment needs. As a member of an alumni association, you can also cultivate an informal relationship with the school's career services department. Even when your school days are in the misty past, don't forget these people and the valuable resource they represent.

Build an Alumni Database

Whenever you upload your resume in response to a job posting, cross-check your alumni database first for members who hold a job title one to three levels above your own, and second for those at or below your level. Using the same approach we discussed with professional association contacts, *you can again double your chances of that job posting turning into an interview* by getting an introduction or referral from a fellow alumnus.

If you don't know the URL of your alma mater, go to *www.utexas.edu/world/univ/*. For community college URLs, you'll find two other useful resources at *www.utexas.edu/world/comcol/state/* and *www.classmates.com*.

Company Alumni Associations

In recent years larger, more widely dispersed companies have seen increased value in maintaining contact with ex-employees, since these people provide a source for future hires or leads on future hires. Corporate HR departments are doing this through online corporate alumni associations. Go to *www.job-hunt.org* for more than 250 corporate alumni associations.

Your Past Managers and Other References As a Networking Resource

It is a major mistake not to speak to your references at all or only at the end of your search, when a job offer is imminent. While as a rule we are confident that our references will speak well of us, the fact is that some might bear us no good will. It isn't wise to discover this by trial and error, as one potential offer after another bites the dust. If these are people you know well and who you *believe* will speak well of you, why not confirm it at the beginning of your job search and leverage that good will throughout your transition?

At the very start of your job search, you should identify as many potential references as possible. The more options, the better the odds of coming up with excellent references. There are other reasons: References can represent great networking resources; everyone you ask to be a reference will be flattered, and they are prime candidates to offer introductions for jobs at their current company. With a little research, you can identify any suitable jobs with the company at which this reference works, putting you in a prime position to ask for a referral or introduction—just not during that first conversation the two of you have had in ten years or more.

KNOCK 'EM DEAD TIP

Of course, when employed, do not use current managers and coworkers as references. It could cost you a job. If you have never worked anywhere else, you can track down people who have already left your current employer. If you explain your situation, they will often act as references for you.

At the beginning of your job search, excellent references, though important, are simply an added bonus. Your real agenda is to use these contacts as another tactic within your overall networking strategy.

The process is simplicity itself, starting with an introduction: "John, this is _____. We worked together at Citibank between 2002 and 2006. How's it going?" It is appropriate here to catch up on gossip and the like. Then broach the subject of your call.

"John, I wanted to ask your advice. [*Everyone loves to be asked for an expert opinion.*] We've had some cutbacks at Fly-By-Night Finance, as you probably heard," or "The last five years at Bank of Crooks and Criminals International have been great, and the _____ project we are just winding down has been a fascinating job. Nevertheless, I've decided this would be a perfect time for a strategic career move to capitalize on my experience."

Then, "John, I realize how important references can be, and I was wondering if you would have any reservations about my using you as one?" It's better to find out now if John doesn't want to be a reference, rather than down the line when it could blow a job offer. The response will usually be positive, so you can then move to the next step. "Thanks, John, I hoped you would say that. Let me update you about what I have been doing recently and tell you about the type of job I'm after." Give a capsule description of what you've done since you worked together and specifically what you can do. Remember that talking too much about what you want in a dream job only reduces your chances of receiving leads. You might also ask John if he would take a look at your resume for you. There are two reasons for this:

1. It gets your resume in his hands so he can pass it on to others.
2. It gives you a reason to follow up with John in two or three weeks, when you can ask for leads.

Notice the goal is *not* to get feedback on your resume, although you often will. If you ask someone his opinion about your resume, in trying to be helpful he will come up with uninformed suggestions that have no basis in an understanding of the world in which your resume must perform. Don't bet your career on your network's good intentions; you now know much more about resume writing than they do. If you completed the Target Job Deconstruction exercise, you have objective criteria against which to judge the quality of your resume. And if you followed the resume-writing directions in Chapter 3 (elaborated on in *Knock 'em Dead Resume Templates*), then you will have checked the story your resume tells against your TJD. It now has all the component parts—the right focus, prioritization of information, and keywords—to make your resume shine.

But while you already have objective benchmarks against which to judge your resume, this doesn't mean you shouldn't listen to suggestions and thank the person who gives them—just that every breeze shouldn't sway you in a new direction. Show appreciation for any advice you receive by following up your call with a thank-you email (see the latest edition of *Knock 'em Dead Job Search Letter Templates* for samples).

With the scene set in this manner, you can network with each of these potential references every month or two, either for input on a particular opportunity or to ask for other intelligence relevant to your search. This might include leads or information about a specific company; for example, "Tina, do you know anyone who went to work at _____?"

Personal/Community Networks

While networking should become an integral part of your life, it will always move into higher gear when strategic career moves are on your front burner. There are a wide variety of personal and community-based networks available to you, depending on your interests and your willingness to become an active member of your local community.

Some are personal: family, friends, and service industry acquaintances.

Others are more formal and socially oriented: such as religious, community, local business, and volunteer groups. Some of these are professional in nature but not restricted to a specific profession (Kiwanis, etc.), while others are community-based groups that focus on a common interest (e.g., Big Brother, Big Sister). You don't necessarily know the people in these groups, but you do have a potential bond based on community involvement. You can find out about these groups in your local newspapers, at the library, through a local school or church, or by searching online.

Family and Friends, Good News/Bad News

It is easy to squander this potentially valuable resource by tapping into it before you have thought through how you can best help your extended family help you. These people aren't stupid, but unlike the contacts you make in your professional networks, they probably don't have a full grasp of what you do for a living. On the other hand, they are highly motivated to help you. Many job hunters make the mistake of confusing the members of this network by giving too much information about their professional life. With the right guidance, your immediate circle will cast a wide net and come up with leads for you, even if they have nothing to do with the professional world.

Here are the steps to help your loved ones help you:

1. Think carefully about what you do for a living and put it in a one- or two-sentence description that even Aunt Aggie can grasp: "I am a computer programmer; I write the instructions that help computers run."
2. Think about the job you want, the kind of company you will work for, and the kind of people you need to talk to. Condense it into a one- or two-sentence explanation: "I'm looking for a job with another computer company. It would be great if you or your friends knew anyone I could talk to who works with computers." Keep it really simple.

3. Give them the information you need to get in touch with these people: "I am looking for the names, email addresses, and telephone numbers of anyone in these areas [*but maybe don't confuse Aunt Aggie with email talk*]. I'm not looking for someone to hire me; I'm just looking for people in my field with whom I can network."

This process of breaking your networking needs into *just three* simple statements gives your immediate circle something they can really work with. You can do this with them one-on-one, or you can get everyone together for a barbecue and get the new program moving in one fell swoop.

Civic, Social, Volunteer, Religious, and Special-Interest Networking Groups

It's good to be involved in your local community, both for your own emotional health and for the health of your community. Your involvement will provide you with a richer personal life, as well as a wide array of networking opportunities. You will find that effective networking with these groups is a little more time-consuming than with professional groups; after all, you have no prior professional relationships, and they don't have a familial obligation to help you out.

At the same time, you can't possibly join all the groups your community has to offer, so you will have to make some decisions about what is practical and which activities are going to be valuable to you in and of themselves; if the activity is personally fulfilling, you are more likely to stick with it over time and reap the personal fulfillment and networking rewards that come from your involvement. These might comprise:

- Service industry acquaintances. Electricians, plumbers, carpenters, accountants, lawyers, hairdressers—anyone whose services you retain is a potential networking resource.
- Religious/community/volunteer groups. These groups connect you with people who wish to make a difference by reaching out to others. Participation in spiritual and volunteer communities helps us achieve a sense of meaning and balance in our lives, and such groups are especially helpful in the emotionally troubled times of job and career change.
- Hobby or special-interest groups. This could be a book club, a women's/men's group, a dance class, a jogging group, or any of the vast number of community-based special-interest groups. It doesn't matter, so long as the activity is one that energizes the inner you by taking you away from the worries of your professional world.
- Business, professional, or civic groups. All communities have networks of professionals joined together in formal groups: Rotarians, Chamber of Commerce, Kiwanis, and many more. These community-based associations, societies, and clubs are professionally oriented in membership, but they aren't focused on one profession; they straddle the line between your professional and community-based networking activities. These groups were conceived as networking tools; they give you another angle of attack for your job search, and perhaps improve your social life.

In your local community networking, your need for job leads should take a back seat to being involved as a productive member. Soon enough, you'll learn what people do for a living, while they learn about you both as a professional and as a human being. As opportunities arise, you can talk about your job search needs.

Your Job Search Network

You will sometimes feel that companies are looking for everyone but you. This can get depressing at times, so you need to be aware of the emotion and manage it. One way is to join or create a support group and job search network with people in the same situation, whether these are online or local community-based networks.

A number of national organizations and many communities support job search networks through religious or other social organizations. Members meet, usually on a weekly basis, to exchange ideas and job leads and, just as important, to share and laugh with others in transition.

You can find groups in your area online at *www.careerjournal.com*, *www.jobbankinfo.org*, or *www.rileyguide.com*. Your local state employment office also maintains lists of job search support groups.

Gathering Leads and Referrals from Networking Conversations

You never know who you're going to meet at the grocery store, coffee shop, hairdresser, or gym. To network effectively in these situations, you need a "networking mindset" that you can get into at a moment's notice. With a networking mindset, you will be surprised at the range of useful people you will meet. Even if they know nothing about your profession, they might know someone involved in the same field as you. Everyone you meet has the potential to know someone who can be useful to your job search.

You can network with people you meet at conventions, association meetings, class reunions, fundraisers, the gym, the coffee shop, continuing-education classes, or at community, social, spiritual, and sporting events. You can talk to them over the telephone, by letter, or via email, online chat, or message posting. While the information-gathering aspects of these conversations will remain fairly constant regardless of the communication medium, there are one or two unique considerations about networking in person.

In-Person Networking

As you never know when you are going to make useful contacts, always maintain a well-put-together appearance in your local community. That doesn't mean that you always have to be dressed for a job interview, just that you should give consideration to your appearance.

Always grab a few of your business cards before leaving the house. Google "create business cards" and you will find suppliers and software for less than $20. When you attend social and professional events, keep those business cards handy. (See *Knock 'em Dead Resumes* for detailed instructions on how to create a "business card resume.") However, for networking in your community, leave your full resume at home: Thrusting one at every new acquaintance will come across as overanxious.

You have to make the effort to reach out to others, and that means working out how you will introduce yourself; at the tennis class, for example: "Hello, I'd like to introduce myself. My name is Mark Germino. I just started playing tennis. How about you?" Always try to end with a question that encourages your contact to introduce and talk about himself. It doesn't really matter what the question is. Once there has been a conversational exchange, you can begin to move forward with your networking agenda, perhaps by saying what you do. Say, "I'm in accounting, how about you?" rather than plunging into a detailed description of your situation.

Keep It Short

Even though gatherings of associations, clubs, and societies provide excellent networking opportunities, they are not scheduled specifically for that activity. Try to keep your initial in-person networking conversations to less than five minutes. You don't want to be known as an overly solicitous bore. You can end a conversation gracefully with an offer of your business card, and you should recognize that a request for your card is a signal for you both to move on. If someone you meet isn't carrying a card, have her write her name and contact information on the back of one of yours, and always try to get a telephone number and an email address.

Whenever you meet someone in person, send an email to thank him for any helpful information you may have gathered from the conversation. It also serves to keep you on his radar.

The Secrets of Successful Networking Conversations

Your networks grow in proportion to the energy you put into them. Networking opportunities can be created on the phone or through email—and for professional networking these communication mediums are far more productive for all concerned—but with local networking, face time will always generate the best results.

Whatever your communication medium, your agenda remains the same. Show interest in your contacts first, and only then move on with your agenda.

The conversation happens in four stages, none of which should be rushed:

Introduction

Recall the last memorable interaction you had with your contact, or mention someone you both know. Ask what is happening in your contact's personal and professional life. Listen to what is said and respond appropriately.

Statement of Your Situation

Prepare a statement that allows you to encapsulate your situation succinctly: "Malcolm, I just got laid off because of the downturn," or "We have a baby on the way, and _____ is a company where there just isn't room for me to grow professionally," or "My job just got sent to Mumbai, so I guess it's time for me to make a move."

Information Gathering

When common professional ground exists through an association or other social network, you can assume that your listener will be well disposed toward you. You can repay this good will by showing respect for that person's time and politely cutting to the chase.

At this point in the conversation you have to be careful to avoid a common gaffe. Don't say something like, "My ideal job would be . . ." or "The next step I'd like to take is . . ."

By describing an ideal job or your desired next step up the professional ladder, you make things more difficult for the listener, who thinks, "This guy is looking for something very specific, and any introductions I can make will probably be a waste of everyone's time." Tell your contacts in general terms what you *do*, not what you *want*. Talking about your aspirations just reduces your chances of getting leads.

Note that I'm assuming you are talking to professional colleagues and seeking leads on job openings, rather than talking to the managers, directors, vice presidents, and presidents who can make those hiring decisions. The conversations with anyone who has the potential to hire you are different because you are then making a marketing presentation.

Ask for Assistance

You can ask for general guidance about your tactics: "If you were in my situation, Charlie, what would you do?" You can ask if he has heard about local companies hiring. You can achieve even more if you are careful to ask your questions in a productive *sequence*.

Great Networking Questions

We are now going to work through a sequence of networking questions that will lead you to jobs you would otherwise never hear about. These are the same question sequences asked every day by headhunters the world over, retooled to fulfill your needs.

These questions follow a logical sequence, but that order might not suit your needs, so as you examine them, figure out what you would ask if you had time for only one question, then if you had time for only two, and so on. The result will be a comfortably prioritized set of questions. Each question you ask should be specific, so avoid time-wasting questions like "How's business these days?" When you're satisfied with your list of questions, have a copy on your computer and/or smartphone, another by your home phone (never at work), and a third that will go in your wallet or purse.

General Questions

You can ask if there are openings in the department or at the company, and with whom you should speak about them.

Don't ask:
- "Can you or your company hire me?"

Do ask:
- "What needs does your company have at present?"
- "Who in the company is most likely to need someone with my background?"
- "Who else in the company might need someone with my background?"
- "Is the company/department planning any expansion or new projects that might create an opening?"
- "When do you anticipate a change in company manpower needs?"
- "Does your company have any other divisions or subsidiaries? Where are they?"
- "I'd appreciate any email addresses or telephone numbers of headhunters you hear from."

Profession-Specific Questions

You might wish to add some profession-specific questions. For instance, people in Information Technology might ask questions about operating systems, communication protocols, programs, and useful foreign languages. In this instance, after receiving an answer, add a similarly focused follow-up question—"Thanks, Gail. Who else do you know that uses these configurations?"— that will lead you to other companies likely to have similar needs. Be sure any question you add to your list is geared toward identifying names, titles, and companies in your areas of interest.

Leads at Other Companies

When you are sure that no job openings exist within a particular department or company, move on to gathering leads in other companies. You can ask, "Do you know of anyone at other banks in town that I might speak to?" but you will get a better response if your question is more focused: "Who do you know at _____?"

If your contact can't think of a person, ask about other companies: "What companies have you heard about that are hiring now?" Or: "If you were going to make a move, which companies would you look at?" Or: "Which are the most rapidly growing companies in the area?"

Whenever you are offered a lead, even if it is an obvious one, say, "Hey, that's a great idea. I never thought of Google as hiring people." Your encouragement is positive reinforcement. Then, after a suitable pause, ask for another company name: "I really appreciate your help, Sam. I never thought of _____. Who else comes to mind?" When people see that their advice is appreciated, they will often come up with more helpful information. When you have gathered two or three company names, you can backtrack with a request for contact names at each of the companies: "Do you know of anyone I could speak to at _____?"

You can also ask for leads at companies you plan to call, or even at those you have already called: "Jack, I was planning to contact _____, Inc. Would you happen to know anyone there who could give me a heads-up on hiring needs?"

When a conversation is going well, and if you are talking to someone in your profession, tacking on a last question that gives you job leads to trade with others can be a good idea: "Jane, I'm a member of a job search network. If you don't have a need for someone with my background right now, perhaps one of my colleagues could be just what you are looking for. What titles is your company looking for right now?"

If you are changing careers or considering a career change, your priorities might be different. In this case you can explain that you are considering a particular profession for a new career direction and ask what it is like working in the profession; what your contact likes least and most about the work; what education, experience, and professional behaviors help people succeed in the profession; who fails and why; and how one gets into and moves ahead in the profession.

The extent of your questioning depends on the willingness of your contact to continue the conversation; I've known these conversations to run for fifty minutes.

When You Get a Referral

When you get leads on companies and specific individuals to talk to, be sure to thank your benefactor and ask to use her name as an introduction. "Thank you, Linda. I didn't know _____ was building a facility in town, and I appreciate getting Holly Barnes's name. May I use your name as an introduction?"

Every time you get a referral, be sure to ask whether you can use your contact's name as an introduction. The answer will invariably be "yes," but asking demonstrates professionalism and will encourage your contact to come up with more names and leads. For example, you can say, "That's very helpful, Bill. Does anyone else come to mind?"

When you get permission to use your contact's name, use it in an introduction. This is a bridge-builder and usually leads to a brief exchange about your mutual contact before you go into your information-gathering agenda.

When you do get help, say thank you. If you do it verbally, it's a nice touch to follow it up with a note (see the latest edition of *Knock 'em Dead Cover Letters* for networking letter examples). The positive impression you make might get you another lead, and it never hurts to include a copy of your resume with the thank-you letter.

Wrapping It Up

When your networking call or face-to-face conversation comes to its natural conclusion, offer your thanks and willingness to return the favor, and leave the door open for future calls: "Christine, thanks so much for your help. I do appreciate it. At times like this you realize how important your colleagues are, so I'd like to give you my telephone number and email so that one day I might return the favor. Let's stay in touch. Might I call you again sometime?"

Other statements that you might use at the end of your conversation include:

- "I'll let you know how it works out with Holly Barnes."
- "Might I get in touch in a couple of months to see if the situation at _____, Inc. has changed?"

When talking to a management contact in your profession, you might suggest, "Would it be worthwhile emailing a copy of my resume for your personal talent database?" All smart managers keep such a database. After all, their job is to get work done through others, and being able to locate good talent is essential.

You are going to get some pleasant surprises when you network, but also a few disappointments. You will be surprised at how someone you always regarded as a real pal won't give you the time of day, and how someone you never thought of as a friend will go above and beyond the call of duty for you. Networking is a numbers game, so keep calling and emailing, and start every communication with an open mind. Stay in touch with your networking contacts, regardless of whether they were able to help you. Let them know when you get a job, and try to stay in contact at least once a year. A career lasts a long time, and next week or a decade from now, when a group of managers (including one from your personal network) talk about filling a new position, they will ask, "Who do we know?" That someone is more likely to be you when you are connected to networks in your profession and local community.

Maintain your social networks once you land that next job on your professional path. This keeps you visible both within your professional community and among the corporate recruiters and head-hunters who may call you down the road with unexpected opportunities. You don't have to accept them, but isn't it better to have the opportunities and contacts even if you don't plan on using them?

CHAPTER 6
NETWORK-INTEGRATED JOB SEARCH TACTICS

IN A COMPETITIVE job market, you cannot rely exclusively on networking or any other single job search tool. You need to use a number of different job search strategies and integrate networking into each of them.

A man who goes fishing and puts one hook in the water has only one chance of catching any of the millions of fish in the sea, and one fish is the best he can ever do. A man with two hooks in the water has double the chances of catching a fish and has also earned himself the opportunity to catch twice as many fish as the first guy.

The more hooks you have in the water, the better your chances of action. All the job search tools and approaches that we discuss in this section of the book—job banks, resume banks, headhunters, direct research and approach—have proven effective. No one alone is a guaranteed silver bullet, and any of them could deliver the ideal opportunity for you. Your plan of attack should embrace as many of these approaches as is practical in your situation. Intelligently pursuing all useful approaches will generate job leads. You can then leverage your networks for leads on and introductions to the hiring managers for the jobs you discover.

It's a Digital World

Corporate recruitment has moved online, so your job search must respond to these recruitment preferences.

With tens of thousands of job sites and resume banks out there, you could spend eternity strolling from one to the next. The danger is that this feels like productive work, and because it involves zero rejection it can be highly addictive. An Internet-based job search can seem magical because the media tell you it is magical, but *job banks and resume banks are not magical*. The Internet increases your ability to gather and disseminate information, but you need to understand, control, and leverage this power, not be controlled by it.

First Get Organized

If you've been through a job search before, you are groaning at starting all over again, but if you follow this plan of attack, apart from having a successful job search, you will be prepared for future job searches. You will have the mechanisms in place to track interesting opportunities; you will have a database of relevant employers and a wide range of networking contacts; plus you'll have a database of relevant job banks, resume banks, and headhunters. You will be more proactive in the management of your career and therefore more successful over the long haul.

If you don't organize properly, you will be buried in an avalanche of information and leads, but it doesn't have to be this way. Organization begins with setting up a career management base of operations for your professional life; this job search will be its first use, but the long-term success of your personal brand, MeInc., demands an organized place for your ongoing professional development and career management activities.

> **KNOCK 'EM DEAD TIP**
> While you know better than to use your office email for a job search, you should also never download your secure email to your office email box. Why? Companies can and do check Internet usage on your computer. Inappropriate activities can cost you a job.

The Importance of Your Email Address and Subject Line, or BinkyPoo Must Die

In a competitive job search, the little things can make a big difference, and the way you introduce yourself is one of them. The majority of job search communications are email based, so your email address and subject line are the first things employers see. They offer a perfect opportunity to quickly define your professional offering and can become powerful marketing tools that your competitors overlook.

As one of the first things any recruiter or potential employer sees, you want the impression it creates to be professional. This might be a good time to restrict addresses like *binkypoo@yahoo.com* and *bigboy@hotmail.com* to nonprofessional activities where they won't detract from your professional reputation.

You have unlimited access to different email addresses, so take advantage of this and add an email account devoted exclusively to your job search and career management affairs.

Your Email Address Is a Primary Brand Identifier

Email addresses act as headlines to tell the reader who is calling, so you need a professional email address for your professional affairs. Create an email address that speaks to your professional identity, for example, *SystemAnalyst@hotmail.com* or *TopAccountant@yahoo.com*. In addition to identifying the sender, a profession-focused email also offers some idea of what the communication is about.

When names like *TopAccountant@yahoo.com* are already taken, you will be encouraged to accept something like *topaccountant1367@yahoo.com*. You can do better; try adding your area code: *TopAccountant516@yahoo.com*; your zip code: *TopAccountant11579@yahoo.com*; or your town, *TopAccountantSeaCliff@yahoo.com*. You might also try an address that is profession specific: *TopAccountantInsurance@yahoo.com* and combinations of these, such as *Top516AccountantInsurance@yahoo.com*, which would tell a local Long Island, NY, employer that you are a top accountant living in Nassau County. Email addresses such as these offer useful information to an employer in your local target market but won't detract for someone outside of that market. In a competitive job search, the little things can make a big difference and the way you introduce yourself is one of them.

Using a profession-oriented email address serves you in another way: It succinctly introduces the *professional you* and, because it refers to a job rather than your name, it has the added benefit of helping to protect your identity.

Subject Lines Are for Teasing

In any written communication, a headline acts to grab your attention and draw you into the story, offering an enticing taste of what's to come. To recruiters and hiring managers buried in junk mail, the right subject line can make the difference between your email getting read or tossed.

If you are responding to a job posting, the job title and job posting number are necessary, and you can combine the required factual information with a brief marketing pitch about your credentials:

Financial Analyst #MB450—CPA/MBA/8 yrs' exp

Posting 2314—MIT Grad is interested

Job #6745—Top Sales Professional Here

Or if there is no job posting:

IT Manager—7 yrs' IT Consulting

Benefits Consultant—Insurance & Corporate

Referral from Tony Banks—Product Manager

Subject Line As Condensed Resume

Your incoming email typically reveals anywhere between thirty-five and sixty characters of the subject line, so you have enough space to include more selling points in your subject line. To be safe, try to get the "must haves" of your headline in the first thirty-five characters, in this example an HR Management job that required specific credentials:

Your next Reg HR Manager—EEOC, FLSA

However, once opened, an email can sometimes show up to 150 characters in the subject line. You can make this space work for you as an abbreviated resume by showcasing the highlights of your resume. This example uses 129 characters, including spaces:

Your next Reg HR Manager—EEOC, FLSA, ADA, OSHA. 10 yrs-arbitration, campus, executive recruitment, selection, compensation, T&D

No one likes to read resumes, but in a competitive job search, the little things your competitors never learned, like an informative email address and enlightening subject line, can make a big difference. They won't get you hired, but they just might get your email and the attached resume read with serious attention.

Security and Confidentiality

Online privacy is an issue for everyone today and is especially important during a job search.

Separate Telephone

Most telephone companies now allow you two or three alternate numbers at no extra charge with your basic service, and usually these come with a distinctive ringtone. This means you can have a dedicated and confidential number for all your job search and career management activities. Note, however, that many still feed into a single message center, so the message you leave for callers needs to be professional and, at the same time, nonspecific about your identity; it should be something like: "Sorry, I can't take your call right now; please leave your name and number and I'll get right back to you."

As many people have dumped their landlines, cell numbers have increasingly become primary phones. Increasingly, two-line phones are becoming available, but currently they are expensive, and buying a burner phone for exclusive ongoing use with your job search and career management activities might not be a bad idea. In this case, only career-related messages will appear, and you can choose to identify yourself in the phone's message center.

A Sanitized Resume

When you are employed—or if you want to create that impression—and involved in a job search, discretion is paramount. Consider sanitizing your resume by removing all "traceable-to-you" contact information (name, address, phone, fax), and replacing them with your career management email.

By removing a current employer's name (all recruiters and employers understand the need for this), you can further protect your identity, replacing it with a generalized description of the company and location. For example, if you work for PepsiCo in Chicago, you could describe this as a "Midwestern Beverage Company."

It usually isn't necessary to sanitize prior employer names. However, if you have a senior title associated with a particularly visible company, it could be a clue as to who you are. In this case replace it with a more generic but recognizable job title.

How to Organize Your Job Search and Career Management Database

It is important for your career that you build and *maintain* a career management database: Keep folders for target companies and your contacts within them, and the same for your contacts within recruitment firms. You might choose to add a Job Leads folder; into this you can put all the job postings you develop. You can add folders that contain contact info for both your on- and offline networking activities.

Additions to these groups can be made at any time; when you see recruiters who work in your industry, put them in the appropriate folder. You're creating a vehicle for launching a massive career blitz tomorrow or four years from now. Organize yourself to capture information today that you can use throughout your work life.

We typically dump job postings or help wanted ads that for whatever reason don't work out. I don't want you to do this for two reasons:

1. You can offer them to others in the course of your networking activities.
2. A company that hires accountants today is just as likely to be hiring them three years from today. Knowing about the company and its contact information gives you a head start next time. This job search and career management database is a tool you create for the benefit of *your entire career*. It is part of gaining control of your professional destiny.

Whenever you respond to a job posting, do exactly as requested, but also copy the job posting and all contact information for the company to a folder. You will need this if an interview occurs. Plus, you can cross-reference the job posting with people in your different networks and perhaps come up with a name and a title to which you can send the resume directly, thus doubling your chances of getting an interview.

On any job site it is a good idea to make your requirements broad to begin with; if a particular site drowns you with inappropriate jobs, gradually refine your target. Alternatively, you might not be getting enough responses from a particular site and might want to recast your needs in broader terms.

Job Sites and Resume Banks

There are so many thousands of job sites, you could never hope to visit them all, so you have to integrate the job site/resume bank aspect of your search intelligently. You start by identifying which sites are relevant to your search. The easiest way to short-list relevant sites is to do Google searches for variations on your target job title, visit the sites that mention an opening, and see what other similar jobs they have. If there are plenty of job postings in your work area and at your level, this is a site worth checking into more closely:

• Does the site have job postings that are suitable for you? If it doesn't, you can move on to the next site. If it does, you will want to keep an eye on the site for relevant job postings as they come in. This means you will want to register with the site and receive job alerts in your email when new jobs matching your criteria get posted to the site.

- When you are asked to define the jobs that interest you, set your sights wide. You may get too many responses initially, but you can gradually narrow the parameters. It's better to plow through a little junk than miss a great opportunity.

KNOCK 'EM DEAD TIP
Remember, those jobs you hear about that aren't quite right for you are not a waste of your time. They are worth saving in a trading file to share with network contacts for whom one of those jobs might be a perfect fit.

- If this is a good site for you, other sites it is linked to might also be useful; check the partners/links pages. These aren't always obvious; if they're not, look for a site map in those little links that always crowd the very bottom of the page.
- Because companies hire more people from smaller niche sites, you must check the specialty sites. You will find a good selection in the Internet Resources at *www.knockemdead.com*.
- You will collect two types of job postings: those that are good for you and those that are suitable to offer to your network. Before you file any of these, go through them carefully, looking for keywords that describe skill sets you have that are not captured as such in your existing resume. List these on a desktop document. You'll use this document to update your resume and to refresh it in the resume banks; more on this in the next section.
- Make a folder for each relevant site you visit, and as postings come in store them in the appropriate folder. You'll quickly see which sites are most productive.
- When you are asked to create a profile—and this is usually part of setting up your account on a site—you essentially cut and paste your resume, as this represents your most carefully considered packaging of the *professional you*. But this requires a little more explanation.

Most job sites are free for you to use. It's the employers who are paying to post their job openings and search the resume bank. The job sites work with employers to develop ever more efficient screening tools. Setting up your account and filling out a profile is part of this process: *Everything you do online is being tracked by someone for some reason.*

Whenever you are filling out a profile or questionnaire on a job site, keep the following in mind.

Multiple Resumes/Profiles

Job sites recognize that many people can do more than one job, and so they frequently allow you to register as many as five separate resumes and/or profiles. It is also a tacit acknowledgment that one "general" resume won't cut the mustard. And yes, it is yet another benefit of the TJD exercises from Chapter 3 that it allows you to create relevant, intelligent, and deep profiles for each option.

Most job sites break up the registration/profile building/resume uploading process into a number of steps: often twelve or more specific dialogue boxes you have to work your way through. They typically include topics like Target Job, Career Objective, Competencies, Relocation, Salary, Ideal Job, Education, and more.

These sites often offer examples to help you fill in the dialogue boxes—but remember that behind all this is the screening process.

Target Job Title

Copy and paste all the different job titles you collected in the first part of the TJD exercise. Putting in more than one title only serves to increase your visibility.

Career/Job Objective/Summary

No one wants to hear about your objectives, and putting them out there is only wasting space. This is the place for your Performance Profile, which you based on your prioritization of employer needs during the TJD process.

This dialogue box often has lots of space, so you can end it by inserting a header that says, "The opportunity to use these skills." Then paste in the entire collection of Core Competencies you identified in Chapter 3.

KNOCK 'EM DEAD TIP

You are not always limited to one answer—even in the case of check boxes. Always test and verify to see if you can select more than one answer. Never assume you are limited— not even if the directions on the screen indicate that you are. Similarly, you might not want to answer a supposedly mandatory question. Try leaving it blank; you'll find out if it really was mandatory when you click "submit."

Salary Requirements

It is always better to give a range rather than a single figure. I show you how to decide on this salary range in Chapter 25, where we discuss salary negotiation. Even though this box is always marked as mandatory, that isn't always the case. Sometimes you can leave it blank if you feel this will be helpful to your cause.

Ideal Job

No one is interested in your ideal job. The recruiter is searching a database and retrieving possible candidates from a list of keywords that they have put into the system. Copy and paste your Performance Profile and follow it with your Core Competencies. Test to see if there is more space by pasting in your Core Competencies again. No person will actually read the repetition (and if they did, they would regard it as a glitch) but the software will catch and reward you for it by increasing your ranking in the search results.

Core Competencies

If they have a separate section for this, paste your Core Competencies . . . as often as space will allow.

Education

Education is the most questioned area of any candidacy. Much prone to exaggeration and outright lies, educational claims *do get checked*. Untruths can cause offers to be withdrawn and jobs to be terminated. Don't fake it.

If you are involved in the pursuit of any postsecondary education but haven't yet achieved it, you can use it if you state the school and the degree, and if you can, also state a projected graduation date . . . you can do this as long as you are enrolled in at least one course toward that degree. Your pursuit of an education while you work is a plus in employers' eyes, and you have a right to show it to them.

Relocation

When completing questions about relocation, don't jump to make a selection: Not all questions are mandatory. If the question is optional, leave it open. If you do answer, select the broadest option possible. Even if you have the ability to list many preferred locations, don't. Choose no preference, and you will get the same responses. Plus:

1. You can always say "no," but you can't say "yes" unless you've been asked.
2. For the right job, opportunity, and money, we would all move to Possum Trot, Kentucky.
3. Any job you interview for but reject will only improve your interviewing skills, which are probably your very weakest professional skill.
4. It gives you leads to trade in your networking initiatives.

Name-dropping

Recruiters often look for candidates who either are working for or have worked for certain companies or competitors. If you work for name companies and products, that is great. You can also drop corporate names and brand names if you have been a vendor or a client.

Resume Banks

If suitable jobs are posted to the job site, it probably means that recruiters are also visiting its resume bank. In that case you may well want to upload your resume. Some considerations to bear in mind:

1. Some resume banks require that you upload your resume to something called an ASCII format. This is not difficult to do, but it is a pain in the neck; you can find step-by-step directions in the latest edition of *Knock 'em Dead Resumes*.

2. Resume banks have purge dates, mostly so that the recruiters who pay for access can be assured that they are not looking at stale resumes. The purge usually happens every ninety days, and you will want to bear the dates in mind so that you can refresh your resume before then.

3. Of course, recruiters also have the ability to restrict their searches by the date a resume was loaded, for example, they might be able to restrict a search to resumes uploaded in the past ten days. This is important when a particular site has job postings suitable for you, because it also means that recruiters will be cruising its resume bank for candidates.

4. In instances where you want to maintain the highest visibility on a site like this, go in once a week and update your resume with new keywords you have identified in other job postings. Make any change to your resume and the database search engine will recognize it as a new document.

5. When there are no new words, you can achieve the same effect quite simply: Log into your account, open your resume, replace a couple of words with a string of x's, and log out. Take a couple of deep breaths, log in again, replace the x's with the original words, and log out again: To all intents and purposes you now have a brand new document.

Finding More Hidden Jobs

In addition to what we've talked about, you can use job sites in other ways. Go to any job site and search their posted openings by putting in minimal keywords and restrictions. For example, if a medical insurance sales manager goes to *www.theladders.com* and does a simple keyword search for "insurance," she may get hundreds of results, and the vast majority will be for jobs that do not interest her. At the same time, those results will reveal recruiters and companies in her profession and target location.

Visit these sites and see if there are suitable job openings posted. Companies all use their own websites as recruitment vehicles and usually have their open jobs posted there. Even if they do not have jobs for someone like you posted, upload your resume anyway. You don't really know what is going on at that company, and at the very least you will be in their database and therefore on their radar when a need arises.

If a company is looking for anyone even remotely connected with your area of professional expertise, they could also be looking for someone like you. Upload your resume and research the company so you can approach the appropriate hiring managers directly.

After visiting a company website, add the link to the appropriate folder in your career management database. Identify all the profession-specific employers at all the job sites you visit, then visit each of those employer websites and add them to a potential employers folder; your hit list of potential employers will grow exponentially.

Websites such as glassdoor.com represent a continuing evolution of the job site. Yes the site has jobs (but only in the tens of millions as yet) and salary calculators.

It also features a database of companies with a sample of the interview questions they ask (supplied by other glassdoor.com members who have interviewed there). You can also get evaluations of companies by current and ex-employees, although I think these must be evaluated very carefully.

> ### KNOCK 'EM DEAD TIP
> This list of companies will also help your social networking activities. You can use the company names in database searches on the social networking sites to find contacts to approach for leads and introductions at these target companies. Everything in a successful job search is geared toward *getting into conversations with people who could make the decision to hire you*—as we have noted, typically someone one to three title levels above your own. Always strive to identify and get into a conversation with anyone who holds any of these target titles at any and every company in your area.

Direct Approach to Target Companies

Everything in a successful job search is geared toward *getting into conversations with the high-value job titles who have the authority to hire you*—and failing that, the people who know and work with them. As we have noted, these titles are typically one to three levels above your own, or people who are otherwise closely involved in the selection cycle.

There will be times when you can't find the right names and titles through your social networks—especially when you first start getting serious about building social networks, and they aren't extensive enough. Additionally, the higher up the corporate ladder of success your high-value job titles are placed, the less likely it is that they are visible or readily accessible through social networking. As a consequence, in this chapter we'll look at alternative ways to connect with potential employers in your target geographic market, and the right names and titles to target within those companies. You can then work back through each of your networks to someone who can give you a referral or an introduction to otherwise inaccessible executives.

We'll begin by sharing tactics to ensure that you know of all the potential employers within commuting distance, and then move on to a number of different ways to identify high-value job titles.

How to Identify Potential Employers

You will never identify all the employers and all the jobs that are suitable for you and located within commuting distance by visiting job sites and networking. Sometimes you have to reverse engineer your job search strategy with these steps:

- Identify all the employers within your commuting range
- Visit their websites and check for jobs and high-value titles
- Upload your resume, whether or not there are suitable jobs posted
- Cross-reference each of those companies with networking contacts in each of your six major social networks (LinkedIn, Google+, Facebook, Twitter, professional, and alumni), looking for contacts who work or have worked there

How to Identify Employers Within Commuting Distance

There are a number of ways to identify all the potential employers in your area:

- Search job sites with a variety of job titles common to your area of professional expertise. As you identify employers, visit each of their websites to look for jobs and to upload your resume. Don't forget to add them to a potential employers folder in your career management database; this procedure of capturing the information for future retrieval applies to most of the following points.
- Search job sites for jobs using just your target job title, then your professional or industry sector, your city, county, state, and the variety of zip codes that cover your target market. This will give you a longer list of employers. You'll visit each of their websites to look for jobs and, as appropriate, upload your resume.
- Use the job aggregator sites like *www.Indeed.com* and *www.SimplyHired.com* whose search engines scan thousands of sites looking for your search terms. Again, you can search by your target job title, then your professional or industry sector, your city, county, state, the variety of zip codes that cover your target market, and other database search term variations as we have discussed throughout the book.
- Search LinkedIn, Google+, Facebook, Twitter, and your professional and alumni networks using the same variety of search terms.
- You can use the apps and dashboard tools available on all your social media sites to search for job postings, and where applicable, employer pages by name, city, county, state, and zip codes.

- You can find lists of employers on your local Chamber of Commerce website.
- You can identify every publicly traded company in the world through the Standard & Poor's (S&P) website (a fee service) or through the S&P reference books at your local library (free). These include the names and titles of V.P. and C-level management.
- Zapdata, owned by Dun & Bradstreet (D&B) is the online version of the D&B Million Dollar Directory (fee based), which you can also find for free in the public library. It contains data on over 15 million U.S. private and publicly held corporations. Includes names and titles of key executives.

  Note: Your alumni and college career services, and some libraries, may be able to give you free online access to the S&P and Zapdata databases, and possibly useful research databases.
- You can find an extensive list of companies by industry on LinkedIn at *www.linkedin .com/companyDir?industries=*. When you find a relevant employer in your target location, link directly to that company's LinkedIn page.

  Note: Not only is this an important step toward a direct approach, you can also look at who is following the company and commenting on their posts. This is useful for expanding your network with other committed professionals in the same field. You should then "like" their comments and link to them. This works on LinkedIn and on your other social media platforms.
- You can also use Google.com, Bing.com, and other search engines to look for job titles in your target market, or just potential employers using phrases like, "Inc., Raleigh, N.C.", "Company, Raleigh, N.C.", "LLC, Raleigh, N.C", and "Partners, Raleigh, N.C." You can also try variations of the previous with a zip code, like "LLC 31405," or use zip codes relevant to your search parameters, like "Employers in 31405." All these variations will generate more lists of employers within your commuting parameters.
- You can also use all these search terms on each of your social networking platforms and the job sites you visit.

Google/Bing Alerts

With "Alerts" from any search engine, you can keep track of news on any topic that interests you, and in the process identify employers and often inside information about those employers, giving you ammunition for a well-considered approach. You can set up alerts for any topic using *www.google.com/alerts* or any other search engine. In a job search this could mean:

- Jobs with specific titles or the names of cities, counties, states, zip codes, or any of the other suggested tactics
- News about your profession or job title
- News about specific companies or people
- News about high-value titles at specific companies or in specific locations
- News about "stock splits"—this often indicates company growth

- News about "Companies," "growing," "hiring"
- News about "Contracts landed"—adding in the other search terms, "Contracts landed Atlanta," or "Contracts landed 45672," etc.
- Use some of the great job search apps mentioned in the last few chapters using these same techniques

After you decide on an Alert topic, you should then think about the channels where you want Google to search for this information: Everything, News, Books, Blogs, Video, Discussions, Applications, and more.

Bing and all the other search engines have similar tools that work in pretty much the same way, but because each search engine is built differently, they will all generate somewhat different results.

New Ways to Identify High-Value Job Titles

Once you have a comprehensive list of employers within commuting distance, you can start identifying high-value job titles. For the moment we'll leave networking contacts as a resource to fall back on while we develop some new approaches to identifying high-value names and titles that we may subsequently be able to approach directly and turn into networking contacts for the future. Alternatively, we can cross-reference such names, titles, and employers with our contacts in our six major social networks for introductions.

Who to Target in Your Job Search

We have already identified that the hiring titles to target during your social networking and job search activities are usually people one to three titles above your target job, because these are the people most likely to be in a position to hire you. We also know that other titles likely to be involved in the selection process include management titles (again, one to three levels above you) in departments that have ongoing interaction with your department, peers holding similar titles to that for which you're applying, colleagues in departments that regularly interact with your department, and internal recruiters and HR professionals.

In fact, any name at one of the employers within your commuting radius is better than no name, and with the Internet at your fingertips there is endless opportunity to identify the names of people who carry either the job titles that would give them the authority to hire you, or titles that can tell you who to talk to, or at least get you one step closer.

Sometimes those job titles one to three levels above yours aren't enough. Sometimes, your job and the corporate structure that towers over it can make for upward of half a dozen pitches to a target company, just to ensure that all the right people know you are available.

For example, let's say you are a young engineer crazy for a job with Last Chance Electronics. It is well within the bounds of reason that any or all of the following job titles could hold responsibility, or be involved with the selection of, your job title, or at the very least could be knowledgeable about what is going on with recruitment in your area of professional expertise:

- Vice President of Engineering
- Chief Engineer
- Engineering Design Manager
- Vice President of Human Resources
- Technical Engineering Recruitment Manager
- Technical Recruiter
- Company President

Apply this thinking to your title and situation, thinking through all the titles that could be suitable for approach in a larger company, then use your networks and the other tactics we've discussed to identify the names that go with each of these titles at a targeted company: The more options you have, the more approaches you can make and the more results you will get, especially when you approach each potential hiring authority in a sequence of different ways, as we'll discuss over the coming pages.

Always strive to identify and get into a conversation with anyone who holds any of these types of high-value hiring titles at any and every company in your area, because getting into these conversations is the shortest path to job interviews, job offers, and getting the hell past the misery of this job search. This "direct approach" tactic is an essential element of your job search strategy.

How to Find High-Value Job Titles

There are a number of different tactics you can use to locate high-value titles relevant to your job search goals:

- Use different versions and combinations of your high-value job titles as search terms with Google and other search engines, such as the acronym, the full phrase, and variations for each of your high-value titles. For example: Chief Marketing Officer, CMO, and C. M. O. You might also try misspellings of these target titles; for instance, "M" is next to "N" on the keyboard and a common typo.
- Use quotation marks around words and phrases to help weed out irrelevant information. For example, if you had an alert for Accounting Manager, you would get alerts for that phrase and also alerts any time the word *Accounting* or the word *Manager* appeared on

the Internet. You can work around this problem by putting quotation marks around the important phrase—"Accounting Manager."

- If there are variations on the job title—Accounting Manager, Manager of Accounting, Manager Accounts, Director Accounting, etc.—you should use "OR" in capital letters: "Accounting Manager OR Manager of Accounting OR Manager Accounts OR Director Accounting." Alternatively, you could do different searches for each.
- If you want to add geographic restrictions—say you only want to hear about jobs in Carle Place or Huntington, NY—put this second choice in parentheses: "Carle Place (OR Huntington, NY)."
- You can search for similar words and phrases by adding the tilde sign: ~. This functions as a symbol for "similar to," so with a phrase like "~accounting jobs," you might get finance jobs in your results. Be sure not to leave a space between the tilde (the squiggly thingy) and the word in question, or the search won't work.

For example: A professional in pharmaceutical sales looking to make direct contact with hiring authorities for a job at a specific company in the Pittsburgh area could try all the following keyword searches and gather new useable information on each search. Try it yourself, first as a Google Search, then as Google News search:

- "Pharmaceutical sales"
- "Sales Manager (OR Account Manager) (OR District Manager)" Pennsylvania (OR Pittsburgh)
- "Sales Manager" _____ [*company name*] Pennsylvania (OR Pittsburgh)
- "Director Sales" _____ [*company name*] Pennsylvania (OR Pittsburgh)
- "Vice President (OR VP OR V.P.) Sales" _____ [*company name*] Pennsylvania (OR Pittsburgh)
- "~Sales Manager" Pharmaceutical (OR Pharma) Pennsylvania (OR Pittsburgh)

You could also:

- Repeat all without "pharmaceutical"
- Repeat all without company name
- Repeat all with just variations on the job title
- Repeat all with separate searches for target title plus: hired, resigned, and deceased

Try these and other keyword phrases suitable to your needs and you will come up with a wide range of job openings, companies, job sites, and recruiters. Just remember that the results on the first pages of a Google search are only those of companies that have spent time and money to ensure high search engine rankings. Continue to dig down in your search results and you'll begin to stumble across people who hold these and similar job titles, usually linked to one of their social media profiles.

- Check out the company website. On the "about us" pages, you can sometimes find names and titles of management.
- Call the company and ask for the name of the titleholder. This may sound old-fashioned, but it works.

Other Online Resources

There are other online resources that can be valuable supplements to the information you get from your personal and professional networks. Sites such as *www.vault.com* will tell you what past and current employees think about their employer. Other online resources such as *www.wetfeet .com* will give you great info about your target companies, as will the contacts in your networks.

These searches will provide useful background information for pitching, and during interviews your homework will be evident. This is always flattering to the interviewer, who sees you've paid attention to detail and shown effort and enthusiasm, each of which can end up being deciding factors in a tight job race. As you develop folders of information on potential employers, be sure to capture the details so that you have retrievable insights for this job search and for future strategic career moves.

Here are some other online resources for researching companies and identifying management titleholders:

www.virtualpet.com/industry/howto/search.htm   *www.superpages.com*
www.standardandpoors.com   *www.zoominfo.com*
www.zapdata.com   *www.corporateinformation.com*
www.hoovers.com   *www.ceoexpress.com*
www.quintcareers.com   *www.infospace.com*
www.vault.com   *www.searchbug.com*
www.thomasnet.com

More Resources for Finding Names of Hiring Authorities

The resources available reach to the horizon. Standard & Poor's also has a far less well-known database of executives by name and title: a Biographical Directory/Database that delivers some amazingly detailed personal information. These higher-level titles will be identifiable through one of the previous resources or through one of the following options:

www.knowx.com
www.lead411.com/about.html
www.business.com/directory/advertising_and_marketing/sales/selling_techniques/lead_generation/

Employee Referral Programs

An increasingly popular recruitment tool is the incentivizing of referrals from employees with corporate Employee Referral Programs, which typically offer a monetary reward for successfully referring employees to the company.

When you have a list of particularly desirable employers, it might be worth doing a few database searches for phrases like "[company name] referral program." If a company has an employee referral program, it can encourage a networking contact to act as a referral for you. This won't work all the time, but when your target is a highly desirable employer, it might be worth the effort.

Don't Approach Dream Employers Too Soon

As you engage in this potential employer research, your database of potential employers within your commuting distance will grow exponentially, and you may also want to create a folder of dream employers in your career management database.

If you are just starting a job search, build the information in these folders and beware of applying for jobs with these "super-desirable" employers right away, even when you have networking contacts who can open doors for you.

I'm sure you sometimes hear about the hit shows on Broadway, but what you may not know is that these shows don't actually start on Broadway: They go through months of rehearsals, previews with selected audiences, and then road trips to cities around Manhattan to iron out the wrinkles. They do this because they don't want to screw up when they open on "the Great White Way"—the most important stage in the world. These experts in seamless performance understand that it doesn't just happen, that we make mistakes and have to iron them out, and that this takes a little time and effort.

This analogy has implications for your job search. Of all the professional skills that are important to landing your next step, your ability to turn job interviews into job offers is both the most important and, at the same time, almost certainly your weakest skill, because you have very little experience and skill in this area. In the early days of a job search, your social media platform, resume, and interviewing skills are probably still in the development and retooling phases, and almost certainly not up to speed. The last thing you need to do is land an interview at the company of your dreams and then screw it up because interview nerves make you trip over your tongue.

It is better to hold off on applying to your dream companies for a few weeks, until you know that your social media profiles and your resume focus on the same target job and reflect complementary messaging. Meanwhile, you can land a couple of interviews and learn not to swallow your tongue in the first few minutes, better preparing you to meet with the people at a dream employer.

All this research has obvious immediate value, but it has significant long-term value as well, because you are building a personalized reference work on your industry/specialty/profession that will help you throughout the twists and turns of a long career.

We'll now turn to employment agencies and what they do for you.

Employment Agencies and Headhunters

There are few clear-cut lines of demarcation in this area:

- *State employment agencies* are staffed by government employees. Their job is to help you find a job; they are almost the only people whose focus is entirely on helping you. They are funded by the state Labor Department and typically carry names like State Division of Employment Security, State Job Service, or Manpower Services. The names vary but the services remain the same. They will make efforts to line you up with appropriate jobs and otherwise help you as best they can. It is not mandatory for employers to list jobs with state agencies, but more and more companies are taking advantage of these free services. These public agencies now list positions that often exceed $100,000 a year, so they're a resource not to be ignored.

  If you are moving across the state or across the country, your local employment office can plug you into the national job bank, or you can connect yourself online at *www.nationjob.com*, which claims to be the largest job bank in the world.
- *Private employment agencies* are for profit, and their source of income derives from the company. They will search on behalf of employers, but typically only in their own databases, and they will market someone to employers only if that person is seen to be in high demand and can be used as a tool to develop other fee-paying assignments.

  When working with an employment agency, choose your agent with the same care and attention with which you would choose a spouse or a lawyer. The caliber of the individual and company you choose could well affect the kind of company you ultimately join. Further, if you choose prudently, an agent can become a lifetime counselor who can guide you step by step up the ladder of success.
- *Career counselors and job search counselors*. Their money comes from you, but while there are charlatans in the business, there are also exemplary, talented, and dedicated professionals in this group. Typically, these people work alone or in very small companies, and they can help you with career choice, resume preparation, job search, and interview preparation.

How do you choose whom to work with? Find out how many years they've been in business, what professional degrees they hold, their affiliations with professional associations, and their professional accreditations. Ideally, they should also have a background as contingency or retained recruiters.

- *Contingency recruiters* gain their income from employers and are largely involved with finding employed professionals for hard-to-fill positions. They do this on a contingency basis, the contingency being that they only collect a fee when they fill the position. Typically, contingency recruiters will search their databases and actively recruit for a percentage of the openings they have to fill. Most contingency recruiters and some contingency firms will market an "in-demand" professional to target companies for a day or two and as a tool to develop other fee-paying assignments. Contingency recruiters are a hybrid, doing search work but not working on a retainer basis, and they are often more professionally sophisticated than local employment agency people.

- *Executive search firms* are also employer paid. They are the only group entirely focused on the employer's needs, and have no interest in you unless you fit an existing requirement. This is because they receive cash upfront, more when a candidate/recruit is hired, and the final payment when that person starts work. They are almost exclusively interested in people currently successful in their jobs, because an employed person is less of a risk (the firms often guarantee their finds to the employer for up to a year) and is a more desirable commodity.

These people rarely deal with salary levels under $100,000 per year. They are more interested in obtaining your resume for their database than seeing you unless you match a specific job they are trying to fill for a client.

You may have heard the term *headhunter*. It is now applied to anyone who provides employment services, but in reality it only fits executive search consultants and a few contingency recruiters.

Whom to Work with, and How to Work with Them

What type of employment services company is best for you? Well, the answer is simple: the one that will get you the right job offer. The problem is, there are thousands of companies in each of these broad categories. How do you choose between the good, the bad, and the ugly?

Fortunately, this is not as difficult as it sounds. A retained executive search firm is not necessarily better or more professional than a contingency search firm, which in turn is not necessarily better or more professional than a regular (EPF) employment agency. Each has its exemplary practitioners and its charlatans. Your goal is to avoid the charlatans and get representation by a company with experience placing professionals like you.

Involvement in professional associations is always a good sign, demonstrating commitment and an enhanced level of competence. In the employment services industry, the high-end employment agencies and contingency search firms—as well as some retained search firms—belong to the National Association of Personnel Services (NAPS), the premier professional organization with state associations in all fifty states. The Association for Executive Search Consultants (AESC) is the premier organization for the retained executive search firms. Career Management Institute (CMI) is the leading association for job search and career management counselors, and NATSS (National Association of Temporary and Staffing Services) is the leading association for temp firms.

Involvement in independent or franchise networks of firms can also be a powerful plus for a job search. For example, an independent headhunter network like NPA (*www.npaworldwide .com*) has hundreds of member firms around the world. Membership in one of the leading franchise groups, such as Management Recruiters, Robert Half, or Dunhill likewise gives you access to a coordinated network of employment services professionals. These networks also have extensive training programs that ensure a high-caliber consultant. Franchise networks can be especially helpful if relocation is in your future, as they tend to have powerful symbiotic relationships with other franchise members around the country and the world.

It is prudent to ask whether your contact has professional accreditations. Most of the national professional associations have training programs that offer accreditation, so these can be another sign that the recruiter is a committed and connected member of her profession. The most widely recognized of all these is the CPC designation. CPC (or its international equivalent, CIPC) stands for Certified Personnel Consultant. The CPC and CIPC designations are recognized as a standard of excellence and commitment only achieved after rigorous training and study.

CIPC designation requires that the holder has already achieved CPC designation, and it requires adherence to an international code of ethics as designated by the International Personnel Association (IPA).

Although certification can be applied for after two years of experience in business, even the newest holders of a CPC usually have five years of experience. The average CPC probably has seven to ten years of experience, and with it come excellent contacts on the corporate side.

Qualified CPCs (like holders of the other accreditations) can also be relied upon to have superior knowledge of the legalities and ethics of the recruitment and hiring process, along with the expertise and tricks of the trade that only come from years of hands-on experience. (I should note that while I hold a CPC accreditation, mine is an honorary one, in recognition of my contributions to the discussion of career management.)

Finally, when dealing with an agency or personnel professional, don't get intimidated. You are not obligated to sign anything, nor are you obligated to guarantee anyone that you will remain in any employment for any specific length of time.

KNOCK 'EM DEAD TIP
For a full list of the accreditations relevant to resume, recruitment, and career management professionals, go to *www.knockemdead.com* on the blog and advice pages.

It Comes Down to the Individual

You can develop mutually beneficial relationships with employment professionals in all of these categories. Their livelihood depends on the people they know in the professional world. Look at how many years of experience they have in employment services and how well they understand your profession. Look for involvement with their professional communities and professional accreditations.

If a recruiter is interested in representing you, expect to provide a detailed analysis of your background, and prepare to be honest. Do not overstate your job duties, accomplishments, or education. If there are employment gaps, explain them. Be circumspect, because an unethical headhunter can create further competition for you when you share information about companies you are talking to. The details of your communications with a company are nobody's business but your own. If the recruiter asks who you are talking with, say your job search is confidential and you'd like to know whom she plans to speak with. Explain that you will happily tell her if you are already in communication with that company.

Find out what the recruiter expects of you in the relationship, and explain what you expect. Reach commitments you both can live with, and stick with them. If you break those commitments, expect the representation to cease. Keep the recruiter informed about all changes in your status: salary increases, promotions, layoffs, or other offers of employment.

Don't consider yourself an employment expert. You get a job for yourself every three or four years. These people do it for a living. Ask for their objective input and seek their advice in developing interviewing strategies with their clients.

Temporary Services Companies

Such companies fill temporary assignments for employers and provide employment services to companies in all industries and at most professional levels, from unskilled and semiskilled labor (referred to as *light industrial*) to administration, finance, technical, sales, and marketing professionals, as well as doctors, lawyers, and management up to the CEO and COO level.

KNOCK 'EM DEAD TIP
This latter part of the business is usually referred to as "interim management." To find companies and associations for the interim management sector, simply key "interim management jobs" into your browser.

Always useful for quickly getting skills up to speed and reestablishing credentials after an absence from the workforce, temp or interim management work can offer a valuable stopgap in a drawn-out job search.

If you are unemployed and need the cash flow for bills, working with a temp company can supply that and expose you to employers in the community that, if you really shine, could ask you to join the staff full-time. This "temp-to-perm" approach is increasingly popular with companies hiring at all levels, as it allows employers to try before they buy.

Here's some advice when considering interim and temp job agencies and services:

- Define the titles and the employment levels they represent, along with geographical areas they cover.
- Determine whether they are members of the National Association of Temporary and Staffing Services (NATSS).
- Select a handful of firms that work in your field; this will increase the odds of suitable assignments appearing quickly.
- Do not overstate your job duties, accomplishments, or education.
- Find out first what the temporary help professional expects of you in the relationship, then explain what you expect. Reach commitments you both can live with, and stick with them.
- Judge the assignments not solely on the paycheck (although that can be important), but also by the long-term benefits to your job search and career. For example, if you have been out of the world of work raising a family, temp work can help you get acclimated and develop some current experience.
- Keep the temporary help counselor informed about any and all changes in your status, such as offers of employment or acquisition of new skills.
- Resolve key issues ahead of time. Should an employer want to take you on full-time, will that employer have to pay a set amount, or will you just stay on as a temporary for a specific period and then go on the employer's payroll?

College Career Services

Career services can help recently graduated students, as well as those about to finish school, and an increasing number of these services also try to help alumni. These dedicated professionals are horrendously overworked. So take the time to stand out by having thought through your issues. Stress your willingness to listen to good advice. If you are then seen to act on that advice, when you come back for more you will have earned the department's respect and will garner yourself more personal attention and guidance.

For students, the best way into corporate America is through internships and on-campus recruiters, who can recommend interns and entry-level hires to the company. Career Services is the best way to learn about these recruiters. Treat your entire interaction with Career Services the same way you intend to treat the interview process. Make a real effort with your appearance and professional demeanor.

Campus recruiters go to society and association meetings on campus all year long to see who is engaged, enthusiastic, and professional in their approach to life and career. Most campus recruiters have already chosen the best before they officially arrive on campus for the job fairs. When you take an active part in campus affairs, you will get to know many of these recruiters. Career Services will usually know which recruiters are involved with which campus activities.

You will also start to build a powerful network of peers for your whole career, because these are likely to be the most successful people in the professional world, as they are already engaged and committed.

Job Fairs

Job fairs (sometimes called career days) are occasions where actively hiring companies get together, usually under the auspices of a job fair promoter, to attract large numbers of potential employees to a one-day-only event. They aren't of much value to senior-level professionals.

Job fairs aren't regular events, except in times of high employment, so they won't take much of your time, but you should become an active participant when they do occur.

They often charge a small entrance fee, in return for which you get direct access to all the employers and formal presentations by company representatives and local employment experts. When you organize yourself properly, take the right attitude, and work all the opportunities, job fairs make for a great job search opportunity.

When you attend job fairs, go prepared with:

- Proper business attire. You may be meeting your new boss, and you don't want the first impression to be less than professional.
- Business cards. If you are currently employed, remember to request discretion and confidentiality.
- Resumes. You should take as many copies of your resume as there are exhibitors, times two. You'll need one to leave at the exhibit booth, and an additional copy for anyone you have a meaningful conversation with. If you have resumes targeted to different jobs, take copies of all of them.
- Laptop or notepad and pen, preferably in a folder.

Job fairs are an opportunity for networking with other job hunters as well. If you know other people going to a job fair (perhaps you are a member of a job search support group), you should go with a collaborative effort in mind. You may be in different professions, but if you all make the effort to speak to and collect business cards from other attendees regardless of their profession, you can help one another find more leads.

If you are attending solo, still make the effort to network with other attendees. Ask them to meet you later in the day to exchange leads that might be mutually beneficial. I have witnessed this in action at job fairs and seen a group of twenty who were total strangers in the morning happily exchanging handfuls of business cards at the end of the day.

It's easy to walk into a job fair and be drawn like a moth to the biggest and most attractive booths, sponsored by the largest and most established companies, and ignore the lesser ones. Remember that *the majority of the jobs in America are generated by companies with less than 500 employees.* You should visit every booth, not just the ones with the flashing lights and all the moths fluttering around.

Attend with specific objectives in mind:

- Talk to someone at every booth. You can walk up and ask questions about company activities, and whom they are looking for, before you talk about yourself. This allows you to present yourself in the most relevant light.
- Collect business cards from everyone you speak to so you can follow up with an email and a call when they are not so harried. Very few people actually get hired at job fairs; for most companies the exercise is one of collecting resumes so that meaningful meetings can take place in the ensuing days and weeks. Nevertheless, you should be "on" at all times, because serious interviews do sometimes occur on the spot.

  If you have a background and resume that matches you for a specific opportunity, make your pitch. If, on the other hand, there's a job you can do but your resume needs some adaptation to better position your candidacy, take a different approach. By all means pitch the company representative, but don't hand over a resume that will detract from your candidacy. Say, "I'm excited that you're interested in the general resume I have on me, but I'm really enthusiastic about your company, and I want to take the time to put what I can do for you in the right light." Then, get the contact's business card and promise to follow up with a resume, which you can then custom fit to the opportunity (see the TJD process in Chapter 3).
- Collect company brochures and collateral materials.
- Arrange times and dates to follow up with as many employers as possible: "Ms. Jones, I realize you are very busy today, and I would like to speak to you further. Your opportunities in _____ sound exactly suited to my skills and interests. I would like to set up a time when we could talk."

In addition to the exhibit hall, there will probably be formal group presentations by employers. As all speakers love feedback, move in when the crush of presenter groupies has died down. You will have more knowledge of the company and the time to customize your pitch to the needs and interests of the employer, plus you'll get more time and closer attention.

Job fairs provide the best opportunities for administrative, professional, and technical people. However, this doesn't mean middle management and executive staff can't gather information, collect cards, and generate leads.

On leaving each booth, and at the end of the day, go through your notes while everything is still fresh in your mind. Review each company and what possibilities it may hold for you. Also review what you have learned about industry trends, new skill requirements, marketplace shifts, and long-term staffing needs. Plan to send emails and make follow-up calls within the week to everyone with whom you spoke.

Email Subject Lines

When sending emails—not just job-related emails but all emails—it is a professional courtesy to provide a revealing and concise subject line. It should immediately tell the receiver who you are and what you want.

The use of a powerful subject line can mean the difference between getting your email opened and not. The intent of a headline in a newspaper is to grab the reader and draw her into the story; in an email, your subject line is your headline: It is what draws the reader into your email and lets her know what she's going to be reading about. Your subject line needs to be intriguing and professional.

Do not use a subject line that states the obvious, like "Resume" or "Jim Smith's Resume." If you are responding to a job posting, the job title and job posting number are necessary, but just a start. Combine this factual information with a little intriguing information, such as:

Financial Analyst #MB450—CPA/MBA/8 yrs exp
Posting 2314—MIT Grad is interested
Job #6745—Top Sales Professional Here

Or if there is no job posting to refer to:

IT Manager—7 yrs IT Consulting
Benefits Consultant—Nonprofit Exp in NY
Referral from Tony Banks—Product Management Job

You can also try longer subject lines, for example:

Your next Reg HR Manager—EEOC, FLSA, & ADA exp

A message in your inbox will typically reveal a maximum of sixty characters; the previous example is just forty-six characters, and an opened message will show up to 150 characters. To be safe, try to get your headline in the first thirty-five characters: "Your next Reg HR Manager—EEOC, FLSA." But feel free to use all this extra headline space for a subhead, for example:

"Your next Reg HR Manager—EEOC, FLSA, ADA, OSHA. 10 years' exp all HR includes arbitration, campus, executive recruitment, selection, compensation, T&D."

> **KNOCK 'EM DEAD TIP**
>
> All the social networking sites have special-interest groups used by recruiters, and it is becoming increasingly common for job hunters to post pitches about themselves in the discussion groups; this helps them become visible to recruiters, Google searches, and the like. So it is common sense to create an extremely abbreviated resume that captures the *professional you* with the most important keywords as identified by your TJD exercises.

This same thinking for extended subject lines will apply to your discussion group posts. These aren't the place for "out-of-the-box thinker" warm-and-fuzzies, but hard-hitting, attention-grabbing statements like this:

"HR Management—EEOC, FLSA, ADA, OSHA, T&D, arbitration, campus/executive recruitment, selection, compensation, restructuring."

Newspapers and Magazines

Almost all recruitment has now moved to the Internet, as have newspapers, so their role in your job search is not as it was in years gone by; however, there are still uses for a local or national newspaper in your job search campaign:

1. Companies that rely on the local community for both customers and employees still use the newspaper as a major recruitment vehicle.
2. The business news stories can tell you about company success stories, new contracts signed, new products and services introduced, and companies coming to town. They keep you informed and mention movers and shakers by name.

    Reminding that person of the article ("I saw you quoted in the *Argus* last week . . .") is flattering and will get you a few minutes of that person's time to make a pitch, get an interview, or get some leads. (If you want to learn how to get yourself quoted in the press, examine the PR chapters in the eBook *Knock 'em Dead Professional Communication* available at *www.knockemdead.com*.)

3. Most local papers have a promotions/movers and shakers column. It will tell you about companies and give you the names of people you can contact. If someone gets promoted or leaves one company for another, that leaves a job to be filled.
4. Industry overviews and market development pieces can tip you off to subtle shifts in your local professional marketplace.

There are still some great job leads in newspapers and magazines, and the fact that most people aren't using them as a job search resource anymore is a good enough reason to at least check them out. A good place to start online is *www.onlinenewspapers.com*, which helps you identify and link to newspapers all over the world.

Passive Marketing with a Web Portfolio or Web-Based Resume

Almost all job search activities take time and effort, so use passive marketing tactics whenever you can to increase your professional visibility and credibility.

For some time now, artists and designers have been creating online portfolios for their work as a cost-effective marketing device. If audio/video/graphics/multimedia can help promote the *professional you*, it might be worth considering an e-resume or e-portfolio for yourself, or have it built for you. This can cost anywhere from $40 up to $3,000.

Think of your web resume as a miniature website (you'll need to update it to reflect current professional activities); it gives you a constant marketing presence and extends your professional visibility and credibility in a couple of other ways. For one, increased visibility increases your credibility. For example, recruiters are doing Google searches on people before meeting them as part of the selection screening process. And for another, a well-put-together web resume will enhance others' perception of you before those initial meetings.

For professionals in the creative arts, a web-based resume/e-portfolio allows you to provide a multimedia proof of your achievements and strengths. With a web-based resume on its own site, you have the opportunity to expand beyond the immediate page, offering access to examples and supporting documents in other media.

It will not replace your main resume, which can offer a link to your multimedia site, but it's a great opportunity to prove that, for example, you have strong presentation skills, because in this format you can support that claim with a video or audio clip of a presentation you gave. Articles, a list of awards, graphics, audio and video clips, blogs, and photos are just some of the options you have to make your multimedia case. Prospective employers, headhunters, clients, and colleagues will get a far more comprehensive picture of the *professional you* in this format, and because a properly delivered e-portfolio is more engaging—at least when the content is good—it speaks of a technologically adapted professional.

PART II
GET THE WORD OUT

IT IS ALWAYS a conversation that generates an interview, and the job offer follows from there. That's why the focus of your job search is always to *get into conversations as quickly and as often as possible with the people who can hire you.*

CHAPTER 7
MAKING CONTACT

LITTLE HAPPENS IN the professional world without conversations taking place; in job searches neither interviews get scheduled nor job offers made without them. That's why the focus of your job search is always to *get into conversations as quickly and as often as possible with the people who can hire you.*

Despite everything you've done up to now, nothing is going to happen without you getting into conversations with these people. You can wait for these conversations to happen or you can make them happen.

Sales and Marketing Strategies

You've posted your resume on resume banks and as your social networking profile on LinkedIn. com and other sites, and you've sent it in response to company and headhunter job postings. Every one of these resumes acts like a baited fish hook, but while positioning your resume where it can be seen is a sensible marketing tactic, just sitting back and waiting for a bite isn't the best way to land your next job.

Jobs in sales exist to generate revenue by getting into conversations with customers and selling them the product, because marketing alone is never enough for profitability.

MeInc. too needs a sales operation to get into the conversations that lead to meetings, then negotiations, contracts, and the sale. Your successful job search, like any sales campaign, depends on *you getting into conversations as quickly and as often as possible with the people/job titles who can make the decision to hire you.*

Who to Approach Within Your Target Companies

Your identified target market should include every company within the geographic boundaries of your job search who could possibly hire someone like you. But companies aren't enough; you need to find people within those companies to talk to.

Getting into conversations with the people who have the authority to hire you is the central goal of all your job search strategies and tactics. It is the most effective way to get job offers and the activity that all job hunters most want to ignore, because talking to strangers on the telephone suddenly seems like a scary thing to do. It's not scary; you do it all the time.

Before you get into a conversation you have to identify whom you want to talk to and how to find them. The people you want to *reach as quickly, directly, and often as possible* are people holding those titles most likely to have the authority to offer you a job: Typically these high-value target hiring titles are one to three levels above your own and in the same department or functional area. *The primary goal of your job search every day is to identify and get into a conversation with anyone who holds any of these target titles at any and every company in your target location:*

- Corporate recruiters; because they are involved in the recruitment and selection cycle, they have a direct relationship with the hiring manager and a stake in completing searches in a timely and efficient manner.
- Titles one to three levels above your own in departments that have ongoing activities with your department. These people are the peers of the titles that will hire you and because of their continuing relations with your department are both likely to know of needs and able to make referrals.
- Titles similar to and one to three levels below your own because these people either have jobs in the departments where you might like to work, or are looking for jobs in the same general area themselves.

• Titles of people in other departments or at other companies that had ongoing communication with you and your title.

Put these titles together and you have a hotlist of at least ten *high-value job titles* that represent the people who have the greatest odds of knowing about suitable jobs for you, being able to make the right introductions, and/or of hiring you. These are the people you want to *get into conversation with as quickly and as often as possible.*

The previous titles represent the people you want to develop networking relationships with; they also represent the titles of job postings you'll stumble across and should snag.

Quick Review of Tools for Finding Names of Hiring Managers

Cross-reference target companies with the members of your social networks to get referrals and introductions. Look for these employers and for your identified high-value networking titles in the special-interest groups you belong to on social networking sites and use the common interest shared by the group to make an initial connection.

You can find a wide array of online search tools to find people, by name, job title, company, industry, and location at *www.knockemdead.com.* Go to the Career Advice pages, then click on Secrets & Strategies where you will find the Internet Resources link.

You can also use search engines to find job titles and names, as we discussed in the last chapter.

While any name and conversation that gets you closer to an interview is valuable, the most valuable job titles to target in your networking are *one to three levels above your own.*

In doing searches of news media that involve the names of your target companies, you will find names and titles plus information that you can use as an icebreaker in your emails, letters, or conversations. Copy an interesting, relevant article and attach it in an email. With a traditional letter, enclose a copy of the article. In both, your letter will open with mention of the media coverage, and this guarantees the rest of your message will be read. It is even more effective when you use it to open a telephone conversation: "I've been meaning to call you ever since I saw the article in . . ."

When you know whom you want to talk to and why, and you know the job and possess the skills that will contribute to the relationship, your irrational fears of talking to strangers on the phone should begin to evaporate.

Always Capture the Information

Capture the information you gather so that you can access and use it in this job search, and perhaps for other job searches down the road. If you stay in this profession and location, most of these companies are still going to be there, and many of the people you find will be too; and these companies and these people are still going to be hiring people like you. Capturing the information is another way in which you become knowledgeable about your profession and connected to the other players.

Beware of Approaching Dream Employers Too Soon

As you build these dossiers of information about individual companies in your target area, one or more of them will emerge as dream employers. Beware of applying for jobs at these "super-desirable" employers right at the start of your search. Most likely your resume and interviewing skills are not up to speed at the beginning of your search. The last thing you need to do is fumble an opportunity to join the company of your dreams. It is better to hold off until you know that your resume is fine-tuned and that you won't swallow your tongue in the first few minutes of the interview. Do this and then, when you feel confident, use network contacts to get insider information and referrals, and your approach to that dream employer is likely to be a smoother experience.

Written Approaches with Emails and Letters

How many emails and letters to send out every week is a difficult question to answer. Two contacts a week is the behavior of the long-term unemployed. Mass emailing 700 employers with one resume isn't the smartest answer either, because you can't ID the right people to reach, personalize the pitches, or be able to follow up in a timely manner.

Every job search is unique; nevertheless, your campaign needs strategy. You should maintain a balance between the *number* of written pitches you send out on a weekly basis and the *types of people to whom they are sent*. Start off with a balanced email and mailing campaign, and your phone follow-ups can maintain equilibrium, too.

The key is to organize and balance your job search activities so that you send as many resumes as possible directly to people by name in a volume that will allow you to make follow-up calls to those people. Start out with modest goals: Try to send between two and ten emails and letters each day addressed to someone by name and spread across each of the following areas:

- In response to job postings
- To the contacts you identify within target companies
- To headhunters
- To miscellaneous networking contacts

Will you need to create and use more than one type of letter in your search? Of course you will, because you will be approaching different types of people for different reasons. However, you don't have to craft every written communication entirely from scratch. You can create great letters quickly from the templates in *Knock 'em Dead Cover Letters*, where you will find letters for just about every job search scenario.

The key is to do each variation once and do it right, then save copies of these letters in folders within your career management database so you can access them at any time.

Multiple Submissions

You will sometimes find it valuable to make a number of contacts within a given company, especially the larger ones, to ensure that all the important players know of your existence. You'll remember the example from the last chapter of the engineer who wants to work for Last Chance Electronics, and the people such an engineer could send a resume to: the company president, the vice president of engineering, the chief engineer, the engineering manager, the vice president for human resources, the technical recruitment manager, and the technical recruiter, to name a few.

You wouldn't necessarily send all these communications out at once but might rather spread them over a period of time. Keep a log of your email (and mail) contacts so you will know when to follow up with a phone call—usually about two days after an email and five days after a traditional letter; exclude Monday mornings from this count, as everyone is busy getting up to speed for the week.

Keep track of these contacts beyond the initial follow-up period. Resumes do get misplaced, and employment needs change. You can comfortably resend emails and traditional mail to everyone on your list every couple of months; when you do this, it isn't necessary to remind them of earlier submissions. Most recipients won't register that they heard from you, and of those who do, most won't take offense. Any who might get upset are people who have no need for your professional skill set and whom you are therefore unlikely to run into anytime soon . . . so who cares.

An organized campaign will proceed on two fronts:

Front One: A carpet-bombing approach to every relevant management title within all the target companies in your location.

Front Two: A carefully targeted approach to a select group of companies. You may choose to hold back on contacting these special employers until comfortable with your developing job search skills—no point in getting into a conversation with a dream employer until you know how to handle that conversation.

You will continue to add to these lists of companies as you unearth fresh opportunities in your day-to-day research efforts, and as you identify new management titles within those companies.

In both these approaches you respond to job postings and upload your resume to their corporate databases in the standard way. Then as your direct research and networking identifies specific individuals within these companies, you begin email/mailing one or two contacts within the company. Repeat the emails/traditional letters to other contacts when your follow-up calls to these people result in referrals or dead ends. Remember, just because Harry in engineering says there are no openings in the company, that doesn't make it so. Any one of the additional contacts you make within that company could be the person *who is the person or who knows the person* with the perfect job for you. Even when a company states it has a hiring freeze there are always, always exceptions.

How to Quadruple Your Chances of an Interview

The more ways you approach your target companies and hiring managers, the faster you will *get into conversations with the people who can and will hire you*. Let's say you respond to a job posting by uploading your resume; that gives you one chance of getting an interview.

You can quadruple your chances of an interview if you also:

- Identify a potential hiring manager and email your resume directly to that manager by name with a personalized cover letter. This doubles your chances of an interview.
- Send a resume and personalized cover letter to that same manager by traditional mail, and you will triple your chances of an interview. Don't smirk at the idea of traditional mail. We all like a break from the computer screen, so delivering your sales message and resume this way can be very effective. When you do this, note in the cover letter that you sent the resume by email and that this additional approach is because you are really interested in the company and "wanted to increase my chances of getting your attention." Doing this demonstrates that you are creative, and not a technological Neanderthal.
- Make a follow-up telephone call to that manager, first thing in the morning, at lunchtime, or at 5 P.M. (when he is most likely to be available and picking up his own phone) and you will quadruple your chances of an interview.

Remember, a successful job search is all about *getting into conversations as often as possible with people in a position to hire you*. The more frequently you approach and get into conversations with managers whose job titles signify that they have the authority to hire you, the faster you will land that new position, because you have skipped right over the hurdle of being pulled from the commercial resume database, you have sidestepped the corporate recruiter's evaluation process, and *as a result* you have the attention of the actual decision maker and the chance to have a conversation, to make a direct and personal pitch.

Getting a resume to someone by name with a personalized pitch gives you a distinct advantage, which is never more important than when the economy is down or in recovery. At such times your competition is fierce and employers actually do recognize and appreciate the initiative and motivation you display by doing these things, especially picking up the phone and calling: All these approaches act as differentiating factors in your candidacy.

Avoid Wishful Thinking

Once your campaign starts to gain traction and you begin to schedule interviews from your calls, your emphasis will change, and you'll spend time preparing for interviews and following up after them.

This is the point at which most job searches stall. We get so excited about an interview and convince ourselves, "This will be the offer." As a result our job search activities slow to a halt. Here's an unsettling fact of life: The offer that can't fail usually does fail, and you are left depressed and without anything happening in your job search.

You *must* keep your job search pump primed with ongoing activity to generate interviews. Apart from this approach helping you get that next job most efficiently, it keeps your psychological pump primed, too.

The more direct contacts you make through email and regular mail, the more follow-up calls you can make to pitch your candidacy, schedule interviews, and get leads for more openings. Don't ignore sending letters through the mail; email has drastically reduced the amount of business mail, so a resume sent this way is going to stand out.

Initiating Conversations with Hiring Managers

Phone conversations are more powerful than resumes, emails, and letters, and they are essential to getting you interviews. Talking with high-value titles who haven't seen your resume and following up on resumes you send out with a phone call are the best ways to get the interviews that lead to job offers.

At the same time as you are uploading to resume databases and emailing and traditional mailing your resume to high-value contacts and hiring managers you identified today, pick up the phone and introduce yourself to the ones you identified and approached with a resume a day or two ago. Make as many of these calls as you send emails and traditional letters pitching your resume. The more often these conversations happen, the quicker your search will end in success.

Don't deceive yourself by thinking this part of the search is not possible because you are terrified of picking up the phone to call strangers. We all talk on the phone every day—these are just calls with a distinct purpose. It is something you can learn to do successfully, and whatever small pain it causes is far outweighed by what you gain: a new job and a fresh start on managing your career more successfully.

In a past professional incarnation as a headhunter, I spent every day on the telephone talking to strangers. Even though I developed a global reputation I was also always absolutely terrified making calls, which of course no one at the time ever knew ;-) The adrenaline rush we associate with fear is usual for anyone engaged in a critical performance. In fact it is a very natural reaction; success comes from harnessing the adrenaline rush you feel at times like these.

I'd be surprised if you, too, weren't a little leery at the prospect of actually calling prospective employers. Three pieces of advice helped me in my hour of abject terror:

- I knew that I would never meet these people unless they were interested in what I had to offer, in which case they'd be happy I called.
- Because I was on the phone, no one would know who I was or how scared I felt and looked.
- The third thing that helped was learning how to make almost every call successful. As outrageous as that sounds, it really is pretty easy.

If you have just a single goal when you pick up the phone—get an interview—you have just one chance of success but many more for failure. But if you have multiple goals for your call, you have multiple chances for success. When headhunters make sales/marketing calls, they usually have five goals in mind, so I have adapted the headhunter's goals to fit your needs:

1. I will arrange an interview date and time.
2. If my contact is busy, I will arrange another time to talk.
3. I will develop leads on promising job openings elsewhere in this and other companies.
4. I will leave the door open to talk with this person again in the future.
5. I will send a resume for subsequent follow-up.

Keep these goals in mind every time you talk with someone during your job search, because every conversation holds the potential to turn into an interview or lead you toward another conversation that will generate first a phone conversation and then a face-to-face meeting.

You might worry about calling people directly because you are concerned that they will be annoyed by the perceived intrusion. This is a misconception: The first job of any manager is to get work done through others, so every smart manager is always on the lookout for talent, and if not for today, then for tomorrow. If that isn't enough to allay your fears, keep in mind that the person on the other end of the line has very possibly been in your position and is sensitive to your situation. If you can be concise and professional, you'll find that the great majority of people you contact will try to be helpful.

Paint a Word Picture

The secret is being succinct. With an initial introduction and presentation that comes in at well under a minute, you won't be construed as wasting anybody's time.

Your aim is to paint a representation of your skills with the widest appeal, keeping it brief out of courtesy, while avoiding giving information that might rule you out.

> **KNOCK 'EM DEAD TIP**
> Writing out something you're going to say aloud is very different from writing something for someone else to read. Speech is more casually structured than the written word. You'll get the best results if you write down the bullet points you want to make rather than full sentences. Once you have written it out, speak it aloud a few times until it sounds conversational and relaxed. Then practice it with a friend or record yourself for critique until it sounds polished and professional.

Step #1

Give the employer a snapshot of who you are and what you do. The intent is to give that person a reason to stay on the phone. You may sometimes have an introduction from a colleague, in which case you will build a bridge with that:

"Miss Shepburn? Good morning, my name is Martin Yate, and our mutual friend Greg Spencer suggested I call . . ."

Or you may have gotten the name and contact information from, for example, a professional association database, in which case you will use that as a bridge:

"Miss Shepburn? My name is Martin Yate. We haven't spoken before, but as we are both members of the _____ Association, I hoped I might get a couple of minutes of your time for some advice . . ."

Never ask if you have caught someone at a bad time because that's offering your contact an excuse to say she is busy. On the other hand, asking whether you have caught someone at a good time will usually get you a positive response, or just pausing after stating the reason of your call, as I did previously, will work. Then you can go into the rest of your presentation. If at any point your contact says or implies that she is harried, immediately ask when would be a good time to call back.

Now we come to the meat of your presentation. Grab the listener's attention now and you are off to a good start. You want to capture a complete picture of the *professional you* in less than one minute, ideally less than forty-five seconds, and the good news is that you already have the text for what you need to say.

In creating your resume you completed TJD exercises that helped you prioritize employers' needs for your job title. When you wrote the Performance Profile for your resume, which introduced the *professional you* succinctly, you condensed the leading employer priorities into three to six short sentences. So you already know what aspects of your experience have widest and most relevant appeal, and we just have to retool them for speaking rather than reading; that's easy. After your introduction:

"Miss Shepburn? My name is Martin Yate. We haven't spoken before, but as we are both members of the _____ Association, I hoped I might get a couple of minutes of your time for some advice . . ."

You pause for agreement, and having taken the opening line from your resume's Performance Profile:

"Ten years' experience in office technology sales, including a successful track record selling B-to-B, including corporations, institutions, and small business." You just make it a little less formal and less specific:

" . . . *I'm in office technology sales, with a successful track record selling B-to-B: corporations, institutions, and small business . . .*"

Then complete the spoken version of your Performance Profile. To create a spoken version, take the sentences and turn them into bullet points so that you can't recite the sentences word for word and sound like you are reading a script.

Once you have your script down, practice speaking it aloud until it sounds conversational and relaxed. Then practice it with a friend or record yourself for critique. Do it in a normal speaking voice until you are comfortable with the content and the rhythm; you'll also know how long it takes. To keep it under the one-minute mark, remember that the idea is just to whet the listener's appetite to know more.

You might take out some information—for example describing yourself as experienced, rather than identifying a specific number of years in your field. This encourages the listener to qualify your statement with a question: "How much experience do you have?" Any question denotes a level of interest and might well mean a job exists or is about to exist.

Step #2

Keeping your presentation short and to the point makes Step #2 optional, depending on the time you have available and on whether you have something impressive to say about your achievements. If you can cover your Performance Profile points and still have a little time left over, add an example of what you can achieve:

"As the number three salesperson in my company, I increased sales in my territory fifteen percent, to over one million dollars. In the last six months, I won three major accounts from my competitors—a hospital, a bank, and a technology start-up."

Note that you always talk about what you can do, but never how you do it.

Step #3

Having introduced yourself professionally and succinctly, get to the reason for your call and move the conversation forward.

"The reason I'm calling is that I'm looking for a new challenge, and as I know a little about your company, I felt we might have some areas of common interest. Are these the types of skills and accomplishments you look for in your sales associates?"

Notice that your presentation finishes not with "Have you got a job? Can you hire me?" but with a question that encourages a positive response and opens the possibility of conversation.

When you make your presentation for real, there will likely be a silence on the other end of the line. Be patient, as the employer may need a few seconds to digest your words.

When the employer does respond, it will either be with a question, denoting interest, or with an objection.

Whatever the voice on the other end of the line says next, try to give short, reasonable answers and finish your reply, when it makes sense to do so, with a question. If a job exists, in answer to your questions the interviewer will tell you a little about that job. This will define what skills and qualities are important to this employer and help you customize your answers with your most relevant skills and experiences.

Conversation is a two-way street, and you are most likely to win an interview when you take responsibility for your half. Just as the employer's questions show interest in you, your questions should show your interest in the work done at the company. By asking questions of your own in the normal course of conversation—questions usually tagged on to the end of one of your answers—you will forward the conversation.

Here's an example of how such a conversation might proceed. Because you and I come from different backgrounds, we will never talk alike, so with the following sample questions and answers just capture the essence so that you can tailor them to your own speech patterns.

"The reason I'm calling is that I'm looking for a new challenge, and as I know and respect your product line, I felt we might have areas for discussion. Are these the types of skills and accomplishments you look for in your staff?"

[Pause]

Miss Shepburn: *"Yes, they are. What type of equipment have you been selling?"* [Buy signal!]

You: *"A comprehensive range from work stations, through routers, modems to printers and ink . . . and all the peripherals you would expect; I sell according to my customers' needs and the capabilities of the technology. I have been noticing a considerable interest in _____ recently. Has that been your experience?"*

Miss Shepburn: *"Yes, I have actually."* [Useful information for you.] *"Do you have a degree?"* [Buy signal!]

You: *"Yes, I do."* [Just enough information to keep the company interested.] *"I understand your company prefers degreed salespeople to deal with its more sophisticated clients."* [Your research is paying off.]

Miss Shepburn: *"Our customer base is very sophisticated, and they expect a certain professionalism and competence from us."* [An inkling of the kind of person the company wants to hire.] *"How much experience do you have?"* [Buy signal!]

You: *"Well, I've worked in both operations and sales, so I understand sales and fulfillment processes, and my customers benefit from not having to deal with false expectations because I understand how to work cooperatively with fulfillment."* [General but thorough.] *"How many years of experience are you looking for?"* [Turning it around, but furthering the conversation.]

Miss Shepburn: *"Ideally, four or five for the position I have in mind."* [More good information.] *"How many do you have?"* [Buy signal!]

You: *"I have two with this company, and one and a half before that, so I fit right in with your needs."*

Miss Shepburn: *"Uh-huh . . . What's your territory?"* [Buy signal!]

You: *"I cover the metropolitan area. Miss Shepburn, it sounds as if we might have something to talk about."* [Remember, your first goal is the face-to-face interview.] *"I am planning to take personal time off next Thursday or Friday. Can we meet then? Which would be best for you?"* [Encourage Miss Shepburn to decide *which* day she can see you, rather than *whether* she will see you.]

Miss Shepburn: *"How about Friday morning?"*

Your questions show interest, carry the conversation forward, and teach you more about the company's needs. By the end of the conversation you have an interview arranged and several key areas you should write down while they are fresh. You can do further research on these areas of interest prior to the interview:

- The company sees growth in _____, so be sure you research what is going on in this particular area.
- They want both professional and personal sophistication.
- They ideally want four or five years' experience.
- They are interested in your metropolitan contacts.

Let's look at the building blocks again before moving on to getting live leads from dead ends:

Step One. Give the employer a succinct verbal snapshot of who you are and what you bring to the table (your Performance Profile).

Step Two. Finish your introduction off with an example of professional achievements.

Step Three. Move the conversation forward by explaining the reason for your call and finishing with a question that elicits a positive response.

At this point, the employer will respond with a question or an objection. If it's a question, it shows that the listener is interested. Among the buy signals that often come up are the following:

- "How much experience do you have?" Too much or too little experience could easily rule you out. Be careful how you answer this question and try to gain time. It is a vague question, and you have a right to ask for qualifications. Employers typically define jobs by years' experience. At the same time there is currently a major move away from simple chronological experience toward the more important concern about what you can deliver on the job. Managers and HR pros are now more open to thinking in terms of "performance requirements" and "deliverables" than ever before.

Here are a couple of ways to handle it:

"I have _____ years' chronological experience, but if you could you give me a brief outline of the performance requirements I can give you a more accurate answer." Then with the information you might be able to answer, *"I am comfortable with all aspects of the pre-sales, sales, and post-sales process and have considerable experience, comfort, and contacts throughout the B-to-B community here in Pittsburgh, including public corporations, institutions, and start-ups."*

Or:

"Could you help me with that question? If you give me a brief outline of the performance requirements, I can give you a more accurate answer." Or, *"I have _____ years' experience, but they aren't necessarily typical. If you'd give me a few details on the performance requirements I'd be able to give you a more accurate answer."*

The employer's response, while gaining you time, tells you what it takes to do the job and therefore what aspects of your experience are most relevant. Take mental notes as the employer talks—you can even write them down if you have time. Then give an appropriate response.

You can move the conversation forward by asking a follow-up question of your own. For example: *"The areas of expertise you require sound like a match to my experience, and it sounds as if you have some exciting projects at hand. What projects would I be involved with in the first few months?"*

- "Do you have a degree?" An easy question if you have one. If not, qualify your answer and point the way forward: "My education was cut short by the necessity of earning a living. However, I'm currently enrolled in classes to complete my degree."
- Buy Signal: "How much are you making/do you want?"

This is a direct question looking for a direct answer, yet it is a knockout question, so you should proceed warily. Earning either too little or too much could ruin your chances before you're given the opportunity to shine in person. There are a number of options that could serve you better than a direct answer. First, you must understand that questions about money at this point in the conversation are being used to screen you in or screen you out. The answers you give now should be geared toward getting you in the door and into a face-to-face meeting. (Handling the serious salary negotiations that are attached to a job offer are covered in Chapter 25, "Negotiating the Job Offer.") For now, your main options are as follows:

- Direct answer: If you know the salary range for the position and there is a fit, give a straightforward answer.
- Indirect answer: "In the 50s." Or "in the 120s."
- Put yourself above the money: "I'm looking for an opportunity to make a difference with my efforts. If I am the right person for the job, I'm sure you'll make me a fair offer. By the way, what is the salary range for this position?"

- Give a range. Come up with two figures: a fair offer considering your experience and job location, and a great offer considering your experience and job location, "Hopefully between $x and $y. What's most important is an opportunity to make a difference. If I am the right person for the job, I'm sure you'll make me a fair offer. By the way, what is the salary range for this position?"

When you give a salary range rather than a single figure, you have more flexibility and a greater chance of "clicking" with the employer's approved range for the position.

When you are pressed a second time for an exact dollar figure, be as honest and forthright as circumstances permit. If you have the skills for the job and you are concerned that your current low salary will eliminate you before you have the chance to show your worth, you might add, *"I realize this is well below industry norms, but it does not reflect on my expertise or experience in any way. It speaks of the need for me to make a strategic career move to where I can be compensated competitively and based on my skills."*

If your current earnings are higher than the approved range, you could say, *"Mr. Smith, my current employers feel I am well worth the money I earn due to my skills, dedication, and honesty. When we meet, I'm sure I can convince you of my ability to contribute to your department. A meeting would provide an opportunity to make that evaluation, wouldn't it?"*

How to Deal with Objections

By no means will every presentation call you make be met with a few simple questions and then an invitation to interview. Sometimes the silence will be broken with an objection. This usually comes in the form of a statement, not a question: "Send me a resume," or "I don't have time to see you," or "You are earning too much," or "You'll have to talk to personnel," or "I don't need anyone like you right now." These seem like brush-off lines, but they can be turned into interviews, and when that isn't possible, they can almost always be parlayed into leads elsewhere.

Notice that all the following suggested response models end with a question, one that helps you learn more about the reason for the objection, perhaps to overcome it and lead the conversation toward a meeting.

In dealing with objections, nothing is gained by confrontation, while much can be gained by an appreciation of the other's viewpoint. Consequently, most objections you hear are best handled by first demonstrating your understanding of the other's viewpoint. Start your responses with phrases like "I understand," or "I can appreciate your position," or "I see your point," or "Of course." Follow up with statements like "However," or "Also consider," or a similar line that allows the opportunity for rebuttal and to gather further information.

It's not necessary to memorize these responses verbatim, only to understand the underlying concept and then put together responses in words that are natural to your character and style of speech.

Objection: "Why don't you send me a resume?"

The employer may be genuinely interested in seeing your resume as a first step in the interview cycle, or it may be a polite way of getting you off the phone. You should identify the real reason without causing antagonism, and at the same time open up the conversation. A good reply would be, *"Of course, Mr. Grant. Would you give me your exact title and your email address? Thank you. So that I can be sure that my qualifications fit your needs, what skills are you looking for in this position?"* or *"What specific job title and opening should I refer to when I send it?"*

Notice the steps:

- Agreement with the prospective employer
- A demonstration of understanding
- A question to further the conversation (in this instance to confirm that an opening actually exists)

Answering in this fashion will open up the conversation. Mr. Grant will relay the aspects of the job that are important to him, and you can use the additional information to move the conversation forward again or to draw attention to relevant skills in:

- Your executive briefing or cover letter
- A customized resume
- Your face-to-face meeting

Following Mr. Grant's response, you can recap the match between his needs and your skills: *"Assuming my resume matches your needs, as I think we are both confident that it will, could we pencil in a date and time for an interview next week? I am available next Thursday and Friday; which would be preferable to you?"*

A penciled-in date and time for an interview very rarely gets canceled, because it doesn't actually get "penciled in"—in this electronic age, it immediately takes up a time slot in the schedule.

Objection: "I don't have time to see you."

If the employer is too busy to see you, it indicates that he or she has work pressures, and by recognizing that, you can show yourself as the one to alleviate some of those pressures through your problem-solving skills. You should avoid confrontation, however; it is important that you demonstrate empathy for the person with whom you are speaking. Agree, empathize, and ask a question that moves the conversation forward:

"I understand how busy you must be; it sounds like a competent, dedicated, and efficient professional [whatever your title is] could be of some assistance. Perhaps I could call you back at a

better time to discuss how I might make a contribution in easing the pressure at peak times. When are you least busy, in the morning or afternoon?"

The company representative will either make time to talk now or will arrange a better time for the two of you to talk further.

You could also try, *"Since you are so busy, what is the best time of day for you? First thing in the morning, or is the afternoon a quieter time?"* Or you could suggest, *"If you would like to see my resume you could study my background at your leisure. What's your email address? Thanks, what would be a good time of day to follow up on this?"*

Objection: "You are earning too much."

Don't give up immediately; follow the process through: *"Oh, I'm sorry to hear that—what is the range for that position?"* Depending on the degree of salary discrepancy, you might reiterate your interest. You can also refer to Chapter 25, "Negotiating the Job Offer," where you will find further advice on dealing with this issue.

If the job really doesn't pay enough—and there will be openings for which you are earning too much—you've gotten "close, but no cigar!" Just a bit further on, I'll tell you how to make a success of this seeming dead end by asking a couple of questions as you wrap up the conversation.

Objection: "We only promote from within."

Your response could be, "[smiling] *Your development of employees is a major reason I want to get in! I am bright, conscientious, and motivated. When you do hire from the outside, and it must happen on occasion, what do you look for?"* or *"How do I get into consideration for such opportunities?"*

The response finishes with a question designed to carry the conversation forward and to give you a new opportunity to sell yourself. Notice that the response logically presupposes that the company does hire from the outside, as all companies obviously do, despite your being told otherwise.

Objection: "You'll have to talk to Human Resources."

In this case, you reply, *"Of course, Mr. Grant. Whom should I speak to in HR, and what specific position should I mention?"*

You cover a good deal of ground with that response. You establish whether there is a job there or whether you are being fobbed off on HR to waste their time and your own. Also, you move the conversation forward again while modifying it to your advantage. Develop a specific job-related question to ask while the employer is answering the first question. It can open a fruitful line for you to pursue. If you receive a nonspecific reply, probe a little deeper. A simple phrase like, *"That's interesting. Please tell me more,"* or *"Why's that?"* will usually do the trick.

Or you can ask, *"When I speak to HR, will it be about a specific job you have, or is it to see whether I might fill a position elsewhere in the company?"*

Armed with the resulting information, you can talk to HR about your conversation with Mr. Grant. Remember to get the name of a specific person in HR with whom to speak, and quote this prior contact by name in any email or verbal contact.

"Good morning, Ms. Johnson. Cary Grant, over in marketing, suggested we should speak to arrange an interview for the open sales associate requisition."

This way you show HR that you are not a time waster, because you have already spoken to the person for whom the requisition is open.

Don't look at the HR department as a roadblock. It may contain a host of opportunities for you. In many companies different departments could use your talents, and HR is probably the only department that knows all the openings. With larger companies you might be able to arrange interviews for two or three different positions!

Objection: "I really wanted someone with a degree."

You should have learned the proper response to "Do you have a degree?" But in case you were abducted by aliens a few pages ago, you could respond by saying, *"Mr. Smith, I appreciate your viewpoint. It was necessary that I start earning a living early in life. If we meet, I am certain you would recognize the value of my additional practical experience."* If you have been smart enough to enroll in a course or two in order to pursue that always-important degree, you should add, *"I am currently enrolled in courses to complete my degree, which should demonstrate my professional commitment, and perhaps that makes a difference?"* In a world of ongoing education it usually will.

You might then ask what the company policy is for support and encouragement of employees continuing their education. Your response will end with, *"If we were to meet, I am certain you would recognize the value of my practical experience, in addition to my ongoing professional commitment. I am going to be interviewing at the end of next week, and I know you will find the time to meet well spent. Is there a day and time that would be best for you?"*

Objection: "I don't need anyone like you now."

Short of suggesting that the employer fire someone to make room for you (which, believe it or not, has been done successfully on a few occasions), the chances of getting an interview with this company are slim. With the right questions, however, your contact will give you a personal introduction to someone else who could use your talents.

Live Leads from Dead Ends

By no means will every hiring manager you call have a job opening that fits your skills, but you can still turn calls that don't result in interviews into successes. Just a couple of pages back we established that your calls have multiple goals: to arrange an interview, to arrange another time for a conversation, to send a resume for future follow-up, and to develop leads on job openings elsewhere. If there isn't a need for someone like you right now you can ask:

- "When do you anticipate new needs in your area?"
- "May I send you my resume and keep in touch for when the situation changes?"
- "Who else in the company might have a need for someone with my background and skills?"
- "What other companies might have a need for someone with my background?"

If the response is positive:

- "Thanks, I appreciate the help. Do you know who I should speak to?"

If the response to *that* is positive:

- "May I mention your name?"

Mentioning a company you plan to call:

- "Do you know anyone I could speak to at _____?"

If you ask just this sequence of questions you will get leads and introductions, and this enables you to open that next call with:

"Hello, Mr. Jones? My name is Martin Yate, Chuck Harris gave me your name and said to tell you hello . . ."

But if you don't ask you can never expect to receive. Your call has been entirely professional, and you haven't wasted anyone's time, because the person has either been in your situation or knows it could well happen. You will find the overwhelming majority of people will try to be helpful if you show them a way to do so.

By adding these questions and others in the same vein you will achieve a measure of success from the call, leaving you energized and with a feeling of achievement after every conversation.

Here are six categories of questions that can lead to job openings, interviews, and offers. Read through them and then develop specific questions you can ask in each area:

1. Leads in department
2. Leads in company
3. Leads in other divisions of company
4. Leads to other companies
5. Contacts in other companies
6. Open door to keep in touch

Remember: Networking and marketing are continuous activities.

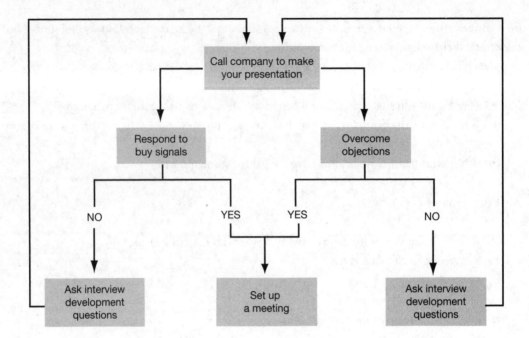

Corporate Gatekeepers

When you are making marketing and networking calls, an overly officious clerical assistant will sometimes try to thwart you in your efforts to present your credentials directly to a potential employer—at least it might appear that way.

In fact, it is very rare that these "corporate gatekeepers," as they are known, are directed to screen calls from professionals seeking employment, as to do so only increases employment costs to the company. What they are there to do is to screen nuisance calls from salespeople and the like.

However, to arm you for the occasional objectionable gatekeeper standing between you and making a living, you might try the following techniques used by investigative reporters, private eyes, and headhunters.

Preempting Questions

Most gatekeepers are trained at most to find out your name and the nature of your business. But when they are asking the questions, they control the conversation. You can remain in control by preempting their standard script: "Good morning. I'm Mr. Yate. I need to speak to Nikki Jones about an accounting matter. Is she there?" Should a truly obnoxious gatekeeper ask snidely, "Perhaps I can help you?" you can effectively use any of the following options: "Thank you, but I'd rather discuss it with Ms. Jones." "It's personal." "It's a professional matter." Or you can blind them with science: "Yes, if you can talk to me about the finer points of [some esoteric aspect of your profession] 10K reporting." They invariably can't, so you're in like Flynn.

Diction, tone of voice, confidence, and clarity are all-important when dealing with clerical staff. They are trained to respect and respond to polite authority, so always demonstrate self-confidence in your manner. When you are clear about whom you want to speak to and can predict possible screening devices, you usually get through. With such gatekeepers you should also avoid using your first name in your introduction, as in "Martin Carlucci"; instead, try "Mr. Carlucci" or "Ms. Carlucci," which is always more authoritative.

When you have been given a name by a networking contact, you can use that introduction to get past corporate gatekeepers: "Tell him Bill Edwards asked me to call."

Go Up the Ladder

If you can't get through to the person you want to speak to, say the accounting manager, instead of wasting the call you can go up the ladder to the controller or the vice president of finance; remember that one, two, and three management titles above you are all likely to be involved in some degree with selection of candidates like you.

Interestingly, the higher you go, the more accessible people are. In this instance, the senior manager may well not schedule an interview with you but instead refer you back down to the appropriate level. Sometimes that VP will switch you directly to the person with whom you want to speak; even if that doesn't happen, the next time you call you have a nice, hefty name to drop when dealing with the pesky gatekeeper: "Your divisional vice president of finance, Mr. Craig Wilde, asked me to call Mr. Jones. Is he there?" Even if you didn't speak directly to that VP up the corporate ladder, and the VP's secretary referred you back down the ladder, you can now say with all honesty, "Mr. [VP's] office recommended . . ." Then the conversation with your target can begin with your standard introduction, but be sure to mention first the name of the person who referred you.

If you haven't yet gleaned any names from a particular company through your networking activities and are being thwarted by a gatekeeper, try these approaches:

- Over time you will develop a list of companies where you have no contacts. You can refer to this list when you run into a brick wall on either a networking or marketing call. "Jack, I was planning to contact _____, Inc. Would you happen to know anyone there who could give me a heads-up?" Or "Jack, do you know anyone at _____ or _____ that I could speak to? Any lead would be most appreciated."
- Check your association membership databases and your online networks and look for members who work or have worked at a target company. Regardless of their titles, these people can bring you one step closer to the right hiring authority contact.
- Visit the company's website and look for names there. Don't forget to read the media clippings that always get posted, since they invariably contain a quote or two from company

representatives. You should also do Google News searches for media coverage of the company and its executives.

- For especially desirable companies, check back with those people who know you well and respect your work: your references. They might know or be able to find out the names of people working within your target.

When none of your research, networking, or marketing activities has presented you with a name, try these techniques:

- There is usually more than one person worth speaking to at any company, so whomever you speak to, ask for more than one name and title. For example, in the finance area (depending on your level), any or all of the following could provide useful contacts: accounting supervisor, accounting manager, assistant controller, controller, vice president of finance, chief financial officer, executive vice president, president, chief operating officer, chief executive officer, chairman. The last eight of these can usually be found on the company website or in reference databases and directories.

Anyone who gives you one name will invariably give you more than one. Some years ago in Colorado I sat with a job searcher who used these techniques to gather 142 names from receptionists in one hour!

- In some companies where security is at a premium, gatekeepers are expressly forbidden to give out names and titles. In this case, you can use some side-door techniques: There are certain people in every company who by the very nature of their jobs have contact with people at all levels of the company and who are not given the responsibility to screen calls. These include people in the mailroom, maintenance, shipping and receiving, second-, third-, and fourth-shift employees, new or temporary employees, advertising and public relations people, sales and marketing people, travel center, Q/A, and customer service employees.

Another approach for getting by pesky gatekeepers is to vary the times when you call a target company. Try before 9 A.M., immediately after 5 P.M., and during lunch hours. Managers often pick up their own lines at these times.

Voice Mail

Voice mail is on the increase. Rather than treating it as a dead end, turn it into a useful means of getting through to your target contact.

When you have an introduction, you can use it to navigate voice mail systems and to leave as a teaser on your voice mail message: *"Good morning, my name is William Powell. Ms. Loy suggested I give you a call. She thought we might have something to talk about. I'll try you later."*

Don't leave long messages; be brief and get on with your job search and make another call. In cases where you don't get a response and need to call back again, do so, but if the person doesn't pick up and you get routed to the voice mail again, hang up and move on to your next call. If you leave countless voice mail messages, it will make you look needy.

When you lack a name, check to see if the system has a directory, and if it does, take note of as many names and extensions as you can. If there is no directory, and the voice mail system tells you to enter an extension key, keep keying until you hit one that results in a human voice. It doesn't matter who answers as long as someone does. The conversation goes something like this:

"Jack speaking."

"Jack, this is Martin Yate. I'm calling from outside and I'm lost on this darned telephone system." [This usually gets a smile.] *"I'm trying to get hold of [whatever the title is]. Could you check who that would be for me?"*

Develop a written list, and keep one on your desktop and one taped by your telephone.

Dealing with Abject Terror

The adrenaline rush you experience when picking up the phone to make the first of these calls is something we associate with fear, and *is normal for anyone engaged in a critical performance activity*. It is a very natural reaction, but because you:

- Know the product you are selling inside out
- Know (from your TJD exercises) exactly what you are going to say and how you are going to say it
- Know it will have the greatest relevance and therefore interest to the listener
  you will be able to harness the adrenaline rush and channel it into peak performance.

The Last Man Standing Wins

It is trite but true that you have never failed until you quit trying. Job searches will always take longer during economic downturns and will take longer the less professionally you approach them. Nevertheless, we have a huge economy, and even in the worst times people are landing new jobs. It's just that they're the ones who are working smarter and harder than everyone else.

If you are in the midst of a long job search, try to keep things in perspective. Although your 224th contact may not have an opening for you, ask questions and you may well discover that he or she has the good lead you need. Don't ask the questions and you'll never know.

In a job search there are only two "yeses": the employer's "we want you to work for us" and your "I can start on Monday." Every other conversation is, in reality, a "no" that brings you closer to the big "yes." Never take rejections of your resume or your phone call as rejections of you. There is a great opportunity right around the corner, so long as you keep turning that corner to maintain your forward momentum.

Stacking the Odds in Your Favor

We all have 168 hours a week to become bagmen or billionaires and to make our lives as fulfilling as they can be. For some of us this means a better job; for others it means getting back to work to keep a roof over our heads. How we manage these hours will determine our success. These job search commandments will see you successfully through the job change and career transition process:

- Start conversations. It has been said that in order to gain that next job it takes on average twenty-five conversations with men or women who have the authority to hire you. What do we learn from this? Make every effort to get into conversations with decision makers with hiring authority and sooner or later you will get that job offer. It doesn't matter if it takes 25 or 125 such conversations, the essential truth still holds: Get into conversations with enough hiring authorities and you will get that desired job offer. Getting into those critical conversations isn't easy; it might take you hundreds of contacts, but if you make the commitment every day of your job search, you will succeed, and you will succeed more quickly than your peers.
- Work at getting a new job. Work forty hours per week at it. Divide your time equally between all the intelligent job search approaches. No one knows which tactic is the one that will work for you, but this integrated approach gives you the shortest odds.
- Research the companies you contact. In a tightly run job race, the candidate who is most knowledgeable and intelligently enthusiastic about the employer has a distinct advantage.
- Follow up on the resumes you send out with phone calls. Resubmit your resume to identified openings after six or seven weeks. Change the format of your resume and submit it again. (See *Knock 'em Dead Resumes* for specific ideas on how to do this.)
- Stay in telephone contact with your job leads. Call them back on a regular basis to maintain top-of-the-mind awareness. If you find yourself needing to call existing contacts more than once every couple of months, you should be putting more emphasis on building your networks and doing direct research.
- Develop examples of your professional profile that make you special—and rehearse building these examples into your interview responses. More on this later.
- Send follow-up notes with relevant news clippings, cartoons, and so on to those in your networks. It's a light touch that helps people keep you in mind. You'll find lots of ideas for follow-up in Chapter 24.
- Work on your self-image. Use this time to get physically fit. Studies show that unfit, overweight people take longer to find suitable work.
- Maintain a professional demeanor during the workweek (clothing, posture, personal hygiene).
- Use regular business hours for making contacts. Use the early morning, lunchtime, after 5 P.M., and Saturday for doing the ongoing research and writing projects that maintain momentum.
- Take off the blinders. We all have two specific skills: our professional/technical skills—for example, computer programming; and our industry skills—for example, banking. Professional/

technical skills can be transferable to other industries, and industry skills can open other opportunities in your industry. For example, that programmer, given decent communication skills, could become a technical trainer and/or writer for programmers or technophobes.

- Don't feel guilty about taking time off from your job search. Just do it responsibly. If you regularly spend Saturday morning in the library doing research, you can take Wednesday afternoon off to go to the driving range once in a while.

- Never stop the research and job search process until you have a written job offer in hand and you have accepted that job in writing with an agreed-upon start date. Even then, continue with any ongoing interview cycles.

- Remember: It's all up to you. There are many excuses not to make calls or send resumes on any given day. There are many excuses to get up later or knock off earlier. There are many excuses to back off because this one's in the bag. But there are no real *reasons*. There are no jobs out there for those who won't look, while there are plenty of opportunities for those who work at it.

- The more you do today, the better you will feel about yourself.

Follow-Up: The Key Ingredient

In theory, the perfect emails you send cold or as a result of phone calls will receive a response rate of 100 percent. Unfortunately, there is no perfect letter, email, or call in this less-than-perfect world. If you sit waiting for the world to beat a path to your door, you may wait a long time.

An IT executive of my acquaintance once advertised for an analyst. By Wednesday of the following week he had over 100 responses. Ten days later he was still plowing through them when he received a follow-up call (the only one he received) from one of the respondents. The job hunter was in the office that afternoon, returned the following morning, and was hired before lunchtime.

What's the takeaway? The candidate's resume was still sitting in the database, waiting to be discovered. The follow-up phone call got it discovered. The IT executive just wanted to get on with his work, and the job hunter in question made it possible by putting himself on the employer's radar. Follow-up calls do work.

Stay the Course

Make phone calls to initiate contact, and you'll get requests for resumes and requests to come right on over for an interview. Make follow-up calls on mailed and emailed resumes and you will generate further interviews.

No one is ever hired without passing through one or a series of formal interviews, and that is where *Knock 'em Dead* is headed next: how to turn interviews into job offers.

CHAPTER 8
ACE THE TELEPHONE INTERVIEW

INTERVIEWERS USE THE telephone to weed out applicants. Your goal is a face-to-face meeting, and these are the methods you must use to get it.

Some aspects of a job search are not clear-cut. For instance, a telephone interview for a job might be scheduled for a certain date and time, so you have plenty of time to prepare for it. Then again, a networking call can turn into a marketing presentation in a flash when you realize that the person on the other end of the phone is in a position to hire you. Likewise, when that marketing presentation progresses past the initial "buy signals" and objections, it can suddenly become a telephone interview. These things happen, but as you understand the steps to take in order to move each of these situations forward, you must be sensitive to the possibility that while telephone interviews can be scheduled in advance, they are just as likely to occur on the fly.

Employers use the telephone as a time management tool. It is easier to cut to the chase and weed out candidates quickly on the telephone than in person. Your goal is a face-to-face meeting, so all you must do is convince the employer she will not be wasting time if she meets with you in person. Here are the techniques you should use to turn the phone conversation into a face-to-face meeting.

Organization for Marketing Calls and Telephone Interviews

Your first substantive contact with a potential employer will usually be by telephone; for entry-level professionals this first meeting will quite often take place at job fairs. For right now, let's concentrate on the telephone interview.

The phone interview happens in one of three ways:

- You are making a marketing or networking call, and the company representative goes into a screening process because you have aroused his interest.
- An employer calls unexpectedly as the result of a resume you have mailed or emailed.
- You have arranged a specific time for a telephone interview.

Odds are that you will experience plenty of telephone interviews during your job search. Whichever activities generate a telephone interview, you must think and act clearly to turn the opportunity into the real thing—a face-to-face meeting. The way you perform will determine whether you move ahead or bite the dust.

A few words about telephone services: call waiting might be nice to have for social use, but responding to its demands during a job search will only annoy the person you have on the line at the time. If you have call waiting, disconnect it or ignore it. More and more telephone companies are also offering additional lines with distinctive rings for your basic service and at no extra charge. With this facility you can have a permanent job search/career management line and keep a constant eye on the job market without compromising day-to-day home life.

Perhaps the most important consideration about telephone interviews is that the employer has only his ears with which to judge you. If the call comes unexpectedly, and screaming kids or barking dogs surround you, stay calm and sound positive, friendly, and collected: "Thank you for calling, Mr. Wooster. Would you wait a moment while I close the door?" You can then take a minute to calm yourself, bring up the company website on your screen, and get your paperwork organized without causing offense. If you need to move to another phone, say so. Otherwise, put the caller on hold, take a few controlled, deep breaths to slow down your pounding heart, put a smile on your face (it improves the timbre of your voice), and pick up the phone again. Now you are in control of yourself and the situation.

If you are heading out the door for an interview, or if some other emergency makes this a bad time for an unexpected incoming call, say so straight away and reschedule: "I'm heading out the door for an appointment, Mr. Bassett. Can we schedule a time when I can call you back?" Beware of overfamiliarity: You should always refer to the interviewer by his surname until invited to do otherwise.

Allow the company representative to guide the conversation and to ask most of the questions, but keep up your end of the conversation. This is especially important when the interviewer does not give you the openings you need to sell yourself. Always have a few intelligent questions prepared to save the situation. The following questions will give you an excellent idea of why the position is open and exactly the kind of skilled professional the company will eventually hire:

- "What are the major responsibilities in this job?"
- "What will be the first project(s) I tackle?"
- "What are the biggest challenges the department faces this year and what will be my role as a team member in tackling them?"
- "Which projects will I be most involved with during the first six months?"
- "Who succeeds in this job and why?"
- "Who fails in this job and why?"

When you get a clear understanding of an employer's needs with questions like these, you can seize the opportunity to sell yourself appropriately: "Would it be of value if I described my experience in the area of office management?"; or "Then my experience in word processing should be a great help to you"; or "I recently completed an accounting project just like that. Would it be relevant to discuss it?"

When you identify an employer's imminent challenges and demonstrate how your skills can lessen the load, you portray yourself as a properly focused employee with a problem-solving mentality, and immediately move closer to a face-to-face interview. Everyone hires a problem solver.

You can also keep up your end of the conversation by giving verbal signals that you are engaged in it; you do this with occasional short interjections that don't interrupt the employer's flow but let her know you are paying attention. Comments like "uh-huh," "that's interesting," "okay," "great," and "yes, yes" are verbal equivalents of the body language techniques you'll use to show interest during a face-to-face meeting.

Always speak directly into the telephone, with the mouthpiece about one inch from your mouth. Numbered among the mystical properties of telephone technology is its excellence at picking up and amplifying background noise. This is excelled only by its power to transmit the sounds of food and gum being chewed, or smoke being inhaled and exhaled. Smokers take note: Nonsmokers instinctively discriminate, and they will assume that even if you don't actually light up at the interview, you'll have been chain-smoking beforehand and will carry the smell with you as long as you are around. They probably won't even give you a chance to get through the door once they hear you puffing away over the phone.

You should take notes when possible; they will be invaluable if the employer is interrupted. You can jot down the topic under discussion, then when he gets back on the line, helpfully recap: "We were just discussing . . ." This will be appreciated and show that you are organized and paying attention. Your notes will also help you prepare for the face-to-face meeting.

The company representative may talk about the corporation, and from your research or the website on your screen you may also know something about the outfit. A little flattery goes a long way: Admire a company's achievements when you can, and by inference you admire the interviewer. Likewise, if any areas of common interest arise, comment on them, and agree with the interviewer when reasonably possible—people usually hire people like themselves.

On the 200 telephone interviews a year that I average (they are radio interviews, not job interviews, but I'm sure you can appreciate the similar level of nervous tension), I've found that standing for the interview calms the adrenaline a little, helps my breathing, and allows me to sound confident and relaxed. It might work for you, too, so give it a try.

How to Handle Skype Interviews

Skype is the fastest, cheapest telecommunications service available, and it has the best voice quality. If you don't have a Skype account, set one up now (free to set up and as little as $2.99 a month to maintain), because the odds of someone wanting to interview over Skype increases daily.

The call can be a simple telephone call or it can be a video call. Recruiters usually want to do video, and this affects how you should dress when attending virtual job fairs.

As I write this, I've just returned from my morning bike ride. I wanted to get the words flowing immediately, so I haven't shaved yet and I'm wearing shorts and a T-shirt and generally look like I slept in a hedge. This doesn't affect my subject-matter expertise, but I sure don't look like a career expert. It is fine for me to dress like a bum when I'm sitting alone typing on my Mac, but if I thought there were a possibility of a Skype interview in my day, I would dress and prepare my environment for it.

Skype Video Interviews

With a Skype video meeting, you simply download the program, open the icon on your desktop, and call a number. You can also enable the video option as needed. If video is at all likely, you need to dress at least semi-professionally. When I have Skype meetings and am not dressed appropriately for the occasion, I simply stick something over my laptop's built-in camera. You could do the same, and if questioned on this, you have my permission to tell a white lie: "I must have some kind of bug because I just can't get the video function to work today. Would you like to reschedule for when I have the issue fixed?" Most of the time the recruiter will want to proceed with the meeting, and if not, you will have avoided making a bad first impression.

I've done a lot of TV over the years, and will never get over my shock and amusement at those oh-so-immaculately-dressed anchors sitting behind their desks. I'd go on set and be introduced to a show's host, who'd be wearing a thousand-dollar suit jacket, shirt, and tie, but I can't tell you how many times he would be wearing shorts or jeans. The moral of the story is that all you need do for Skype interviews is dress for "above the desk."

Your Skype Set

If you are on video, it will be a head-and-shoulders close-up with the area behind you framing the shot. Think about where you will be doing the interview and what will be behind you; a plain blank wall is usually the best option.

Your Skype Performance

I do media all the time, and even with all my on-camera experience, what I am going to tell you still took me a while to figure out. When you talk to someone on Skype, you tend to look at the person onscreen and not the camera lens on top of your laptop or tablet. This is a mistake. From the other end of the line you are seen to be looking down and can appear to be avoiding eye contact—not the impression you want to create.

The camera lens is usually at the top center of your laptop/tablet; if not, you will need to clip a separate lens to the top of your device. This means the simple solution is to put your laptop on a pile of books so that the lens on your device is at about eye level and looking straight at your face.

Train yourself to look into the lens, not at the interviewer's onscreen image. Imagine that the lens represents the interviewer's eyes. Look straight into it and smile as you talk, just as you would in normal conversation. What the interviewer will experience is a warm and confident candidate who isn't afraid to make eye contact. This may take some practice, but job searches are going to increasingly use Skype for screening interviews, so it's worth taking the time to get this right.

No matter how much practice you get, you'll still be drawn to look at the onscreen image of the interviewer, but at the very least be sure that you look into the lens of your machine:

- When you say hello
- When you are being asked a question
- When you ask a question
- When you are making a critical point
- When you are finishing an answer
- When you make your closing statement about wanting the job
- When you say goodbye

You won't do this successfully without practice, so I strongly urge doing a few Skype video calls with friends to get a feeling for how you and others typically come across, and to practice looking into the lens rather than at your interviewer's image.

Answering Questions

Beware of giving yes-or-no answers, as they give no real information about your abilities and do nothing to forward your agenda. At the same time, don't waffle; your answers need to be concise. Understanding someone over the telephone can sometimes be a challenge, so if you didn't hear or didn't understand a question, ask the speaker to repeat it. If you need time to think about your answer—and that is quite acceptable—say so: "Let me think about that for a moment."

Whenever possible, you should give real-world examples to illustrate your points: "That's interesting. I was involved in an audit like that a couple months back and it presented some interesting challenges."

There are some 200 questions you are likely to be asked during an interview, which we'll cover in detail in the coming pages. Meanwhile, there are a handful of questions often asked during telephone interviews in addition to the ones that will come right after you make a marketing presentation. Let's look at them in light of your probable lack of information about the company and the job:

"What are you looking for?"

With so little real knowledge about the company at this point, you need to be careful about specificity. Don't say, "I want to move into marketing," unless you know such opportunity exists. Otherwise keep your answer general and focused on (a) improving yourself professionally and (b) becoming a productive member of a respected team.

"What are your strengths?"

If you know about specific skill requirements, emphasize them; if not, stick to a brief outline of your key *technical skills* and a selection of the *transferable skills and professional values* that support them.

"What's your greatest weakness?"

This is one of the toughest and most common of all interview questions, and it often comes right after you have been tossed that softball, "What's your greatest strength?" Every conceivable slick answer has already been used a hundred times, so saying you "work too hard" isn't going to impress anyone.

The truth of the matter is that we all have weaknesses, even you and I, and this is one instance where any interviewer is going to appreciate an honest answer like a breath of fresh air. So your goal is to be honest without torpedoing your candidacy—a tall order, but you can do this. You do it by talking about a real weakness that we all share (even your interviewer), and then explaining what you are doing about it.

Two Weaknesses We All Share

We all face two professional challenges:

1. Staying current with the rapid pace of technological change.
2. Meeting the ever-increasing demands for improved productivity.

Getting up to speed and keeping pace with new skills are universal challenges, and so they're weaknesses we all share.

The Technology Challenge Response

Your answer to the ongoing challenges presented by technological change starts by addressing how changing technology affects your particular job and profession.

You then follow your statement of the problem with examples that show what you are doing to keep up with the technological changes that affect your productivity:

"I'm currently studying . . ."

"I just attended a weekend workshop . . ."

"I'm signed up for classes in . . ."

"I just finished reading . . ."

To take a more fully fleshed-out example: *"I'm currently studying Dragon's advanced voice recognition tools. With its ability to transcribe conversation into text on a Word doc, it improves record keeping and dramatically increases my efficiency in creating written follow-up communications. I'm also learning to use voice commands to control my computing devices. These are very small efficiencies, but they add up to something significant. I'm not fully up to speed yet, but I can already see what an asset it will be."*

With this type of answer, you identify a genuine weakness that anyone can relate to; and in addressing what you are doing about it you demonstrate the kind of effort that *is only of concern to the most dedicated and forward-looking people in your profession.*

The Increasing Productivity Challenge

The problem of increasing productivity is also universal. You can use it as an alternative to the technology challenge response, or as an additional answer. You start by talking about the general difficulties in keeping up with all the deliverables of the job, and then move on to address what you are doing about it: You are working on your *multitasking skills.*

Used alone or in combination, these answers address the question honestly, while also displaying your self-awareness and commitment to your job and profession—a commitment shared only by true professionals.

"I don't think you'll be suitable because you lack _____ skill."

If the statement is true, acknowledge it, then follow with an example of a similar skill you picked up quickly and apply with consummate skill: "Yes, I understand. When I joined my current company I knew nothing about _____, but I studied on my own and with the help of a mentor within the department I was up to speed in a matter of weeks. Given my proven ability to learn quickly and my willingness to invest my own time, would you consider talking to me in more detail about this topic when we meet face-to-face?" With this type of response you are putting a positive spin on your shortcoming, which gives you a good shot at overcoming the objection. If you are successful in arranging a face-to-face interview, you'll now have time to bone up on the subject and identify a sensible development program before you meet with the employer.

Under no circumstances, though, should you ask about salary or benefits and vacation time; that comes much later. Your single objective at this point is to meet face-to-face; money is not an issue. If the interviewer brings up a direct question about how much you are earning, you can't get around it, so be honest. On the other hand, if you are asked how much you want, answer truthfully that at this point you don't know enough about the company or the job to answer that question. There is a whole chapter in this book on negotiation (Chapter 25) that covers the money issue in some detail.

The telephone interview has come to an end when you are asked whether you have any questions—perhaps, "What would you like to know about us?" This is a wind-down question, so it is a good opening to get some specific questions of your own answered that can advance your candidacy:

- "What are the most immediate challenges of the job?"
- "What are the most important projects of the first six months?"
- "What skills and behaviors are most important to success on the job?"
- "Why do some people succeed and others fail doing this work?"

By discovering answers to these questions now, you will have time before the face-to-face meeting to package your skills according to the needs at hand and to create an appropriate executive briefing for distribution with your resume to the different interviewers you meet.

If you have not already asked or been invited to meet the interviewer, now is the time to take the initiative.

"It sounds like a very interesting opportunity, Ms. Bassett, and a situation where I could definitely make a contribution. The most pressing question I have now is when can we get together?"

When an invitation for an interview is extended, there are practical matters that you need to clarify with a handful of simple questions that address the when (date and time) and where (don't assume the interview will take place at a facility that you associate with the company). You will also want to inquire about the interview procedure:

- "How many interviews typically occur before a decision is made?"
- "Who else will be part of the selection process, and what are their roles within the department or company?"
- "What is the time frame for filling this position, and how many other people are in consideration at this time?"

Follow with a casual inquiry as to what direction the meeting will take. You might ask, "Would you tell me some of the critical areas we will discuss on Thursday?" The knowledge gained will help you to package and present yourself, and it will allow you time to bone up on any weak or rusty areas. This is also a good time to establish how long the meeting is expected to last, which will give you some idea of how to pace yourself.

Once the details are confirmed, finish with this request: "If I need any additional information before the interview, may I feel free to get back to you?" The company representative will naturally agree. No matter how many questions you get answered in the initial conversation, there will always be something you forgot. This allows you to call again to satisfy any curiosity—it will also enable you to increase rapport. Don't take too much advantage of it, though: One well-placed phone call that contains two or three considered questions will be appreciated; four or five phone calls will not.

In closing your conversation, take care to ascertain the correct spelling and pronunciation of the interviewer's name. This shows your concern for the small but important things in life—and it will be noticed, particularly when the interviewer receives your follow-up thank-you note. (See the latest edition of *Knock 'em Dead Cover Letters* for a comprehensive selection of samples.)

It is difficult to evaluate an opportunity properly over the phone, so even if the job doesn't sound right, go to the interview; it will give you practice, and the job may look better when you have more facts. You might even discover a more suitable opening elsewhere within the company.

CHAPTER 9
DRESS FOR JOB INTERVIEW SUCCESS

WHEN YOU DRESS like a professional, you are likely to be treated as one, and that's a good head start before saying a word.

The moment you set eyes on someone, your mind makes evaluations and judgments with lightning speed. Potential employers also make the same lightning-speed evaluations when you first meet at the beginning of a job interview. It's a fair estimate that nine out of ten of today's employers will reject an unsuitably dressed applicant without a second thought.

"What You See Is What You Get!"

The initial respect you receive at the interview will be in direct proportion to the image you project. The correct professional appearance won't get you the job offer—but it will lend everything you say that much more credence and weight. Wearing a standard business uniform instantly communicates that you understand one of the paramount unwritten rules of professional life and that you have a confident self-image.

Employers rarely make overt statements about acceptable dress codes to their employees, much less to interviewees. Instead, there is a generally accepted but unspoken dictum that those who wish to succeed will dress appropriately, and those who don't, won't.

There are a few professions where on-the-job dress (as opposed to interview dress) is somewhat less conservative than in the mainstream: Fashion, entertainment, and advertising are three examples. In these and a few other fields, there is a good deal of leeway with regard to personal expression in workplace attire. But for 95 percent of us, jobs and employers require a certain level of traditional professionalism in our wardrobes. While you need not dress like the chairman of the board (although that probably wouldn't hurt), adopting "casual Friday" attire on the day of your interview is not in your best professional interests. For a job interview, it is generally accepted that you should dress one or two levels up from the job you are applying for, while remaining consistent with the type of occupation it is within. To maximize your career options over the long haul of a career you must aim to consistently meet or exceed these standards.

Your Interview Advantage

Your appearance tells people how you feel about yourself as an applicant, as well as how you feel about the interviewer, the company, and the interview process itself. By dressing professionally, you tell people that you understand the niceties of corporate life, and you send a subtle "reinforcing" message that you can, for example, be relied on to deal one-on-one with members of a company's prized client base.

How you dress sends signals about:

- How seriously you take the occasion, and, by extension, how much respect you feel for your interviewers and all others whom you meet at the interviews.
- How well you understand the confidence a look of traditional professionalism gives clients, customers, peers, and superiors.

Yet no matter how important these concerns might be, they pale in comparison to the impact a sharp appearance can have on your own sense of self. When you know you have taken care of your appearance and that you look the best you can, you feel pride and confidence: Your posture is better, you smile more, and you feel more "in control" of your destiny. In turn, others will respond positively to the image of professionalism and self-confidence that you present. Portraying the correct image at an interview will give you a real edge over your competition. You can expect what you say to be strongly influenced in the mind of your interviewer by the way you present yourself. Appearances count.

The Look

The safest look for both men and women at interviews is traditional and conservative. Look at investing in a good-fitting, well-made suit as your first step to a successful strategic career move. With your business clothes, quality matters far more than quantity; it's better to have one good outfit than two mediocre ones. Your professional wardrobe is a long-term career asset, so add quality items, and over time the quantity will come.

Up until recent years, this was fairly easy for men, as their professional fashions tended to remain constant. These days, men's fashions are experiencing a metamorphosis, with designers of high fashion offering affordable lines of updated, professionally acceptable looks. However, a man can always interview with confidence and poise in his six-year-old Brooks Brothers suit, provided it isn't worn to a shine.

For women, things are more complicated. Appropriate female attire for the interview should reflect current professional fashions if the applicant is to be taken seriously. Moreover, in selecting a current professional look, a woman must walk a fine line, combining elements of both conformity (to show she belongs) and panache (to show a measure of individuality and style).

The key for both sexes is to dress for the position you want, not the one you have. This means the upwardly mobile professional might need to invest in the clothes that project the desired image.

The correct appearance alone probably won't by itself get you a job offer, but it does go a long way toward winning the attention and respect you need to land the offer. When you know you look right, you can stop worrying about the impression your clothes are making and concentrate on communicating your message.

Every interview and every interviewer is different, so it isn't possible to set down rigid guidelines for exactly what to wear in any given situation. However, there are a handful of common-sense guidelines that will ensure you are perceived as someone savvy, practical, competent, reliable, and professional.

General Guidelines

The right look varies from industry to industry. A college professor can sport tweed jackets with elbow patches on the job, and an advertising executive may don the latest designer dress or wear wild ties as a badge of *creativity* (that is what they are being paid for). Nevertheless, that same college professor is likely to wear a suit to an important interview, and even professional men and women in advertising and the media are likely to dress more conservatively for a job interview.

Most of us are far more adept at recognizing the dress mistakes of others than at spotting our own image failings. When you look for a second opinion, you often make the mistake of asking only a loved one. Better candidates for evaluation of your interview attire are trusted professional friends who have proven their objectivity in such matters.

Whenever possible, find out the dress code of the company you are visiting. For example, if you are an engineer applying for a job at a high-tech company, a blue three-piece suit might be overpowering. It is perfectly acceptable to ask someone in Human Resources about the dress code (written or informal) of the company. You may even want to make an anonymous visit to get a sense of the corporate style of the company; if that isn't practical, you can always visit the website to see how the company likes to be perceived by its public.

I have been asked, "If everyone wears sweaters at the company where I am interviewing, shouldn't I wear the same if I want to be seen to fit in?" In fact, very few companies allow a very relaxed dress code for all their employees all the time. An increasing percentage allows a somewhat relaxed dress code on a particular day (often Friday), when "casual professional" attire is allowed, if not always encouraged. Sometimes, some younger professionals mistake this to mean they can dress for the beach at all times. Even if the company is casual all the time for all its employees, do not dress casually for a job interview. There are two big reasons to avoid casual interview attire:

1. The company is considering an investment that will probably run into hundreds of thousands of dollars if the hire works out, and potentially as much as tens of thousands of dollars if it doesn't—hardly a casual event.
2. Companies sometimes allow casual dress at times and in circumstances that will not jeopardize business. They are comfortable doing this because they already know everyone on the payroll knows how to dress appropriately. The interview is where the company needs to know you appreciate the niceties of business dress; they already have a fair idea that you own a sweater and a pair of khakis.

Tattoos and Piercings

If you are contemplating a professional career, recognize that visible body piercings and tattoos will forever close many doors to your entry, and most of the rest to your ascent. While tattoos and piercings are an individual expression and your right, corporations also have a right not to hire people who they feel are unable to represent company interests in the best light. Like it or not, *any and all body decoration is frowned upon by the vast majority of employers.*

In other words, if you sport tats or piercings, conceal them during the interview and at all times during your professional endeavors. If you are considering body decoration, ask yourself if in the history of humankind there has ever been one item in any man or woman's wardrobe that he or she has willingly worn every day for the rest of his or her life. Soberly weigh your personal interests against your professional success.

Perspiration

It isn't uncommon to have excess perspiration under the arms, on your chest, and on your hands when you find yourself in a tension-inducing situation like a job interview. This can be a problem for both sexes and for people of any age, although for most the problem does seem to lessen as the years roll by. However, for some in their twenties and thirties it can be pretty bad; I have a colleague who tells of his suit getting drenched with nervous sweat when he was a young man.

Now I cannot think of another time when I have recommended a personal hygiene product. But my friend tells me that he used Certain Dri for two nights before an interview and also put it on his right hand both nights to eliminate sweaty palms. It worked like magic, a report I have received from other sources too. I address the perspiration issue later in the chapter from other perspectives.

Men

The following are the best current dress guidelines for men preparing for a professional interview.

Men's Suits

A *Wall Street Journal* survey of CEOs showed a 53 percent preference for navy blue and dark blue, while 39 percent favored gray or charcoal gray. Brown can be acceptable for subsequent interviews at some companies. In summer months, a lightweight beige suit is fine at second or third interviews; you would never wear a light-colored suit except during the warmer months. Ideally, wear a 100-percent wool suit, as wool looks and wears better than any other material. The darker the suit, the more authority it carries. (Beware: A man should not wear a black suit to an interview unless applying for an undertaker's job.) Pinstripes and solids, in dark gray, navy, or medium blue, are equally acceptable, although many feel a dark solid suit is the best option because it gives authority to the wearer and is seen as less stuffy than a pinstripe suit. Somewhat less common but also acceptable are gray-colored glen plaid (also called "Prince of Wales") or hound's-tooth suits.

A well-cut two-piece suit is preferable (with the standard two-button suit jacket, although the older three-button, single-breasted jacket is quite acceptable) to a three-piece suit that includes a vest or waistcoat. The three-piece is seen as ultraconservative, which might be a useful tool in some situations, but the extra layer of clothing brings in the heat and sweat factor, which argues against it for more practical reasons. Double-breasted jackets are seen as more edgy, and you are more likely to wear them to an interview at an advertising agency than at the local bank.

Above all, it's the quality and fit of your suit that matters. Current fashions favor a slimmer cut, particularly in the trousers. However, the fit and cut must complement your own build. The leaner, tapered look elongates your appearance; the looser cuts add bulk. There should be no pull at the jacket shoulders and no gape at the back, and the jacket cuffs should break at your wrists. Your trousers should fit comfortably at the waist. A flat front is most flattering (unless you are enviably scrawny), and there should be only a slight break where the trouser hits the shoe. If your ankles are visible in the mirror, the pants are too damn short! Cuffed trousers add a very sophisticated and conservative look, but an important consideration might be that uncuffed trousers are seen to enhance your height.

Men's Shirts

The principles here are simple:

Rule One: Always wear a long-sleeved shirt, never wear a short-sleeved shirt.

Rule Two: Always wear a white, cream, or pale blue shirt.

By white, I do not mean to exclude, for instance, shirts with very thin red or blue pinstripes; nevertheless, there is a presence about a solid white shirt that seems to convey honesty, intelligence, and stability; it should be your first choice. It is true that artists, writers, software engineers, and other creative types are sometimes known to object to white shirts because they feel that it makes it look like "the suit is wearing them." If this is you and you can't get over it, pale blue may be the best option. Remember—the paler and more subtle the shade, the better the impression you will make. Pale colors draw attention, and your collar is right next to your face, which is where you want the interviewer to stay focused.

While monograms are common enough, those who don't wear them may feel strongly about the implied ostentation of stylized initials on clothing; the great valet Jeeves once commented on the topic, saying, "I thought the practice was restricted to those in danger of forgetting their names."

Cotton shirts look better and hold up under perspiration more impressively than their synthetic counterparts. If at all possible, opt for a cotton shirt that has been professionally cleaned and starched. A cotton and polyester blend can be an acceptable alternative, but keep in mind that the higher the cotton content, the better the shirt will look. While these blend shirts wrinkle less easily, you are advised to ignore the "wash-and-wear" and "no need to iron" claims you'll read on the front of the package when you purchase them.

Make sure your shirt fits the neck properly; the sleeve cuff should end at the wrist. Details such as frayed fabric and loose buttons will not go unnoticed when you are under professional scrutiny. It's best to choose your interview clothes well in advance, make any minor repairs, have them cleaned, and keep them ready.

Ties

While a cheap-looking tie can ruin an expensive suit, the right tie can do a lot to pull the less-than-perfect suit together for a professional look. When you can't afford a new suit for the interview, you can upgrade your whole look with the right tie.

A pure silk tie makes the most powerful professional impact, has the best finish and feel, and is easiest to tie well. A pure silk tie or a 50-percent wool/50-percent silk blend (which is almost wrinkle-proof) should be your choice for the interview. Linen ties are too informal, can only be tied once or twice between cleanings because they wrinkle easily, and only look right during warmer weather anyway. A wool tie is casual in appearance and has knot problems. Most man-made fibers are too shiny, with harsh colors that may undercut your professional image.

The tie should complement your suit. This means that there should be a physical balance: The rule of thumb is that the width of your tie should approximate the width of your lapels. The prevailing standard, which has held for over a decade now, is that ties can range in width between 2 and 3½ inches. Wearing anything wider may mark you as someone still trapped in the disco era. Currently, ties are being worn narrower in the pages of the fashion magazines, but that really doesn't have to concern you.

While the tie should complement the suit, it should not match it. You would never, for instance, wear a navy blue tie with a navy blue suit. Choose an appropriate tie that neither vanishes into nor battles with your suit pattern. The most popular and safest styles are solids, foulards, stripes, and paisleys.

Do not wear ties with large polka dots, pictures of animals such as leaping trout or soaring mallards, or sporting symbols such as golf clubs or (God forbid) little men on polo ponies. Avoid wearing any piece of apparel that has a manufacturer's symbol emblazoned on the front as part of the decoration.

Other considerations include the length of the tie (it should, when tied, extend to your trouser belt), the size of the knot (smaller is better), and whether you should wear a bow tie to an interview (you shouldn't).

Men's Shoes

Shoes should be either black leather or brown leather. Stay away from all other materials and colors. Lace-up wingtips are the most universally acceptable. Slightly less conservative, but equally appropriate, are slip-on dress shoes—not to be confused with boating shoes. The slip-on, with its low, plain vamp or tassel is versatile enough to be used for both day and evening business wear. Those who are hyperconscious of fashion will say that a lace-up wingtip can look a bit cloddish at dinner. This may be true if you have a dinner interview with the senior law partner of a firm in Chicago, Los Angeles, or New York, but otherwise don't lose sleep over it.

In certain areas of the South, Southwest, and West, heeled cowboy boots are not at all unusual for business wear, and neither are those Grand Ole Opry versions of the business suit.

But beware: Outside of Dallas, Nashville, Muskogee, and similar municipalities, you will attract only puzzled stares—so try to be aware of the regional variations in professional dress.

Men's Socks

Socks should complement the suit. Accordingly, they should be blue, black, gray, or brown. When they match the suit color, they extend the length of your leg, giving more height and authority. They should also be long enough for you to cross your legs without showing off bare skin, and should not fall in a bunch toward the ankle as you move. Elastic-reinforced, over-the-calf socks are your best bet.

Men's Accessories

The right accessories can enhance the professional image of any applicant, male or female, just as the wrong accessories can destroy it. The guiding principle here is to include nothing that could be misconstrued or leave a bad impression. For instance, you should not wear obvious religious or political insignias in the form of rings, ties, or pins, as they draw attention to matters that employers are forbidden to address by federal law. This does not necessarily apply when you are aware that a particular spiritual association will establish connectivity, such as wearing a cross when you interview with the archdiocese.

The watch you wear should be simple and preferably plain, which means that funky Mickey Mouse is out. Sports- and Swatch-style watches, or digital monsters, are acceptable nowadays but aren't the best choice. Don't be afraid to wear a simple, slim analog watch with a leather strap; you will notice it is what the most successful and sophisticated business professionals wear.

A briefcase is always perceived as a symbol of authority and can make a strong professional statement. Leather makes the best impression, with brown and burgundy being the colors of choice. The case is best unadorned—embellishments can only detract from the effect of quiet confidence and authority.

It's a good idea to take a cotton or linen handkerchief on all interviews. Plain white is best because it looks crisp, but the color isn't really that important. You aren't taking a handkerchief to put in a breast pocket but for far more practical reasons. That handkerchief can be used to relieve the clammy-hands syndrome so common before an interview—anything to avoid the infamous "wet fish" handshake. Keep it in an inside pocket, avoiding the matching tie-and-pocket-square look of a dyed-in-the-wool doofus at all costs.

Belts should match or complement the shoes you select. Accordingly, a blue or gray suit will require a black belt and black shoes, while brown, tan, or beige suits call for brown. Wear a good-quality leather belt if you can. The most common mistake made with belts is the buckle; an interview is not the place for your favorite Harley Davidson, Grateful Dead, or Bart Simpson buckle. Select a small, simple buckle that doesn't overwhelm the rest of your look or make personal statements that you cannot be certain will resonate with an interviewer.

Men's Jewelry

Men may wear a wedding band, and cuff links are acceptable with French cuffs. Anything more in the way of jewelry can be dangerous. Necklaces, bracelets, neck chains, and earrings can send the wrong message, and tie tacks and clips are passé in most areas of the country.

Men's Raincoats

The safest and most utilitarian colors for raincoats are beige and blue; stick to these two exclusively. If you can avoid wearing a raincoat, do so (it's an encumbrance and adds to clutter), but it is better to have a raincoat than to have your suit drenched.

Women

The following are the best current dress guidelines for women preparing for a professional interview.

Women's Suits

You have more room for *creativity* in this area than men do, but also more room for mistakes. Until recent years, your professional fashion *creativity* had to remain within certain accepted guidelines dictated not by the fashion industry, but by the consensus of the business world—which trails far behind the pages of fashion magazines. And while there are still the limits of good taste and necessary conservatism for the interviewer, the fashion designers have worked hard to create workable professional alternatives for the ever-growing female workforce.

A woman's business wardrobe need no longer be simply a pseudo-male selection of drab gray skirts and blouses. With the right cuts, pinstripes and even ties can look both stylish and professional.

Wool and linen are both accepted for professional women's suits, but 100 percent linen and cotton garments can present a problem. They're cool, but they retain stains, show sweat, and wrinkle so quickly that you may feel as though you leave the house dressed for success and arrive at your destination looking like a bag lady. Cotton-polyester blends are great for warm climates; they look like linen but lack the wrinkle factor. Combinations of synthetics and natural fabrics have their advantages: Suits made of such material will certainly retain their shape better. Ultra-lightweight wool gabardine is the most versatile and rugged natural fabric you can opt for. In a basic seasonless color, it will become a wardrobe staple. When it comes to the quality of fabric you choose, pay attention to detail as the interviewer may draw unwarranted conclusions about your personality and taste based on your standards of dress. It would be better to invest in one or two suits of fine quality than multiple suits of lower quality. You can get a lot of mileage out of one classic suit and completely change the look and personality of it with different tops and accessories.

Like her male counterpart, the professional woman should stick to solids or pinstripes in gray, navy, and medium blues. At the same time, a much wider palette of colors is open for consideration by the professional woman, from purple to coral to lipstick red. While there are situations where you will want to choose one of the more powerful colors, it might be best at one of the subsequent interviews, rather than the first.

A solid skirt with a coordinating subtle plaid jacket is also acceptable, but make sure there is not too much contrast or it will detract from the focus of your meeting: the interview. Colors most suitable for interview suits include charcoal, medium gray, steel gray, black (whereas a man is advised against black, the color is open and acceptable for the professional woman), and navy blue. Of all these looks, the cleanest and most professional is the simple solid navy or gray suit with a white blouse.

Jackets should be simple, well tailored, and stylish, but not stylized. This is probably not the time to wear a peplum-style jacket—a standard length that falls just at the hips is preferable. The cut and style should flatter your build and reflect your personal style without detracting from what you have to say. Attention to details such as smooth seams, even hemlines, correctly hanging linings, and well-sewn buttons is essential.

How long a skirt should you wear? Any hard-and-fast rule I could offer here would be in danger of being outdated almost immediately, as the fashion industry demands dramatically different looks every season in order to fuel sales. (After all, keeping the same hemlines would mean that last season's clothes could last another season or two.) It should go without saying that you don't want to sport something that soars to the upper thigh if you want to be taken seriously as an applicant. Your best bet is to dress somewhat more conservatively than you would if you were simply showing up for work at the organization in question. Hemlines come and go, and while there is some leeway as to what is appropriate for everyday wear on the job, the safest bet is usually to select something that falls at or no more than two inches above the knee.

Increasingly popular is the one-piece business dress with a matching jacket. This outfit is particularly useful for the "business day into evening crowd," but can be perfectly suitable for interviews if it is properly styled and fitted. It is particularly important to stick with subtle solid colors for this look.

Blouses

Blouses with long sleeves will project a responsible and professional look. Three-quarter-length sleeves are less desirable, followed in turn by short sleeves. Never wear a sleeveless blouse to an interview; you may be confident that there is absolutely no chance that you will be required to remove your jacket, but why take the risk of offending someone with unexpected glimpses of undergarments?

Solid colors and natural fabrics, particularly cotton and silk, are the best selections for blouses—although silk is warm and therefore raises perspiration concerns for a nervous interviewee.

Combinations of natural and synthetic fabrics are wrinkle resistant but do not absorb moisture well, so with these choices you will need to take perspiration countermeasures into account.

The acceptable color spectrum is wider for blouses than for men's shirts, but it is not limitless. The most prudent choices are still white or cream or gray; these offer a universal professional appeal. Pale pink or light blue can also work, but should be worn only if it fully blends into your overall look. Light colors are "friendly" and draw attention to your face, yet will not distract the interviewer from what you have to say. The blouse with a front-tie bow is a little fussy and has become dated; a classic softened shirt collar works best with a suit. The button-down collar always looks great, particularly if you are interviewing with a conservative company or industry.

Women's Neckwear

While a woman might choose to wear a string of pearls instead of a scarf to an interview, the scarf can still serve as a powerful status symbol and does a few things jewelry does not. It can change the entire look of an outfit to give your wardrobe basics more mileage. If you choose a color that flatters your face, it will automatically give you a more energized look. You can also use a scarf to de-emphasize things that could detract from your presentation, such as aging, saggy skin on the neck, or a vestigial tattoo. Opting to wear a scarf says something dramatic about you, so make sure it's something positive. A good-quality scarf will offer a conservative look, a good finish, and drape nicely. Tying a scarf can be tricky but there are plenty of easy YouTube tutorials out there to show you how to do it with panache. As with men's ties, the objective is to complement the outfit, not match it. Avoid overly flamboyant styles, and stick with solids or basic prints (foulards, small polka dots, or paisleys) in subtle colors that will complement—not compete with—your outfit or your conversation.

Women's Shoes

The professional woman has a greater color selection in footwear than does her male counterpart. The shoes should preferably be leather, but in addition to brown and black, a woman is safe in wearing navy, burgundy, forest green, or even, if circumstances warrant—and it is not a first interview—red. The color of your shoes should always be the same or a darker tone than your skirt.

It is safest to stay away from faddish or multicolored shoes (even such classics as two-toned oxfords). First, all fashion is transitory, and even if you are up-to-date, you cannot assume that your interviewer is. Second, a good proportion of your interviewers might be men, who are less likely to appreciate vivid color combinations. As with the rest of your wardrobe, stay away from radical choices and opt for the easily comprehensible professional look.

Heel height is important, as well. Flats are fine; a shoe with a heel of up to about 2½ inches is perfectly acceptable. Stay away from high heels; at best you will wobble slightly, and at worst you will walk at an angle. The pump, or court shoe, with its closed toe and heel, is perhaps the safest and most conservative look. A closed heel with a slightly open toe is acceptable, too, as is the slingback shoe with a closed toe. The toe on any style should not be overly pointed. Just think moderation in all things; the goal is to look like a professional, not a pin-up.

Pantyhose

These should not make their own statement. Neutral skin tones are the safest, most conservative choice, though you are perfectly within the realm of professional etiquette when wearing a sheer white or cream if it complements your blouse or dress. You may make an exception if you are interviewing for a job in the fashion industry, in which case you might coordinate colors with your outfit, but be very sure of the company dress code that is already in place. Even in such an instance, avoid loud or glitzy looks.

As you well know, pantyhose and stockings are prone to developing runs at the worst possible moment, so keep an extra pair in your purse or briefcase.

Women's Accessories

Because a briefcase is a symbol of authority, it is an excellent choice for the professional woman. Do not, however, bring both your purse and a briefcase to the interview. (You'll look awkward juggling them.) Instead, transfer essential items to a small clutch bag or wristlet you can store in the case. In addition to brown and burgundy (recommended colors for the men), you may include navy and black as possible colors for your case, which should always be free of personal, expensive, or distracting embellishments.

Belts should match or complement the shoes you select. A black or gray suit will require a black belt and black shoes; brown, tan, or beige suits will call for brown; and navy looks best with navy or burgundy accessories. In addition, women may wear snakeskin, lizard, and the like (though beware of offending animal rights activists). Remember that the belt is a functional item; if it is instantly noticeable, it is wrong.

Women's Jewelry

As far as jewelry goes, less is more. A woman should restrict rings to engagement or wedding bands if these are applicable, but she can wear a necklace and earrings, as long as these are subdued and professional looking. A necklace should be conservative and tasteful: a strand of pearls, a small-scale status necklace, or a thin chain with a nonreligious metal pendant. Avoid bright gemstones, CZs, or other sparkles that will distract the interviewer. Earrings should be small, discreet, and in good taste. If you have noticeably pierced ears, don't skip the earrings. It could look like an overlooked detail. A conservative wristwatch is acceptable, as is one small bracelet. Avoid costume jewelry, oversized pieces, excessive sparkle, dangles, anything with your name or initials on it, and anything religious. Remember, too much of the wrong kind of jewelry could cost you a job offer or inhibit your promotional opportunities once on the team.

Makeup

Take care never to appear overly made-up; natural is the key word. Eye makeup should be subtle, so as not to overwhelm the rest of the face. As a general rule, I advise very little lipstick at an interview because it can cause negative reactions in some interviewers, and because it can smudge and wear off as the hours wear on. (Who can say, going in, how long the meeting will last?) However, women tell me that as they advance into their thirties and beyond, the natural pinkness of the lips can fade; you might feel you look pale and washed-out without lipstick. So if you feel "undressed" without your lipstick, use some, but apply it sparingly and carefully, choose a neutral or subdued color, and, of course, never apply it in public.

For Men and Women: A Note on Personal Hygiene

Bad breath; dandruff; body odor; and dirty, unmanicured nails have the potential to undo all your efforts at putting across a good first impression. These and related problems all speak to an underlying professional slovenliness, which an interviewer may feel will manifest itself in your work. You want to present yourself as an appealing, self-respecting, and enjoyable professional to be around. You can't achieve this if the people you meet have to call on their powers of self-control in order to stay in the same room with you.

What was that old TV body odor commercial tag line: "What even your best friend won't tell you"? So don't ask yourself whether any friend or colleague has actually come out and suggested that you pay more attention to personal hygiene; it is such a touchy issue that most people will avoid you rather than discuss it. Ask yourself how you felt the last time you had to conduct business of any sort with someone who had a hygiene problem. Then resolve never to leave that kind of impression.

Personal grooming of hair, skin, teeth, and nails is easy and straightforward, but body odor is a different challenge. When it comes to body odor you are literally what you eat; onions, garlic, cilantro, and junk food can all give your bodily odors a distinctly unpleasant pungency. Because it takes time for your body to rid itself of such smells, the best advice is to start paying attention to diet as you begin to put your wardrobe together.

CHAPTER 10

BODY LANGUAGE

LEARN TO CONTROL negative body movements and encourage positive ones. Discover the seven guidelines for good body language during your interview.

As human beings, we rely to a remarkable degree on our ability to gather information visually. This really is not all that surprising, because while speech is a comparatively recent development, humans have been sending and receiving nonverbal signals since the dawn of the species. In fact, the language of the body is the first means of communication we develop after birth. We master the spoken word later in life, and, in so doing, we forget the importance of nonverbal cues—but the signals are still sent and received, usually at a subconscious level.

It is common to hear people say of the body language they use, "Take me or leave me as I am." This is all very well if you have no concern for what others think of you. For those seeking professional employment, however, it is important to recognize that your body is constantly sending messages, and you must make every effort to understand and control the information stream. If your mouth says, "Hire me," but your body says, "I'm not being truthful," you are likely to leave the interviewer confused. "Well," she will think, "the right answers all came out, but there was something about that candidate that just rubbed me the wrong way." Such misgivings are generally sufficient to keep a candidate from making the short list. The interviewer may or may not be aware of what causes the concern, but the messages will be sent, and your cause will suffer.

Of course, interviewers will listen carefully to what you say, too. When your body language complements your verbal statements, your message will gain a great deal of impact, but when your body language *contradicts* what you say, the interviewer will be skeptical. In short, learning to use positive body signals and control negative ones during an interview can have a significant impact on your job search and on the new job.

Under the Microscope

The challenge for the interviewer is to determine, using every means at her disposal, what kind of an employee you would make. Your task as a candidate is to provide the clues most likely to prompt a decision to hire.

Let's begin at the beginning. When you are invited to an interview, you are probably safe in assuming that your interviewer believes you meet certain minimum standards and could conceivably be hired.

In this context, the adage that actions speak louder than words is something you should take quite literally. Studies done at the University of Chicago found that more than 50 percent of all effective communication relies on body language. Since you can expect interviewers to respond to the body language you employ at the interview, it is up to you to decide what messages you want them to receive.

There are also studies that suggest the impression you create in the first few minutes of the interview is the most lasting. Since the first few minutes after you meet the interviewer is a time when she is doing the vast majority of the talking, you have very little control over the impression you create with your words—you can't say much of anything! It is up to your body to do the job for you.

The Greeting
For a good handshake:

1. Your hands should be clean and adequately manicured.
2. Your hands should be free of perspiration.

It is professional protocol for the host (interviewer) to initiate the handshake. If, through nerves, you find yourself initiating the handshake, don't pull back, as you will appear indecisive. Instead, make the best of it, smile confidently, and make eye contact.

Your handshake should signal cooperation and friendliness. Match the pressure extended by the interviewer—never exceed it. A typical professional handshake lasts for between two and five seconds, just two or three reasonably firm up-and-down pumps accompanied by a smile. The parting handshake may last a little longer; smile and lean forward *very* slightly as you shake hands before departing.

Certain professional and cultural differences should be considered as well. Many doctors, artists, and others who do delicate work with their hands can and do give less enthusiastic handshakes than other people. If you work in the media, you'll notice that quite frequently, on-air personalities don't want to shake hands at all; it's the easiest way to catch a cold and they depend on their voices and appearance more than most. Similarly, the English handshake is considerably less firm than the American, while the German variety is typically firm.

Use only one hand and always shake vertically. Do not extend your hand parallel to the floor with the palm up, as this conveys submissiveness. By the same token, you may be seen as too aggressive if you extend your hand outward with the palm facing down.

While a confident and positive handshake helps break the ice and gets the interview moving in the right direction, proper use of the hands throughout the rest of the interview will help convey an above-board, "nothing-to-hide" message.

Watch out for hands and fingers that take on a life of their own, fidgeting with themselves or other objects such as pens, paper, your tie, or your hair. Pen tapping is interpreted as the action of an impatient person; this is an example of an otherwise trivial habit that can take on immense significance in an interview situation. Rarely will an interviewer ask you to stop doing something annoying. Instead, she'll simply make a mental note that you are an annoying person and congratulate herself for picking this up before making the mistake of hiring you.

Other negative hand messages include:

- Clasping your hands behind your head. You'll expose perspiration marks, and you run the risk of appearing smug, superior, bored, and possibly withdrawn.
- Showing insecurity by constantly adjusting your tie. When interviewing with a woman, this gesture might be interpreted as displaying something beyond a businesslike interest in the interviewer.
- Slouching in your chair, with hands in pockets or thumbs in belt. This posture can brand you as insolent and aggressive (think of any teenage boy). When this error is made in the presence of an interviewer of the opposite sex, it can carry sexually aggressive overtones as well.
- Pulling your collar away from your neck. This may seem like an innocent enough reaction to the heat of the day, but the interviewer might assume that you are tense or masking an untruth. The same goes for scratching your neck during, before, or after your response to a question.

- Moving your hands toward a personal feature that you perceive as deficient. This is a common unconscious reaction to stress. A man with thinning hair, for example, may thoughtlessly put his hand to his forehead when pondering how to respond to the query ("Why aren't you earning more at your age?"). This habit may be extremely difficult for you to detect in the first place, much less reverse, but make the effort. Such protective movements are likely to be perceived—if only on a subliminal level—as an acknowledgment of low self-esteem.
- Picking at invisible bits of fluff on your suit. This gesture looks exactly like what it is, a nervous tic. Keep your focus on the interviewer. If you do have some bit of lint somewhere on your clothing, the best advice is usually to ignore it until you can remove it discreetly.

By contrast, employing the hands in a positive way can further your candidacy:

- Subtly exposing your palms now and then as you speak can help demonstrate that you are open, friendly, and have nothing to hide. You can see this technique used to great effect by politicians and television talk show hosts.
- It can, very occasionally, be beneficial to "steeple" your fingers for a few seconds as you consider a question or when you first start to talk. Unless you hold the gesture for long periods of time, it will be perceived as a neutral demonstration of your thoughtfulness. Of course, if you overuse or hold this position for too long, you may be taken as condescending. Steepling also gives you something constructive to do with your hands; it offers a change from holding your pad and pen.

Taking Your Seat

Some thirty inches from my nose
The frontier of my person goes.
Beware of rudely crossing it,
I have no gun, but I can spit.
—W. H. Auden

Encroaching on another's "personal zone" is a bad idea in any business situation, but it is particularly dangerous in an interview. The thirty-inch standard is a good one to follow: It is the distance that allows you to extend your hand comfortably for a handshake. Maintain this distance throughout the interview, and be particularly watchful of personal-space intrusions when you first meet, greet, and take a seat.

A person's office is an extension of her personal zone; this is why it is not only polite but also sound business sense to wait until the interviewer offers you a seat.

It is not uncommon to meet with an interviewer in a conference room or another supposedly "neutral" site. Again, wait for the interviewer to motion you to a spot, or, if you feel uncomfortable doing this, tactfully ask the interviewer to take the initiative: "Where would you like me to sit?"

The type of chair you sit in can affect the signals your body sends during an interview. If you have a choice, go with an upright chair with arms. Deep armchairs can restrict your ability to send certain positive signals and encourage the likelihood of slumping. They're best suited for watching television, not for projecting the image of a competent professional.

Always sit with your bottom well back in the chair and your back straight. Slouching, of course, is out, but a slight forward-leaning posture will show interest and friendliness toward the interviewer. Keep your hands on the arms of the chair; if there are no arms on the chair, keep your hands in your lap or on your pad of paper.

Crossed legs, in all their many forms, send a mixture of signals, most of which are negative:

- Crossing one ankle over the other knee can show a certain stubborn and recalcitrant outlook (as well as the bottom of your shoe, which is not always a pretty sight). The negative signal is intensified when you grasp the horizontally crossed leg or—worst of all—cross your arms across your chest.
- Some body language experts feel crossed ankles indicate that the person doing the crossing is withholding information. Of course, since the majority of interviews take place across a desk, crossed ankles will often be virtually unnoticeable. For women, some dress fashions encourage decorous ankle crossing. This posture is probably the most permissible body language faux pas, so if you must allow yourself one body language vice, this is the one to choose.
- When sitting in armchairs or on sofas, crossing the legs may be necessary to create some stability amid all the plush upholstery. In this instance, the signals you send by crossing your legs will be neutral, as long as your legs are not crossed ankle over knee.
- Some of us (and I'm one of "us") have something called nervous leg syndrome. Sit me at a desk and one leg will be flexed at the knee snapping up and down like the drummer in a thrash metal band shredding the hell out of that bass drum. If you have nervous leg syndrome, you know it is nothing more than a soothing soundtrack to the beat of an agile mind, but to others it can be annoying and offensive, to the point that it will cost you job offers—it really is that annoying to others.

The solution is to give a friend/loved one permission to call you on it every time you start drumming to the beat of your life. Learn to be conscious of when you are doing it, and don't do it at any point during a job interview. It is an indulgence that you can overcome . . . at least when you have to deal with the rhythm-less at job interviews.

Facial Signals

Once you take your seats, most often across a desk, and the conversation begins, the interviewer's attention will be focused on your face.

Our language is full of expressions testifying to the powerful influence of facial mannerisms. When you say that someone is shifty-eyed, tight-lipped, has a furrowed brow, flashes bedroom eyes, stares into space, or grins like a Cheshire cat, you are speaking in a kind of shorthand and using a set of archetypes that enable us to make judgments—consciously or unconsciously—about that person.

Tight smiles and tension in the facial muscles often bespeak an inability to handle stress; little eye contact can communicate a desire to hide something; pursed lips are often associated with a secretive nature; and frowning, looking sideways, or peering over one's glasses can send signals of haughtiness and arrogance. Hardly the stuff of which winning interviews are made!

The Eyes

Looking at someone means showing interest in that person, and showing interest is a giant step forward in making the right impression. Remember: We are all our own favorite subjects!

Looking away from the interviewer for long periods while she is talking, closing your eyes while being addressed, and repeatedly shifting focus from the subject to some other point are all likely to leave the wrong impression.

There is a difference between looking and staring at someone. Rather than looking at the speaker straight on at all times, create a mental triangle incorporating both of the eyes and the mouth; your eyes will follow a natural, continuous path along the three points. Maintain this approach for roughly three-quarters of the time; you can break your gaze to look at the interviewer's hands as points are emphasized or to refer to your notepad. This is the way we maintain eye contact in nonstressful situations, and it will allow you to appear attentive, sincere, and committed.

Be wary of breaking eye contact too abruptly and of shifting your focus in ways that will disrupt the atmosphere of professionalism. Examining the interviewer below the head and shoulders, for instance, is a sign of overfamiliarity. This is especially important when being interviewed by someone of the opposite sex.

The eyebrows send messages as well. Under stress, one's brows may wrinkle; this sends a negative signal about your ability to handle challenges in the business world. The best thing to do is take a deep breath and collect yourself. Most of the tension that people feel at interviews has to do with anxiety about how to respond to what the interviewer will ask.

The Head

Nodding your head slowly shows interest, validates your interviewer's comments, and subtly encourages her to continue. Tilting the head slightly, when combined with eye contact and a natural smile, demonstrates friendliness and approachability. The tilt should be momentary and not exaggerated, almost like a bob of the head to one side. (Do not overuse this technique unless you are applying for a job in a parrot shop!) Rapidly nodding your head can leave the impression that you are impatient and eager to add something to the conversation if only the interviewer would let you.

The Mouth

One guiding principle of good body language is to turn your mouth upward rather than downward. Look at two boxers after a fight: The victor's arms are raised high, his back is straight, and his shoulders are square. His smiling face is thrust upward and outward, and you see happiness, openness, warmth, and confidence. The loser, on the other hand, is slumped forward, brows knit and eyes downcast, and the signals you receive are those of anger, frustration, belligerence, and defeat.

Your smile is one of the most powerful positive body signals in your arsenal, and it exemplifies the up-is-best principle. Offer an unforced, confident smile as frequently as opportunity and circumstances dictate; avoid grinning idiotically, as this indicates that you may not be quite right in the head.

You should be aware that the mouth also provides a seemingly limitless supply of opportunities to convey weakness. This may be done by touching the mouth frequently, "faking" a cough when confronted with a difficult question, or gnawing on one's lips absentmindedly. Employing any of these "insincerity signs" when you are asked about, say, why you lost your last job, might instill or confirm suspicions about your honesty or openness.

Glasses

People who wear glasses sometimes leave them off when going on an interview in an attempt to project a more favorable image. There are difficulties with this approach. Farsighted people who don't wear their glasses will (unwittingly) seem to stare long and hard at the people they converse with, and this is a negative signal. Also, pulling out glasses for reading and peering over the top of your glasses—even if you have been handed something to read and subsequently asked a question—carries professorial connotations that can be interpreted as critical. If you wear glasses for reading, you should remove them when conversing, replacing them only when appropriate.

Wearing dark glasses to an interview will paint you as secretive, cold, and devious. Even if your prescription glasses are tinted, the effect will be the same. You might consider untinted glasses for your interview, or contacts. At the same time, glasses on a younger-looking person can add an air of seriousness and might be considered a plus.

Body Signal Barricades

Folding or crossing your arms, or holding things in front of the body, sends negative messages to the interviewer: "I know you're there, but you can't come in. I'm nervous and closed for business."

It is bad enough to feel this way, but worse to express it with blatant signals. Don't fold your arms or "protect" your chest with hands, clipboard, briefcase, or anything else during the interview.

You can, however, keep a pad and pen on your lap. It makes you look organized and gives you something to do with your hands. Holding a pad and pen and keeping your arms on the arms of the chair, will also help you avoid slouching. Remember to show one or both of your palms occasionally as you make points, but do not overuse this gesture.

Feet

Some foot signals can have negative connotations. Women and men wearing slip-on shoes should beware of dangling the loose shoe from the toes; this can be distracting, and, as it is a gesture often used to signal physical attraction, it has no place in a job interview. Likewise, avoid compulsive jabbing of floor, desk, or chair with your foot; this can be perceived as a hostile and angry motion, and is likely to annoy the interviewer.

Some people (your author is included in the front ranks on this one) have an annoying habit of jiggling one leg up and down on the ball of the foot. Those of us who do this know it is a tic that says we are totally engaged and excited about some topic (and sometimes even the one under discussion), but those forced to endure it find it distracting and can interpret it as impatience. If you are a dreaded jiggler, you must get this under control for your job interviews!

Walking

Many interviews will require that you walk from one place to the next—on a guided tour of facilities, from one office to another, or to and from the table in a restaurant. (Of course, if you are interviewing in a restaurant, you will have to walk with your interviewer to and from the dining facility.) How long these walks last is not as important as how you use them to reinforce positive professional behaviors and impressions.

Posture is your main concern: Keep your shoulders back and stay erect. Smile and make eye contact as appropriate. Avoid fidgeting with your feet as you move, rubbing one shoe against the other, or kicking absentmindedly at the ground if you stand to talk; these signals will lead others to believe that you are anxious or insecure. Crossing your arms or legs while standing carries the same negative connotations as it does when you are sitting. Hands-in-pockets, hands-on-hips, or thumbs-in-belt postures are all to be avoided. These send messages that you are aggressive and dominating.

Putting It All Together

Now you have the big picture, and you can begin to be more aware of the signals your body can unwittingly send. Let's reduce all this information into a handful of simple recommendations. Positive signals reinforce one another; employing them in combination yields an overwhelming positive message that is truly greater than the sum of its parts.

So far we have focused primarily on the pitfalls to avoid—but what messages *should* be sent, and how? Here are seven general suggestions on good body language for the interview:

1. Walk slowly and stand tall upon entering the room.
2. On greeting your interviewer, give a smile, make eye contact, and respond warmly to the interviewer's greeting and handshake.
3. As you sit, get your butt well back in the chair; this allows the chair back to help you sit upright. Increase the impression of openness ("I have nothing to hide!") by unbuttoning your jacket as you sit down. Keep your head up. Maintain eye contact a good portion of the time, especially when the interviewer begins to speak and when you reply. Smile naturally whenever the opportunity arises.
4. Use mirroring techniques to reproduce the positive signals your interviewer sends. Say the interviewer leans forward to make a point; a few moments later, you too lean forward slightly, demonstrating that you don't want to miss a word. Perhaps the interviewer leans back and laughs; you "laugh beneath" the interviewer's laughter, taking care not to overwhelm your partner by using an inappropriate volume level. This can seem contrived at first, but through observing those in your own social circle, you'll notice that this is natural behavior for good communicators.
5. Keep your head up and don't slouch in your seat.
6. Try to remain calm and do not hurry your movements; you'll look harried and are more likely to knock things over. Most people are more klutzy when they are nervous, and consciously slowing your body movements will lessen the chances of disaster and give you a more controlled persona.
7. Remember to breathe. When we are nervous we can forget to do this, which leads to oxygen deprivation and obviously screws up cognitive processes.

Open for Business

The more open your body movements during the interview, the more you will be perceived as open yourself. Understanding and directing your body language will give you added power to turn interviews into cooperative exchanges between two professionals.

Just as you interpret the body language of others, both positive and negative, your body language makes an indelible impression on those you meet. It tells them whether you like and have confidence in yourself, whether you are pleasant to be around, and whether you are more likely to be honest or deceitful. Like it or not, your body carries these messages for the world to see.

Job interviews are reliable in one way: They bring out insecurities. All the more reason to consciously manage the impressions your body sends. You will absorb the lessons in this chapter very quickly if you take the time to observe and interpret the body signals of friends and family. When you see and can understand body language in others, you'll be more aware of your own, and more capable of controlling it.

CHAPTER 11
THE CURTAIN RISES ON THE JOB INTERVIEW

FIRST IMPRESSIONS are the strongest. Here are the preparations to make before heading out to the interview.

Backstage in the theater, the announcement "Places, please" is made five minutes before the curtain rises. It's the performers' signal to psych themselves up, complete final costume adjustments, and make time to reach the stage. They are getting ready to go onstage and *knock 'em dead*. You should go through a similar process to get thoroughly prepared for your time in the spotlight.

Winning a job offer depends not only on the things you do well but also on the mistakes you avoid. As the interview approaches, settle down with your resume and the exercises you performed in building it. Immerse yourself in your past successes and the *transferable skills and professional values* that made them possible. Interview nerves are to be expected; the trick is to use them to your benefit by harnessing that nervous energy for your physical and mental preparation.

Here's what you should bring with you:

The company dossier: Always take copies of the resume you customized for this job and an executive briefing that clearly defines how you match the job's requirements: one for you and one for each of the interviewers you might meet. Your main interviewer will invariably have a copy of your resume, but you can't be certain of that with other people you meet. It is perfectly acceptable to have your resume in front of you at the interview; it shows you are organized, and it makes a great cheat sheet. It is not unusual to hear, "Mr. Jones wasn't hired because he didn't pay attention to detail and couldn't even remember his employment dates"—just the kind of thing you are likely to forget in the nervousness of the moment.

A decent folder with pad of paper and writing instruments: These demonstrate your preparedness, and they give you something constructive to do with your hands during the interview; you can keep your resume in the folder.

Reference letters: If you have reference letters from past employers, take them along. Some employers don't put much stock in written references and prefer a one-on-one conversation with past employers. Nevertheless, having them with you and getting them placed in your candidate file can't do any harm.

A list of job-related questions: Asking questions that give you insight into the day-to-day realities of the job shows your engagement with the work. It also helps you advance your candidacy because our judgments about people are based, in part, on the questions they ask since those questions speak to the depth of their interest and understanding. Additionally, asking questions gives you insight into how you should best focus your answers to the interviewer's queries.

You can find more questions to ask at the end of Chapter 13.

KNOCK 'EM DEAD TIP

In the early rounds of interviewing, stay away from questions about where the job can lead and what the pay and benefits are. It's not that these questions aren't important, just that the timing is wrong. It won't do you any good to know what a job pays when you aren't going to get a job offer. Instead, ask the questions that will lead to a job offer being extended, and then ask the questions you need to evaluate that offer. For questions to ask during the negotiation phase, see Chapter 25, "Negotiating the Job Offer."

Any additional information you have about the company or the job: If time permits, visit the company website, review any company literature and research you might have, and do a Google search for news articles mentioning the company by name and for articles that relate to your profession.

Directions to the interview: Decide on your form of transportation and finalize your time of departure, leaving enough time to accommodate travel delays. Check the route, distance, and travel time. If you forget to verify date, time, and place (including floor and suite number), you might not even arrive at the right place, or on the right day, for your interview. Write it all down legibly and put it with the rest of your interview kit.

To arrive at an interview too early indicates overanxiousness, and to arrive late is inconsiderate, so arrive at the interview on time, but at the location early. This allows you time to visit the restroom (usually your only private sanctuary at an interview) and make the necessary adjustments to your appearance, review any notes, and put on your game face. Remember to add contact numbers to your interview kit, so if you are delayed on the way to the interview, you can call and let the interviewer know.

Your dress should be clean-cut and conservative. As you could be asked to appear for an interview at a scant couple of hours' notice, keep your best outfit freshly cleaned, shirts or blouses wrinkle free, shoes polished, and all readied for interviews at a moment's notice.

Visit the hairdresser once a month so that you always look groomed, and keep your nails clean and trimmed at all times (even if you work with your hands). While you will naturally shower or bathe prior to an interview, and the use of an unscented deodorant is advisable, you should avoid wearing aftershave or perfume; you are trying to get a job, not a date. Never drink alcohol the day before an interview. It affects your eyes and skin tone, as well as your wits.

When you get to the interview site, visit the restroom to check your appearance and take a couple of minutes to do the following:

- Review the company dossier.
- Recall your commitment to the profession and the team, and the professional behaviors that help you succeed.
- Breathe deeply and slowly for a minute to dispel your natural physical tension.
- Review the questions you will need to identify first projects and initial needs.
- Smile and head for the interview—you are as ready as you are ever going to be. Afterward you will review your performance to make sure the next one goes even better.

Under no circumstances should you back out because you do not like the receptionist or the look of the office—that would be allowing personal insecurities to triumph. You are here to improve one of your most critical professional skills—turning interviews into job offers. Whatever happens, you can and must learn from this experience.

> **KNOCK 'EM DEAD TIP**
> It is inappropriate and distracting for you and for the interviewer to have a cell phone ring during an interview. If for any reason you forget and it does ring, just apologize and turn it off. *Never answer a personal call at a job interview.*

As you are shown into the office, you are on!

This potential new employer wants an aggressive and dynamic employee, but someone who is less aggressive and dynamic than he is, so take your lead from the interviewer.

Do:

- Give a firm handshake—respond to the interviewer's grip and duration.
- Make eye contact and smile. Say, "Hello, Ms. Larsen. I am John Jones. I've been looking forward to meeting you."

Do Not:

- Use first names (unless asked).
- Smoke (even if invited).
- Sit down (until invited).
- Show anxiety or boredom.
- Look at your watch.
- Discuss equal rights, sex, race, national origin, religion, or age.
- Show samples of your work (unless requested).
- Ask about benefits, salary, or vacation.

Now you are ready for anything—except for the tough questions that are going to be thrown at you next. We'll handle those in the following pages.

PART III
GREAT ANSWERS TO TOUGH INTERVIEW QUESTIONS

IN THIS PART of the book you will learn why interviewers do the things they do. You'll also learn the formulas for answering tough interview questions in ways that are honest, unique to you, and advance your candidacy without making you sound like a snake-oil salesman. Along the way you will also learn some useful strategies to make a greater success of your career.

"LIKE BEING ON TRIAL FOR YOUR LIFE" is how many people look at a job interview. With the interviewer as judge and jury, you are at least on trial for your livelihood, so you must have winning strategies. F. Lee Bailey, one of America's most celebrated defense attorneys, attributes his success in the courtroom to preparation. He likens himself to a magician going into court with fifty rabbits in his hat, not knowing which one he'll really need, but ready to pull out any single one. Bailey is successful because he is ready for any eventuality and because he takes the time to analyze every situation and every possible option. He never underestimates his opposition, he is always prepared, and he usually wins.

Another famous attorney, Louis Nizer, successfully defended all of his fifty-plus capital offense clients. When lauded as the greatest courtroom performer of his day, Nizer denied the accolade. He claimed for himself the distinction of being the *best prepared*.

You won't win your day in court just based on your skills. As competition for the best jobs increases, employers are comparing more candidates for every opening and becoming more skilled in the art of selection. To consistently win against stiff competition, like Bailey and Nizer, you have to be prepared for the questions that can be thrown at you, and that requires understanding what is behind them.

During an interview, employers ask you dozens of searching questions—questions that test your knowledge, skills, confidence, poise, and professional behaviors (we'll address this in some detail in a few pages). There are questions that can trick you into contradicting yourself and questions that probe your analytical skills and integrity. They are all designed so the interviewer can make decisions in these critical areas:

- Can you do the job?
- Are you motivated to take the extra step?
- Are you manageable and a team player?
- Are you professional in all your behaviors?
- Are you a problem solver?

Being able to do the job is only a small part of getting an offer. Whether you are motivated to make an extra effort, whether you are manageable and a *team player*, and whether you think of yourself as a problem identifier and problem solver are just as important to the interviewer. In this era of high unemployment and deep specialization, companies look more actively at the way you behave in the workplace and your professional behavioral profile. Specific desirable professional behaviors cannot be ascertained by a single question or answer, so the interviewer will seek a pattern in your replies that shows your possession of such behaviors—I discuss them in detail in Chapter 13.

You not only have to make a case for yourself in these five areas, you need to avoid these deadly traps that can damage your candidacy:

- Failing to listen to the question.
- Answering a question that was not asked.
- Providing superfluous, inappropriate, or irrelevant information.
- Being unprepared for the interview.

The effect of these blunders is cumulative, and each reduces your chance of receiving a job offer.

The number of offers you win in your search for the ideal job depends on your ability to answer a staggering array of questions in terms that have value and relevance to the employer: "Why do you want to work here?" "What are your biggest accomplishments?" "How long will it take you to make a contribution?" "Why should I hire you?" "What can you do for us that someone else cannot do?" "What is your greatest weakness?" "Why aren't you earning more?" and "What interests you about this job?"

The questions and answers in the following chapters come from across the job spectrum. Though a particular example answer might come from the mouth of an administrator, while you are a scientist or in one of the service industries, the commonality shared by all job functions in contributing to the bottom line will help you draw a parallel to your job. I'll give you the question and explain what is behind it and the types of information the employer will be looking for in your answers.

Notice that many of the example answers teach a small lesson in professional survival—something you can use both to get the job and to help you climb the ladder of success.

The answers provided in the following chapters should not be repeated word for word, exactly as they come off the page. You have to tailor them to your profession, and illustrate them with examples from your own real-world experience, and, as you have your own style of speech, you'll need to put the answers into your own words.

CHAPTER 12
THE FIVE SECRETS OF THE HIRE

UNDERSTANDING HOW AN interviewer thinks, and on what criteria hiring decisions are based, is an important career management skill.

No employer wakes up in the morning saying, "It's a wonderful day in the neighborhood; I think I'll hire an accountant in need of a job." Staff is only ever added to the payroll in the belief that the additional costs inherent in a new hire will be exceeded by the contributions that hire makes to the bottom line, by earning or saving money, saving time, or otherwise increasing *productivity*.

An integral part of every employee's responsibility is the *identification, prevention, and solution of problems* within her area of responsibility: problems that throw a wrench into the moneymaking machinery. Because these responsibilities are integral to every job, they are part of your job, too. You get hired to contribute to the bottom line in some small way, to prevent any problems within your area of expertise that get in the way of this, and, when prevention isn't an option, to solve these problems.

Whatever your job title, that job is a small but important cog in the complex moneymaking machinery of the corporation. Your cog has its own *problem identification, prevention, and solution* functions and must simultaneously mesh seamlessly with other cogs, working in harmony to execute tasks beyond the scope of individual effort.

There are five criteria that smart hiring managers apply to every hiring decision to help ensure a successful outcome; for you, these are the five secrets to turning a job interview into a job offer. These secrets are based on the logical evaluations that interviewers make when hiring for any job, at any level, and in every profession. Understanding the five secrets of the hire will revolutionize the way you perform at job interviews; and applying them every day in your work will propel your climb up the professional ladder on your next job and throughout your career.

The First Secret: Ability and Suitability

Saying, "Hey, I can do this job—give me a shot and I'll prove it to you" is not enough to land a job offer. You have to prove it by demonstrating a combination of all the skills that define your ability to do that job. You bring two sets of skills to a job:

1. You must demonstrate an *ability* to do the work, that you are in full possession of the *technical skills* required for execution of your responsibilities. And you have to show a clear grasp of the job and the role it plays in the department, as a small but important cog in the complex moneymaking machinery of the corporation.

2. You must also establish your *suitability* for the job. You possess a body of professional/ industry knowledge that helps you understand "the way things get done in banking/ agribusiness/pharmaceuticals." These ways differ from one industry to the next. It must be obvious that you speak the language and understand the protocols of your profession.

For example, a computer programmer working in a bank has *technical skills*. She shows *ability* to do the job by demonstrating possession of the skills and how to apply them in writing good code. She shows *suitability* for the job by demonstrating an understanding of how the program will be used in application and why it will be used that way. That comes from a *familiarity with the operations of the financial world and the terminology used to communicate within that professional community.*

Ability, Suitability, and Career Change

But wait, you say, a computer programmer doesn't have to know banking: She can pick that up fairly quickly. It's the programming skills that are important. I don't disagree, but if you were hiring and you had to pick between two programmers with equal technical skills, who would *you* hire, the one who knew your business or the one who didn't?

Given the transferability of certain *technical skills*, suitability is one of the biggest hurdles career changers have to overcome in both their resumes and in the ensuing interviews.

If you are considering a career change, you can use understanding of this first secret of the hire as part of your preparation to make that career change. Take time to find people already doing this work in your target industry/profession who can explain the mechanics of the business and the reasons for those mechanics, the professional protocols that have been developed to deal with the realities and contingencies of that world, and the terminology professionals in the field use to discuss them, so that in turn you can make the connections between your credentials and the new world in which they will be applied.

The Second Secret: Every Job Is about Problem Anticipation, Identification, Prevention, and Solution

Regardless of profession or title, at some level we are all hired to do the same job: We are all problem solvers, paid to *anticipate, identify, prevent, and solve problems* within our areas of expertise. This applies to any job, at any level, in any organization, anywhere in the world, and being aware of this is absolutely vital to job search and career success in any field.

Once you have identified the particular problem-solving business you are in, you've gone a long way toward isolating what the interviewer will want to talk about. The TJD exercises helped you identify the problems that are the meat and potatoes of your work and gave you plenty of examples of your use of *critical thinking skills* in the problem resolution process. When you can tell stories of problems you've dealt with efficiently, it helps interviewers visualize you solving their problems—on their payroll, as a member of the team.

Identify and list for yourself the typical problems you tackle on a daily basis. Come up with plenty of specific examples. Then move on to the biggest, dirtiest problems you've faced. Recall specifically how you solved them.

Here's a technique used by corporate outplacement professionals to help people develop examples of their problem-solving skills and the resulting achievements (you went through a similar exercise while developing your resume):

1. State the problem. What was the situation? Was it typical of your job, or had something gone wrong? If the latter, be leery of apportioning blame.
2. Isolate relevant background information. What special knowledge or education were you armed with to tackle this dilemma?

3. List your key qualities. What professional skills and professional behaviors did you bring into play to solve the problem?
4. Recall the solution. How did things turn out in the end?
5. Determine what the solution was worth. Quantify the solution in terms of money earned, money saved, or time saved. Specify your role as a team member or as a lone gun, as the facts demand.

Interviewers are impressed by candidates who ask intelligent questions about the job, because those *questions demonstrate the depth of that candidate's understanding*. You can definitely help your candidacy by asking questions about the problems that lie at the heart of your job; it turns a one-sided examination of skills into a two-way conversation between professionals with a common interest. Very few candidates understand this. When you ask about the problems, challenges, projects, deadlines, and pressure points that will be tackled in the early months, you demonstrate the *critical thinking skills* that underlie your problem-solving abilities, which proves you will be able to hit the ground running on those first critical projects.

Show this in the way you answer questions, and in the questions you ask, and bells will ring for the interviewer; indeed, the poor old dear might drop dead and go to heaven on the spot.

The Third Secret: Professional Behavior

Professionals are seen to be professional because they behave in a certain way. Solid possession of the *transferable skills and professional values* informs your judgment, opinions, and conduct; it is your embodiment of them in everything you do that does most to convey quiet professional confidence. These are the skills and values that get you hired, get you noticed, land you top assignments, and lead to promotions and raises; they enable you to succeed in all your professional endeavors. Just to refresh your memory, here are those skills and values again. Keep referring back to them—they're one of the most valuable things you'll take away from this book.

Transferable Skills	Professional Values
Technical	*Motivation and Energy*
Critical Thinking	*Commitment and Reliability*
Communication	*Determination*
Multitasking	*Pride and Integrity*
Teamwork	*Productivity*
Leadership	*Systems and Procedures*
Creativity	

Showing your possession of *transferable skills and professional values*, with illustrative examples you give in answers to interviewers' questions, is your passport to success at any interview. They give your answers substance and a ring of truth.

KNOCK 'EM DEAD TIP
Transferable Skills and Career Change
There are seven *transferable skills*. Apart from the *technical skills* of the job, all these skills are transferable between all jobs in the same profession *and* all jobs in different professions. However, with *technical skills*, it is likely that only some of them will apply to jobs in different professions.

The Fourth Secret: Motivation and Intelligent Enthusiasm

Motivation is one of the *professional values* that all employers like to see in their employees. From the employer's side of the desk, the preference for *motivated, intelligently enthusiastic* candidates is roughly this:

- The motivated and *intelligently enthusiastic* candidate will work harder and will turn in a superior work product.
- Someone who really enjoys his work and is engaged in his profession will be easier to work and get along with, and that will be a positive influence and a welcome, happy addition to the team.
- Someone who is enthusiastic and motivated by his work is likely to have a greater understanding of the job and therefore a greater commitment to taking the rough with the smooth.

In a tightly run job race, when there is really nothing to choose between two top contenders, the job offer will always go to the most *intelligently enthusiastic* candidate. However, interviews are stressful situations, and when you are stressed, your defenses are up and you retreat behind a wall of stiff professionalism: The natural enthusiasm and motivations that normally are part of your *professional persona* are restrained.

So, the fourth secret of the hire is an admonishment to allow your natural enthusiasm for your work and for this job opportunity to shine through, rather than hide it because of interview nerves or a misconstrued sense of professionalism.

When it comes to a tightly run job race between equally qualified candidates, remember that *the offer will always go to the most intelligently enthusiastic candidate.* Show enthusiasm for your work, your profession, and the opportunity; it just might be the tiebreaker for your ideal job.

The Fifth Secret: Teamwork and Manageability

Teamwork relates to your ability to function productively as a member of a group focused on achieving large-scale goals. Working on a team takes patience, balance, tolerance, and an ability to assert your own personality without overpowering everyone else's. You don't have to like everyone on your team; but you have to be able to work with them, and that requires emotional maturity. Your willingness to be a *team player* and your ability to function as an integrated member of the team is critical because many of the contributions your department must make toward the smooth running of the corporate machine are beyond the scope of your individual contribution.

When you embrace and apply the five secrets, you will turn job interviews into job offers, and applying these secrets on your new job will steadily increase your credibility and visibility, simultaneously delivering greater job security, forward momentum, and marketability.

Why You Go to Job Interviews

You need to have the right focus going into the interview. *You are not going to the interview to decide if you want the job*, because you have nothing to decide until an offer is on the table. You go to any job interview for one reason only: to get a job offer. Nothing else matters. Turning interviews into job offers is a critical professional survival skill, and *of all the professional skills you possess, this one is almost certainly a weakness, and needs to be strengthened*. In the following chapter, I'll show you how to make it one of your most powerful tools.

Last-Minute Interview Prep

If you read and absorb this entire section on interviewing you will be well prepared for the worst that any interviewer can throw at you. That won't stop you worrying on your way to an interview or waiting in the lobby. Much better that you focus on positive matters that can impact your interview performance. Here are seven meditations for before battle that will get you in fighting trim:

1. The job you are interviewing for exists to help the company make money, save money, or increase productivity in some small way. When you increase productivity you save time and money, and that makes more time to make more money. Your job fits into one or more of these categories—decide which.
2. The department you are interviewing with is a cog in this moneymaking machinery. Think through how it contributes to the overall company goal of achieving profitability.

3. Your target job is a smaller cog within the department's machinery that contributes to profitability. When you understand how this target job relates to the department's role, you are also able to relate your work to the company's overriding mission: making payroll and a profit.

4. You know the experience and skills for which the company is looking and the deliverables that are expected as a result. And you know that your job exists to help the company make money within your area of expertise, by your anticipation, prevention, and solution of the problems that get in the way of the profit.

5. Look at each of the job's requirements in turn and determine what you do with each to anticipate, prevent, and solve the problems that get in the way of profitability. You deliver on all these requirements with the way you do your job—by the way you anticipate and solve the problems that are dumped on your desk every day.

6. These issues are what your job is about, and you *love* dealing with them. Knowing the issues allows you to talk intelligently about the job and simultaneously gives you intelligent questions to ask.

7. When your answers are built on this awareness, you come across as informed, thoughtful, and intelligent. Tag questions about the real guts, the real challenges of the job, and you turn a job interview from a one-sided examination of skills into a two-way conversation between a couple of professionals with a common interest—this is interpreted as intelligent enthusiasm.

In every tightly run job race, when there is nothing to choose between the skills of two top contenders, the job offer will *always* go to the most intelligently enthusiastic candidate because that candidate will be seen to work harder and smarter, produce better results, be a better team player, and be easier to manage. That candidate is you.

CHAPTER 13
WHY INTERVIEWERS DO THE THINGS THEY DO

SITTING IN FRONT of the interviewer as he looks over your resume, your mind racing with the possibilities of what could happen next, you're probably thinking, "This is crazy. Why am I here? I'd rather be abducted by aliens." What probably won't occur to you is that quite a lot of the time the interviewer feels the same way.

There is no getting around the fact that job interviews are scary events, but you are already way ahead of many other candidates because you are seriously investing yourself in developing that critical skill of turning job interviews into job offers.

On the other side of the desk is not an adversary but someone who really would like to hire you. You know that the interviewer you are facing hates to interview. I guarantee that secretly he is thinking, "Please god let this be the one, so I can get back to that pile of work on my desk." You just have to help him make the right decision.

In this part of the book, you'll get right inside the interviewer's head to understand why interviewers do the things they do. And you'll learn the formulas for answering tough interview questions in ways that are honest, unique to you, and advance your candidacy without making you sound like a snake-oil salesman.

There's a mistaken belief that any person, on being promoted into the ranks of management, becomes mystically endowed with all the skills of management, including the ability to interview and hire the right people. This is a fallacy; perhaps only half of all managers have been taught how to interview. Most just bumble along and pick up a certain proficiency over time. Consequently, at any job interview you are quite likely to run into one of two types of interviewer:

1. The untrained interviewer who doesn't know what he is doing and worse, *doesn't know* he doesn't know what he is doing.
2. The competent interviewer who knows exactly what he is doing and has a plan for the interview.

They both present challenges—and opportunities, when you know how to handle them.

Interview Strategies

There are a number of interview strategies that interviewers can use to help gather information:

1. Behavioral
2. Stress
3. Situational

We'll look at them in order.

Behavioral Interview Strategies

Behavioral interviewing has become an integral part of almost every job interview today. It is based on the reasonable premise that your past behavior can predict your future performance: "If I know how you behaved in specific situations on someone else's payroll I'll know how you will behave on mine." To get this insight, an interviewer examines your behavior in general work situations—"Are you comfortable with your accounts receivable skills?"—then looks for examples: "Tell me about a time when you had a problem with an account."

Behavioral interviewing also looks for balance. If the interviewer is feeling impressed, he will try to temper a positive response with, "Great, now tell me about a time when things didn't work out so well." Fortunately, you prepared for this line of questioning when you completed TJD exercises earlier.

Stress Interview Strategies

While every job interview is a stress interview, if the ability to function under stress is part of your job—for example, sales—then the interviewer might reasonably be expected to try to create a temporary environment that reveals how you perform under stress. He is most likely to do this with questions or demands, for example:

"Sell me this pen."

"What would you say if I told you your presentation was lousy?"

"I'm not sure you're right for this job."

Whenever you feel stress rising in an interview, stay calm:

- Breathe evenly and calmly. Shortness of breath will inhibit your thinking process and make you sound nervous.
- If you are offered a beverage at the beginning of the interview, always accept some water. Then if, at any time, you need a moment to collect your thoughts, you can take a sip; besides buying you time to think, swallowing helps reduce any tension you might be feeling. (There are more techniques to gain time later in this chapter.)
- Keep your body posture relaxed and open. Many people have a tendency, when under stress, to contract their bodies. This adds to the tension and sends the wrong message.
- Think through the question. Consciously remove any perceived intimidating verbal inflection. For example, depending on the tone of voice used, the question, "I'm not sure you are right for the job. What do you think?" can be heard as, "You just aren't right for this job." Or you could hear it as, "I'd like to hire you and you're one of my top candidates, but I'm not sure you're the one, so please convince me."

The stress interview is covered in more detail in Chapter 16.

Situational Interview Strategies

Situational strategies give the interviewer an opportunity to see you in something close to a real work situation, with the goal of getting a better idea of how you perform your duties. The situational strategy will always relate to a frequently executed task, something at the very heart of your job, and it can happen as a formal part of the interview or very casually.

Customer service and sales jobs are prone to situational interviewing strategies more than most; if you face one of these, you'll panic a little, but the situational role-play is going to re-create a task or situation that is at the core of your work, so try to relax. Ask a few questions for clarification and to get nerves under control. If it's going to take more than a few minutes, you can ask for a restroom break. Then, as much as you can, relax, step up, and do your job. Remember, what is being sought is confirmation that you understand the building blocks of that task: You aren't expected to deliver an Oscar-worthy performance.

The Experienced Interviewer

A manager's job is to get work done through others, and the first step is to hire the right people. If you cannot hire effectively, you can never manage productively, and if you can't manage productively . . . you lose your job. Consequently, more and more managers are learning how to interview effectively. You can also rely on just about all headhunters, corporate recruiters, and HR people to run competent interviews because it's what they do every day.

Competent interviewers have a plan: They know what they are going to ask, when they are going to ask it, why they are asking it, and what they hope to find. They follow a set format for the interview process to ensure objectivity in the selection process, and a set sequence of questions to ensure the facts are gathered logically and in the right areas. They have all been in many more interviews than you have. We gain three pointers from this:

- You don't need to exaggerate or fabricate. What you have to say is going to capture their full attention; besides, they can tell fact from fiction and truth from dreams.
- Interviewing can get boring if you do a lot of it. The majority of candidates make this worse. You don't need to be uptight or stiff; try to relax and become the friendly, competent, outgoing person you are on your best days. Just don't be a wise-ass.
- This is a job: It needs to be completed so they can go on to the next one. Your interviewers are hoping, praying, that you will be the one.

Competent interviewers always have a plan for the interview, and this is what it looks like from the other side of the desk:

How interviews are organized

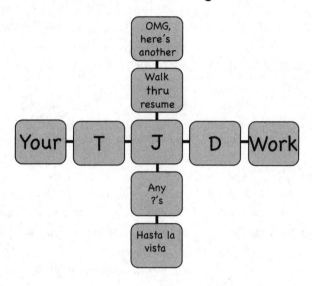

"OMG, Here's Another One"

Yes, that's the first thought in the interviewer's mind as you sit down to begin the interview. It continues, "I pray to the baby Jesus that this is the one. All I want is someone who 'gets' the job, can do it and wants to do it, comes to work on a regular basis, and gets on with people. I just need to hire someone and get back to the emergencies on my desk!"

Contrary to what you may think, *the interviewer wants you to relax*. That's because a more relaxed you is a more communicative you, and the interviewer needs information on which to base her decision. So at the beginning of an interview you'll move through some formulaic small talk and the offer of a beverage to prepare the way for the actual questioning to begin. Always accept the beverage, and ask for water. You *are* nervous, your throat is more prone to dryness, and water is the best remedy.

The interview gets underway with a statement from the interviewer, who will say something along the lines of "We're looking for a _____, and I want to find out about your experience and the strengths you can bring to our team." She will then explain a bit about how the interview itself will go: whether you'll be talking to other people and if so, who they are. This is the time when you offer a nicely formatted version of your resume printed on decent paper, because next the interviewer is going to glance down at the resume, and say, "So tell me a little bit about yourself . . ."

Walk Through Your Resume

Using your resume as a reference point, interviewers will often have you walk through your work history, asking you questions about different aspects of your experience. These early questions are designed to get you comfortable with talking, so they will mostly be straightforward, since a good interviewer wants to limit her contributions to about 20 percent of the interview, leaving you to talk the other 80 percent of the time—offering plenty of time to analyze your answers. Your answers should be similarly straightforward, and you'll make an effort here to show an understanding, in general terms, of your job's role within the department, and that in essence the job is about *problem anticipation, identification, prevention, and solution.*

Some interviews end after this journey through the resume, either because the interviewer has enough information to rule you out, or because she doesn't know any better. Skilled interviewers use this walk through the resume as a qualifying round. If you pass, they'll take the interview to the next level.

Your TJD Work Pays Off

Next the interviewer, examining your resume, will want to look at your qualifications and experience in each of the critical deliverables of the job. Since you already invested time in working back and forth among the job description you're interviewing for, your TJD document, and your resume, you will be able to connect real-world experiences to the *problems anticipated, identified, prevented, and solved* in each area by the intelligent application of the appropriate *technical* and *transferable skills.*

If you make the time to do this, you will be able to connect any question or issue the interviewer raises to the qualifications you bring to the table and illustrate them with real-world examples, explaining:

- What you did and why you did it
- The underlying transferable skills you used to get it done
- The professional values that helped you make the right judgment calls
- What you learned and how you grew professionally from the experience

Any Questions?

You know the interview is drawing to a close when you are asked if you have any questions. In Chapter 11 I suggested you make a list of such questions. Bringing the list out and checking off what hasn't been covered demonstrates the kind of *intelligent enthusiasm* that, again, helps set you apart from other candidates. The list you develop for your first interview can be the template for all subsequent interviews.

Hasta la Vista, Baby

The interviewer will thank you for your time and may give you some idea of next steps. If this information isn't offered, ask for it. If there is another round of interviews:

- Recap your understanding of the job
- What you bring to the table

- That you are qualified and very interested
- Ask to schedule the next interview

If there are no more interviews, ask when the decision will be made. Then repeat the previous steps, but instead of asking for the next interview ask for the job. You have everything to gain and nothing to lose; showing *motivation* and *intelligent enthusiasm* for the job now could be the decisive factor.

KNOCK 'EM DEAD TIP
If you are entering the world of work for the first time, or making a substantial career shift, you might not have the knowledge to analyze the job's deliverables. In this case go back to your networks and call people already in the profession to identify the *transferable skills and professional values* necessary to succeed in the initial target job of your new career.

Facing an Interview Panel

There will be situations where you will face more than one interviewer at a time. When these occur, remember the example of an attorney who had five law partners all asking questions at the same time. As the poor interviewee got halfway through one answer, another question would be shot at her. Pausing for breath, she smiled and said, "Hold on, ladies and gentlemen. These are all excellent questions, and, given time, I'll answer them all. Now I believe the managing partner has a question?" In so doing, she showed the interviewers exactly what they wanted to see—someone who remains calm and can function efficiently in stressful situations.

You never know when an interview can take a more stressful turn. It might appear that way because you are tense and tired (remember, it's okay to ask for a restroom break, to recharge yourself, at any time during a day of interviews); or it can be that rubber-stamp meeting with the senior vice president at the end of a series of grueling meetings. That is not surprising. While other interviewers are concerned with determining whether you are able, willing, and a good fit for the job in question, the senior executive who eventually throws you for a loop may be looking at your promotion potential.

This is how competent interviewers are trained to develop structured interviews. So much for the interviewer who knows what she's doing. Now for the hard part: dealing with the interviewer who doesn't know that she doesn't know what she is doing.

What Is Your Psychological Capital Quotient?

Your success at work can depend on many factors: the *technical skills* of your profession, *transferable skills*, and *professional values*, to name a few. Now new research has discovered that how you perceive your colleagues and coworkers may be just as important. It suggests that your ability to get work done is connected to how you see those around you.

Do you see your coworkers as capable, professional, decent people or incompetent jerks?

Behavioral psychologists tell us that these considerations can reflect your ability to solve problems and push yourself to achieve. This is referred to as psychological capital. Psychologists have developed tests and questions designed to use an appraisal of psychological capital to identify the candidates most likely to have the ability to develop competencies fast, pursue professional knowledge, grow professionally, work well with other team members, experience greater satisfaction from involvement in groups, and experience and display less disruptive cynicism. Psychological capital tests and questions essentially examine three areas:

1. Self-confidence—you believe you can achieve your goals
2. Resilience—you believe you can overcome setbacks
3. Optimism—you expect the future to bring good things

For example, managers who see themselves as self-confident, resilient, and optimistic are more likely to believe in and encourage success in their staff, while managers who believe their reports are incompetent and lazy will end up with a demoralized team. Apply this to yourself and you can see that how you interact with others either energizes and empowers or demoralizes them.

We will look at this a little more in Chapter 20, which discusses acing psychological tests. However, this awareness can be applied immediately to how you think about yourself, the people you work with, and how you answer interview questions. Think about this: Whether you choose to see your coworkers as capable, professional, decent people or as incompetent jerks can influence how you come across in answering all interview questions.

The Unconscious Incompetent

Do you ever remember leaving an interview and feeling that you could do the job but that the interviewer didn't ask you the questions that would allow you to showcase your skills? You were probably facing an Unconscious Incompetent: an interviewer who doesn't know that he doesn't know how to interview and who bases hiring decisions on "experience" and "knowing people" and "gut feeling."

Facing an untrained interviewer, you must understand how he thinks if you want to turn the situation to your advantage. Untrained interviewers reveal themselves in six distinct ways:

1. The interviewer's desk is cluttered, and he can't find the resume or application that was handed to him a few minutes before.

Response: Sit quietly through the bumbling and searching. Check out the surroundings. Breathe deeply and slowly to calm any lingering interview nerves. As you bring your adrenaline under control, you bring a calming tone to the interview and the interviewer.

2. The interviewer experiences constant interruptions from the telephone or people walking into the office.

Response: Interruptions provide opportunities to review what's been happening and plan points you want to make; it's a good time to review the list of questions you want to ask. The interruptions also give you time to think through a question that has just been asked or to add new information to a point made prior to the interruption.

When an interruption occurs, make a note on your pad of where you were in the conversation and refresh the interviewer on the point when conversation resumes. He will be impressed with your level head and good memory.

3. The interviewer starts with an explanation of why you are both sitting there, and then wanders into a lengthy lecture about the job and/or the company. This interviewer is nervous and doesn't know how to ask questions.

Response: Show interest in the company and the conversation. Sit straight, look attentive, make appreciative murmurs, and nod at the appropriate times until there is a pause. When that occurs, comment that you appreciate the background on the company, because you can now see more clearly how the job fits into the overall scheme of things and how valuable this or that skill would be for the job. Could the interviewer please tell you some of the other job requirements?

This is now an interview that you can guide without the interviewer feeling you have taken control of the proceedings. All you have to do is ask the questions from your list. They will demonstrate a real grasp of what is at the heart of this job; this interviewer will be impressed by the grasp of the job that your questions demonstrate.

Use questions like these: "Would it be of value if I described my experience with _____?" or "Then my experience in _____ should be a great help to you," or "I recently completed an accounting project just like that. Would it be relevant to discuss it?"

4. The interviewer begins with, or quickly breaks into, the drawbacks of the job. The job may even be described in totally negative terms. That is often done without giving a balanced view of the duties and expectations of the position. This usually means that the interviewer has had bad experiences hiring for the position.

Response: Listen, then ask why some people fail in this job. The interviewer's answers tell you exactly how to sell yourself for this position. Address each of the stated negatives and ask what kind of person handles this best. Then illustrate your proficiency in that particular aspect of the job with a short example from your work history.

5. The interviewer keeps asking closed-ended questions—questions that demand no more than a yes-or-no answer and offer little opportunity to establish your skills. Now, every other candidate is facing the same problem, so if you can finesse the situation, your candidacy will really stand out.

    Response: The trick is to treat each closed-ended question as if the interviewer has added, "Please give me a brief yet thorough answer." Closed-ended questions are often mingled with statements followed by pauses. In those instances, agree with the statement in a way that demonstrates both a grasp of your job and the interviewer's statement. For example: "That's an excellent point, Mr. Smith. I couldn't agree more that the attention to detail you describe naturally affects cost containment. My track record in this area is . . ."

6. You can also run into "situationally incompetent interviewers," usually when a hiring manager asks colleagues or team members for evaluations without detailing the deliverables of the job clearly. This problem can be compounded when such interviewers do not know how to interview.

    Response: Always take additional copies of your resume with you to the interview to aid extra interviewers in focusing on the appropriate job functions. Be ready to hold up your end of the conversation by asking intelligent questions, the answers to which will enable you to sell your candidacy.

Keeping Up Your End of the Conversation

There are a number of techniques you can use to keep up your end of the discussion.

1. You can show engagement with what the interviewer is saying by giving verbal signals. You do this with occasional short, quiet interjections that don't interrupt the employer's flow but let him know you are paying attention: "uh-huh," "that's interesting," "okay," "great," and "yes, yes" all work. But be careful not to overdo it.

2. If you don't fully understand a question or if you need time to think, ask, "Would you run that by me again?" The question is not only repeated, it is usually repeated with more detail, giving additional information and time to formulate an answer.

3. If a question stumps you, and having it repeated still doesn't help, it is better to say, "I'd like to come back to that later, I'm not used to interviewing and I'm nervous and drawing a blank right now." Odds are the interviewer will forget to ask again. If he remembers, at least your mind will have been working on it in the background and with the extra time will probably come up with an answer. If you have a great answer and the interviewer doesn't bring it up again, you can bring it up yourself.

Conversation Etiquette

Speak clearly and be careful not to mumble or shout, either of which can happen when you are nervous.

1. If you find your throat gets dry, stop and take a drink of water. The interviewer will be patient.
2. If for any reason you become flustered, stop for a moment and collect your thoughts before continuing. It's better to take a few seconds to calm down than to dig a hole deeper and deeper with babbling.
3. Keep in mind that the 80/20 rule applies to you as well. It's all right to talk a lot—that's what the interviewer expects—but don't dominate the conversation to the exclusion of anyone else. If the interviewer signals that he wants to communicate something, let him do so.
4. *Never* interrupt. You want all information possible before engaging your mouth, and often the most important part of a statement or question comes in the latter part of the sentence. Get in the habit of listening to what is being said all the way through, rather than just waiting your turn to talk.

Information-Gathering Questions

Demonstrate a good understanding of the job's deliverables and your possession of all the *technical* and *transferable skills and professional values* that help you do the job well, and you will be a top contender. If you want to turn a one-sided examination of skills into a two-way conversation between professionals with a common interest, you'll need to ask questions of your own, and the more they go to the heart of the job, the stronger the impression you will make.

Don't be afraid to ask questions. Your questions show interest, and we make our judgments of people based on both the statements they make and the questions they ask. The questions you ask show that you *get* the job and take it seriously. The interviewer's answers deliver insights into the job that you wouldn't otherwise have, giving you a better focus for your responses and the points you want to make.

This is especially important when the interviewer does not give you the openings you need to sell yourself. Always have a few intelligent questions prepared to save the situation. The following questions will give you an excellent idea of why the position is open and exactly the kind of skilled professional the company will eventually hire:

- "Who succeeds in this job and why?"
- "Who fails in this job and why?"
- "What do you consider the most important day-to-day responsibilities of this job?"

- "What is the hardest part of the job?"
- "What will be the first projects I tackle?"
- "What will you want me to have achieved in the first ninety days?"
- "What are the biggest challenges the department faces this year and what will be my role as a team member in tackling them?"
- "Which projects will I be most involved with during the first six months?"
- "What will you want me to have achieved in the first six months?"
- "What skills and values do you consider critical to success in this job?"

When you get a clear understanding of an employer's needs with questions like these, you can seize the opportunity to sell yourself appropriately, using the same techniques you would use when an interviewer talks but doesn't ask questions. Using that list as a starting point, make a list of your own to take to your job interviews.

The most important questions to ask at the end of an interview are to determine if:

- There is another interview—in which case you must ask for it, with an intelligent and enthusiastic explanation of why you are qualified and why you are interested in pursuing the opportunity.
- This is the final interview—in which case you must ask for the job with an intelligent and enthusiastic explanation of why you are qualified and why you are interested in pursuing the opportunity.

CHAPTER 14

HOW TO KNOCK 'EM DEAD: GREAT ANSWERS TO TOUGH INTERVIEW QUESTIONS

ONE OF THE two bad seats at a job interview is sitting in front of the interviewer wondering what she is going to ask next; the other is sitting across from a candidate wondering what kind of phony, canned platitudes you are going to be fed in response to a serious question. All any interviewer really wants is to find someone who can do the job, wants to do the job, and can get along with others. All you need to do to win the job offer is show the interviewer you are this person.

Fortunately you have already done the lion's share of the work. You know exactly who gets hired for this job and why. Your TJD revealed how employers prioritize their requirements and how they express them. You determined the experience and skills you possess in each of the deliverable areas of the job, you developed examples of assignments that show you tackling that area's typical problems successfully, and you created a behavioral profile of the person everyone wants to work with and the person nobody wants as an employee. All this is supported by a clear understanding of how your *transferable skills and professional values* impact every aspect of your daily professional life. Showing these universally admired skills and values in action as you make passing reference to them in your answers gives those answers substance and a ring of truth.

Armed with this knowledge, you are already better prepared than the vast majority of other candidates. Apart from a healthy and perfectly natural case of pre-performance nerves, the only rational worry you have left is fear of the unknown: not knowing what questions you might be asked, what is behind them, and how to answer them. That will be our focus for the next few chapters.

I will help you understand what is behind each question—the kind of information an employer is likely to be seeking—and I'll give an example of the kind of points you might want to make in your answers. The idea is not to memorize my sample answers; they are meant to reveal the logic of the questions and to point the way toward answers that work for you.

Tell me about yourself.

This is one of the first questions you will answer, and how you answer will set the tone for the whole interview. The interviewer wants to know about your experience and qualifications for this job, and whether bringing you in for a face-to-face meeting is going to be a waste of time.

Answering well will require a little careful thought. If you haven't thought the answer through, you'll ramble, and if you ramble right out of the starting gate, you'll lose the interviewer's attention and can usually kiss the job goodbye.

Plan Your Response

Answer the question well and you create a good first impression and set the tone for your candidacy; you'll also immediately feel more confident when the interviewer's body language subtly signals interest and attention. Everything you say should be job focused. Your response should tell the interviewer about your professional abilities and the analytical and *communication skills* that support them.

What Is Your Customer Buying?

The first lesson we all learn on entering the world of work is "The customer is always right." The second lesson is "Find out what the customers want and sell it to them." In this context, that means: Think carefully about the job's requirements and deliverables, and be prepared to address how your skills and experience have prepared you for this job. The work you do in preparation for this opening question will arm you with great ammunition for the rest of the interview.

Get Inside the Customer's Head

You need to know exactly how employers prioritize, think about, and express the responsibilities of the job and the deliverables that they expect to see fulfilled. You start by collecting four to six job postings for your target job, and then prioritizing the needs these job postings all have in common. What you'll come up with is a list of skills and responsibilities that all employers seek when looking to hire for this position.

Every Job Is the Same

At their core, all jobs are the same: They all exist to help the company make money, save money, or increase *productivity* in some way, and they all exist to *identify, prevent, and solve the problems* that typically occur every day within that job.

Your job is to think through each duty and identify:

1. All the problems that regularly crop up when doing that aspect of the job
2. The ways you execute your responsibilities every day to identify these problems and prevent them from arising
3. How you deal with the problems when they do arise

A Cog in the Machine

A corporation is a complex moneymaking machine, and each department is a cog in that machine that helps it run. In turn, your job is a still smaller cog that must mesh effectively with all the other cogs with which it comes into contact. Think about your job's role in the department and the other titles with which you have to interact effectively and harmoniously.

Putting Your Answer Together

Take the four or five most common responsibilities and turn them into bullet points, reflecting your understanding and experience in each major area of responsibility.

This gives you a condensed professional work history that focuses on what this customer is most likely looking for. An accountant might start her answer this way: "I have twelve years' experience with accounts payable, accounts receivable, quarterly P&Ls, and compliance."

Then add chronology—"I spent x years at _____ and this is where I learned how to . . ." With this structure you'll show the *professional development* that brought you to the point you are at today.

You might finish with something along the lines of, "Over the years, I've developed an ever-growing frame of reference for these critical areas, and as we talk, I hope to show you that I have a real understanding of the challenges each aspect of the job presents."

This question is often followed by another:

"What do you know about us?" *or* "What do you know about the company?"

If you don't know anything about the company, you will lose out to candidates who do. When you are asked, "What do you know about us?" and you reply, "Not much," you have quite likely killed your candidacy because you've shown a lack of real interest in the job. As well, you are directly showing disrespect to the interviewer who spends the majority of his or her waking hours there.

Gather Information

If a job interview is worth going to, it's worth knowing something about the company and the people who work there. Your knowledge of the company and its products is another piece of the jigsaw puzzle that helps an interviewer evaluate your enthusiasm and motivation for your work and this job. Read media coverage on the company and its key executives and look for industry commentary as well. But don't forget to check out what employees are saying at websites like *glassdoor.com* and *techcrunch.com*.

You want to gather information that empowers you to talk intelligently about company activities and why it is of interest to your professional and personal goals. Your research will raise as many questions as it answers, and you can use this by adding questions of your own to the end of your answer: "I read that _____, and wonder how this is affecting you . . . ?" "Everyone talks about how the workplace is focused, professional, and a fun place to be, can you tell me . . . ?" Such questions demonstrate engagement with your profession and with this specific opportunity.

Your research should take you beyond the ability to regurgitate facts and empower you, so that during the interview you show an understanding of the company as a group of people united for a common cause. This can help you have more meaningful discussions and encourage a sense that you are their kind of person.

As you answer, remember that by admiring the company's achievements you are, by inference, admiring the interviewer. A little flattery goes a long way. It's okay to throw in relevant personal details—perhaps that working for the company will bring you closer to family.

Use Your Knowledge Throughout the Interview

The knowledge you gathered to answer this question, which comes at the beginning of the interview can often be used throughout the conversation. As the meeting progresses, the interviewer will talk about the company, and your research will allow you to throw in an intelligent comment or ask a relevant question.

Likewise, when areas of common interest arise, comment on them, and agree with the interviewer when possible—people extend job offers to people like themselves.

Walk me through your job changes. Why did you leave/want to leave this job?

This question comes early in an interview and helps the interviewer understand the chronology and reasoning behind your career moves and gaps in employment. Don't worry about gaps; everyone has to deal with them. You must be ready to walk through your resume without hesitation, making two statements about each employer:

1. What you learned from that job that applies to this one; in other words, the experience you gained from past jobs is an indicator of how you will perform in this one.
2. Why you left. You should have an acceptable reason for leaving every job you have held. The following LAMPS acronym identifies acceptable reasons for leaving a company:
   - Location: The commute was unreasonably long.
   - Advancement: You weren't able to grow professionally in that position, either because there were others ahead of you or there was no opportunity for growth.
   - Money: You were underpaid for your skills and contribution.
   - Pride or prestige: You wanted to be with a better company.
   - Security: The company was not stable.

For example: "My last company was a family-owned affair. I had gone as far as I was able to go. It just seemed time for me to join a more prestigious company and accept greater challenges."

Under no circumstances should you badmouth a manager—even if she was a direct descendant of Attila the Hun. Doing so will only raise a red flag in the interviewer's mind: "Will he be complaining about me like this in a few months?"

Why did you leave _____ company?

This is a "checkbox" question: The interviewer wants to ask the question, check the box, and move on. You get into trouble with too much information. Any answer longer than two short sentences is too long. Use a phrase from the LAMPS acronym, keep it short and simple, and then shut up; if the interviewer wants more, she will ask. Use a phrase noted previously.

Why have you changed jobs so frequently?

If you have been caught in mergers and layoffs, simply explain. If you have jumped around, blame it on youth (even the interviewer was young once). Now you realize what a mistake your job-hopping was, and with your added domestic responsibilities you are now much more settled. Or you may wish to impress on the interviewer that your job-hopping was never as a result of poor performance and that you grew professionally as a result of each job change.

You could reply: "My first job had a long commute. I soon realized that, but I knew it would give me good experience in a very competitive field. Subsequently, I found a job much closer to home where the commute was only half an hour each way. I was very happy at my second job. However, I got an opportunity to really broaden my experience base with a new company that was just starting up. With the wisdom of hindsight, I realize that move was a mistake; it took me six months to realize I couldn't make a contribution there. I've been with my current company a reasonable length of time. So I have broad experience in different environments. I didn't just job-hop; I have been following a path to gain broad experience. So you see, I have more experience than the average person of my years, and a desire to settle down and make it pay off for me and my employer."

Or you can say: "Now I want to settle down and make my diverse background pay off in my contributions to my new employer. I have a strong desire to contribute and I am looking for an employer that will keep me challenged; I think this might be the company to do that. Am I right?"

Why do you want to come back?

It sometimes happens that you make a move, regret it, and look back fondly at a company you were with, sometimes years ago. When you re-apply to a past employer, you can expect to be asked about your reason for wanting to return.

It's a tricky question. You can't complain about a current or recent employer, but neither do you want to be seen as lacking judgment. The best advice is to talk about the *work* and *people factor* in your response.

Position this last job positively, identifying how it has helped you develop new skills (because this adds to your desirability), and introduce personal factors as a reason for returning.

For example, my wife Angela switched school districts for a job that would build her skills and pay more, but it wasn't working out. When asked about this in a job interview, she said, "I really loved working here. The only reason I left the district was for a great opportunity to broaden my skill set and learn more about school district finance. In the last year and a half I have managed accounts payable, receivable, bookkeeping, auditing, payroll, taxes, purchasing, cash management, financial reporting, and grants. It has been a great experience that has helped me grow considerably.

"But I also learned that the people I work with are just as important as the paycheck and developing new skills. I still have friends here, and I have this deep feeling that I want to come back home with my new skills. I know I can make real contributions right away."

Why were you fired?

If you were fired and you don't try to clean up the mess *and* change your ways, it can dog you for years.

Firing someone is unpleasant and never a decision any manager makes lightly, so in the majority of cases the employee bears a degree of responsibility. The first and most important thing is to take responsibility for the actions or behavior that led to your dismissal. If you do not take responsibility for your actions, you cannot change them.

If you take responsibility for your actions, you can clean up your act and clean up the past. Call the person who fired you; your aim is to clear the air, so whatever you do, don't be antagonistic. Reintroduce yourself and explain that you are looking (or, if you have been unemployed for a while, say you are "still looking") for a new job. Say that you appreciate that the manager had to do what was done, *that you want to apologize for being such a problem*, and that you learned from the experience.

Then address what you learned and ask, "If you were asked as part of a pre- or post-employment reference check, what would you say about me? How would you describe my leaving the company? Would you say that I was fired or that I simply resigned? You see, every time I tell someone about my termination, whoosh, there goes another chance of getting back to work!" Most managers will plump for the latter option. Taking responsibility and cleaning up the past really works and is the first step in putting yourself back on a success track.

Have you ever been asked to resign?

When someone is asked to resign, it is a gesture on the part of the employer: "You can quit, or we will can you, so which do you want it to be?" Because you were given the option, that employer cannot later say, "I had to ask him to resign," since that is tantamount to firing and could lead to legal problems; that's the point of the gesture. If you answer, "Yes," it's a mark against you and can derail your candidacy, so answer, "No." If you are in doubt about what would be said in a reference check, call Human Resources at the company and verify.

Why were you out of work so long? Why does your resume have a gap?

This question always has you scrambling for an answer; it touches a raw spot and can be humiliating, but you can turn it around by facing and using the facts of the matter.

The facts are that you are a hardworking, competent professional who had always been led to believe that was enough. You'd never had a problem finding work before and no one had ever told you that job search skills were something you needed to develop—not at school, college, or anywhere.

Then you got sideswiped by the biggest recession in eighty years and on top of this, the sudden move to Internet-based recruitment (while you were working and not paying attention to such things) had changed all the rules of job search anyway.

You might try something along the lines of, "If you look at my work history, you'll see it has been steady for _____ years. Then I lost my job. The big problem for me was my complete lack of understanding about how to find a job in the worst recession in eighty years, at a time when recruitment had moved entirely online and changed all the rules of job search.

"I'd never had a problem finding a job before, but because of the changes in how you find a job today, when I did apply for jobs, most of the time my resume got stuck in a database and was never even seen by recruiters. I didn't understand that my resume had to be written differently. The big reason I've been out of work is that my resume didn't work in this new environment and I just haven't been getting interviews."

Then move the conversation forward to what's most important to the interviewer: what you can do and how long it will take you to be productive. You might finish with a question of your own, asking about the most difficult and/or urgent responsibilities of the job and why people fail in this job, "but put me to work and I'll get right back to doing what I do best: identifying, preventing, and solving problems. What are some of the recurring problems your people have to deal with in this job?" The interviewer's answer should give you ammunition to talk about how well suited you will be for the position.

Your answer should emphasize that while you may not have been in the corporate workplace, neither have you been idle. Talk about how you have kept current with classes or part-time work, and/or what you have been doing to keep the specific *technical skills* of the job honed. You can also talk about how you used other *transferable skills* and applied *professional values* in whatever work you were doing, noting that these skills are fresh, current, and needed in every job.

What aspects of your work do you consider most crucial?

All jobs exist to support profitability; you need to determine whether your job is chiefly concerned with generating revenue, protecting assets, improving productivity in some way, or is perhaps a combination of these imperatives. Once you have determined this, you have the framework for an answer.

But to answer effectively, you need to grasp the true guts of your job, which is to *identify, prevent, and solve problems* that occur within your area of expertise, and in the process to *help your employer achieve and maintain profitability.*

Your answer begins with an explanation of why the job exists and what role it plays in achieving departmental and company goals. Then itemize the most important responsibilities of the job (you prioritized these in your TJD).

You then proceed to address:

- The technical skills you need to deliver on these responsibilities: "I need to be able to do _____ to execute my responsibilities."
- "Of course, crucial to the job is my ability to identify, prevent, and solve the problems that crop up in each of these areas every day . . ."
    a. You anticipate the ways that problems can arise in your area of responsibility and explain how you execute your work in ways that prevent many of the problems typical to your job from arising in the first place. You have an example or two ready.
    b. You tackle and solve problems that do occur, because they cannot be prevented, in a timely, effective, and professional manner. You'll have an illustration ready for this too.
  You do this in a way that is courteous to customers and vendors and considerate to those coworkers who, in their jobs, must deal with the results of your work. Again, you'll have examples.
- Finally, make mention of one or two of the *transferable skills and professional values* that help you deliver on these crucial responsibilities: "So my multitasking, communication, and critical thinking skills help me do this every day . . ."

How do you manage your work deadlines?

This examines the *time management* and *organization abilities* that enable you to *multitask* productively. You should address the Prioritize, Do, Review cycle: You set time at the end of every day to review that day's activities and plan tomorrow's. You prioritize all the planned activities and stick to those priorities to make sure the important work is attended to first.

Describe to me how your job contributes to the overall goals of your department and company.

Every company is in business to make a profit. Every company depends on individual initiative being harnessed to *teamwork* to achieve the complex tasks that result in corporate profitability. Describe how your job makes individual contributions and its role as an important cog in the machinery that is your department. Your cog needs to mesh with all the other cogs (your colleagues) for the gears of productivity to engage and move the department toward its goals.

Show that you are aware of the problems that crop up in your job every day and get in the way of company productivity. Identify how your job, at its core, is to *anticipate and prevent problems* from arising and to *solve them* when they do.

What is your greatest strength?

First talk about a must-have *technical skill*. For example, a sales professional might talk about prospecting for new clients, illustrating the answer with the tactics and strategies used. Second, talk about one or more of the *transferable skills* that help you execute this critical part of your job; for example, you could talk about the roles that *communication, critical thinking,* and *multitasking skills* play in helping you execute your "greatest strength." This way you give a complete and believable answer that also speaks of skills you apply in other aspects of your work.

What is your greatest weakness?

The greatest-strength question is often followed by asking about your greatest weakness. While this question is handled at the start of Chapter 16, "How to Handle Stress and Illegal Questions," you can start thinking about what might constitute an acceptable answer to this awful question: What parts of your job are an ongoing challenge for everyone in your profession? This can help you position weakness as a challenge shared by all conscientious people in the profession.

What is your role as a team member?

Think for a moment about why the job exists. It is there to contribute to the bottom line in some way. Your department, in turn, has a similar but larger role in the company's bottom line. Your ability to link your job's role to that of the department's larger responsibilities, and then to the overall success of the company, will demonstrate your sense of the importance of *teamwork*. The department depends on *teamwork*, so describe yourself as a *team player*.

What kinds of decisions are most difficult for you?

The most difficult decisions always relate to the most crucial responsibilities of your work. The employer is looking for people who can make decisions and solve problems, not those who'll dither instead of do. You want to position yourself as someone who's decisive but not precipitate, who considers the implications of decisions, any side effects they might have on other activities, and whether the decision conflicts with existing *systems and procedures* or other company priorities. Emphasize that, having analyzed the situation and reached a logical conclusion, you act.

The question almost demands that you explain how you make these difficult decisions, and that you give an illustration, and if you don't give one, it might well come in a follow-up question. Your example should relate to one of the crucial responsibilities of your job, and itemize the logical steps you take in analyzing the problem to help you reach the right decision.

What bothers you most about your job?

Think about those aspects of your work that *everyone* in your profession agrees are an annoying but important part of the job. Use one of these as the basis for your answer and end on a positive note about how you deal with them: You take the rough with the smooth, and take the time to do _____ well so you don't have to do the damn thing over. It is important that your answer show that you remain objective and don't take shortcuts.

Tell me about a time things went wrong.

You are being asked to talk about something that went wrong, but that doesn't mean you can't do so with an example that turned out fine. Your TJD process identified a number of such examples you can use. Choose an example and paint it black, but don't point the finger of blame; crap happens.

End with how you solved the problem or contributed to its solution. Get in a subtle plug for *transferable skills*: " . . . so sticking with it and doing it by the book helped us put things right in the end."

You can go on to explain that the next time you faced the same kind of problem you had a better frame of reference, knew what to avoid, what to do more of, and what other new approaches you could try. Finish your answer with a statement about what you learned.

How have you benefited from your disappointments/mistakes?

You learn more from failures, mistakes, and errors than you do from successes, so this is an opportunity for you to demonstrate your *emotional maturity* (you stay calm) and *critical thinking skills* (you think things through objectively).

Your answer will explain how you treat setbacks as learning experiences: You look at what happened, why it happened, and how you can do things differently at each stage. Edison once explained his success as an inventor by claiming that he knew more ways *not* to do something than anyone else living; you can do worse than to quote him. In any event, sum up your answer with, "I treat disappointments as a learning experience. I look at what happened, why it happened, and how I would do things differently in each stage should the same set of circumstances appear again. That way, I put disappointment behind me and am ready with renewed vigor and understanding to face the new day's problems."

You don't need to be specific about your failures, but be prepared with an example in case of a follow-up question starting, "Tell me about a time when . . ."

What are you looking for in your next job?

Ask not what your company can do for you; ask what you can do for your company. You are there to get a job offer, and you only want to address your needs when an offer is on the table and negotiation likely.

With so little real knowledge about the company—your research isn't the same as insights explained by a company representative—you need to be careful about specificity.

Keep your answer general and focus on the fulfillment you experience from a job well done, with a team similarly committed, working for a company with a solid reputation. If you're lower on the success ladder, add learned and earned professional growth to this—although if your future boss is the next step up . . . not such a good idea. You can add that you have observed that good people seem to move forward in groups and you'd like to earn a place within this inner circle and earn the opportunity to grow as circumstances allow by making a consistent difference with your presence.

What do you spent most of your time on, and why?

Your answer obviously needs to show that you focus your attention on top priorities, and you can make additional points by noting that you don't ignore the important but time-consuming repetitive tasks. You can mention some small thing that has to be done frequently, because if it has to be done frequently, it is obviously critical to success. But don't do this at the expense of those top priorities, or you're likely to be pegged as someone who gets bogged down in minutiae.

Another tactic is to use an example of *multitasking* to emphasize how you manage the priorities of the job. For example, "Like a lot of businesspeople, I work on the telephone and meetings take up a great deal of time. What's important to me is prioritization of activities based on the deliverables of my job. I find more gets achieved in a shorter time if a meeting is scheduled, say, immediately before lunch or at the close of business. I try to block my time in the morning and the afternoon for main-thrust activities. At four o'clock, I review what I've achieved, what went right or wrong, and plan adjustments and my main thrust for tomorrow."

What are your qualifications for this job?

The interviewer is interested in your experience and your possession of the *technical skills* to do the job, your academic qualifications, and the *transferable skills/professional values* that enable you to do any task well. This is why you need a clear recall of which *transferable skills* help you execute each aspect of your job.

When you are confident in your skills, you can learn more about the job and make points for your candidacy by asking a question of your own: "If you could tell me about specific work assignments I'll be involved with early on, I can show exactly how I can make real contributions in this job."

What can you do for us that someone else cannot do?

You cannot know other candidates' capabilities, so smilingly disarm your interviewer with this fact, then say, "But what I bring is . . ." Your answer will then demonstrate your grasp of the job's responsibilities, the problems that occur in each area, and how you are prepared to deal with them.

You can finish your answer with reference to the *transferable skills and professional values* you also bring to the job: "I also bring to this job a *determination* to see projects through to a proper conclusion. I *listen* and take direction well. I am *analytical* and don't jump to conclusions. I understand we are in business to make a *profit*, so I keep an eye on cost and return." End with: "How do these qualifications fit your needs?" or "What else are you looking for?" If you haven't covered the interviewer's hot buttons, she will cover them now, and you can respond accordingly.

How do you stay current?

We live in an age of technological innovation, in which the nature of every job is changing as quickly as you turn these pages. This means you must look to professional education as the price of sustained employability. In your answer, talk about the importance of keeping abreast of changes in the profession. You can refer to:

- Courses you have taken or are planning to take
- Books you have read or are reading
- Membership in professional associations
- Subscriptions to professional journals or online groups you belong to

If you're not already doing some of these things, you need to start *now*.

What achievements are you most proud of?

Use an example of something that is at the core of your job and central to its success, where you were part of a team working on some larger project beyond the scope of individual contribution, or where you accepted responsibility for some dirty/ignored project that nevertheless also had importance to the success of your department. Don't exaggerate your contributions to major projects—share the success and be seen as a *team player*. Be honest, and to guarantee your illustrations are relevant, take them from your TJD. For example, you might say something like, "Although I feel my biggest achievements are still ahead of me, I am proud of my involvement with _____. I made my contribution as part of that team and learned a lot in the process."

Tell me about the most difficult project you've tackled.

The interviewer wants to know:

    a. If you have experience relative to current projects
    b. How you handle them

When possible, discuss projects that parallel work you are likely to do at the new job. State the project, then identify its challenges (in some detail), your *critical thinking* process to isolate causes of the problem and possible solutions, the story of your implementation of the solution, and the value it delivered to your employer.

Tell me about an important goal you set recently.

Your answer should cite a goal that relates to productivity or another aspect related to the more important deliverables of your job in some way. You might use a skill-development goal, explaining why you chose it, how it helped you grow, and the benefits of completion. Or you can talk about a productivity/performance standard goal, why you chose it, and how it helped. You can add to this how you integrated achieving this goal into all your other activities, which allows you to talk about your *multitasking skills*.

What have you done to become more effective in your job?

Similarly to the prior question, behind this is an interest in your *motivation* to do the work being offered. The interviewer is looking for a fit between your dreams and her reality.

All worthwhile jobs require hard work and a desire to learn. Technology changes mean your job skills must always be in development if you want to remain current and viable. The interviewer wants to know if you are *committed* to your profession, and is looking for *at least* one example. You can also talk of the mentor relationships you have formed, the books and professional commentary you've read, the professional organizations you belong to, the certifications you're earning, the courses you are enrolled in, and the webinars you attend. If you aren't doing some of these things, wake up and start *now*.

How do you rank among your peers?

The interviewer is examining your self-esteem. In some cases (for instance in sales) it may be possible for you to quantify this: "I'm number two in the region." In other cases, you'll be more subjective, but you should strive to be realistic. You might slip in a real-life detail such as, "There are two groups in my department: those who make a difference, and those who watch. I'm in the first group."

How do you feel about your progress to date?

Your answer should illustrate a commitment to productivity and professional development. Explain how you ensure that your work is executed effectively and, if you can, cite endorsements given you by managers. You see each day as an opportunity to learn and contribute, and you see the environment at this company as conducive to your best efforts. Perhaps say something like, "Given the parameters of my job, my progress has been excellent. I know the work, and I am just reaching that point in my career where I can make significant contributions."

You might finish by saying that being at this interview means you've gone as far as you can with your present employer and that this environment at _____ and its new ways will encourage a new spurt of growth.

Is it ever necessary to go above and beyond the call of duty in terms of effort or time to get your job done?

If you hope to get ahead in your professional life, any job you ever hold will every now and then deliver opportunities to reschedule your personal life and otherwise mess up your weekends.

But these invasions of personal time are nevertheless opportunities to show your *commitment* and *team spirit*, so you always step up when these sometimes unwelcome opportunities present themselves; doing so increases professional success . . . and that gives you better personal time. Answer "Yes," and then illustrate with a story of making extra and special efforts with good humor.

Tell me about a time when an emergency caused you to reschedule your workload/projects.

The question examines *multitasking skills* and how you handle emergency imperatives. You'll make points when you explain how your *planning* and *time management skills* help you stay on top of your regular responsibilities even when emergency priorities throw normal scheduling off.

The story you tell should illustrate your flexibility and willingness to work extra hours when necessary. Demonstrate that your *multitasking skills* allow you to change course without having a nervous breakdown.

How long will it take you to make a contribution?

It takes time to understand *systems and procedures*, who the power players are, and why things are done the way they are. Be sure to qualify the question: In what area does the interviewer need rapid contributions? You might ask, "Where are your greatest areas of need right now?" You give yourself time to think while the interviewer explains priorities.

What is the most difficult situation you have faced?

You're really being asked two different questions: "What do you consider difficult?" and "How did you handle it?" This means the interviewer will be evaluating both your *critical thinking* and *technical skills*.

Don't talk about problems with coworkers. Instead, focus on a job-related problem. Throughout the book, we have talked about the importance of problem solving and the steps a professional takes to identify the most appropriate approaches and solutions; you should have numerous examples from your TJD and the resume creation process with which to illustrate your answer. Make sure to identify the benefits of your solution.

What do you think determines progress in a good company?

The interviewer needs to see that you understand progress is earned over time, and does not come as a result of simply showing up to work on a regular basis. Begin with each of the *technical skills* required to do the job, briefly citing the *transferable skills* that allow you to do the job well. Finish with your *willingness* to take the rough with the smooth that goes with every job, and the good fortune of having a manager who wants you to succeed.

What are some of the problems you encounter in doing your job, and what do you do about them?

There's a trap in this question and two areas you need to cover in your response, so your answer has three steps.

1. First the trap: Note well the old saying, "A poor workman blames his tools," and don't find problems with the job itself or the tools you have to execute that job. Next, the two areas you need to cover:
2. Whatever your title, at its heart your job is about *problem identification, prevention, and solution*. Make this statement with details of the problems you are a specialist in preventing and solving. This part of your answer demonstrates your deep understanding of your work.
3. Your awareness that careless mistakes cost the company good money means you are always on the lookout for potential problems caused by oversight. For example: "Some parts of my job are fairly repetitive, so it's easy to overlook problems. Lots of people do. However, I always look for them; it helps keep me alert and motivated, so I do a better job. To give you an example, we make computer-memory disks. Each one has to be machined by hand, and, once completed, the slightest abrasion will turn one into a reject. I have a steady staff and little turnover, and everyone wears cotton gloves to handle the disks. Yet about six months ago, the reject rate suddenly went through the roof. Is that the kind of problem you mean? Well, the cause was one that could have gone unnoticed for ages. Jill, the section head who inspects all the disks, had lost a lot of weight and her diamond engagement ring was slipping around her finger, scratching the disks as she passed them and stacked them to be shipped. Our main client was giving us a big problem over it, so my looking for problems and paying attention to detail really paid off."

In your last job, how did you plan to interview?

If you are a manager, getting work done through others is at the very heart of your job. Recruitment and selection are part of your job description, and you can expect this question. Your answer should give a description of how the skilled interviewer prepares, as we discussed in Chapter 13. You might also read *Hiring the Best* and the eBook *Knock 'em Dead Breaking Into Management: The Essentials of Survival & Success* (details at *www.knockemdead.com*).

If I hired you today, what would you accomplish first?

Gear your answer to first getting settled in the job, understanding how things are done, and becoming a member of the team. You would mention that of course this includes a clear priority on all your responsibilities. Then finish with a question, "What are the most critical projects/problems you'll want me to tackle?" The response to that becomes your final answer to what you will accomplish first.

What type of decisions do you make in your work?

This examines the extent of your authority and how *critical thinking* enters into your work. With the TJD, you will have a clear understanding of the job's deliverables and can determine the decision-making events that are integral to your job. The interviewer will certainly follow with a request for an example; your answer will address the types of decisions you make and include an example that shows how you approach making them.

How do you handle rejection?

This question is common if you are applying for a job in sales, including face-to-face sales, telemarketing, public relations, and customer service. If you are after a job in one of these areas and you really don't like the heavy doses of rejection that are any salesperson's lot, consider a new field. The anguish you will experience will not lead to a successful career or a happy life.

With that in mind, let's look behind the question. The interviewer simply wants to know whether you take rejection as rejection of yourself or whether you simply accept it as a temporary rejection of a service or product. Here is a sample answer that you can tailor to your particular needs and background: "I accept rejection as an integral part of the sales process. If everyone said 'yes' to a product, there would be no need for the sales function. As it is, I see every rejection as bringing me closer to the customer who *will* say 'yes.' Sales is a profession of communication, determination, and resilience; rejection is just part of the process, it's nothing personal. I always try to leave the potential customer with a good feeling, as no sale today can well become a sale next month."

Tell me about a situation that frustrated you at work.

This question is about *emotional maturity*. The interviewer wants to know how you channel frustration into productivity. Give an example of a difficult situation in which you remained diplomatic and objective and found a solution that benefited all concerned. Show yourself to be someone who isn't managed by emotions—you acknowledge the frustration, then put it aside in favor of achieving the goals of the job you are paid to do.

What interests you least about this job?

The question is potentially explosive but easily defused. Regardless of your occupation, there is at least one repetitive, mindless duty that everyone groans about but that nevertheless goes with the territory. Use that as your example. " _____ are probably the least demanding part of my job. However, I know they are important for _____, so I do them at the end of the day as part of my performance review and next-day planning." Notice how this response also shows that you are *organized* and possess *critical thinking* and *multitasking skills*; it also shows you understand that it is necessary to take the rough with the smooth.

I'm not sure you're suitable for the job (too inexperienced).

In a job search you quickly develop a feeling for whether a particular position is a close match, a job you've already done for so long that you might be perceived as too experienced (too heavy), or a job that might be a bit of a stretch (too light). If you can see a potential problem with an opportunity, the employer probably can too. Nevertheless, you were close enough to get the interview, so make every effort to land the offer.

This could also be used as a stress question (to see how you handle adverse situations on the job). The interviewer's "I'm not sure" could really mean, "I'd like to hire you, so here's a wide-open opportunity to sell me on you." Either way, remain calm and accept this as another opportunity to set you apart from other candidates.

Put the ball straight back into the interviewer's court, "Why do you say that?" You need more information and time to organize an appropriate reply, but it is also important to show that you are not intimidated.

When you might be too light, your answer itemizes all the experience and skills you bring, and offsets weaknesses with other strengths and examples of how efficiently you develop new skills.

You can also talk about the *motivation* you bring to the job, and that you will expect to be motivated for some considerable time because of the opportunity the job offers for your professional development, while someone with all the skills is going to need a quick promotion to keep him happy. You can finish your answer with a reflexive question that encourages a "yes" answer, "Wouldn't you agree?"

I'm not sure you're suitable for the job (too experienced).

If you are told you have too much experience, respond with the positives: how your skills help you deliver immediately and why the position fits your needs; perhaps, "I really enjoy my work, so I won't get bored, and I'm not looking for a promotion, so I'm not after anyone's job. I'll be a reliable and trustworthy person to have at your back. I have excellent skills [itemize], so I can deliver quickly and consistently. My experience makes me a steadying member of the team, and when you think I'm ready I can help mentor." Finish with a smile, " . . . and let's not forget I've already made my mistakes on somebody else's payroll."

Do you have any questions?

A sign that the interview is drawing to a close. Take the opportunity to make a strong impression. Ask questions that help advance your candidacy by giving you information about the real-world experience of the job: "Yes I do have one or two questions." Go through the list of questions you developed after reading the interview preparation chapter and brought with you:

- Who succeeds in this job and why?
- Who fails in this job and why?
- What are the major projects of the first six months?

- What will you want me to have achieved after ninety days?
- What will you want me to have achieved after six months?
- What will my first assignment be?

For a longer list of the sort of questions you might want to ask, check out Chapter 25.

Most candidates ask questions about money and benefits. These are nice-to-know questions that an interviewer is not really interested in discussing at this point. As your goal at every interview is to bring the interviewer to the point of offering you the job, such questions are really irrelevant because they don't bring you closer to the job offer. Better that you concentrate on gathering information that will help you further your candidacy.

Ask about next steps if there are more interviews. If there are, match your skills to the needs of the job, explain your interest in the job and desire to pursue it, and ask for the next interview.

If there's not another interview, cite your understanding of the job, how your skills match each of the deliverables, state that you want the job and want to join the team, and ask for the job.

For Job Seekers in the Nonprofit World

As a headhunter many years ago, I took an assignment from a nonprofit foundation and was completely surprised when the client made a point of telling me: "Nonprofit is not a goal." Yes, nonprofit organizations may have laudable and altruistic goals, and expect their employees to be motivated by more than just money, but because money is often harder to come by in the nonprofit world, making a dollar work at peak efficiency certainly is a concern for everyone trying to change our world for the better by working in a nonprofit environment.

I've discussed this issue with many senior people throughout the nonprofit world (when they approach me for speeches or services), and one of their biggest concerns is lack of concern for cost containment, productivity, and efficiency, and this leads us right back to why jobs exist: to make money, save money, or increase productivity. In the nonprofit world, the motive may not be the financial reward. The major difference in working for a nonprofit is not to make money, save money, or increase productivity *for the benefit of the executives and stockholders* of that company, but rather to make money, save money, or increase productivity so that it can *empower the nonprofit to do more good with their resources.*

Perhaps the profit messaging is not so strong in the nonprofit world, but making a dollar go further and work harder most certainly is. Consequently, you can easily customize your answers to all the most common interview questions.

CHAPTER 15
QUESTIONS OF MANAGEABILITY AND TEAM SPIRIT

"WHAT ARE YOU like to work with, Mr. Jones?" Learn the techniques interviewers use to find out if you are manageable, if you will fit in, and most important, whether you are the type of person who is able to work toward common goals and with whom others like to work.

If you are offered the job and accept, you will be working with the other employees of the company, quite possibly including the interviewer, for fifty weeks of the year, so the interviewer really wants to know if you are going to reduce his life expectancy. Every employer wants to know whether you will fit in with the rest of the staff, whether you are a *team player*, and most of all, whether you are manageable. Fortunately, you have carefully thought through the behaviors of professional success and failure; and as a result, you have a clear idea of who you are and how you behave professionally. This self-awareness will help you handle the questions addressed in this chapter.

A big part of your job as that small but important cog in the moneymaking machinery of the corporation is to mesh with the other cogs in your department (and beyond) to support those departmental deliverables that are beyond the scope of individual effort. Once your ability and suitability are considered up to scratch, the final and most significant overall consideration of hiring managers is your willingness to take direction and work for the common good of the group. Here are the questions your interviewers will ask to assess this.

How do you take direction?

The interviewer wants to know whether you are open-minded and can be a *team player*. Can you follow directions, or are you a difficult, high-maintenance employee? The employer hopes that you are a low-maintenance professional who is motivated to ask clarifying questions about a project before beginning and who then gets on with the job at hand, coming back with requests for direction as circumstances dictate.

This particular question can also be defined as "How do you accept criticism?" Your answer should cover both points: "I take direction well and recognize that it can come in two varieties, depending on the circumstances. There is carefully explained direction, when my boss has time to lay things out for me in detail; then there are those times when, as a result of deadlines and other pressures, the direction might be brief and to the point. While I have seen some people get upset with that, personally I've always understood that there are probably other considerations I am not aware of. As such, I take the direction and get on with the job without taking offense, so my boss can get on with his job."

Would you like to have your boss's job?

It is a rare boss who wants his livelihood taken away. On my own very first job interview, my future boss said, "Mr. Yate, it has been a pleasure to meet you. However, until you walked in my door, I wasn't out on the street looking for a new job." You see, I had this case of wanting to start at the top rather than actually work my way up.

The interviewer wants to know if you are the type of person who will be confrontational or undermining. He also seeks to determine how goal oriented and motivated you are in your work life—so you may also want to comment on your sense of direction. But while ambition is admired, it is admired most by those far enough above the fray not to be threatened. Be cautiously optimistic; perhaps, "Well, if my boss were promoted over the coming years, I would hope to have made a consistent enough contribution to warrant his consideration. It's not that I am looking to take anyone's job; rather, I am looking for a manager who will help me develop my capabilities."

What do you think of your current/last boss?

Be short and sweet and shut up. People who complain about their employers are recognized as the people who cause the most disruption in a department. This question is the interviewer's way of finding out if you're going to cause trouble. "I liked her as a person, respected her professionally, and appreciated her guidance." The question is often followed by one that tries to validate your answer.

Describe a situation where your work or an idea of yours was criticized.

This is a doubly dangerous question because you are being asked to describe how you handle criticism, and to detail inadequacies. If you have the choice, describe a poor idea that was criticized, not poor work.

Put your example in the past, make it small, and show what you learned from the experience. Show that you go through these steps to become maximally productive:

- Listen to understand
- Confirm the understanding
- Ask for guidance
- Confirm the desired outcome
- Show a satisfactory resolution
- Address what you learned and how the experience helped you grow

You might end with something that captures the essence of your example: "I listened carefully and asked a couple of questions for clarification. Then I fed back what I heard to make sure the facts were straight. I asked for advice, we bounced some ideas around, then I came back later and represented the idea in a more viable format. My supervisor's input was invaluable." Those are the steps you go through to become maximally productive in these situations.

How do you get along with different kinds of people?

You don't have to talk about respect for others, the need for diversity, or how it took you ten years to realize Jane was a different sex and Charley a different color, because that is not what this question is about. If you respect others, you will demonstrate this by explaining to your interviewer how you work in a team environment (because this is, in reality, a "team player" question) and how you solicit and accept input, ideas, and viewpoints from a variety of sources. Give a quick, honest illustration of working productively with a person who is different from you in terms of personality or in terms of the demands his job places on him—and how you respond to maximize productivity and a harmonious work environment.

Rate yourself on a scale of one to ten.

This question is meant to plumb the depths of your self-esteem and self-awareness. If you answer ten, you run the risk of portraying yourself as insufferable. On the other hand, if you say less than seven, you might as well get up and leave. Your best bet is probably an eight. Say that you always give of your best, which includes ongoing personal and professional development, so that in doing so you always increase your skills and therefore always see room for improvement. It helps to give an example: "I just read a great book on time management called *How to Get Control of Your Time and Your Life*, and found that a daily plan/do/review cycle is a really useful tool for staying on top of and prioritizing multiple projects."

What kinds of things do you worry about?

Some questions, such as this one, can seem so off-the-wall that you might start treating the interviewer as a confessor in no time flat. Your private phobias have nothing to do with your job, and revealing them can get you labeled as unbalanced. It is best to confine your answer to the sensible worries of a conscientious professional. "I worry about deadlines, staff turnover, tardiness, backup plans for when the computer crashes, or that one of my auditors will burn out or defect to the competition—just the normal stuff. It goes with the territory, so I don't let it get me down." Whatever you identify as a worry might then be the subject of a follow-up question, so think through the worry you state and how you cope with it.

What have you done that shows initiative?

The question probes whether you are a doer, someone who will look for ways to increase revenue and/or productivity—the kind of person who makes a difference for good with her presence every day. Be sure, however, that your example of initiative does not show a disregard for company *systems and procedures*.

The story you tell shows you stepping up to do a necessary job others didn't see as important or didn't want to do. For example, "Every quarter, I sit down with my boss and find out the dates of all his meetings for the next six months. I immediately make the hotel and flight arrangements, and attend to all the web-hosting details. I ask myself questions like, 'If the agenda for the July meeting needs to reach the attendees at least six weeks before the meeting, when must it be finished by?' Then I come up with a deadline. I do that for all the major activities for all the meetings. I put the deadlines in his Blackberry and in mine two weeks earlier to ensure everything is done on time. My boss is the best-organized, most relaxed manager in the company."

If you could make one constructive suggestion to management, what would it be?

What matters here is less the specific content of your answer than the tone. Suggest what you know to be true and what your interviewer will appreciate as a breath of fresh air: Most people want to do a good job. Management should create an environment where striving for excellence is encouraged *and* where those retired on the job have the opportunity to change their ways or leave. Everyone would benefit.

Why do you feel you are a better _____ than some of your coworkers?

The trick is to answer the question without showing yourself in anything but a flattering light. "I don't spend my time thinking about how I am better than my colleagues, because that would be detrimental to our working together as a team. I believe, however, some of the qualities that make me an outstanding _____ are . . ." From here, go on to itemize specific *technical skills* of your profession in which you are particularly strong, and a couple of the *transferable skills* that apply to doing these aspects of your work so well.

What are some of the things that bother you? / What are your pet peeves? / Tell me about the last time you felt anger on the job.

It is tremendously important that you show you can remain calm. Most of us have seen a colleague lose his cool on occasion—not a pretty sight, and one that every sensible employer wants to avoid. This question comes up more and more often the higher up the corporate ladder you climb and the more frequent your contact with clients and the general public. To answer it, find something that angers conscientious workers. "I enjoy my work and believe in giving value to my employer. Dealing with clock watchers and people who regularly get sick on Mondays and Fridays really bothers me, but it's not something that gets me angry." An answer of this nature will help you much more than the kind given by one engineer who went on for some minutes about how he hated the small-mindedness of people who don't like pet rabbits in the office.

What are some of the things about which you and your supervisor disagreed?

You did not disagree.

In what areas do you feel your supervisor could have done a better job?

The same goes for this one. No one admires a Monday-morning quarterback.

You could reply, though: "I have always had the highest respect for my supervisor. I have always been so busy learning from Mr. Jones that I don't think he could have done a better job. He has really brought me to the point where I am ready for greater challenges. That's why I'm here."

What are some of the things your supervisor did that you disliked?

If you and the interviewer are both nonsmokers, for example, and your boss isn't, use it. Apart from that: "You know, I've never thought of our relationship in terms of like or dislike. I've always thought our role was to get along together and get the job done."

How well do you feel your boss rated your job performance?

This is one very sound reason to ask for written evaluations of your work before leaving a company. Some performance-review procedures include a written evaluation of your performance—perhaps your company employs it. If you work for a company that asks you to sign your formal review, you are quite entitled to request a copy of it. You should also ask for a letter of recommendation whenever you leave a job; you have nothing to lose. If you don't have written references, perhaps say: "My supervisor always rated my job performance well. In fact, I was always rated as being capable of accepting further responsibilities. The problem was there was nothing available in the company—that's why I'm here."

If your research has been done properly you can quote verbal appraisals of your performance from prior jobs. "In fact, my boss recently said that I was the most organized engineer in the work group, because . . ."

How do I get the best out of you/did your boss get the best out of you?

The interviewer could be envisioning you as an employee. Encourage the thought by describing a supportive manager who outlined projects and their expected results at the start, noted deadlines, shared her greater experience and perspectives, and told you about potential problems. She always shared the benefit of experience. You agreed on a plan of attack for the work, and how and when you needed to give status updates along the way. Your boss was always available for advice and taught you to take the work seriously but encouraged a collegial team atmosphere.

How interested are you in sports?

The interviewer is looking for your involvement in groups, as a signal that you know how to get along with others and pull together as a team.

"I really enjoy most team sports. I don't get a lot of time to indulge myself, but I am a regular member of my company's softball team." A recently completed survey of middle- and upper-management personnel found that the executives who listed group sports/activities among their extracurricular activities made an average of $3,000 per year more than their sedentary colleagues. Don't you just love baseball suddenly?

Apart from team sports, endurance sports are seen as a sign of determination: Swimming, running, and cycling are all okay. Games of skill (bridge, chess, and the like) demonstrate analytical skills; despite the recent popularity of poker and recognition of it as a game of analytical, math, communication, and negotiation skills, I feel that mentioning poker should be avoided.

What personal characteristics are necessary for success in your field?

You know the answer to this one: It's a brief recital of your *transferable skills and professional values.*

You might say: "To be successful in my field? Drive, motivation, energy, confidence, determination, good communication, and analytical skills. Combined, of course, with the ability to work with others." Your answer will be more powerful if you relate *transferable skills and professional values* to the prime needs of the job.

Do you prefer working with others or alone?

This question is usually used to determine whether you are a *team player*. Before answering, however, be sure you know whether the job requires you to work alone. Then answer appropriately. Perhaps: "I'm quite happy working alone when necessary. I don't need much constant reassurance. But I prefer to work in a group—so much more gets achieved when people pull together."

Explain your role as a group/team member.

You are being asked to describe yourself as either a *team player* or a loner. Think for a moment about why the job exists in the first place: It is there to contribute to the bottom line in some way, and as such it has a specific role in the department to contribute toward that larger goal. Your department, in turn, has a similar, but larger, role in the company's bottom line. Your ability to link your small role to that of the department's larger responsibilities, and then to the overall success of the company, will demonstrate a developed professional awareness. Most departments depend on harmonious *teamwork* for their success, so describe yourself as a *team player*: "I perform my job in a way that helps others to do theirs in an efficient manner. Beyond the mechanics, we all have a responsibility to make the workplace a friendly and pleasant one, and that means everyone working for the common good and making the necessary personal sacrifices for it."

How would you define a motivational work atmosphere?

This is a tricky question, especially because you probably have no idea what kind of work atmosphere exists in that particular office. The longer your answer, the greater your chances of saying the wrong thing, so keep it short and sweet. "One where the team has a genuine interest in its work and desire to turn out a good product/deliver a good service."

Do you make your opinions known when you disagree with the views of your supervisor?

If you can, state that you come from an environment where input is encouraged when it helps the team's ability to get the job done efficiently. "If opinions are sought in a meeting, I will give mine, although I am careful to be aware of others' feelings. I will never criticize a coworker or a superior in an open forum; besides, it is quite possible to disagree without being disagreeable. However, my last manager made it clear that she valued my opinion by asking for it. So, after a while, if there was something I felt strongly about, I would make an appointment to sit down and discuss it one-on-one."

What would you say about a supervisor who was unfair or difficult to work with?

"I would make an appointment to see the supervisor and diplomatically explain that I felt uncomfortable in our relationship, that I felt he was not treating me as a professional colleague, and therefore that I might not be performing up to standard in some way—that I wanted to right matters and ask for his input as to what I must do to create a professional relationship. I would take responsibility for any communication problems that might exist and make it clear that, just as I took responsibility for the problem, I was also taking responsibility for the solution."

Do you consider yourself a natural leader or a born follower?

Ouch! The way you answer depends a lot on the job offer you are chasing. If you are a recent graduate, you are expected to have high aspirations, so go for it. If you are already on the corporate ladder with some practical experience in the school of hard knocks, you might want to be a little cagier. Assuming you are up for (and want) a leadership position, you might try something like this: "I would be reluctant to regard anyone as a natural leader. Hiring, motivating, and disciplining other adults and at the same time molding them into a cohesive team involves a number of delicately tuned skills that no honest person can say they were born with. Leadership requires first of all the desire; then it is a lifetime learning process. Anyone who reckons they have it all under control and have nothing more to learn isn't doing the employer any favors."

Of course, a little humility is also in order, because just about every leader in every company reports to someone, and there is a good chance that you are talking to just such a someone right now. So you might consider including something like, "No matter how well developed any individual's leadership qualities, an integral part of leadership ability is the ability to take direction from your immediate boss, and also to seek the input of the people being supervised. The wise leader will always follow good advice and sound business judgment, wherever it comes from. I would say that the true leader in the modern business world must embrace both." How can anyone disagree with that kind of wisdom?

You have a doctor's appointment arranged for noon. You've waited two weeks to get in. An urgent meeting is scheduled at the last moment, though. What do you do?

What a crazy question, you mutter. It's not. It is even more than a question—it is what I call a question shell. The question within the shell—in this instance, "Will you sacrifice the appointment or sacrifice your job?"—can be changed at will. This is a situational-interviewing technique, which poses an on-the-job problem to see how the prospective employee will respond. A Chicago company asks this question as part of its initial screening, and if you give the wrong answer, you never even get a face-to-face interview. So what is the right answer to this or any similar shell question?

Fortunately, once you understand the interviewing technique, it is quite easy to handle—all you have to do is turn the question around. "If I were the manager who had to schedule a really important meeting at the last moment, and someone on my staff chose to go to the doctor instead, how would I feel?"

It is unlikely that you would be an understanding manager unless the visit was for a triple bypass. To answer, you start with an evaluation of the importance of the problem and the responsibility of everyone to make some sacrifices for the organization, and finish with: "The first thing I would do is reschedule the appointment and save the doctor's office inconvenience. Then I would immediately make sure I was properly prepared for the emergency meeting."

How do you manage to interview while still employed?

As long as you don't explain that you faked a dentist appointment to make the interview you should be all right. Beware of revealing anything that might make you appear at all underhanded. Best to make the answer short and sweet, and let the interviewer move on to richer areas of inquiry. Just explain that you had some vacation time due, or took a day off in lieu of overtime payments. "I had some vacation time, so I went to my boss and explained that I needed a couple of days off for some personal business and asked her what days would be most suitable. Although I plan to change jobs, I don't in any way want to hurt my current employer in the process by being absent during a crunch."

How have your career motivations changed over the years?

This question only crops up when you have enough years under your belt to be regarded as a tenured professional. The interviewer's agenda is to examine your *emotional maturity* and how realistic you are about future professional growth.

Your answer requires self-awareness. While the desire to rule the world can be seen as *motivation* in young professionals, it may not be interpreted so positively coming from a tenured corporate soldier from whom more realism is expected.

Your answer should reflect a growing maturity as well as a desire to do a good job for its own sake and to make a contribution as part of the greater whole. Here's an example you can use as a starting point in crafting your own:

"I guess in earlier years I was more ego driven, with everything focused on becoming a star. Over the years I've come to realize that nothing happens with a team of one—we all have to function as part of a greater whole if we are to make meaningful contributions with our professional presence. Nowadays I take great pleasure in doing a job well, in seeing it come together as it should, and especially in seeing a group of professionals working together in their different roles to make it happen. I've discovered that the best way to stand out is to be a real team player and not worry about standing out."

How do you regroup when things haven't gone as planned?

At times we can all react to adversity in pretty much the same way we did as kids, but that isn't always productive, and it isn't what an interviewer wants to hear. Here's a way you can deal with setbacks in your professional life and wow your interviewer in the process:

"I pause for breath and reflection for as long as the situation allows—this can be a couple of minutes or overnight. I do this to analyze what went wrong and why. I'm also careful to look for the things that went right, too. I'll examine alternate approaches and, time allowing, I'll get together with a peer or my boss and review the whole situation and my proposed new approaches."

You can go on to explain that the next time you face the same kind of problem you'll know what to avoid, what to do more of, and what other new approaches you can try.

You might consider finishing your answer with a statement about the beneficial effects of experiencing problems. "Over the years I've learned just as much from life's problems as from its successes."

Have you ever had to make unpopular decisions?

Inherent in the question is a request for an example, in which you'll demonstrate how *critical thinking* and *leadership skills* help you make the unpopular decisions, while *teamwork* and *communication skills* help make them palatable. Your answer needs to show that you're not afraid to make unpopular decisions when they are in the best interests of your job or the department's goals.

Simultaneously, stress your effort to make the decision workable for all parties, and finish by explaining how everyone subsequently accepted its necessity and got onboard.

What would your coworkers tell me about your attention to detail?

Say that you are shoddy and never pay attention to the details and you'll hear a whoosh as your job offer flies out the window.

Your answer obviously lies in the question. You pay attention to detail, your analytical approach to projects helps you identify all the component parts of a given job, and your *multitasking skills* ensure that you get the job done in a timely manner without anything falling through the cracks.

What do you do when there is a decision to be made and no procedure exists?

You need to show that even though you're more than capable of taking initiative, you're not a rogue missile. Explain that the first thing you'll do will be to discuss the situation with your boss or—if time is tight and this isn't possible—with peers. That's exactly what the hiring manager wants to hear. Make clear that in developing any new approach/procedure/idea you'll stick to the company's established *systems and procedures*.

When do you expect a promotion?

Tread warily, show you believe in yourself, and have both feet firmly planted on the ground. "That depends on a few criteria. Of course, I cannot expect promotions without the performance that marks me as deserving of promotion. I also need to join a company that has the growth necessary to provide the opportunity. I hope that my manager believes in promoting from within and will help me grow so that I will have the skills necessary to be considered for promotion when the opportunity comes along."

If you are the only one doing a particular job in the company, or you are in management, you need to build another factor into your answer. "As a manager, I realize that part of my job is to have done my succession planning, and that I must have someone trained and ready to step into my shoes before I can expect to step up. That way, I play my part in preserving the chain of command." To avoid being caught off-guard with queries about your having achieved that in your present job, you can finish with: "Just as I have done in my present job, where I have a couple of people capable of taking over the reins when I leave."

Tell me a story.

Wow. What on earth does the interviewer mean by that question? You don't know until you get her to elaborate. Ask, "What would you like me to tell you a story about?" To make any other response is to risk making a fool of yourself. Sometimes the question is asked to evaluate how analytical you are. People who answer the question without qualifying show they do not think things through carefully. The interviewer may also ask it to get a glimpse of the things you hold important. The answer you get to your request for clarification may give you direction, or it may not; but either way it demonstrates your *critical thinking skills*.

You need to have a story ready that portrays you in an appropriate light. If you speak of your personal life, tell a story that shows you like people, are engaged in life, and are determined. Do not discuss your love life. If the story you tell is about your professional life, make sure it shows you working productively as a member of a team on some worthwhile project that had problems but which came out okay in the end. Alternatively, tell stories that show you employing *transferable skills and professional values* in some subtle way.

What have you learned from jobs you have held?

You've learned that little gets achieved without *teamwork* and that there's invariably sound thinking behind *systems and procedures*. To get to the root of problems it's better to talk less and listen more. Most of all, you've learned that you can either sit on the sidelines watching the hours go by or you can get involved and make a difference with your presence. You do the latter because you're goal oriented, time goes quicker when you're engaged, and besides, the relationships you build are with better people. You might finish with: "There are two general things I have learned from past jobs. First, if you are confused, ask—it's better to ask a dumb question than make a dumb mistake. Second, it's better to promise less and produce more than to make unrealistic forecasts."

Define cooperation.

The question examines *manageability* and asks you to explain how you see your responsibilities as a *team player*, both taking direction and working for the overall success of your department. Your answer will define cooperation as doing your job in a way that enables your colleagues to do theirs with a minimum of disruption. It's your desire to be part of something significant: Through hard work and good will, you help make the team something greater than the sum of its parts.

What difficulties do you have tolerating people with backgrounds and interests different from yours?

Another "team player" question with the awkward implication that you do have problems. Say, "I don't have any." But don't leave it there.

"I don't have any problems working with people from different backgrounds. In fact I find it energizing; with different backgrounds you get different life experiences and different ways of coming at problems. The opportunity to work with people different from yourself is golden."

In hindsight, what have you done that was a little harebrained?

You are never harebrained in your business dealings, and you haven't been harebrained in your personal life since graduation, right? The only safe examples to use are ones from your deep past that ultimately turned out well. One of the best, if it applies to you, is: "Well, I guess the time I bought my house. I had no idea what I was letting myself in for and didn't pay enough attention to how much work the place would need. Still, there weren't any big structural problems, though I had to put a lot of work into fixing it up the way I wanted. Yes, my first house—that was a real learning experience." Not only can most people relate to this example, but it also gives you the opportunity to sell one or two of your very positive and endearing professional behaviors.

You have been given a project that requires you to interact with different levels within the company. How do you do this? What levels are you most comfortable with?

This is a two-part question that probes communication and self-confidence skills. The first part asks how you interact with superiors and motivate those working with and for you on the project. The second part is saying, "Tell me whom you regard as your peer group—help me categorize you." To cover those bases, include the essence of this: "There are two types of people I would interact with on a project of this nature. First, there are those I would report to, who would bear the ultimate responsibility for the project's success. With them, I would determine deadlines and a method for evaluating the success of the project. I would outline my approach, breaking the project down into component parts, getting approval on both the approach and the costs. I would keep my supervisors updated on a regular basis and seek input whenever needed. My supervisors would expect three things from me: the facts, an analysis of potential problems, and that I not be intimidated, as this would jeopardize the project's success. I would comfortably satisfy those expectations.

"The other people to interact with on a project like this are those who work with and for me. With those people, I would outline the project and explain how a successful outcome will benefit the company. I would assign the component parts to those best suited to each, and arrange follow-up times to assure completion by deadline. My role here would be to facilitate, motivate, and bring the different personalities together to form a team.

"As for comfort level, I find this type of approach enables me to interact comfortably with all levels and types of people."

Tell me about an event that really challenged you. How did you meet the challenge? In what way was your approach different from that of others?

This is a straightforward, two-part question. The first part probes your *critical thinking skills*. The second asks you to set yourself apart from the herd. Outline the root of the problem, its significance, and its negative impact on the department/company. The clearer you make the situation, the better. Having done so, explain your solution, its value to your employer, and how it was different from other approaches:

"My company has offices all around the country; I am responsible for seventy of them. My job is to visit each office on a regular basis and build market-penetration strategies with management, and to train and motivate the sales and customer service forces. When the recession hit, the need to service those offices was greater than ever, yet the traveling costs were getting prohibitive.

"Morale was an especially important factor: You can't let outlying offices feel defeated. I reapportioned my budget and did the following: I dramatically increased telephone contact with the offices and instituted weekly sales-technique emails and monthly training webinars—how to prospect for new clients, how to negotiate difficult sales, and so forth. I increased management training, again using webinars and concentrating on how to run sales meetings, early termination of low producers, and so forth.

"While my colleagues complained about the drop in sales, mine increased, albeit by a modest 6 percent. After two quarters, the new media/coaching approach was officially adopted by the company."

Give me an example of a method of working you have used. How did you feel about it?

You have a choice of giving an example of either good or bad work habits. Give a good example, one that demonstrates your understanding of corporate goals and your organizational or *critical thinking skills*. If you have taken the time to develop the time management and organization skills that underlie *multitasking* abilities, you have a great illustrative example to use.

You could say: "Maximum productivity requires focus and demands organization and time management. I do my paperwork at the end of each day, when I review the day's achievements; with this done, I plan for tomorrow, prioritizing all projected activities. When I come to work in the morning, I'm ready to get going without wasting time and sure that I will be spending my time and effort in the areas where it is most needed to deliver results. I try to schedule meetings right before lunch; people get to the point more quickly if it's on their time. I feel this is an efficient and organized method of working."

In working with new people, how do you go about getting an understanding of them?

Every new hire is expected to become a viable part of the group, which means getting an understanding of the group and its individual members. Understanding that everyone likes to give advice is the key to your answer. You have found that the best way to understand and become part of a new team is to be open, friendly, ask lots of questions, and be helpful whenever you can. The answers to your questions give you needed insights into the ways of the job, department, and company, and they help you get to know the person.

What would your references say about you?

You have nothing to lose by giving a positive answer. If you checked your references, as I recommended earlier, you can give details of what your best references will say. When you demonstrate how well you and your boss got along, the interviewer does not have to ask, "What do you dislike about your current manager?"

Every interview is a stress interview, but sometimes interviewers will ratchet up the stress level. You need to be ready, and that's where we're headed next.

CHAPTER 16
How to Handle Stress and Illegal Questions

THERE IS NO greater fear than fear of the unknown, and that is exactly what you worry about going into a job interview; this worry increases your anxiety level.

While interviewers categorically deny conducting stress interviews, they readily admit that if there is stress on the job, they need to know how a candidate will react to it. Often they will try to re-create it by throwing in the occasional question to see how a candidate maintains her balance: Does she remain calm and analytical? Does her mind still process effectively when under pressure? Can she express herself effectively, and is she in control while managing stressful situations?

Any question you are unprepared for can cause stress. Interviewers can create stress unintentionally, or can consciously use stress to simulate the unexpected and sometimes tense events of everyday business life. Seeing how you handle the unexpected in a job interview gives a fair indication of how you will react to the unexpected when it crops up in real life.

The sophisticated interviewer talks very little, perhaps only 20 percent of the time, and that time is spent asking questions. Few comments, and no editorializing on your answers, means that you get no hint, verbal or otherwise, about your performance.

Interviewers are looking for the candidate who stays calm and continues to process incoming information during stressful events, and having processed it, asks questions for clarification or responds professionally with actions and/or words suitable to the situation and capable of moving it toward a desirable conclusion.

If you are ill prepared for an interview, no one will be able to put more pressure on you than you do on yourself. The only way to combat the stress you feel from fear of the unknown is to be prepared, to know what the stress questions might be, what the interviewer is trying to discover with the question, and to prepare your strategies for these situations. Remember: A stress interview is just a regular interview with the volume turned all the way up—the music is the same, just louder.

What is your greatest weakness?

This is one of the toughest of all interview questions and often comes right after you have been tossed that softball "What is your greatest strength?" question (see Chapter 14).

Every conceivable slick answer has already been used a hundred times, so saying you work too hard isn't going to impress anyone. The truth of the matter is that we all have weaknesses, even you and I, and this is one instance when any interviewer is going to relish an honest answer like a breath of fresh air. Your goal is to be honest and forthright without torpedoing your candidacy.

We all share a weakness: staying current with rapid changes in technology. Changes in technology give everyone an ongoing challenge: getting up to speed with the new skills demanded if you are to do your job well. Your answer can address this very issue and in the process still show that you are someone capable of staying on top of things in a rapidly changing workplace.

First talk about these constantly evolving challenges, then follow with examples that show how you *are* keeping up with technologies that affect your productivity. "I'm currently reading about . . ."; "I just attended a weekend workshop . . ."; or "I'm signed up for classes at . . ."

With this type of answer you identify your weakness as *something that is only of concern to the most dedicated and forward-looking professionals in your field*.

You could also talk about the general difficulties in keeping up with all the deliverables of the job and use it to talk about what you are doing to develop your *multitasking skills*. You can also consider the following as effective alternatives or as additional illustrations if they are demanded:

- If there is a *minor* part of the target job where you lack knowledge—but knowledge you will pick up quickly and can prove that you will pick up quickly—use that.
- Identify a weakness that has no possible relation to the needs of this job. Although if you do this, you might be asked for another example, which will bring you back to the first two options.

How do you go about solving problems in your work?

Every position, from CEO to fast-food server, has its problems and challenges. This question examines your grasp of *critical thinking*, and asks you to explain your approach to problem solving. There is an established approach to problem solving that everyone who gets ahead in her professional life learns. When confronted with a problem, you take these steps:

- Define the problem.
- Identify why it's a problem and whom it's a problem for.
- Identify what's causing the problem.
- Seek input from everyone affected by the problem.
- Identify possible solutions.
- Identify the time, cost, and resources it will take to implement each option.
- Evaluate the consequences of each solution.
- Decide upon the best solution.
- Identify and execute the steps necessary to solve the problem.

Your answer should cover these steps. If asked for a real-world example, you'll have plenty in mind from your TJD exercises. Remember to recall the results and benefits of your solution and the *transferable skills* that came into play.

With hindsight, how could you have improved your progress?

This is a question that asks you to discuss your commitment to success. As professional success affects so many other parts of your life, take time to think through the mistakes you have made and commit to getting better control of your career for the future. Whatever you choose to say, when it comes to questions asking for information detrimental to your candidacy, always put your answer in the past: You woke up, took responsibility, and corrected the situation. Show that, having learned from the experience, you are now committed to ongoing professional development.

What kinds of decisions are most difficult for you?

You are human—admit it, but be careful what you admit. The employer is looking for people who can make decisions and solve problems, not those who'll dither instead of do. You want to come off as someone who's decisive but not precipitate, who considers the implications of actions on outcomes, any side effects those actions might have on other activities, and whether they conflict with existing *systems and procedures* or other company priorities.

If you have ever had to fire someone, you are in luck, because no one likes to do that. Emphasize that, having reached a logical conclusion, you act. If you are not in management, tie your answer to *transferable skills and professional values*: "It's not that I have difficulty making decisions—some just require more consideration than others. A small example might be vacation time. Now, everyone is entitled to it, but I don't believe you should leave your boss in a bind. I think very carefully at the beginning of the year when I'd like to take my vacation, and then think of alternate dates. I go to my supervisor, tell him what I hope to do, and see whether there is any conflict. I wouldn't want to be out of the office for the two weeks prior to a project deadline, for instance. So by carefully considering things far enough in advance, I make sure my plans jibe with my boss and the department for the year."

Here you take a trick question and use it to demonstrate your consideration, analytical abilities, and concern for the department—and for the company's bottom line.

Tell me about the problems you have living within your means.

If you have experienced severe financial difficulties, you'll need to address them and how they have been handled. The answer needs to be carefully thought out and short, emphasizing that you are in control of the situation. Otherwise, say that you continually strive to improve your skills and your living standard: "I know few people who are satisfied with their current earnings. As a professional, I am continually striving to improve my skills and my living standard. But my problems are no different from those of this or any other company—making sure all the bills get paid on time and recognizing that every month and year there are some things that are prudent to do and others that are best deferred."

What area of your skills/professional development do you want to improve at this time?

Another "tell me all your weaknesses" question. Don't damage your candidacy with careless admissions of weakness. Choose a skill where you are competent but that everyone, including the interviewer, knows demands constant personal attention. *Technology skills* as they apply to your job could be a good example of a "weakness" that every committed professional shares. Cite the importance and challenge of staying current in this area and finish with saying, "_____ is so important, I don't think I will ever stop paying attention to this area." Be prepared to explain how you are working on this skill development right now. "In fact, I'm reading a book on this now," or "I'm taking another course next . . ." There are plenty of books and online courses on every topic under the sun, so if you are engaged in your career, you should be able to give some details.

One effective answer to this is to say, "Well, from what you told me about the job, I seem to have all the necessary skills and background. What I would really find exciting is the opportunity to work on a job where . . ." At this point, you replay the skill-development area you cited. This approach allows you to emphasize what you find exciting about the job and that you have all the required *technical skills* and are proactively committed to professional skill development. It works admirably.

You can finish with saying, "These areas are so important that I don't think anyone can be too good or should ever stop trying to polish their skills."

Your application shows you have been with one company a long time without any appreciable increase in rank or salary. Tell me about this.

Analyze why this state of affairs exists. It may be that you like your professional life exactly as it is. You take *pride* in your work and haven't pushed for promotions. If so, tell it like it is, because most people are eager for a promotion—someone who isn't could make for a good hire; it could be your ace.

Here are some tactics you can use. First of all, try to avoid putting your salary history on application forms. No one is going to deny you an interview for lack of a salary history if your skills match those the job requires. And of course, you should never put such unnecessary information on your resume.

Now, we'll address the delicate matter of "Hey, wait a minute; why no promotions?" The interviewer has posed a truly negative inquiry. The more time either of you spend on it, the more time the interviewer gets to devote to concentrating on negative aspects of your candidacy. Make your answer short and sweet, then shut up. For instance, "My current employer is a stable company with a good working environment, but there's minimal growth there in my area—in fact, there hasn't been any promotion in my area since _____. Your question is the reason I am meeting here with you; I have the skills and ability to take on more responsibility, and I'm looking for a place to do that."

In your current job, what should you spend more time on and why?

Without a little self-control you could easily blurt out what you consider to be your greatest weaknesses. Tricky question, but with a little forethought your answer will shine.

Enlightened self-interest dictates that your ongoing career management strategies identify and develop the skills demanded in a constantly changing work environment that make you desirable to employers, and that each of your job changes should occur within the context of an overall career management strategy.

So your answer might address the fact that existing skills always need to be improved and new skills acquired, citing an example of some skill development initiative you are working on now. Unless you are in sales/marketing, you could add that with networking seen as so important by everyone today, you should probably be investing more time in that; in sales and marketing, of course, this is your very lifeblood.

Your answer might include, "With the fast pace of change in our profession, existing skills always need to be improved and new skills learned. For instance, in this job I think the organizational software now available can have a major impact on personal productivity. If I stayed with my current employer this would be a priority, just as it will be when I make the move to my next job; it's in my own best interests to have good skills." With an answer along these lines you show foresight instead of a weakness. You can then end with:

- Courses you have taken and are planning to take
- Books you have read or book clubs to which you belong
- Memberships in professional associations
- Subscriptions to professional journals

Such an answer will identify you as an aware, connected, and dedicated professional.

Are you willing to take calculated risks when necessary?

Confirm your understanding of the question by qualifying it: "How do you define calculated risks? Can you give me an example?" or "Would you run that by me again?" This will give you more information as well as more time to think while the interviewer repeats the question in more detail. You can use this "qualifying the question" technique with tough questions when you want a little recovery time.

Once you understand the question, you'll probably answer, "Yes" if you want the job offer. Be prepared with an example for the possible follow-up question showing how your calculations and preparation minimize potential risk. Whatever your answer, the risk taken must be within the normal bounds of the execution of your duties and in no way jeopardize colleagues or company.

See this pen I'm holding? Sell it to me.

This question often comes up for sales professionals, but every employee needs to know how to *communicate* effectively and sell appropriately—sometimes products, but more often ideas, approaches, and concepts. This is what the interviewer is getting at with this apparently out-of-the-blue request.

As such, you are being examined about your understanding of constitutive/needs-based/ features and benefits sales, how quickly you think on your feet, and how effectively you use verbal communication. For example, say the interviewer holds up a yellow highlighter. First you will want to establish the customer's needs with a few questions like, "What sort of pens do you currently use? Do you use a highlighter? Do you read reports and need to recall important points? Is comfort important to you?" Then you will proceed calmly, "Let me tell you about the special features of this pen and show you how it will satisfy your needs. First of all, it is tailor-made for highlighting reports, and that will save you time in recalling the most important points.

The case is wide for comfort and the base is flat so it will stand up and be visible on a cluttered work area. It's disposable—and affordable enough to have a handful for desk, briefcase, car, and home. And the bright yellow means you'll never lose it." Then close with a smile and a question of your own that will bring a smile to the interviewer's face: "How many gross shall we deliver?"

How will you be able to cope with a change in environment after _____ years with your current company?

Another chance to take an implied negative and turn it into a positive: "That's one of the reasons I want to make a change. After five years with my current employer, I felt I was about to get stale. I have exemplary skills in _____, _____, and _____. It's just time for me to take these skills to a new and more challenging environment and experience some new thinking and approaches. Hopefully, I'll have the chance to contribute from my experience."

Why aren't you earning more at your age?

Accept this as a compliment to your skills and accomplishments. "I have always felt that solid experience would stand me in good stead in the long run and that earnings would come in due course. Also, I am not the type of person to change jobs just for the money. At this point, I have a set of desirable skills [*itemize them as they relate to the job's priorities*] and the time has come for me to join a team that needs and values these skills. How much *should* I be earning now?" The figure could be your offer.

What is the worst thing you have heard about our company?

This question can come as something of a shock. As with all stress questions, your poise under stress is vital: If you can carry off a halfway decent answer as well, you are a winner. The best response to this question is simple. Just say with a smile and a laugh: "You are a tough company to get an interview with, and you demand a lot of your employees. But I actually like that about you, because I'm looking to gain the sort of expertise that will facilitate my professional growth." This way you compliment the company and pass off the negative judgment as a misperception by all those *other* jerks who think hard work is a bad thing.

Why should I hire an outsider when I could fill the job with someone inside the company?

The question isn't as stupid as it sounds. Obviously, the interviewer has examined existing employees with an eye toward their promotion or reassignment. Just as obviously, the job cannot be filled from within the company. If it could be, it would be, and for two very good reasons: It is cheaper for the company to promote from within, and it is better for employee morale.

Hiding behind this intimidating question is a pleasant invitation: "Tell me why I should hire you." Your answer should include two steps. The first is a recitation of your *technical* and *transferable skills*, tailored to the job's needs.

For the second step, realize first that whenever a manager is filling a position, he is looking not only for someone who can do the job, but also for someone who can benefit the department in a larger sense. No department is as good as it could be—each has weaknesses that need strengthening. So in the second part of your answer, include a question of your own: "Those are my general attributes. However, if no one is promotable from inside the company, you must be looking to add strength to your team in a special way. How do you hope the final candidate will be able to benefit your department?" The answer to this is your cue to sell your applicable qualities.

Have you ever had any financial difficulties?

A common question, especially if you deal with money. Tell the truth because when references are checked, salary and credit are at the top of the list. Your answer succinctly gives the circumstances, the facts of your difficulties, and where you stand today in resolving those issues. Do not bring up financial problems until this question is asked or an offer is on the table and references are to be checked.

For someone to check your credit history, he must have your written consent. This is required under the 1972 Fair Credit and Reporting Act. Invariably, when you fill out a job application form, sign it, and date it, you've also signed a release permitting the employer to check your credit history.

If you have had to file for bankruptcy, it will show up in a credit check, so be honest, professional, and as brief as possible. Don't give any information about the circumstances: It isn't necessary and no one wants to know. What employers do want to hear is that you have turned the corner and everything is under control now. They also want to know, very briefly, what you learned and have done to rebuild your credit and get back on your feet.

Financial difficulties aren't the deal breaker they used to be, unless they affect the employer's insurance obligations, and in light of the corporate and personal financial crises of recent years, many corporations are re-evaluating and taking a more realistic stance on these matters. Once it's behind you, get it expunged from your record.

How should I handle a DWI?

Find out if it will show up on a background check, as procedures differ from state to state. If the application asks, answer and leave it be; if not, don't offer this information until background checks are close. Then be brief—"It happened, I was young, etc."—and stress what you learned from it. Try to get it expunged: Google "DWI expunge."

How should I handle a felony?

First, determine if it's on your record, if it will show up in a background check, and what employers in your state can take into consideration. States handle felony records differently, as they do the information an employer may inquire about. Learn what you have to disclose to an employer and don't disclose more than you have to. Briefly, tell the employer what you've learned and that it is behind you. Discrepancies between your application and convictions can cause problems.

There's no need to discuss issues that didn't result in conviction or anything that has been expunged.

Tell me about a time things didn't work out well.

There are two techniques that every skilled interviewer will use, especially if you are giving good answers. With this first technique, the interviewer is looking for negative balance, partly to get a more balanced view of you as a fallible human being, and partly because smart people learn at least as much from their mistakes as from their successes. The trick is to pull something from the past, not the present, and to finish with what you learned from the experience. For example: "That's easy. When I first joined the workforce, I didn't really understand the importance of *systems and procedures*. There was a sales visit report everyone had to fill out after visiting a customer. I always put a lot of effort into it until I realized it was never read; it just went in a file. So I stopped doing it for a few days to see if it made any difference. I thought I was gaining time to make more sales for the company. I was so proud of my extra sales calls, I told the boss at the end of the week. My boss explained that the records were for the long term, so that should my job change, the next salesperson would have the benefit of a full client history. It was a long time ago, but I have never forgotten the lesson: There's always a reason for *systems and procedures*. I've had the best-kept records in the company ever since."

To look for negative confirmation, the interviewer may then say something like, "Thank you. Now can you give me another example?" He is trying to confirm a weakness. If you help, you could cost yourself the job. Here's your reaction: You sit deep in thought for a good ten seconds, then look up and say firmly, "No, that's the only occasion when anything like that happened." Shut up and refuse to be enticed further.

Tell me about a time when you put your foot in your mouth.

Answer this question with caution. The interviewer is examining your ability and willingness to interact pleasantly with others. The question is tricky because it asks you to show yourself in a poor light. Downplay the negative impact of your action and end with positive information about your candidacy. The best thing to do is to start with an example outside of the workplace and show how the experience improved your performance at work.

"About five years ago, I let the cat out of the bag about a surprise birthday party for a friend, a terrific faux pas. It was a mortifying experience, and I promised myself not to let anything like that happen again." Then, after this fairly innocuous statement, you can talk about communications in the workplace: "As far as work is concerned, I always regard employer-employee communications on any matter as confidential unless expressly stated otherwise. So, putting my foot in my mouth doesn't happen to me at work."

What was there about your last company that you didn't particularly like or agree with?

Be careful not to criticize a manager, or you might be seen as a potential management problem. It is safest to say that you didn't have any of these problems. If there was an unhappy work environment and this opinion was shared by many, you can mention it, but remain nonspecific, although you might discuss that some people didn't seem to care about anything they did, and you found this difficult.

Another option: "I didn't like the way some people gave lip service to the 'customer comes first' mantra, but really didn't go out of their way to keep the customer satisfied. I don't think it was a fault of management, just a general malaise that seemed to affect a lot of people."

What do you feel is a satisfactory attendance record?

There are two answers to this question—one if you are in management, and one if you are not. As a manager: "I believe attendance is a matter of management, motivation, and psychology. Letting the employees know you expect their best efforts and won't accept half-baked excuses is one thing. The other is to keep your employees motivated by a congenial work environment and the challenge to stretch themselves. Giving people pride in their work and letting them know you respect them as individuals have a lot to do with it, too."

If you are not in management, the answer is even easier: "I've never really considered it. I work for a living, I enjoy my job, and I'm rarely sick."

What is your general impression of your last company?

Always answer positively. There is a strong belief in management ranks that people who complain about past employers will cause problems for their new ones. Your answer is, "A good department and company to work for." Then smile and wait for the next question. If pressed for more, add, "I had gone as far as I could and could see no opportunities opening up, so I determined it was time to make a strategic career move."

What are some of the things you find difficult to do? Why do you feel that way?

This is a variation on a couple of earlier questions. Remember, anything that goes against the best interests of your employer is difficult to do. Your answer should share a difficulty common to the job and everyone who does that job, and at the same time advance your candidacy; difficult, but not impossible. "That's a tough question. There are so many things that are difficult to stay current with, considering the pace of business today and pace of change technology brings to our profession. One of my problems has been staying on top of the customer base in a productive and responsible fashion. I built my territory and had 140 clients to sell to every month, and I was so busy touching base with all of them that I never got a chance to sell to any of them. So I graded them into three groups. I called on the top 20 percent of my clients every three weeks. The balance of my clients I called on once a month, but with a difference—each month, I marked ten of them to spend time with and really get to know. I still have difficulty reaching all my clients in a month, but with time management, prioritization, and organization, my sales have tripled and are still climbing."

Jobs have pluses and minuses. What were some of the minuses on your last job?

A variation on the question, "What interests you least about this job?" which was handled earlier. Potentially explosive but easily defused. Regardless of your occupation, there is at least one repetitive, mindless duty that everyone groans about but which has to be done. You just need to show that you recognize its importance despite the boredom factor and take care of business responsibly. For example, "Client visit reports are probably the least exciting part of my job. However, I know they are important for reference and continuity, so I do them at the end of the day as part of my daily performance review and next-day planning." This response answers the question without shooting yourself in the foot, and shows that you possess *critical thinking* and *multitasking skills*. You can finish with a nod toward your *professional values* and *teamwork skills*, "Besides, if I don't do the paperwork, that holds up other people in the company."

Or perhaps, "In accounts receivable, it's my job to get the money in to make payroll and good things like that. Half the time, the goods get shipped before I get the paperwork because sales says, 'It's a rush order.' That's a real minus to me. It was so bad at my last company that we tried a new approach. We met with sales and explained our problem. The result was that incremental commissions were based on cash in, not on bill date. They saw the connection, and things are much better now."

What kinds of people do you like to work with?

This is the easy part of what can be a tricky three-part question. Obviously, you like to work with people who are fully engaged in their work and who come to work with a smile and to make a difference with their presence, with people who are there to get results, not just mark time till the end of the day. You like to work with people who have *pride*, honesty, *integrity*, and *commitment* to their work.

What kinds of people do you find it difficult to work with?

This question can stand alone or can be the second part of a three-part question. Your answer comes from understanding why your job exists: It's a small cog in the complex machinery of making a company profitable, so you might say, "People who don't care about their work and don't care about being part of something larger than themselves, people who have the time to find fault but not to find solutions." End by noting that while they aren't the best coworkers, you don't let them interfere with your *motivation*.

Or, "People who don't follow procedures, or slackers—the occasional rotten apples who don't really care about the quality of their work. They're long on complaints, but short on solutions."

How have you successfully worked with this difficult type of person?

Sometimes this question stands alone; other times it's the third part of a three-part question. First, you don't let such people affect your *motivation* or quality of work. Second, you don't buy into their negativism by encouraging them. You are polite and professional but prefer to ally yourself with the people who come to work to make a difference. You maintain cordial relations but don't go out of your way to seek close acquaintance. Life is too short to be de-motivated by people who think their cup is half empty and it's someone else's fault.

Or you might reply with something like: "I stick to my guns, stay enthusiastic, and hope some of it will rub off. I had a big problem with one guy—all he did was complain, and always in my area. Eventually, I told him how I felt. I said if I were a millionaire, I'd clearly have all the answers and wouldn't have to work, but as it was, I wasn't, and had to work for a living. I told him that I really enjoyed his company but I didn't want to hear it anymore. Every time I saw him after that, I presented him with a work problem and asked his advice. In other words I challenged him to come up with positives, not negatives."

You might even end by noting that sometimes you've noticed that such people simply lack enthusiasm and confidence, and that energetic and cheerful coworkers can often change that.

How did you get your last job?

The interviewer is looking for initiative. Show that you went about your search with planning, *organization*, and intelligence, the same way you'd approach a work project. At least show *determination*. For example: "I was turned down for my last job for having too little experience. I asked the manager to give me a trial for the afternoon, then and there. I was given a list of companies they'd never sold to. I picked up the phone and didn't get close to a sale all afternoon, but she could see I had guts."

How would you evaluate me as an interviewer?

The question is dangerous, maybe more so than the one asking you to criticize your boss. If you think the interviewer is a congenital imbecile whom you wouldn't work for on a bet, don't tell the truth, because behind this question is a desire to see your verbal and diplomacy skills in action. This is an instance when honesty is not the best policy: Remember, you are there to get a job offer. It is best to say, "This is one of the toughest interviews I have ever been through, and I don't relish the prospect of going through another. I have great professional skills, but interviewing is not one of them; it's not something I have had much experience doing. Yet I do realize that you are just trying to determine if I have the skills you need." Then go on to explain how your skills match the job. You may choose to finish the answer with a question of your own: "I think I can do this job, and I think I would like it. What do you think?"

Wouldn't you feel better off in another company?

Relax, things aren't as bad as you might assume. This question is usually asked if you are really doing quite well or if the job involves a certain amount of stress. A lawyer, for example, might well be expected to face this one. The trick is not to be intimidated. Your first step is to qualify the question. Relax, take a breath, sit back, smile, and say, "You surprise me. Why do you say that?" The interviewer must then talk, giving you precious time to collect your wits and come back with a rebuttal.

Then answer "no," and explain why. All the interviewer wants to see is how much you know about the company and how determined you are to join its ranks. Overcome the objection with an example showing how you will contribute to the company. You could reply: "Not at all. My whole experience has been with small companies. I am good at my job and in time could become a big fish in a little pond. But that is not what I want. This corporation is a leader in its business. You have a strong reputation for encouraging skills development in your employees. This is the type of environment I want to work in. Coming from a small company, I have done a little bit of everything. That means that no matter what you throw at me, I will learn it quickly."

Then end with a question of your own. In this instance, the question has a twofold purpose: first, to identify a critical area to sell yourself; and second, to encourage the interviewer to imagine you working at the company: "For example, what would be the first project you'll need me to tackle?"

You end with a question of your own that gets the interviewer focusing on those immediate problems. You can then move the conversation forward with an explanation of how your background and experience can help.

What would you say if I told you your presentation this afternoon was lousy?

This question is asked to help a manager understand how emotionally mature you are. When it is a manager's duty to criticize performance, he needs to know that you will respond in a professional and *emotionally mature* way.

"If" is the key word here. The question tests your poise, *critical thinking*, and *communication skills*. Don't assume you are being criticized. An appropriate response would be: "First of all, I would ask which aspects of my presentation were lousy. I would need to find out where you felt the problem was. If there were a miscommunication, I'd clear it up. If the problem were elsewhere, I would seek your advice, confirm that I understood it, and be sure that the problem did not recur."

Building Stress Into a Sequence of Questions

Sometimes an interviewer will build stress into a sequence of questions. Starting off innocently enough, the questions are layered and sequenced to dig deeper and deeper, but these stress question sequences will hold few surprises for you. Let's take the simple example of "Can you work under pressure?"

This example will use a reporter's technique of asking who, what, where, when, why, and how. The technique can be applied to any question you are asked and is frequently used to probe those success stories that sound too good to be true. You'll find them suddenly tagged on to the simple closed-ended questions as well as to the open-ended ones. They can often start with phrases like "Share with me," "Tell me about a time when," or "I'm interested in finding out about," followed by a request for specific examples from your work history.

Can you work under pressure?

A simple, closed-ended question that requires just a yes-or-no answer, but you won't get off so easy.

Good, I'd be interested to hear about a time when you experienced pressure on your job.

An open-ended request to tell a story about a pressure situation. After this, you will be subjected to the layering technique—six layers in the following instance.

Why do you think this situation arose?

It's best if the situation you describe is not a peer's or manager's fault. Remember, you must be seen as a *team player*.

How do you feel others involved could have acted more responsibly?

An open invitation to criticize peers and superiors, which you should diplomatically decline.

Who holds the responsibility for the situation?

Another invitation to point the finger of blame, which should be avoided.

Where in the chain of command could steps be taken to avoid that sort of thing happening again?

This question probes your analytical skills and asks whether you are the type of person who takes the time to revisit the scene of the crime to learn for the next time.

After you've survived that barrage, a friendly tone may conceal another zinger: "What did you learn from the experience?" This question is geared to probe your judgment and *emotional maturity*. Your answer should emphasize whichever of the key professional behaviors your story was illustrating.

When an interviewer feels you were on the edge of revealing something unusual in an answer, you may well encounter "mirror statements." Here, the last key phrase of your answer will be repeated or paraphrased, and followed by a steady gaze and silence. For example, "So, you learned that organization is the key to management." The idea is that the silence and an expectant look will work together to keep you talking. It can be disconcerting to find yourself rambling on without quite knowing why. The trick is knowing when to stop. When the interviewer gives you an expectant look in this context, expand your answer (you have to), but by no more than a couple of sentences. Otherwise, you will get that creepy feeling that you're digging yourself into a hole.

The Illegal Question

Of course, one of the most stressful—and negative—questions is the illegal one, a question that delves into your private life or personal background. Such a question will make you uncomfortable if it is blatant and could also make you angry.

Your aim, however, is to overcome your discomfort and avoid getting angry. You want to get the job offer, and any self-righteous or defensive reaction on your part will ensure that you don't. You may feel angry enough to get up and walk out, or say things like, "These are unfair practices; you'll hear from my lawyer in the morning." But the result will be that you won't get the offer and therefore won't have the leverage you need. Remember, no one is saying you can't refuse the job once it's offered to you.

So what is an illegal question? Title VII is a federal law that forbids employers from discriminating against any person on the basis of sex, age, race, national origin, or religion. More recently, the Americans with Disabilities Act was passed to protect this important minority:

- An interviewer may not ask about your religion, church, synagogue, or parish, the religious holidays you observe, or your political beliefs or affiliations. He may not ask, for instance, "Does your religion allow you to work on Saturdays?" But he may ask something like, "This job requires work on Saturdays. Is that a problem?"
- An interviewer may not ask about your ancestry, national origin, or parentage; in addition, you cannot be asked about the naturalization status of your parents, spouse, or children. The interviewer cannot ask about your birthplace. But he may ask (and probably will, considering the current immigration laws) whether you are a U.S. citizen or a resident alien with the right to work in the United States.
- An interviewer may not ask about your native language, the language you speak at home, or how you acquired the ability to read, write, or speak a foreign language. But he may ask about the languages in which you are fluent if knowledge of those languages is pertinent to the job.

- An interviewer may not ask about your age, your date of birth, whether you are married or pregnant, or the ages of your children. But he may ask you whether you are over eighteen years old.
- An interviewer may not ask about maiden names or whether you have changed your name; your marital status, number of children or dependents, or your spouse's occupation; or whether (if you are a woman) you wish to be addressed as Miss, Mrs., or Ms. But the interviewer may ask about how you like to be addressed (a common courtesy) and whether you have ever worked for the company before under a different name. (If you have worked for this company or other companies under a different name, you may want to mention that, in light of the fact that this prospective manager may check your references and additional background information.)

As you consider a question that seems to verge on illegality, take into account that the interviewer may be asking it innocently and may be unaware of the laws on the matter. Even more likely is that the interviewer really likes you, and is interested in you as a person. When we meet someone new, often some of the first questions will be: Where are you from? Are you married? Have kids? What church do you go to? Bear this in mind so that you don't overreact.

Your best bet is to be polite and straightforward, just as you would be in any other social situation. You also want to move the conversation to an examination of your skills and abilities, and away from personal issues. Here are some common illegal questions—and possible responses. Remember as you frame your answers to the odd illegal question that your objective is to get job offers; if you later decide that this company is not for you, you are under no obligation to accept the position.

What religion do you practice?

In most instances, an interviewer may not ask about religious beliefs. However, as with most illegal questions, it's sometimes in your interest to answer.

You might say, "I attend my church/synagogue/mosque regularly, but I make it my practice not to involve my personal beliefs in my work." Or, "I have a set of beliefs that are important to me, but I do not mix those beliefs with my work and understand this is something employers don't want their people discussing."

If you do not practice a religion, you may want to say something like, "I have a set of personal beliefs that are important to me, but I do not attend organized services at present. And I do not mix those beliefs with my work, if that's what you mean."

Are you married?

If you are, the company is concerned about the impact your family duties and future plans will have on your tenure there. Although illegal if it is asked, it's best to answer this question and remove any doubts the interviewer might otherwise have. Your answer could be, "Yes, I am. Of course, I make a separation between my work life and my family life that allows me to give my all to a job. I have no problem with travel or late hours; those things are part of my work and family obligations have never interfered. My references will confirm this for you."

Do you have/plan to have children?

Most often asked of women in their childbearing years. This isn't any of the interviewer's business, but he may be concerned about whether you will leave the company early to raise a family. Behind the question is the impact of absences on departmental deliverables. You could always answer "no." If you answer "yes," you might qualify it, "but those plans are for way in the future, and they depend on the success of my career. Certainly, I want to do the best, most complete job for this company I can. I consider that my skills are right for the job and that I can make a long-range contribution. I certainly have no plans to leave the company just as I begin to make meaningful contributions."

If the questions become too pointed, you may want to ask—innocently—"Could you explain the relevance of that issue to the position?" That response, however, can seem confrontational; you should only use it if you are extremely uncomfortable, or are quite certain you can get away with it. Sometimes, the interviewer will drop the line of questioning.

Illegal questions tend to arise not out of brazen insensitivity but rather out of an interest in you. The employer is familiar with your skills and background, feels you can do the job, and wants to get to know you as a person. Outright discrimination these days is really quite rare. With illegal questions, your response must be positive—that's the only way you're going to get the job offer.

CHAPTER 17
ANSWERING UNANSWERABLE QUESTIONS

JOB INTERVIEWS ARE consistently scary affairs: You are being judged professionally, and it's easy to *feel* you're being judged as a person too. Almost everyone feels invalidated when things don't pan out. And then every year you read something about the "stupid questions" employers ask, questions like:

"How many children are born every day?"

"If you were asked to unload a 747 full of jelly beans, what would you do?"

"Why are manholes round?"

"What kind of tree would you like to be and why?"

How the hell do you answer questions like these? How do such questions help employers make good hiring decisions? Actually, *most* of these questions aren't as whack-a-doodle as they might sound, and yes, they do all have answers.

Engage with Your Profession, the World, and Your Life

We live in a post-industrial era alternatively known as "the Knowledge Era," "the Digital Age," "the Information Age," and other names. What they all convey is that our jobs increasingly speak to the analysis, manipulation, and movement of information. This makes our analytical and processing abilities increasingly important to potential employers. Some of us have these skills naturally, and some of us don't; however, we can all increase our analytical and processing skills.

Successful professionals consistently engage with professional journals, podcasts, and blogs that address issues relating to their profession. Reading, watching, listening, and engaging in professional discussion with your peers will keep you informed about all the critical issues of your professional arena, the world in which it operates. It will make you a more competent professional with a far wider frame of reference, and together these will hone your analytical skills. It will also make you a more interesting colleague for others who share the same commitment. You've heard of these people before; they all belong to the Inner Circle we talk about in the context of *Knock 'em Dead* professional growth strategy.

If you are thoroughly engaged in your profession and take an interest in the world around you, answering the following mind-boggling questions will become much easier as you become a better-informed and smarter person.

It is also useful to engage in analytical thinking as an integral part of your day by doing things that make you think and feed your mind. Here are a few ideas:

- Watch *Jeopardy!* It is on TV every night and it's thirty minutes of brainteasers. Hell for a week or two because you feel like such a dummy, but then addictive, fun, and educational.
- Read the *New Yorker* magazine online or in print. Killer cartoons and comprehensive coverage of everything from technology to the arts. Read this magazine for a year and you can walk into a reception at the White House and hold conversations with anyone. Okay, I'm exaggerating a bit, but you get the point.
- Lumosity.com is a brain-training website that develops your cognitive skills with puzzles and games.

The point of all this is that these seemingly absurd questions are invariably conceived with a purpose: to evaluate intelligence, analytical, and processing skills as they relate to individual and team performance. We'll start with the easy ones.

What kind of tree would you like to be?

I've never heard it asked and never communicated with anyone who has been asked it, so this one may well be apocryphal, but people claim that it is asked, so what would you say? Think through all the building blocks of the *Knock 'em Dead* approach, things like:

- Think with your professional hat on
- The values and behaviors most valued by employers
- As a manager what makes a good team member

With these thoughts in mind imagine yourself to be a hiring manager asking this question. What are you be thinking? You're wondering about all the obvious issues surrounding skills and the deliverables of the job, and you're wondering about a candidate's values and how she sees herself. With this in mind it isn't really very hard to come up with a reasonable answer.

Remembering that interviews are focused on evaluating the *professional you*, it might be worth skipping ahead to Chapter 20 ("How to Ace the Psychological Tests"), which addresses how employers use aptitude and psychological evaluation as part of the selection process.

Put yourself across the desk. It is easy to see that asking, "How do you see yourself?" is likely to generate a canned answer. But by asking the question in an unusual way you throw the candidate off-guard, and you are likely to get a more revealing answer. This is the thinking that leads interviewers to ask many of the very unsettling questions discussed in this chapter.

In developing ideas for what your answer might be, focus on the behaviors and values that are relevant to your profession and that (in our example) might be applied to a tree—I know this sounds mighty strange but just bear with me and it will all start to make sense.

Enough theory already; let's get to an answer. Determine a tree onto which you can apply *professional values and transferable skills*, something like this:

"I would like to be an American live oak. It is strong with a deep root system that keeps it steady and it survives no matter what the weather. It doesn't matter what you throw at it (even lightning bolts); the live oak can and does take it. Living more than 200 years, it is reliable and provides support and sustenance to many different plants and animals, and its permanence supplies shade and shelter to anyone who needs it.

"It is strong, substantial, deep, reliable, and is always a good landmark."

Finish on a lighter note:

"Oh, and it never sheds all its leaves, so I'd have a head of hair no matter what ;-)."

And you end with a smile (don't use the tag line if the interviewer is bald or thinning unless you too are follically challenged).

Even a crazy-ass question like this can be answered if you know what is important to your work and to being a productive *team player*. In fact, all these seemingly crazy questions have roots in these considerations, because that is what is important to a hiring manager: Find someone who can do the job, play well with others, and not give me headaches.

Why are manhole covers round?

This question examines logic and analytical skills. Asked in the context of a job that deals with design, building, or manufacturing, it also examines spatial intelligence and your understanding of basic design principles. Manhole covers are round because:

- Rectangular manhole covers can fall into the hole
- Round manhole covers cannot fall into the manhole
- Rectangular manhole covers have to be aligned to fit back into the manhole once work is completed
- Round manhole covers don't need to be aligned
- Manhole covers are made of cast iron and are incredibly heavy. If you have to move a heavy object you can either lift it or roll it; rectangular covers have to be lifted to be moved
- Round covers don't have to be lifted and can be rolled

In making these points in an answer you demonstrate analytical skills that nail the problems, causes, and solutions. If you ever face this question, answer it with pleasure in your voice over the elegant simplicity of the design and the very real problem it solves. Your answer will be correct, and your tone of voice will show that you appreciate such thinking.

Name three previous Nobel prize winners.

Who can answer this question and how they answer it holds the solution to how you should approach it.

The only people who can readily answer this question are people who love absorbing information for its own sake; people who are attuned to what is going on in their profession and with an interest in the activities and figures who help make the world a better place—exactly what we have been talking about previously.

Why you give the answer you do is just as important as your answer itself.

There are 573 Nobel prize winners in six categories (Physics, Chemistry, Medicine, Literature, Peace, Economic Sciences). Consequently, I don't think the interviewer will necessarily know if you actually named three Nobel prize winners.

Now, if you just give names, you will probably be asked for your reasoning, so this is one of those questions where you want to forestall further questions and get onto the next topic ASAP. I'd recommend a response and a reason, for example: "Alfred Nobel—he invented dynamite and then left his fortune to making amends via the Nobel Prize. Nelson Mandela, because of all he did to achieve racial equality and peaceful resolution of conflict. Marie Curie, for her discovery of radium and all the implications of that for our modern society."

You tell me, are these all Nobel Prize winners? I honestly don't know. But who cares? The answer shows wide knowledge covering divergent fields and speaks to desirable behaviors and values: getting along with people, finding peaceful resolutions to conflict, making a change for good.

"What If" Questions

We now come to questions that everyone asks about what you would do in different situations. The key to answering them all is showing that when presented with a challenge, you automatically examine it from different perspectives (evaluating the upside and downside of each) before offering a solution.

Let's start with a question that managers from the grocery chain Trader Joe's are famous for asking candidates:

If I came to your house for dinner what would you serve?

This is not about mentioning their products; it is, of course, about how you decide what to serve. So you'd ask about food allergies, refreshment preferences, dietary restrictions for religious or other reasons, favorite and least favorite foods. Then you'd devise a menu and run it by the manager's administrative assistant to double-check the choices before you started implementation. You'd even go a little further and ask about environmental allergies—so you have time to put those ten cats outside and vacuum your home.

If you had a choice between two superpowers (being invisible or able to fly) which would you choose?

This one sometimes gets asked by product managers for high-tech companies, as well as in interviews for evangelist sales and marketing positions. Again it is not so much the answer as your reasoning. You might say, "If I were invisible no one would see what I am doing, which would be a negative, and I could also be perceived as deceptive. On the other hand, flying? That's going to get anyone's attention, plus you can get much more done."

A variation of this question is, "If you could be a superhero, who would you be?" Your answer can be the same—just give a name to the dude that can fly, and no, it's not Mighty Mouse.

Who would win in a fight between Spiderman and Batman?

There is no right answer. I checked this out online and found hundreds of pages of people arguing this issue—go figure. Marc Hughes, the film critic at *Forbes*, has been quoted as saying, "It's impossible to accurately answer a question about comic book characters." So what do you say? I'd quote Marc Hughes in response to this question.

Who's your favorite Disney Princess?

Cinderella, Esmeralda, Rapunzel . . . there have to be a hundred of them. Who knows and who even cares? All that matters is that you have a name and a reason. Fortunately, princesses are usually sickeningly perfect, so pick a name, any name, and align her behaviors and values with behaviors and values we talk about elsewhere in the book. The important thing is to show you think about the answer and that the answer you give reveals something about the *professional you*.

Describe the color yellow to somebody who is blind.

This one is about listening and analytical skills. So you turn the challenge into questions: "I would ask whether or not you can experience colors; what colors you do you 'see.' I'd ask how you experience each of these colors. With this information I can identify how you cognitively experience color and also understand the vocabulary you use to express your understanding. This would give me the base data to evaluate and turn into metaphors that you're most likely to interpret accurately."

If you were shrunk to the size of a pencil and put in a blender, how would you get out?

Any eight-year-old kid can answer this, but we adults have forgotten what the undersides of chairs and tables look like. With that change of viewpoint as we got older, we lost the fantasy and invention that went with being short (remember underneath that table, when it was a cave, a fort, a tepee?). We also lose our sense of wonder and creativity.

The question poses a fantasylike situation. Once you work your way into it, the question becomes an exercise in basic logic. You'll kick yourself if you haven't worked out the answer: "A pencil is about seven inches long, and a blender runs six to twelve inches tall on the inside and rarely more than five inches across at the mouth. If I were shrunk small enough to fit in a blender it would mean that my legs would still be long enough to reach out and brace against the sides; gradually I could work my way up a few inches until I could reach the lip and haul myself out."

Why are there ridges around a quarter?

Unless you are a numismatist you won't know this one, which is perhaps why the only known occurrences of this question occur in financial houses. This is a question that inquires into a candidate's involvement with the arcane details of coins and money.

The ridges around the outside of some coins are called *reeded edges*, and they are there to:

- Make counterfeiting that much more difficult.
- Prevent theft and fraud. Look at any old gold or silver coins without reeded edges and you will see that many of them have tiny slivers of the gold or silver shaved off. The precious metal was stolen and the coin then fraudulently passed on at its face value.

Reeded edges were invented to prevent this theft and fraud when our coinage was gold and silver based.

What would you do if you were the one survivor in a plane crash?

Always look for what is behind the question: A plane crash is a disaster and by applying the question to the workplace you can translate it this way: Things go wrong in the best-run departments, and the interviewer wants to know about your reactions to stress. Your answer, then, should be about remaining calm under stress, taking calmly considered actions that exhibit leadership, creativity, practicality, and logic.

First of all you display common sense: For safety you get yourself away from the wreckage and regroup. What do you need? Water, shelter, communication, and heat, so you return to the wreckage and search for water, food, clothing or other coverings, lighters, and matches.

Most problematic is going to be finding matches or lighters because of security regulations, so you look for emergency supplies that exist in every cabin and look for the carry-on baggage of the flight crew. As you do these things you look for signs of life.

Next you withdraw and decide on where you will establish a base of operations: somewhere that offers defense against the elements and predators. In short you stay calm enough to make sensible decisions that can help resolve a bad situation.

If you were asked to unload a Boeing 767 full of jelly beans, what would you do?

It's about how well you listen to the question, which is not how you would do it but what you would do. This means the short answer is, "I'd do it." But the smart candidate would answer, "I'd do it of course, but I'd want to do the best job possible as efficiently as possible so I'd want to know where the jelly beans are to be moved to, how they are packed now, if I need to be concerned about repackaging, and the time by which the task needs to be completed."

"Next I'd want to get onsite and evaluate the problem firsthand and discover what resources are available to help execute the task—equipment, people, and money."

You'd finish with something along the lines of, "Then I'd devise a plan of attack that would deliver the desired outcome in the time available. From there I would roll up my sleeves and start work, constantly evaluating and revising as I went along."

How many children are born every day?

We started the chapter with discussion of taking an interest in the world around you, and that answering these mind-boggling questions will become much easier if you do.

You might not know the answer but you can think of global associations involved with the well-being of children and say that you would consult these resources. Incidentally, UNICEF estimates 353,000 children are born a day. That's 225 a minute or 4.3 babies every second.

Design a spice rack for the blind.

This is a question that seeks your ability to think like your customer so that you can deliver what that customer needs; it also requires you to think of cost of solutions from the company perspective.

There are a number of common-sense approaches to this question. You want to suggest some options and a means of evaluating them. Since it all begins with the customer, you would want to know what suggestions blind people have? You could create a focus group to generate some starter ideas and ask participants to enrich their suggestions.

Perhaps the most utilitarian approach is already in use:

- Most often used
- Less frequent but necessary
- Hot and spicy

Blind people can read and write so three broad categories based on usage that incorporates an alphabetical system coupled with peel-off braille stickers would certainly be a front-runner. Finally, you'd need to construct a cabinet to hold the spices and their labels, one without any sharp edges or fittings that could cut or snag.

Questions to Determine High Analytical Skills

Behavioral questions ("Tell me about a time when . . .") examine past performance to predict future behaviors while situational questions ("What is the problem with this invoice?") strive to confront candidates with typical on-the-job challenges.

There are also a limitless number of questions that examine analytical skills. You could face these types of questions in any job interview, but you are far more likely to face them if you work in professions that demand high analytical skills: Technology, Science, Research, Finance, Auditing, and Accounting. These and other statistics- and research-oriented occupations that demand superior analytical skills are the most likely to present you with seemingly odd questions.

Additionally, these questions are intended to examine your love of problem solving and the approaches to analytical examination that you have mastered.

Defining Problems

Many of these questions, by their very nature ("How many windows are there in Seattle?") have no definitively "correct" answer. How you explain your approach to answering the question or solving the proffered problem is just as important as any final answer you might offer. The interviewer is just as interested in how you define the problem and break it down into problems small enough that there are business, common-sense, and analytical tools available to process them.

These questions all require that you define the problem from different perspectives; in other words, stepping back from the challenge, examining what has to be achieved by whom, for whom, in what time frame, and the potholes to be avoided along the way.

How many piano tuners are there in Chicago?

Just like the "number of windows in Seattle," no one knows. This question and others like it (some to follow) have become known as *Fermi* equations or estimates. A Fermi estimate seeks to quantify problems that would be extremely difficult, if not impossible, to actually measure.

Enrico Fermi was a physicist, who as Wikipedia says, was known for his ability to make good approximate calculations with little or no actual data. Fermi problems typically involve making logical guesstimates about the upper and lower ranges of likely quantities.

This type of estimate involves careful analysis of the problem to break it down into challenges that can be defined and therefore are more likely to be fairly accurately measured. In this instance we would need to know the number of households owning pianos, the number of public buildings housing pianos, the frequency with which pianos are typically tuned (usually on an annual basis), and how long a tuning takes (1–2 hours).

We should also know how many a single piano tuner could expect to tune in an average work week.

Such a series of rough estimates are then multiplied together (by some mathematical chicanery way above my pay grade) to deliver an answer that is within the bounds of reason. A Fermi estimate takes each of the above considerations and turns them into a series of equations that will generate an answer that is within the right range without any claim to precise numerical accuracy.

Other Fermi questions might include, "How many basketball[s] can you fit in this room?" which poses the challenges of evaluating spheres fitting into rectangles. Or, "If you had a machine that produced $100 for life, what would you be willing to pay for it today?" This would require estimates of life expectancy, expected standard of living, inflation, and cost of living based on locale. "How many cows are in the United States?" How do we break this down? How many states? How many farms per state? How many cows per farm, etc. Your answer would begin, "Let's say there are . . ."

There is an endless supply of Fermi-style questions. When you hear an incredibly complex question, you are likely facing a Fermi equation. Your initial challenge is to break it down into component challenges that are small and defined enough to be evaluated (even a dummkopf like me can do that), then depending on your mathematical abilities to go as deep into creating and solving the equations as your professional skills will allow.

CHAPTER 18
WELCOME TO THE REAL WORLD

AS A RECENT graduate, most likely entering the professional world for the first time, you can expect questions designed to determine your potential.

Corporate recruiters liken the gamble of hiring recent graduates to laying down wines for the future: Some will develop into full-bodied, excellent vintages, but others will be disappointments. When hiring professionals with work experience, there is a track record to evaluate; with recent graduates, there is little or nothing. Often, the only solid things an interviewer has to go on are the degree, SAT scores, and that ubiquitous burger-flipping job. That's not much on which to base a hiring decision.

Of all the steps a recent graduate will take up the ladder of success over the years, none is more important or more difficult than getting a foot on that first rung. You have no idea how the professional game is played and you are up against thousands of other grads with pretty much the same to offer. Differentiating yourself by demonstrating your understanding of the professional world and your motivation and potential will be important tools in helping get your career off to a good start.

Interviewers will look at what you have done to show initiative, and how willing you are to learn, grow, and get the job done.

Your goal is to stand out from all the other entry-level candidates as someone altogether different: You are more engaged in the success of your professional life, more knowledgeable about the job and the world in which it functions, and more prepared to listen, learn, and do whatever it takes to earn your place on a professional team. Don't be like thousands of others who, in answer to questions about their greatest strength, reply lamely, "I'm good with people" or, "I like working with others." Answers like this brand you as average. To stand out, a recent graduate must recount a past situation that illustrates *how* she is good with people, or one that demonstrates an ability to be a *team player*.

Fortunately, the *transferable skills and professional values* discussed throughout the book are just as helpful for getting your foot on the ladder as they are for increasing your employability and aiding your climb to the top.

It isn't necessary to have snap answers ready for every question, and you never will. It is more important for you to pause after a question and collect your thoughts before answering: That pause shows that you think before you speak, an admired trait in the professional world. Remember that *critical thinking* is one of the *transferable skills*.

Asking for a question to be repeated is useful to gain time and is quite acceptable, as long as you don't do it with every question. And if a question stumps you, as sometimes happens, do not stutter incoherently. It is sometimes best to say, "I don't know" or, "I'd like to come back to that later." Odds are the interviewer will forget to ask again; if he does come back to it, at least your mind, processing in the background, has had some time to come up with an answer.

The following questions are commonly asked of entry-level professionals, but these are not the only questions you will be asked, so you will still need to study the other chapters on turning interviews into offers. For example, the first two questions you are likely to face at most of the job interviews you go to over your entire career are likely to be, "Tell me a little about yourself" and "What do you know about our company?" The questions in this chapter are just those aimed exclusively at entry-level professionals.

How did you get your summer jobs?

Employers look favorably on recent graduates who have any work experience, no matter what it is. In fact internships are the new entry-level jobs; it is getting increasingly hard to get full-time professional work right out of college without having had internships. Employers always say, "If they have had internship experience, they manage their time better, are more realistic, and more mature. Any work experience gives us much more in common." So, as you think about some of those crummy jobs you held, take the time to consider, in hindsight, about what you actually learned about the professional world from that experience.

It's not the job that defines you, it's what you bring to the job that defines you; countless successful people in all professions trace their big breaks back to going above and beyond with menial jobs. At any job you can learn that business is about making a profit, that making a profit means taking care of the little things . . . and that when you are starting out, your job is just dealing with the little things. You also learned about doing things more efficiently, *working together as a team*, *solving problems*, adhering to *systems and procedures* (which are always there for good reason), and putting in whatever effort it took to get the job done right. In short, you treated your summer jobs, no matter how humble, as a launch pad for greater things.

In this particular question, the interviewer may also be looking for initiative, *creativity*, and flexibility. Here's an example: "In my town, summer jobs were hard to come by, but I applied to each local restaurant for a position waiting tables, called the manager at each one to arrange an interview, and finally landed a job at one of the most prestigious. I was assigned to the afternoon shift, but because of my quick work, accurate billing, and ability to keep customers happy, they soon moved me to the evening shift. I worked there for three summers, and by the time I left, I was responsible for the training and management of the night-shift waiters, the allotment of tips, and the evening's final closing and accounting. All in all, my experience showed me the mechanics of a small business and of business in general."

Which of the jobs you have held have you liked least?

It is likely that your work experience has contained a certain amount of repetition and drudgery, as all starter jobs do. So beware of saying that you hated a particular job "because it was boring." Regardless of your occupation, there is at least one repetitive, mindless duty that everyone groans about, but which nevertheless goes with the territory. The job you liked least or what you liked least about a job, and how you express it, speaks to your willingness to take the ups and the downs that go with every job. Put your answer in the past; perhaps, "Burger King—hated smelling of french fries . . ." Then show that you learned something, too. "When you get involved, there's always something to learn. I learned that _____." End by moving the conversation forward. "Every job I've held has given me new insights. All of my jobs had their good and bad points, but I've always found that if you want to learn, there's plenty to pick up every day. Each experience was valuable." Notice how this response also shows that you are *organized* and possess *critical thinking* and *multitasking skills*.

You should be prepared with examples of things you have learned from those Burger King jobs, and if examples don't jump to your mind as you read this, refer back to the *transferable skills and professional values*.

If the question is, "What interests you least about this job?", it's because interviewers want to gauge your understanding of the work, and when you don't have any real-world experience this also evaluates your motivation in researching the job and the profession.

One way to prepare for this question is to make it part of your social networking research; in fact, it might make a good question to ask in one of your LinkedIn group discussions: "What's the least interesting part of the job, and how do you make yourself pay attention to the boring but necessary details?"

What are your future vocational plans?

The mistake all entry-level professionals make is to say, "In management," because they think that shows drive and ambition. But it has become such a trite answer that it immediately generates a string of questions most recent graduates can't answer, questions like, "A manager in what area?" and, "What is a manager's job?" Your safest answer identifies you with the profession you are trying to break into and shows you have your feet on the ground: "I want to get ahead in _____, but without real experience it is difficult to see where the opportunities will be and how my skills will develop to meet them. I intend to quickly develop a clear understanding of how to deal with the problems and challenges that lie within my area of responsibility. I know that I want to make a home in this profession and channel my skills into my profession's areas of growth, and with the support of a good manager, I think these plans will unfold in a logical manner. Right now I need the opportunity to roll up my sleeves and start earning that expertise."

What college did you attend, and why did you choose it?

The college you attended isn't as important as your reasons for choosing it—the question examines your reasoning process. Emphasize that it was your choice, and that you didn't go there as a result of your parents' desires or because generations of your family have always attended the Acme School of Welding. Focus on the practical: "I went to _____; it was a choice based on practicality. I wanted a school that would give me a relevant education and prepare me for the real world. _____ has a good record for turning out students fully prepared to take on responsibilities in the real world. It is [or isn't] a big school, and [or but] it has certainly taught me some big lessons about the value of [*transferable skills and professional values*] in the real world of business."

Are you looking for a permanent or temporary job?

This question is often asked of young candidates. The interviewer wants reassurance that you are genuinely interested in the position and won't disappear in a few months. Go beyond saying, "Permanent." Explain why you want the job: "Of course, I am looking for a permanent job. I intend to make my career in this field, and I want the opportunity to learn the business, face new challenges, and learn from experienced professionals like you." You will also want to qualify the question with one of your own: "Is this a permanent or a temporary position you are trying to fill?" Don't be scared to ask. The occasional unscrupulous employer will hire someone fresh out of school for a short period of time—say, for one particular project—then lay him off.

How did you pay for college?

Avoid saying, "Oh, Daddy handled all of that." Your parents may have helped you out, but if you can, emphasize that you worked part-time as much as you could. People who paid for their own education make big points with employers, because it shows *motivation*, and the experience always delivers a better grasp of the professional world. If this isn't you, find and listen to someone who can tell you what working in the professional world teaches you, and use the knowledge.

How do you rank among your peers?

The question examines your self-esteem. Look at yourself and your peers in different ways until you can come up with a viewpoint that gives you an edge. In some cases it may be possible for you to quantify this—"I graduated twelfth in my class at MIT with a 4.0 GPA." If you can't say something like this, and perhaps came from a background where such a start was never in the cards, you might talk about being the first person in your family to graduate, or working since you were ten. Your goal is to differentiate yourself from your peers, and in this example to show that you are professionally grounded with a life experience that gives you greater professional maturity than many of your peers.

I'd be interested to hear about some things you learned in school that could be used on the job.

The interviewer wants to hear about *real-world* skills, so explain what the experience of college taught you about the world of work, rather than specific courses. Use internships or any work experience to differentiate yourself.

You can find examples in every college activity that gave you the opportunity to develop *transferable skills and professional values*. Your answer might say, in part, "Within academic and other on-campus activities, I always looked for the opportunity to apply and develop some of the practical skills demanded in the professional world, such as _____."

Do you like routine tasks/regular hours?

The interviewer knows from bitter experience that most recent grads hate routine and are hopeless as employees until they come to an acceptance of such facts of life. Explain that routine is the efficient cycle of procedures that deliver services and products to the company's customer base, you appreciate that the routine and the repetitive have a role in even the most creative of jobs, and you understand that it is only by paying attention to the repetitive details that the work gets done. If regular hours are required, respond, "A company expects to make a profit, so the doors have to be open for business on a regular basis."

What have you done that shows initiative and willingness to work?

You can tell a story about how you landed or created a job for yourself, or got involved in some volunteer work. Your answer should show that you both handled unexpected problems calmly and anticipated others. Your *motivation* is demonstrated by the ways you overcame obstacles. For example: "I was working in a warehouse and found that a shipment was due; I knew that room had to be made. I came in on a Saturday, figured out how much room I needed, cleaned up the mess on the loading dock, and made room in the warehouse. When the shipment arrived, the truck just backed in."

After your illustration, recap with something similar to, "I stick with my *commitments*. I am invested in doing good work and commit whatever time and effort is necessary to finish tasks properly, because I know other people's productivity depends on all aspects of my work being done properly."

After an effort above and beyond the call of duty, a manager might congratulate you; if so, you can conclude your answer with that endorsement: "The manager happened along just when I was finishing the job and said she wished she had more people who took such pride in their work."

How do you take direction?

Can you take direction and criticism not only when it is carefully and considerately given, but more importantly when it *isn't*? Can you follow directions and accept constructive criticism, or are you a difficult, high-maintenance young know-it-all?

If you take offense easily or bristle when your mistakes are pointed out, you won't last long with any employer. Competition is fierce at the entry level, so take this as another chance to set yourself apart: "Yes, I can take instruction—and more important, I can take constructive criticism without feeling hurt. Even with the best intent, I will still make mistakes, and at times someone will have to put me back on the right track. I know that if I'm ever to rise in the company, I must be open to direction."

Have you ever had difficulties getting along with others?

This question examines your people skills and, by extension, your *manageability*. Are you a *team player*, or are you going to be a cog that doesn't mesh, and so disrupts the department's functioning and makes the manager's life miserable?

You can give a yes-or-no answer and shut up, but if you think through what you are going to say, your answer can also emphasize your *transferable skills and professional values*. In this case, you say that there are two types in every department: the type who is engaged and committed to peak performance every day, and the type who does his job but without the same level of *commitment*. You can and do get on with everyone, but tend to bond more with the people who take a genuine *pride* in becoming their best.

What type of position are you interested in?

Another entry-level question that tempts you to mention management. Tell the interviewer you are interested in an entry-level job, which is what you will be offered anyway. "I am interested in an entry-level position that will enable me to learn this business from the ground up and will give me the opportunity to grow professionally when and as I prove myself."

What qualifications do you have that will make you successful in this field?

There is more to answering this question than reeling off your academic qualifications. You will also want to explain that your skills match the job's responsibilities, and talk about the *transferable skills and professional values* that will help you do the job well. Include any relevant work experience to support your argument; even a little experience is a better argument than none. It's a wide-open question that says, "Hey, we're looking for an excuse to hire you. Give us some help."

Why do you think you would like this type of work?

Answering requires you to have researched job functions. One thing you can do is prepare by networking with people already doing this job. Ask what the job is like and what that person does day-to-day, what are the challenges related to each major responsibility of the job, and how that person executes his work in ways that *anticipate and prevent these problems* from arising. Armed with these insights into the realities of the job, you can show that you understand what you are getting into. "I think the big challenges with this job are _____, and helping people solve their problems is just the kind of work I enjoy."

What's your idea of how this industry works?

The interviewer does not want a dissertation, just the reassurance that you don't think this company and the business world in general work along the same lines as a registered charity. Your understanding should be something like this: "The role of any company is to make as much money as possible, as quickly and efficiently as possible, and in a manner that will encourage repeat business from the existing client base and new business from word of mouth and reputation." Finish with the observation that it is every employee's role as a team member to help achieve those goals: "I am a small but important cog within this moneymaking machinery. I need to mesh well with the other cogs in my department so that we can collectively deliver on the department's responsibilities. On an individual basis my job is to enhance productivity and profitability by the timely identification, anticipation, prevention, and solution of the problems that arise within my areas of professional expertise."

Why do you think this industry will sustain your interest over the long haul?

You can expect interviewers to ask questions that gauge your level of interest. You need to know what is going on in whatever profession and industry you intend to enter, because you will be asked.

Your answer should speak both to your pragmatism and your motivation. "I have always been interested in [*your new profession/industry*]. I believe it offers stability and professional growth potential over the years [*explain why*]. Also, I'll be using skills [*itemize strong skill sets that are relevant to the job*] that are areas of strength, from which I derive great personal satisfaction."

What do you think determines progress in a good company?

These pages have given you a clear blueprint for professional advancement. Your answer will reference the deliverables of the job as defined in your TJD and the *transferable skills* that help you execute every aspect of your job effectively, thereby becoming a productive member of the team.

Finish by referring to the *professional values* of *integrity*, *commitment*, and a willingness to play by the rules (*systems and procedures*).

Do you think grades should be considered by first employers?

If your grades were good, the answer is obviously "yes." If they weren't, your answer needs a little more thought: "Of course, an employer should take everything into consideration. Along with grades there should be an evaluation of real *motivation* and *manageability*, the candidate's understanding of how business works, and actual work experience; plus, the best academics don't always make the most productive professionals. Einstein and Edison, two of the most intellectually and economically productive minds of modern times, had terrible academic records."

Many candidates are called for entry-level interviews, but only those who prepare themselves with an understanding of their target jobs will be chosen. Preparation takes time, so don't leave preparing for them until the last minute. You are taking a new product to market. Accordingly, you've got to analyze what it can do, who is likely to be interested, and how you are going to sell it to them. Start now and hone your skills to get a head start on your peers; you'll get more interviews, and the more you interview, the better you'll get.

CHAPTER 19
STRANGE VENUES FOR JOB INTERVIEWS

LEARN THE TIPS that will help you master interviews in noisy, distracting hotel lobbies, restaurants, at poolside, and in other unusual settings.

Why are some interviews conducted in strange places? Are meetings in noisy, distracting hotel lobbies designed as a form of torture? What are the real reasons that an interviewer invites you to eat at a fancy restaurant?

For the most part, these tough-on-the-nerves situations happen because the interviewer is a busy person, fitting you into a busy schedule. A woman I know had heard stories about tough interview situations but never expected to face one herself. It happened at a retail convention in Arizona, to which she had been asked for a final interview. The interview was conducted by the pool. The interviewer was there, taking a short break between meetings, in his bathing suit. The first thing the interviewer did was suggest that my friend slip into something comfortable.

That scenario may not lurk in your future, but the chances are you will face many tough interview situations in your career. They call for a clear head and a little gamesmanship if you want to stay ahead of the competition. The interviewee at the pool used both. She removed her jacket, folded it over the arm of the chair, and seated herself, saying pleasantly, "That's much better. Where shall we begin?"

It isn't easy to remain calm at such times. On top of interview nerves, you're worried about being overheard in a public place, or (worse) surprised by the appearance of your current boss. That last item isn't too far-fetched. It actually happened to a reader from San Francisco. He was being interviewed in the departure lounge at the airport when his boss walked through the arrivals door. Oops—he had asked for the day off "to go to the doctor."

Could he have avoided the situation? Certainly, if he had asked about privacy when the meeting was arranged. That would have reminded the interviewer of the need for discretion. The point is to do all you can in advance to make such a meeting as private as possible. Once that's done, you can ignore the rest of the world and concentrate on the interviewer's questions.

Hotel Lobbies and Other Strange Places

Strange interview situations provide other wonderful opportunities to embarrass yourself. You come to a hotel lobby in full corporate battle dress: coat, briefcase, perhaps an umbrella. You sit down to wait for the interviewer. "Aha," you think to yourself, opening your briefcase, "I'll show him my excellent work habits by delving into this computer printout."

That's not such a great idea. Have you ever tried rising with your lap covered with business papers, then juggling the briefcase from right hand to left to accommodate the ritual handshake? It's quite difficult. Besides, while you are sitting in nervous anticipation, pre-interview tension has no way of dissipating. Your mouth will become dry, and your "Good morning, I'm pleased to meet you" will come out sounding like a cat being strangled.

To avoid such catastrophes in places like hotel lobbies, first remove your coat on arrival. Instead of sitting, walk around a little while you wait. Even in a small lobby, a few steps back and forth will help you reduce tension to a manageable level. Keep your briefcase in your left hand (unless you are a leftie) at all times—it makes you look purposeful, and you won't trip over it when you meet the interviewer.

If, for any reason, you must sit, breathe deeply and slowly. This will help control the adrenaline that makes you feel jumpy.

A strange setting can actually put you on equal footing with the interviewer. Neither of you is on home turf, so in many cases the interviewer will feel just as awkward as you do. A little gamesmanship can turn the occasion to your advantage.

To gain the upper hand, get to the meeting site early to scout the territory. By knowing your surroundings, you will feel more relaxed. Early arrival also allows you to control the outcome of the meeting in other subtle ways. You will have time to stake out the most private spot in an otherwise public place. Corners are best. They tend to be quieter, and you can choose the seat that puts your back to the wall (in a physical sense, that is). In this position, you have a clear view of your surroundings and will feel more secure. The fear of being overheard will evaporate.

The situation is now somewhat in your favor. You know the locale, and the meeting place is as much yours as the interviewer's. You will have a clear view of your surroundings, and odds are that you will be more relaxed than the interviewer. When she arrives, say, "I arrived a little early to make sure we had some privacy. I think over here is the best spot." With that positive demonstration of your organizational abilities, you give yourself a head start over the competition.

The Meal Meeting

Breakfast, lunch, and dinner are the prime choices for interviewers who want to catch the seasoned professional off-guard. In fact, the meal is arguably the toughest of all tough interview situations. The setting offers the interviewer the chance to see you in a non-office (and therefore more natural) setting, to observe your social graces, and to consider you as a whole person. Here, topics that would be impossible to address in the traditional office setting will surface, often with virtually no effort on the part of the interviewer. The slightest slip in front of that wily old pirate—thinly disguised in a Brooks Brothers suit—could get your candidacy deep-sixed in a hurry.

Usually you will not be invited to a "meal meeting" until you have already demonstrated that you are capable of doing the job. An invitation to a meal means that you are under strong consideration, and therefore intense scrutiny.

This meeting is often the final hurdle and could lead directly to the job offer—assuming that you properly handle the occasional surprises that arise. The interviewer's concern is not whether you can do the job but whether you have the growth potential that will allow you to fill more senior slots as they become available.

But be careful. Many have fallen at the final hurdle in a close-run race. Being interviewed in front of others is bad enough; eating and drinking in front of them at the same time only makes it worse. If you knock over a glass or dribble spaghetti sauce down your chin, the interviewer will be so busy smirking that he won't hear what you have to say.

To be sure that he remains as attentive to the positive points of your candidacy as possible, let's discuss table manners.

Your social graces and general demeanor at the table can tell as much about you as your answer to a question. For instance, over-ordering food or drink can signal poor self-discipline. At the very least, it will call into question your judgment and maturity. High-handed behavior toward waiters and busboys could reflect negatively on your ability to get along with subordinates and on your *leadership skills*. Those concerns are amplified when you return food or complain about the service, actions which, at the very least, find fault with the interviewer's choice of restaurant.

By the same token, you will want to observe how your potential employer behaves. After all, you are likely to become an employee, and the interviewer's behavior to servers in a restaurant can tell you a lot about what it will be like on the job:

- Alcohol: Soon after being seated, you will be offered a drink—if not by your host, then by the waiter. There are many reasons to avoid alcohol at interview meals. The most important reason is that alcohol fuzzes your mind, and research proves that stress increases the intoxicating effect of alcohol. So, if you order something to drink, stick with something nonalcoholic, such as a club soda, Coke, or Pepsi, or simply a glass of water.

  If you do have a drink, never have more than one. If there is a bottle of wine on the table, and the waiter offers you another glass, place your hand over the top of your glass. It is a polite way of signifying no.

  You may be offered alcohol at the end of the meal. The rule still holds true—turn it down. You need your wits about you even if the interview seems to be drawing to a close. Some interviewers will try to use those moments, when your defenses are at their lowest, to throw in a couple of zingers.
- Smoking: Don't smoke unless encouraged. If both of you are smokers, and you are encouraged to smoke, never smoke between courses, only at the end of a meal. Even the most confirmed nicotine addicts, like the rest of the population, hate smoke while they are eating.
- Utensils: Keep all your cups and glasses at the top of your place setting and well away from you. Glasses are knocked over at a cluttered table most often when one stretches for the condiments or gesticulates to make a point.

Here are some other helpful hints:

- Never speak with your mouth full.
- To be on the safe side, order something that is easy to eat, as you are there for talking, not eating. Of course, while this rule makes sense in theory, you probably will be asked to order first, so ordering the same thing can become problematic. Solve the problem before

you order by complimenting the restaurant during your small talk and then, when the menus arrive, asking, "What do you think you will have today?"

- Do not change your order once it is made, and never send the food back.
- Be polite to your waiters, even when they spill soup in your lap.
- Don't order expensive food. Naturally, in our heart of hearts, we all like to eat well, especially on someone else's tab. But don't be tempted. When you come right down to it, you are there to talk and be seen at your best, not to eat.
- Eat what you know. Stay away from awkward, messy, or exotic foods (e.g., artichokes, long pasta, and escargot, respectively). Ignore finger foods, such as lobster or spare ribs. In fact, you should avoid eating with your fingers altogether, unless you are in a sandwich joint, in which case you should make a point of avoiding the leaky, overstuffed menu items.
- Don't order salad. The dressing can often get messy. If a salad comes with the meal, request that the dressing be on the side. Then, before pouring it on, cut up the lettuce.
- Don't order anything with bones. Stick with fillets; there are few simple, gracious ways to deal with any type of bone.
- Checks and Goodbyes: I know an interviewer whose favorite test of composure is to have the waiter, by arrangement, put the bill on the interviewee's side of the table. She then chats on, waiting for something interesting to happen. If you ever find yourself in a similar situation, never pick up the check, however long it is left by your plate. When ready, your host will pick it up, because that's the protocol of the occasion. By the same token, you should never offer to share payment.

When parting company, always thank the host for her hospitality and the wonderful meal. Of course, you should be sure to leave on a positive note by asking good-naturedly what you have to do to get the job.

Strange interview situations can arise at any time during the interview cycle, and in any public place. Wherever you are asked to go, keep your guard up. Your table manners, listening skills, and overall social graces are being judged. The question on the interviewer's mind is: Can you be trusted to represent the company gracefully and with a professional demeanor?

CHAPTER 20
How to Ace the Psychological Tests

CAREFUL! ANSWERING THESE questions casually can be hazardous to your professional health.

Most private-sector applications of the polygraph test, voice-stress analysis, and other electronic screening methods have been banned by Act of Congress. While many government personnel (for instance, those involved in drug interdiction activities) are still subject to these tests, the majority of private employers use psychological tests to weed out what they consider to be undesirable job applicants. These tests may be known as aptitude tests, personality profiles, personnel selection tests, or skills, aptitude, and integrity tests, but in the end they are all the same thing: an attempt to find out if you show signs of being a "risky" hire.

Psychological exams come in two flavors. One is a face-to-face meeting with a psychologist, and the other (far more common) is a written test, often multiple choice.

While these examinations cannot be regarded as definitive litmus tests of your employability, many companies are grafting the imprecise discipline of psychological testing onto the equally imprecise one of employment selection. The result is cheap and easy to administer. Those seeking employment are often asked to answer "a few routine questions," which end up being anything but routine. The tests, which should not be used as the sole basis for a hiring decision, are nevertheless often used in a pass-or-fail way and have a huge effect on people's livelihoods. In your case, let's do everything we can to make sure they don't have a negative effect on your job prospects.

It isn't surprising that many of the companies using these tests are concerned about the honesty of prospective employees. Each year, American industry loses an estimated $40 billion from employee theft. While honesty is often one of the behavioral profiles examined, the tests can also examine aptitude and suitability for a position. Often, the exams are geared toward evaluating the amount of energy a person might bring to the job; how he or she would handle stress; and what his or her attitudes toward job, peers, and management would be.

Unfortunately, answering a psychological test with complete personal honesty may very well threaten your chance of being offered employment. That's the bad news. Here's the good news: You can ace the tests without having to compromise your personal integrity.

Not long ago, I did an in-house employee selection and motivation seminar for a large corporation. When asked for my opinion on the subject of psychological testing, I replied the tests were often used inappropriately as a pass-or-fail criterion for hiring, and anyone with half a brain could come up with the desired or correct answers. "The question is," I concluded, "how many people who could have served you well will you miss out on because of a test?"

The managers assured me they had a test that was "virtually infallible" in helping to identify strong hires and certainly not subject to the machinations of the average applicant. They asked if I would be prepared to take it. I not only agreed but also promised to prove my point. "Let me take the test twice," I said. "The first profile you get will tell you to hire me; the second will say I'm a bad risk."

I took the test twice that day. "Applicant #1" came back with a strong recommendation for hire. "Applicant #2" came back with a warning to exercise caution.

How was this possible? Simple: None of us is the same person in the workplace as in our personal life. Over a period of time at work, we come to understand the need for different behavioral patterns and different ways of interacting with people.

Sometimes our *professional persona* spills over into our personal life, but this is not a stream that flows both ways. When personal preference trumps professional protocol, we get warnings and terminations. In other words, as professionals, we are inculcated with a set of behavioral patterns that enable us to be successful and productive for our employers.

Did I really "fool" the test? No. I was completely honest both times. The "winning" test was the one in which I viewed myself—and, thus, described myself—as a thoroughly professional white-collar worker in the job for which I was applying. The "losing" test was the one I used to describe myself as the kind of person I see myself as in my personal life.

This was not a hoax perpetrated by a smart aleck. *I am* that person they would have hired, and I possess a strong track record to back up my claim. I simply learned the behaviors necessary to succeed, adopted them, and made them my own—just as you have undoubtedly done, or are in the process of doing.

Many of the tests lack an awareness of the complexity of the human mind. They seem to miss the point when they ask us to speak honestly about our feelings and beliefs. They do not take into account that our learned behaviors in our professional lives are, invariably, distinct from the behaviors we display in our personal lives.

If you understand what you are likely to face, you can prepare and present yourself in the most effective way, and you can do it without compromising your integrity.

How to Prepare For, Read, and Respond to the Tests

There are six different types of tests, designed to plumb different aspects of your doubtless troubled psyche:

- Personality
- Personnel selection
- Aptitude
- Skills
- Integrity
- Psychological capital

Let's take a look at each of these.

Personality Tests

Are you a people person? Do you get upset easily? Are you quick to anger? Employers are using tests of general personality more frequently these days to screen job candidates. They use these tests because they believe that certain personality traits are required for success in a particular position.

There are two basic kinds of personality tests: projective and objective.

Projective Personality Tests

The projective tests ask you to tell a story, finish a sentence, or describe what you see in a blob of ink. These tests, in some form or other, have been around for decades, and psychologists use them a great deal to help understand how we deal with tough issues.

One popular test shows you pictures of a scene and asks you to describe what's going on. The psychologist may ask you to "tell me more about it." These areas of your mind are also accessed through the use of incomplete sentences, where you are given the beginning of a sentence and have to fill in the rest of it on your own. So, for instance, you may be asked to complete a sentence such as "When I am at work, I . . ."

In an employment-selection context, these tests are generally looking for leaders, achievers, and winners. They search for analytical and system-thinking skills, and look at decision-making and consensus-building styles.

Objective Personality Tests

Objective personality tests ask dozens, sometimes hundreds, of questions using some sort of rating scale—like strongly agree to strongly disagree, true-or-false, or yes-or-no. These tests usually have good reliability and validity. They were not designed to be used for employee screening, although they often are.

Knowing the names of the most common tests can tip you off to the type of screening being done. Personality tests you might run into include:

- *NEO Personality Inventory*: measures adjustment, extroversion, openness, agreeability, and conscientiousness.
- *16 PF*: measures sixteen personality factors, including a lie scale.
- *California Psychological Inventory*: measures twenty personality scales such as empathy, tolerance, responsibility, and dominance. (This is a good personality test, but it can be expensive for an employer, so it isn't used as often as some others.)
- *Minnesota Multiphasic Personality Inventory*: a very long, heavy-duty test of major psychological problems, often (wrongly) used in employee selection.

Personnel Selection Tests

Personnel selection tests are personality tests designed specifically to screen job candidates. These tests measure psychological behaviors such as trustworthiness, reliability, and conscientiousness. Some of them also psychologically screen you for potential alcohol or substance abuse. Tests you might run into that examine these areas include:

- Hogan Personality Inventory
- Employee Reliability Inventory
- PDI Employment Inventory

Aptitude

If you don't have the skills it takes to do the job, do you have the aptitude to learn? In a work world where the learning curve for new skill development becomes increasingly interesting to potential employers, we can expect to see the use of aptitude tests on the upswing. Judging your ability to develop skills in general or skills in a particular area is the premise behind these aptitude tests.

Some of the aptitude tests you might run into include:

- Wechsler Adult Intelligence Scale—Revised
- Raven's Progressive Matrices
- Comprehensive Ability Battery
- Differential Aptitude Tests

Skills

If the job calls for typing seventy-five words per minute, you may be given a typing test. If you are a programmer, you may be asked to take an objective test of programming skills or asked to debug a program. There are tests to measure every possible skill: filing, bookkeeping, mechanical comprehension, specific computer programs, math, credit rating, and so on. Some of them are typical paper-and-pencil written tests. Newer tests present the information using a software program.

It's hard to argue against some of these tests. After all, if the job calls for you to type letters and reports all day, the employer wants to hire the best typist. If you're supposed to use Microsoft Word on the PC all day, the employer will look for the person with the best knowledge of that program. As long as the employer is measuring an important skill, testing skills makes sense. If this is a problem area for you, you have found another *professional development project*.

Integrity Tests

Integrity tests are increasingly popular. Some companies are leery of personality tests, so they turn to integrity tests to screen out liars, cheats, and thieves. Some tests measure honesty or integrity, while others measure different psychological traits.

The problem with these integrity tests is that they don't work. A psychologist wrote that in one case using an integrity test would eliminate 2,721 honest applicants so that 101 potentially dishonest applicants would be denied employment. I should point out that the integrity test itself is actually okay; it's just that so few people actually steal that the use of the test eliminates a heck of a lot of good applicants. Another major study found that 95.6 percent of people who take these tests and get a failing score are actually incorrectly classified!

Here are a couple of integrity tests consistently in use today:

- Personnel Selection Inventory
- Personnel Reaction Bank

Listen carefully and apply what you learn in this chapter so that you don't become an incorrectly classified statistic.

Psychological Capital Tests

A new field of psychological research is being applied to employee selection. This research has determined that your success at work can depend on many factors: The *technical skills* of your profession and the *transferable skills and professional values* that underlie success in any profession are the most significant. Now behavioral research psychologists have discovered that how you perceive your colleagues and coworkers may be just as important.

This research tells us that these perceptions can reflect your ability to achieve, overcome setbacks, and get along with others in a productive manner. Referred to within the testing profession as Psychological Capital Tests, they can analyze your ability to develop competence, learn new skills quickly, pursue professional knowledge, grow professionally, work well with other team members, experience greater satisfaction from your involvement in groups, and experience and display less disruptive cynicism—all based on how you perceive and interact with others. Evaluating your psychological capital focuses on:

- Self-confidence—you believe you can achieve your goals
- Resilience—you believe you can overcome setbacks
- Optimism—you expect the future to bring good things

How Psychological Capital Tests Work

These tests are based on a belief that people know how to answer straightforward questions, so these *imaginary friend* tests put you in hypothetical work situations and ask questions about imaginary people sharing that situation with you. The psychologists say that with this approach candidates won't know how to fake their answers because, as one of them memorably put it, "With an imaginary person, test takers don't know whether they are supposed to be positive, so they respond honestly"!

Should you face one of these tests, you'll be asked to evaluate situations about an imaginary colleague/manager/subordinate. Then you will answer questions about your imaginary friend and how that person is experiencing the situation on a 7-point scale from strongly agree to strongly disagree. You can expect questions keyed to self-confidence, resilience, and optimism, such as, "Is he feeling confident about succeeding in this new job?" or, "Does she believe she can bounce back from this negative review?" You may be talking about an imaginary person, but here's a hint: *They're confident, optimistic, resilient, and enthusiastic about work.*

Getting to Know Yourself and Acing the Mind Readers

Born independently wealthy, very few of us would be doing the jobs we do. But we are doing them, and we have learned certain sets of skills and behavioral traits that are critical to our ability to survive and succeed professionally. The first thing you must do, then, is identify and separate the *professional you* from the personal you.

1. Step One: Never answer a test question from the viewpoint of your innermost beliefs. Instead, use your learned and developed professional behavior traits and *modus operandi*. Ask yourself, "How has my experience as a professional taught me to think and respond to this?" To do this effectively (and to understand ourselves a little better in the process), we need some further insights into the three critical skill sets that every professional relies on to succeed:
   - Professional/*technical skills*, which examine the skills required to execute your daily duties.
   - Industry knowledge (such as—if you happen to be in banking—your overall knowledge of the world of banking: how things work, how things get done, what is accepted within the industry, and so on).
   - *Transferable skills* (the traits discussed in Chapter 2), such as the skills that underlie success in every job (for example *communication skills*) and *professional values* such as *honesty* and *integrity*.

2. Step Two: Look at yourself from the employer's point of view. (Review Chapter 12, "The Five Secrets of the Hire" for some helpful ideas.) Evaluate the traits that enable you to discharge your duties effectively. Examine the typical crises/emergencies likely to arise: What supportive behavioral traits are necessary to overcome them? As you do this, you will almost certainly relive some episodes that seemed to put you at a disadvantage for a time. When it was tough to do things the right way, you had to buckle down and see the problem through, even though doing so did not necessarily "come naturally." But the fact is that you *did* overcome the obstacle. Remember how you did it, and keep that in mind as you answer the questions.

   Conversely, you will want to look at those instances where a crisis had a less-than-successful outcome. What traits did you swear you would develop and use for the next time?

   Highlighting such traits constitutes your acknowledgment of the supremacy of learned behaviors in the workplace. It does *not* constitute lying: Why do you think so many professionals strive to keep their business lives separate from their personal lives? What is the point of such a separation if the two lives are identical?

3. Step Three: Think of people you've known who have failed on the job. Why did they fail? What have you learned from their mistakes and made a part of the *professional you*?

4. Step Four: Think of people you've known who have succeeded on the job. Why did they succeed? What have you learned from their success and made a part of the *professional you*?

Once you have completed this exercise in detail, you will have determined how a professional would react in a wide range of circumstances, and identified the ways in which you have, over time, developed a *professional persona* to match that profile.

Getting Ready for the Test

Any test can be nerve-racking, but when it comes to these tests your livelihood is in the balance, so tip the odds in your favor with these tried-and-true techniques:

- The tests instruct you to answer quickly, offering the first response that comes to mind. Don't. Following this path may cost you a job. Instead, look at the test in terms of the exercises outlined previously; provide reasoned responses from the viewpoint of the *professional you*.
- Time limits are usually not imposed. On the contrary, those administering the test will often begin the proceedings with a soothing "take your time, there's no pressure." (Except, of course, the minor pressure of knowing a job offer is on the line!)
- If there is a time limit, find out how much time you have. Figure out roughly how much time per question or section you have. Pacing yourself helps, because you won't panic when you realize you've only got five minutes to complete the second half of a fifteen-minute test. Of course, you'll bring your watch.
- When in doubt, guess. Some of the really sophisticated tests you may have taken to get into college nailed you if you guessed wrong, but skill tests usually work differently. They add up all your right answers to get your test score. So, when in doubt, eliminate any of the obviously wrong answers, and take your best shot.
- With skill tests, ask for a warm-up or practice section. If the test is on a computer, adjust your chair, keyboard, and monitor before the timer starts, and take a deep breath.
- For paper-and-pencil tests, make sure you have enough desk space and sharp pencils.
- If the test is going to be done with other applicants in a group situation, stay focused on what you are doing. If you have to sit in the front of the room so no one else distracts you,

do it. If the test will be long and there's no break, make sure you won't get hungry (take a power bar) or have to use the bathroom.

- No matter what, use all your allotted time! Check your answers, and make sure they are written in the right places. Depending on your remaining time, review every other, or every fourth, question. Of course, if you can recall at the end which questions you were unsure about, review those first.
- You may not even realize you're taking an integrity test until the direction of the questions gives it away: "Have you ever stolen anything?" "Have you ever felt guilty?" "Have you ever told a lie?" Avoid the temptation to respond impulsively with something like "Lies? No, I prefer to chop down the damned cherry tree." The truth is, we have all done these things in our lives. When you are asked, for instance, whether there is anything you would ever change about yourself, or whether you think everyone is dishonest to some degree, the overwhelming likelihood is that your own honesty is being tested: The best answer is probably "yes."

In fact, if you never admit to these behaviors, you could be pegged as a faker. While fakers may be kept in the running, they've earned a question mark. Fakers are sometimes viewed as being too eager to please or simply a bit out of touch with their true feelings.

Many of the better tests in use today also use lie scales that can detect when someone is faking. How do they do this? One way is to include questions like "I always tell the truth" or "I never have a negative thought about a coworker." When the test is developed, hundreds or thousands of people take it, and the researchers figure out what the typical response is to these questions. Anyone who deviates from the average response on enough of these faking questions is also flagged as a faker.

If you must answer questions about ethics in a face-to-face encounter, explain your answer, placing it far in the past where appropriate, and talk about what you have learned from any negative experience. If such questions must be answered on paper, the best approach is to follow the dictates of your own conscience and try to bring the issue up after the test. You might say something like this:

"Gee, that question about lying was a tough one. I guess everyone has told a lie at some time in the past, and I wanted to be truthful, so I said 'yes.' But I'd be lying if I told you it didn't make me nervous. You know, I saw a show on television recently about these tests. It told the story of someone who lost a job because of answering a question just like that; the profile came back with an untrustworthy rating."

This may reduce the odds of your being denied the job in the same way. If the test does come back with a question about your honesty, you will at least have sown seeds of doubt about the validity of such a rating in the interviewer's mind. That doubt, and your disarming honesty, might just turn the tables in your favor.

Be careful, and take a balanced approach as you answer integrity test questions. Honesty is the best policy:

- In a face-to-face meeting with a psychologist, use the same techniques we have discussed throughout *Knock 'em Dead* to qualify and clarify the question before answering.
- The written tests may contain "double blinds," where you are asked a question on page one, and then asked a virtually identical one thirty or forty questions later. The technique is based on the belief that most of us can tell a lie, but few of us can remember that lie under stress, and are therefore likely to answer differently later. This could paint you as untruthful. The problem isn't that one answer is likely to deny you employment; the questions are asked in patterns to evaluate your behavior and attitudes on different topics.
- Assuming the test isn't timed, read the test through before you start answering questions! (There's "plenty of time" and "no pressure," remember?) Review the material at least three times, mentally flagging the questions that seem similar. This way you will be able to answer consistently.
- Watch out for words like *always* and *never*—this is very black and white: Always means 100 percent of the time, and never means 0 percent of the time. You will recall earlier discussions about psychological capital and the importance of a self-confident, resilient, and optimistic self-image. Check the *Always* box too often and you will be seen as having an overly favorable impression of yourself. Check the *Never* box too often and you will be seen as having an overly negative impression of yourself. Moderation in all things works, so aim for a strong tilt toward optimism and self-confidence, but don't go overboard and come across as a narcissist. California Psychological Inventory and 16 Personality Factors are both tests that put emphasis on these considerations.
- Resist any temptation to project an image of yourself as an interesting person. These tests are not designed to reward eccentricity, so think sliced white bread. You are happy at work and home. You enjoy being around people. You don't spend all your evenings watching movies. You don't spend your weekends with a computer or pursuing other solitary pastimes (unless you are a programmer or an aspiring Trappist monk). You have beliefs, but not too strong. You respect the beliefs of all others, regardless of their age, sex, race, political persuasion, or religion.
- Relax. One part of the Wechsler test (a developmental aptitude test) asks you to repeat back a string of numbers to the psychologist. If you're too hyped up, you'll get flustered and blow it. These tests measure intelligence plus your test-taking behavior. And you can certainly improve your test-taking behavior!
- Learn to visualize success in advance. Picture yourself at the test. Go through each step: You hear the instructions; the examiner says to begin. You read the test questions and realize you will do well. You get to a really tough part of the test. Visualize your success, and visualize your setbacks. Realize that you can and you will pull through because you

have a clear vision of the *professional you*. When you finish the test, read through your answers a few times. If you don't like any answers, change them.

• Remember to use your professional, working mindset when you take these tests. Answer as you would if you were on the job and your boss was asking the questions.

Everything I have said here takes for granted that the overriding goal of the employer is to determine whether or not you are suitable for the job. If you can give an accurate, affirmative answer to that question, the approach you take in doing so is—to my way of thinking—of little consequence. If you have learned and applied what it takes to prosper in your profession, it is your right to provide an honest profile of your *professional self*, in whatever forum you are to be evaluated.

CHAPTER 21
THE GRACEFUL EXIT

TO PARAPHRASE SHAKESPEARE, all the working world's a stage. Curtains rise and fall, and your powerful performance must be capped with a professional and memorable exit. To ensure that you leave the right impression, this chapter will review the dos and don'ts of leaving an interview.

A signal that the interview is drawing to a close comes when you are asked whether you have any questions. Ask questions, and by doing so, highlight your strengths and show your enthusiasm. Remember, your goal at the interview is to generate a job offer. Make sure your exit is as graceful as your entrance.

Dos:

1. *Ask appropriate job-related questions.* When the opportunity comes to ask any final questions, review your notes. Bring up any relevant strengths that haven't been addressed.

2. *Show decisiveness.* If you are offered the job, react with enthusiasm. Then sleep on it. If it's possible to do so without making a formal acceptance, lock the job up now and put yourself in control; you can always change your mind later. Before making any commitment with regard to compensation, see Chapter 25, "Negotiating the Job Offer."

3. *When more than one person interviews you, be sure you have the correct spellings of their names.* "I enjoyed meeting your colleagues, Ms. Smith. Could you give me the correct spellings of their names, please?" This question will give you the names you forgot in the heat of battle and will demonstrate your consideration.

4. *Review the job's requirements with the interviewer.* Match them point by point with your skills and attributes.

5. *Find out whether this is the only interview.* If so, you must ask for the job in a positive and enthusiastic manner. Find out the time frame for a decision and finish with, "I am very enthusiastic about the job and the contributions I can make. If your decision will be made by the fifteenth, what must I do in the meantime to ensure I get the job?"

6. *Ask for the next interview.* When there are subsequent interviews in the hiring procedure, ask for the next interview in the same honest and forthright manner: "Is now a good time to schedule our next meeting?"

7. *Keep yourself in contention.* A good leading question to ask is, "Until I hear from you again, what particular aspects of the job and this interview should I be considering?"

8. *Always depart in the same polite and assured manner in which you entered.* Look the interviewer in the eye, put on a smile (there's no need to grin), give a firm handshake, and say, "This has been an exciting meeting for me. This is a job I can do, and I feel I can contribute to your goals, because the atmosphere here seems conducive to doing my very best work. When will we speak again?"

Don'ts:

1. *Don't discuss salary, vacation, or benefits.* It is not that the questions are invalid, just that the timing is wrong. Bringing up such topics before you have an offer is asking what the company can do for you—instead, you should be saying what you can do for the company. Those topics are part of the negotiation (handled in Chapter 25, "Negotiating the Job Offer"); remember, without an offer you have nothing to negotiate.

2. *Don't press for an early decision.* Of course, you should ask, "When will I know your decision?" But don't press it. Don't try to use the "other opportunities I have to consider" gambit as leverage when no such offers exist—that annoys the interviewer, makes you look foolish, and may even force you to negotiate from a position of weakness. Timing is everything; the issue of how to handle other opportunities as leverage is explored in detail later.

3. *Don't show discouragement.* Sometimes a job offer can occur on the spot. Usually it does not. So don't show discouragement if you are not offered the job at the interview, because discouragement shows a lack of self-esteem and determination. Avoiding a bad impression is the foundation of leaving a good one, and the right image to leave is one of enthusiasm, guts, and openness—just the professional behaviors you have been projecting throughout the interview.

4. *Don't ask for an evaluation of your interview performance.* That forces the issue and puts the interviewer in an awkward position. You can say that you want the job, and ask what you have to do to get it.

GET A FREE RESUME REVIEW FROM MARTIN YATE!
Go to the website of the store where you bought the book, write an honest review,
and send the link with your resume to *MartinYate@KnockEmDead.com*.

PART IV
FINISHING TOUCHES

ONCE THE JOB interview is over, you move on to the next step in the process for securing job offers. You are never the only qualified candidate for a job, and the better the job, the stiffer your competition is likely to be. On top of this, interviewers expect that a candidate who is interested in the job will make an effort to follow up on the interview in a professional manner.

THE SUCCESSFUL COMPLETION of every interview is a big stride toward getting job offers, yet it is not the end of your job search. Following up after your interviews isn't being needy, it is being professional.

A company rarely hires the first competent person it sees. A hiring manager will sometimes interview as many as fifteen people for a particular job, but the strain and pace of conducting interviews naturally dim the memory of each applicant. Unless you are the last person to be interviewed, the impression you make will fade with each subsequent interview the interviewer undertakes. And if you are not remembered, you will not be offered the job. You must develop a strategy to keep your name and skills constantly in the forefront of the interviewer's mind. These finishing touches often make all the difference.

Some of the suggestions here may not seem earth-shattering: just simple, sensible demonstrations of your manners, enthusiasm, and determination. But remember that today all employers are looking for people with that extra little something. You can avoid a negative or merely indifferent impression, and be certain of creating a positive one, by following these guidelines.

CHAPTER 22
HOW TO FIGHT AGE DISCRIMINATION IN YOUR JOB SEARCH

THE CURSE OF silent discrimination. It's not that interviewers will tell you to your face they think you are too old; more often the discrimination is silent.

The appearance of age can give rise to some valid unspoken concerns from the other side of the desk: that you could be a management problem, that perhaps you won't fit in, that you aren't technologically up-to-date, and that you aren't there for the long haul.

Since lots of reasons for this discrimination have nothing to do with your ability to do the job, it is easy to point the finger of blame and slowly resign yourself to diminished horizons. The smarter course is to fight back with some of the hard-won street smarts that come with age, experience, and understanding.

What Can You Do about Age Discrimination?

Ever since Title VII of the 1964 Civil Rights Act was passed into law, it has been illegal to discriminate in employment against someone because of, amongst other things, her age. This was necessary to combat the rampant discrimination at that time, but despite the laws only a buffoon would say that same discrimination isn't still alive and well.

Here are the not-so-pleasant facts:

- You live in a youth-oriented culture and don't look as young as you used to.
- The higher you climb professionally, the fewer the opportunities, the tougher the competition, and the more people there are standing behind you with dagger in hand.
- You can be seen as a know-it-all and as a potential management problem, especially to younger managers.
- You can be seen as lethargic and without drive.
- You make more money, and this costs the company more.
- You may not be current with the profession's applications of technology.

The impact of technology on all jobs has brought with it the pressure of staying technologically current; boomers are the most likely to fall behind. Even joking about the pressures of technology on everyday life can have negative connotations.

Those are the facts; now let's see what you can do about them.

Look at Yourself from Someone Else's Point of View

Looking for a job when you don't have one is a hellish experience that can tear your ego to shreds, especially when you meet interviewers who seem to have an irrational (some would say immature) bias against maturity. It's normal to feel frustration and anger in those situations, but acting on it is the best way to torpedo your job search. Instead, you need to understand where the person on the other side of the desk is coming from, and how he sees you.

Now walk over to the other side of the desk and go back in your mind twenty years. Think about what it must be like to have someone maybe two decades your senior telling you how much he knows. The emotion you feel is likely to be intimidation, accompanied by warning sirens. You probably aren't feeling enthusiastic about bringing this person onboard.

The older you get, the greater the chance that your interviewer will be younger and quite possibly intimidated about the management threats you could pose. You, on the other hand, are so sensitive to the age issue that you may overcompensate.

With age comes a wider frame of reference and greater maturity, but with it can also come a blind spot for the insecurities you felt not so many years ago. That younger interviewer may very well be feeling just as intimidated and defensive as you are, resulting in you both feeling uptight and neurotic. Obviously, this is not a recipe for success. Use your maturity to deal with your own feelings and remain alert to the possible discomfort on the interviewer's side of the desk.

Age Discrimination at a Job Interview

Age discrimination at job interviews comes in two flavors, spoken and unspoken. Learning to address both types can make the difference between job offers and rejection.

Because age discrimination is illegal, with few exceptions ("Are you between the ages of sixteen and sixty-five?"), questions about age at an interview can usually be considered illegal. However, that doesn't stop them being asked, so the question is how to handle them.

You could say, "That's an illegal question, and I'm not going to answer it." But a response like this isn't going to get you a job offer; you sound like a troublemaker already.

The best way to answer any question is to demonstrate that you understand what is behind it. You want to show your understanding of the job's deliverables, and at the same time make a positive statement about yourself.

Illegal age-related questions can indicate that the interviewer is concerned about your age, but they can also mean that the interview is going well—the interviewer is looking at you favorably, probably thinks you can do the job, and is just showing an interest in you as a human being. With age being such a sensitive issue in the workplace, interviewers rarely ask an illegal question intentionally; these questions can slip out for the most innocent of reasons.

Before you start thinking I'm crazy, let's step back from the job interview, just for a moment, and imagine yourself at a barbecue. You meet a stranger and make small talk: "Where are you from? What do you do? You married? Kids? What, you have grandchildren? You don't look old enough. How old are you?"

In a social setting like this, these are natural conversational questions that indicate a genuine interest in you as a person—and they could mean the very same thing at an interview. Yet when asked during a job interview, every one of the previous questions could be interpreted as illegal.

Since it won't advance your candidacy to take offense, just tell yourself that the interviewer is showing interest in you as a person, and look for ways that you can answer and make a contribution toward your candidacy at the same time.

Let's look at ways you could answer the age question:

"I'm forty-nine."

That's okay as far as it goes, but it doesn't do anything to advance your candidacy, so let's examine an alternative, where you answer the question and show that your age is a plus to your candidacy:

"It's interesting that you should ask. I just turned forty-nine. That gives me _____ years in the profession, and _____ years doing exactly the job you're trying to fill. In those years I've gained experience in all kind of situations and environments, made my share of mistakes on someone else's payroll, and learned from them. [Smile.] I guess the great benefit of my experience and energy level is _____ ."

Then finish with a benefit statement(s) about what you bring to the job.

Unspoken Age Discrimination

Even if questions about age remain unspoken, you know they are still being asked—it's only human. In my coaching practice, I tell clients that, if age-related questions are not asked, they have two options:

1. Say nothing and hope age isn't an issue. Right, now let me tell you about a bridge I'd like to sell you . . .
2. Face the fact that age discrimination exists and find ways to make your age a benefit to this manager.

You should own your age and seize appropriate opportunities to share how it can be a benefit to the department and to the manager personally. I suggest you personalize an answer along the lines of:

"Jack, if I sat in your chair looking at me, a seasoned professional, I'd have a bunch of age-related questions that I couldn't ask. I'd be considering issues like energy, drive, manageability, how well you'd get on with a team where everyone looks to be _____ years younger, and I'd be thinking about your ability to keep current professionally."

If you don't have a chance earlier in the interview, raise this point when asked, "Do you have any questions?"

You can then proceed, as in the previous example, with the benefits of your experience and maturity as they relate to the job under consideration. You can add comments about the following issues too, as they relate to your circumstances:

Emergencies
- "My experience means that I have already lived through panics, emergencies, and times when the poop hits the paddle wheel. When crises occur, as they do in even the best-run operations, I know how to handle them calmly. I've been there and lived through them and learned from the experience."
- "Because I've been through panics and emergencies before, you'll find me a steadying influence who won't get flustered about a little extra effort and who will do my part in bringing the team together to tackle the issue."

Loyalty

- "The average professional stays in a job four years, and the younger your workforce, the faster the turnover; the older the worker, the slower the turnover. Employee churn is disruptive to meeting the deliverables of this department and it affects your job and your reputation."
- "Hire another Young Turk and you know that she will constantly be haggling for promotions and possibly your job, and on top of this, she will be gone in four years."
- "I don't want your job, I want this job, and I'm not looking to change again in four years. I just want to find a first-class team, settle down, and, over time, earn my place as a trusted member of your inner circle—as someone you can count on."

Your Right Hand

- "I'm competent, experienced, conscientious, calm, and motivated."
- "You'll come to see me as someone you can rely on to get the job done and who is a positive influence."
- "You'll see me as someone who can be trusted, and most of all, someone who will stand at your back in all things."
- "At your request I could mentor less-experienced team members."

You can indeed bring all these benefits to a hiring manager and a department. Take the time to think about each of these points and personalize them to your profession and work experience. The result will be an increased awareness of your unique selling points, and this will increase your self-confidence.

Make statements such as the previous ones, as they apply to you and your profession, and you will do more than answer that hiring manager's unspoken questions. You will make a series of compelling arguments in favor of your candidacy. You will show yourself to be unusually perceptive, balanced, focused on the issues, and to the point, and you will doubtless score some other points in your favor.

Timing Is Everything

I said earlier that you can raise these issues toward the end of the interview when asked, "Do you have any questions?" However, if things happen that make you think the interviewer is concerned about age, you can speak up earlier.

At whatever point you choose to make your case about the merits of an experienced professional, you should be prepared with a question you might ask at the end of your argument that will move the conversation forward, perhaps a question that goes to the heart of the job's deliverables.

Ability is judged partly by what you say in answer to questions and partly on the questions you ask, because your questions, like your answers, show your understanding of and engagement with the job.

For example, an accountant dealing with accounts receivable might say, "This is all interesting food for thought, but what is most interesting to me now is: What are the biggest problems accounts receivable is experiencing? What percentage of payables is aging over thirty days? Over forty-five days?"

Prepare such questions in advance, and only ask ones that lead in the direction of your positive qualities as an employee.

Manage Your Appearance

Fighting age discrimination is not just about answering unspoken questions; your appearance is going to have an impact too.

You live in a youth-oriented, telegenic world, and the appearance of your clothes, hair, and skin can say an awful lot about your ability to fit in and keep the pace. Look back to when you were thirty and a Young Turk on the fast track. Do you remember how ancient those fifty-year-old wrinklies and crumblies looked with their sagging, sallow skin, eye bags like Vuitton steamer trunks, and hair sprouting everywhere except their heads?

Age discrimination in a youth-oriented society will not go away, and that means you have to fight back: You need to do everything you can to stack the odds in your favor, and it starts with facing the facts and doing whatever is necessary to maintain an air of vibrancy about your appearance.

Women tend to be more sensitive to these issues than men, who by and large are woefully ignorant of maximizing their appearance. Most tips in this section apply to men and women alike, but I'll also address a few that apply only to one sex. As a woman reading the following, you'll take any good advice you can from it and you will also appreciate that the somewhat blunt tone is not aimed at you but at your sometimes less-evolved male counterparts for whom many of these ideas, like getting rid of nose and ear hair, are still revolutionary concepts.

Your goal is to look sharp—not for a social date, but sharp for the professional world; so if you need to update some aspects of your wardrobe, there is no time like the present for wardrobe shopping or committing to a more age-appropriate hairdo. Chapter 9 deals extensively with dress and professional appearance, so we are just going to address age-related factors.

Got Hair?

With age, the texture of your hair changes. It often becomes frizzier and the sheen disappears along with the color—damn but aging sucks. Many people (mostly men) lose hair and mistakenly comb over those last three strands like Homer Simpson. The best advice for a man with thinning hair is to crop or even shave your head. Not only is cropped and shaved hair accepted as stylish, it is also businesslike, because a subtle association with sports and the military adds an air of virility and action.

If you are still lucky enough to have hair, it is probably going or has gone gray. Some men and women can carry their gray hairs with distinction, but others hate it as another visible sign of mortality. If you proudly keep your hair gray, you can't let it seem like you no longer care about your appearance. Rather, you have to pay special attention to maintaining an air of vibrancy in other ways.

If you have hair and choose to dye it, just be careful how you do it. Hair coloring has to look natural and therefore in balance with your skin tone (your skin is aging too; we'll talk about that shortly). You don't fool anybody with the hair color of your youth slapped on top of your now-mature face and body. For example, you may have had dark hair in your teens and twenties, but re-creating that color will not shave ten years off your appearance; it will only make you look unnatural and a doofus.

Your hair faded gradually over the years, passing through increasingly muted shades of its former glory. So for the most natural-looking coloring, you must find tones somewhere between where you are now and what you used to look like back in the day. These tones need to be blended to create a natural look.

It isn't possible to do this convincingly with an off-the-shelf bottle of hair color. You need to go to a professional colorist who will blend in lowlights (and sometimes highlights too) with your current color. This will give you a new look that doesn't hide the gray but just blends it and, while taking off maybe five years, also sharpens your style. Remember, you are fighting an intelligent rear-guard action, not playing make-believe that you are thirty instead of fifty.

I've noticed that younger colorists don't always understand this challenge and think you just want the gray covered; the result is less than spectacular. The best way is to find a more experienced colorist, who is far more likely to understand and handle the issues.

Color Maintenance

If you choose to color your hair, you need to maintain it on a monthly basis. If you are a man, I don't recommend getting this done at the barbershop; instead, you will need a full-service salon. You'll get a better cut, and the colorists will be more accomplished and have a better choice of products.

Trumpish Eyebrows

Eyebrows are another aging concern that men almost always overlook. Eyebrows are hair, and they grow: Do nothing about it and you end up looking like Donald Trump. Unattended to, your eyebrows gradually grow wild and bushy and long. This gives an unkempt and aging impression to everyone who sees them.

You have two options: trimming or plucking. Often your hairdresser will keep your eyebrows trimmed. Most sophisticated women are horrified by this, saying that razor-trimmed eyebrows don't look natural, and that instead they need to be carefully plucked every week.

I agree with this, and as a man who spends big chunks of his life entirely alone and big chunks in the spotlight, I have even tried to do it; but the truth is I could never stick to the regimen—too much time and too much pain. I have the hairdresser trim them every month and try to pluck the odd one that grows wild between visits.

If you are feeling plucky (pun intended), it might be worthwhile to start the process by having someone at a salon do your eyebrows for you once so you can watch the technique; it costs between $15 and $35. You start with the longest and pluck them out, then do the outer edges where they straggle down toward your ears and cheekbones, then work on the bridge of your nose to give a clean separation and erase that unibrow look so fashionable in prehistoric times. Then, of course, you want to pluck out the gray hairs whenever they appear.

Nose and Ear Hair

It's the damnedest thing: For a man, as the hair gradually disappears from your head, it sprouts in your ears and nose. This only happens with the passage of the years, so it is a clear signal of your aging process, and it is not an attractive look. It is compounded by failing eyesight from years of staring at computer screens, which results in an inability to see the problem. But everyone else can see it, and nothing in the world says "old fart" louder than nose and ear hair.

No one is going to keep this under control for you; it's something you will have to do yourself. At the very least, get a nose hair trimmer to whack away some of that undergrowth. However, this is not the best solution, as cutting the hair makes it stronger and you end up with a nasty little stubble field that will give people the impression that you are trying to grow a Hitler moustache—not a good idea.

There are two options: If you have a couple of hundred bucks to spare, get a few laser treatments and be done with it. Otherwise, the only sensible solution is to pluck the little buggers out every week without fail—horribly painful, but very necessary and probably good for your personal relationships too. A good pair of tweezers helps, as does a magnifying mirror. To begin with, you'll probably have to do this religiously every day until you thin things out. Once it's under control, you move to the once-a-week schedule.

The same applies to hair that grows on or in the ears. You need to get these things under control and then keep them that way. Getting rid of all this unwanted facial hair will have a subtle but significant effect on the youthfulness of your appearance.

Take Care of Your Skin

If you ignore your skin over the years it will show the ravages of age far more than if you take care of it, and it is never too late to start. This is going to be new information for most men, but don't get squeamish: This can really help your appearance and self-confidence.

Your pores get bigger with age and you get skin discoloration from sun damage. Also, men don't clean their faces as carefully as women. Without careful cleansing it is easy to leave dirt and also soap scum; the pores get clogged and will get larger and more unsightly due to oxidation (i.e., blackheads). These problems are exacerbated if you drink or smoke.

The result is dirty, oily dead skin just sitting there on the surface of your face, and it really helps you look your age. You have to clean your skin more thoroughly and carefully. Any woman in your life will happily help you get started or improve the regimen you currently follow.

It's a good idea to use an exfoliation treatment on a regular basis; this helps make the skin look smoother and rids it of excess keratin (dead cell buildup). Exfoliate with a soft face brush while cleansing or by using an AHA or BHA product to promote cell turnover.

Men also tend to rub their faces too vigorously when washing and drying. The tugging and pulling contribute to loss of elasticity—in other words, sagging. This is one of those areas in life where men should pick up some of the habits of women:

- Wash your face thoroughly, ideally with a gentle foam or cream cleanser, depending on skin type. Foam is typically for normal/oily skin, while cream is typically for dry skin.
- Always treat your skin gently: Pat (don't rub) it dry.
- Apply moisturizer or sunblock.

The sun is the number one factor that contributes to skin aging, followed by cigarette smoke and environmental pollutants. A broad-spectrum sunblock, with a formula that blocks UVA rays (rays that damage skin cells) and UVB rays (rays that burn) is recommended.

Different skin types have different needs. The skin types are normal, oily, and dry. And then there are combination skins: normal/oily, oily with a dry surface, etc. This latter is caused by overtreatment of oily skin, often with too-harsh cleansers or toners with alcohol. Many people have combination skin: oily in patches, dry in patches, and normal in patches. If you don't treat these areas separately, in helping one area you'll be damaging another. Once you understand your skin's real needs, you can find products that will really help your skin, and in the process improve your appearance.

Eye Wrinkles

The skin around the eye area is thin and fragile and frequently lacks adequate moisture. This only increases the prominence of your wrinkles. Taking care of your skin and moisturizing properly around the eyes won't eradicate these particular signs of aging, but over the course of a month you can achieve a quite noticeable improvement. You will need a separate treatment for this area, as a regular moisturizer is not enough for the delicate eye area.

Wrinkled Neck and Hands

Remember to moisturize your neck and hands. They have gotten more wrinkled than you realize and are a dead giveaway of aging. For hands, get a hand cream with at least SPF 8, which will help prevent sun damage and the age spots that come from it. Use fade creams to diminish age spots on your hands and face, a cream with a natural extract such as cranberry or pear leaves (arbutin) or one with hydroquinone. When using fade creams, it is easy to over-apply, and this can be harsh on the skin, causing redness; follow the directions.

As the skin ages, some women mistakenly apply too much or overly pink blush and lip tones or the wrong shade of foundation. The key is to find a color that looks natural. Blending is key, so lip color should be complementary and from the same color family as the blush color: warm/warm, or cool/cool.

Four Rules for Maintaining Healthy Skin

Once you have cleaned up your skin and started using moisturizers and protectants, there are four rules for maintaining a healthful, glowing, younger-looking skin. You won't look thirty again, but I promise that you will look as if you still have a full tank of gas.

1. Drink plenty of water

Eight glasses a day, and coffee and caffeinated beverages don't count, as they dehydrate your skin. This is important even in winter, when most people don't think they need as much water. Central heating dehydrates skin and the winter climate makes your skin more prone to chapping and redness, all of which are more visible with the less-resilient skin of age.

2. Massage your skin

If you can't get a professional facial on a regular basis, learn to do self-massage, as this promotes blood flow and helps your circulation. A little research on Google will yield countless books, blogs, and YouTube videos on self-massage techniques . . . and your new skill can also be applied to your personal life, to the romantic delight of your partner!

3. Exercise

With increased exercise comes better circulation, which increases blood flow and lends a healthy glow to your skin.

This could mean going to the gym, bike riding (don't street jog; it leads to joint replacements, and I can tell you from personal experience they are painful and expensive), or integrating exercise into your personal routine. Take the stairs, not the elevator; walk when you can; maintain your own house and yard—it can be fun, really. Let's face it, you can probably do with a little more exercise. Plus, you'll be paying yourself for doing it with the money you save from a gym membership—not to mention yard maintenance fees.

4. Maintain a balanced diet

If you are healthy within, you will look better on the outside. Eating a balanced diet and taking vitamin supplements can also positively impact the appearance of your skin. You might also consider seeing a nutritionist; you'd be surprised at the number of foods your body might be intolerant of—foods that might be difficult to digest, leading to bloating and skin irritations.

Pre-Interview Workout

If possible, always try to work out on the morning of an interview. It will help eradicate the impression of a tired old warhorse who has been carrying the weight of the world on his shoulders for half a century. Your posture will improve, as well as your skin tone, and the sense of well-being will add spring to your step, which sends a signal of vibrancy. Put all these ideas into practice and your appearance will shed a few years. You'll feel healthier and more self-confident too.

Job Search and the Changing Homes of Opportunity

Earnings and social prestige are traditionally associated with job title and company: Exalted job titles at well-known companies always top the list with higher pay and greater social prestige. These considerations are pretty much ingrained into the psyches of working professionals.

There are obvious pluses, but also minuses to pursuing this path with these types of companies, but once you hit your fifties, age and wage discrimination kick in and many people get pushed out of those blue-chip companies to which they gave thirty years of their life. Of course there is nothing personal in throwing you on the scrapheap after a lifetime of sacrifice and service, nothing personal at all—it's just business. Bullshit! It's personal all right, but your only revenge is to transmute this stab in the back into a greater level of success and perhaps independence, than the people who conned you. It is going to require an adjustment in thinking.

Mistakenly, the job search focus of many who undergo this experience is to get back into the same type of company. This where they made their reputations, this is the world they know, so it's where they largely continue to look for opportunity.

However, the majority of the jobs in America are generated by companies with fewer than 500 employees, and the greatest period of growth for new companies is in their first ten years—especially from the third year, once they have become established and begun to grow in earnest.

Working for a Small Company

Just as with big companies, there are pluses and minuses to working for a smaller company.

Minuses: They are lesser known and are therefore less socially prestigious. Usually they haven't established the sort of revenues that lead to the mind-boggling benefits of corporate success in a publicly traded company. Often the salary isn't as high or the health care as comprehensive.

Pluses: On the plus side, smaller companies are more likely to be growth companies making money by increasing sales, whereas established, mature companies focus more on cost cutting to maintain and grow income. Consequently, growing companies position the mature man or woman with the benefit of likely having faced and solved such problems before, with the added advantage of having done it on someone else's payroll.

The leaders at young companies are more likely to be men forced out by age and wage discrimination, women forced out by sex, age, and wage discrimination, or younger entrepreneurs who can be convinced of the wisdom of hiring maturity and depth of experience—just so long as you don't come across as an old know-it-all who is going to create management problems. This means that two-thirds of the time hiring managers are more likely to be in your age range and see the benefit of all your experience and the different hats you can wear. Properly handled, 100 percent of the hiring managers you face can be brought to appreciate the benefits that your maturity delivers, experience that can be especially potent with smaller, younger companies.

Where to Find Smaller Companies

The website *www.referenceusa.com* gives you access to 25 million-plus American and Canadian companies, including 4 million new businesses. If you work in health care, it identifies almost a million doctors and dentists. It also has a jobs database with 2.5 million-plus jobs. You are required to have a library card to access the database.

In addition:

- *www.Zapdata.com*, owned by Hoovers.com, has a directory of approximately 17 million private and publicly held U.S. companies.
- *www.bizjournals.com* has forty regional editions and focuses on growing companies.
- *www.startuphire.com* focuses on start-ups (duh) and has a job bank that exceeds 40,000 jobs. It's easy to use: Just plop in a job title and enter a city or zip code.
- *www.rileyguide.com* helps you search a wide range of companies by profession.
- *www.ventureloop.com* gives you access to over 40,000 jobs at 3,000+ venture-backed companies.
- Finally, let's not forget *www.thesearchparty.com*, a site that does two things: helps you find headhunters who will screen and represent you, and connects headhunters with employers. Much cheaper than traditional headhunting, this is a new and potentially disruptive approach to recruitment and therefore job search. The company claims to cut recruitment fees in half and recruitment time by 75 percent. This is attracting a lot of employers.

Opportunities in Dying Industries

Who wants a career in a dying industry? How to get out of and avoid dying jobs and dying industries is an evergreen topic in the world of career management, and looking at the long term, this makes a lot of sense. However, when your professional horizon shrinks from thirty years to ten or five years, what makes for a viable career choice changes too.

If you are in your fifties or sixties and corporate America has thrown you on the scrapheap because of age and wage discrimination, your long-term outlook is very different from that of a pimply twenty-something. You need to work, but your focus is no longer on making it to mahogany row; now it is about economic survival, living a meaningful life, or both.

Those industries that are leaving the United States—apparel, paper and pulp, etc. (*www.bls .gov* can give you the complete picture)—are avoided like the plague by younger professionals intent on climbing the ladder of professional success. This actually leaves lots of opportunity at all levels, but especially at the higher levels in companies within these dying industries. There are some great career opportunities for mature professionals in the very industries everyone else is running away from. This is supported by bls.gov, which says that the available jobs in such industries won't come from job growth but from the need to replace employees who will transfer to other industries or retire.

For example, take paper, pulp, and mills. Surely these are dead industries. I always thought so, till I spent some time catching up with a headhunter I hadn't spoken to for a while. He told me that he was still thriving in his old specialty of executive recruitment in the dying paper and pulp industry.

As he explained it, talented people were leaving those companies in droves, and this made it extremely difficult for those surviving companies to attract and develop good talent, leaving significant leadership vacuums at all levels. So while these industries were dying, they still existed, and they still needed talent—and their situation made them more open to bringing in talent from outside their industry sector.

More important, they often had openings in management ranks and would look at candidates that other industries might not. Furthermore, these industries are dying because they are being exported, and this means that the professional manager with international or multicultural experience has additional special sauces to bring to the table.

Entrepreneurial Options

Try this test: Make a list of ten people you know who are in their fifties. These can be people you went to grade school or college with, or worked with at the peer, subordinate, or superior level—just so long as they are your age. If you and your list are fifty-four to fifty-five years old, the odds are that perhaps up to three of these people are still working in traditional corporate jobs (with benefits); if fifty-six, between two and three; if age fifty-seven to fifty-eight, no more than two; if fifty-nine to sixty, one at best is still in a traditional corporate job.

This is an important message for the professional in his or her middle years. It says that corporate jobs at the level you are used to are likely to become increasingly scarce. One option is to consider putting those hard-earned skills to work at smaller companies, where your depth and breadth of experience might be better appreciated.

Contracting

Not so long ago I spent an evening with Dave Theobald, the founder of Netshare (*www .netshare.com*), a career site for executives. As we compared our various aches and pains, we also talked about the very real issues of age discrimination and what a man or woman can do about it, above and beyond the approaches already discussed. Here are the salient points of our conversation (captured on the tablecloth and later transcribed):

1. For those over fifty-three, mass-mailing recruiters is a waste of time and money. The only time a recruiter is going to present a candidate in the mid-fifties—except when this candidate is at very senior levels—is when she has an excellent relationship with the client and can say, "I know he is fifty-six, but I want you to interview him anyway, because I think he is an excellent candidate."

2. Contacting contract/project recruiters, however, is a different story. "Gray is in." (In some instances, you don't need to dye your hair any longer.) There are some real advantages for the mid-fifties people looking for contract jobs. First, the job can be anywhere. Second, you can size up the company just as the company is sizing you up—evaluating the culture, chemistry, and philosophical fit. Third, it may turn into a full-time job.

3. The disadvantages of contract work are: (a) no benefits, medical in particular, and (b) no security. (This disadvantage is somewhat moot because there's no real job security anywhere today.)

4. A big advantage to contract work is that if it doesn't work out beyond the agreed-upon period, say six months, your ego isn't bruised, and you can talk about recent consulting assignments in subsequent interviews.

The idea of contract and consulting may come as culture shock to an executive raised with decades of corporate identity and teamwork. However, unending corporate employment is no longer the only option, nor necessarily the norm, as you're about to see. Search terms like:

Senior level contractor company
and
Senior level contractor jobs
will generate thousands of hits. Vary the search terms to get more.

Consulting

Consulting is the same as contracting, only you are selling yourself (more work) and keeping more of the pie. Because you are bringing the money in your own front door, you are achieving real financial security, perhaps the only real financial security there is in this new age.

You'll need to adapt another version of that resume to position yourself as a consultant and apply the very same techniques you use for job search toward landing consulting assignments. The structure of our corporations has changed so much in recent years that there is far more discretionary money for outsourcing services than ever before.

Consulting with Smaller Companies

Small companies, including both those that are growing and those that are struggling to adapt to the digital era, are frequently in need of consulting help. Working as a consultant is scary hard work, but the work and the checks are there; plus you are bringing in money through your own front door—and that, my friend, short of becoming a trustafarian, is the only way to gain any kind of financial security.

There's a great site, *www.expert360.com*, that specializes in matching you with smaller companies and shorter-term assignments. Such assignments:

- Give you current work experience
- Bring in money
- Can turn into full-time jobs
- Build consulting experience

It's worth considering, because when you bring money in your own front door, no employer can snatch it away.

Surprising Entrepreneurial Opportunity in Dying Industries

We talked earlier about shrinking industries and how they might not always be a losing proposition as an employment option. Here are a couple more examples: one from the shrinking financial services industry, and the other from the down-for-the-count appliance repair industry; in both instances we look at the exciting entrepreneurial opportunities people have discovered for themselves. These are both true stories of guys I know: one in New York, one in rural Georgia. You can't find two worlds more dissimilar, so the logic may apply in your world too.

Appliance Repair

Here is an example, not of finding an office or factory job within the shrinking appliance industry, but of turning it into a successful entrepreneurial endeavor. I know a guy who, when he got pushed out of his professional world, started fixing things: because he liked it and because he couldn't afford new ones.

I met him when I hired him to fix my dishwasher. A year later he was over to do the microwave, and this time, instead of having him fix it, I had him replace it with a reconditioned one. He took away my old one for free. A few days later it hit me: If he fixes an appliance, he makes money; and if he replaces an appliance, he not only makes money but gets some new stock to recondition for another customer down the road.

He lives about a mile from me, where he has a storefront and a yard. The storefront is where he runs the business. The yard in the back is where he keeps his—no joke—growing collection of classic Rolls Royces.

This is America; it is a huge country, and there is always opportunity, even when everyone tells you that opportunity is dead for someone like you. Just look around your neighborhood: The men and women who have the hairdressing, carpentry, plumbing, and lawn-care businesses are just as well off over the long haul as the suits enslaved in the high-rise salt mines.

As I write this, I have seen two new home-appliance repair trucks around town and have spoken to both of the drivers. They were both the owners of the businesses—one was a franchise (tithe about 10 percent of your income but have a proven methodology, branding, and support system to rely on); the other was a guy who just saw it as a community need that he could fill. They are both doing fine.

White Collar Professional to Blue Collar Business Owner

Some years ago in New York, I met a guy who had been laid off from the financial services industry. As the money got tight, he painted his house to get it ready to sell. Then someone at Home Depot mistook him for a painter and offered him a job, which led to another. Last time I saw him, he had a thriving house-painting business with ten vans and almost fifty employees. He told me it was a cakewalk: "Most of the guys in the house-painting business are drunks; dammit, haven't you ever noticed a paint can opener is also built to open beer bottles? Either that or they don't speak English.

"All I did was take what I learned in the financial services world—'Find out what the customer wants and sell it to him'—and applied it in local services."

A World of Entrepreneurial Options

The fifties are an age that breeds a surprising number of successful entrepreneurs, who become successful because they have no other choice.

You don't live in an either/or world, and there is nothing to stop you pursuing full-time employment just as you pursue consulting/contract assignments and consider buying or setting up your own business. You can make the same money (or better money), keep more from the tax man (write-offs), and have far more freedom in your life. The work is largely the same, the approaches for getting it are pretty much identical, and you are at that point in your career when you can offer real value as an outside authority. Pursuing contract, consulting, and entrepreneurial options are well worth consideration as a parallel activity in conjunction with your job search. The opportunities for success in these worlds are almost infinite.

Stack the Odds in Your Favor

Age discrimination will not go away, but you can become more aware of how you are perceived and manage the image you project more effectively. You need to do everything you can to stack the odds in your favor, and that includes maintaining an air of vibrancy about your appearance.

- Change is constant. You must adapt to the realities of a professional world where there is no certainty but perhaps more opportunity. With continual rapid change becoming a constant in our lives, those who learn to live with uncertainty and who can adapt to the needs of an ever-changing professional landscape are perfectly positioned to seize the abundant opportunities that always accompany a changing of eras. Recognize that change is constant; grasp the fact that by taking responsibility for your destiny and continuing to adapt and evolve, you can change your situation today and your tomorrows forever.
- Assuming you go back to work for a corporation, in the future it would be wise to invest yourself in identifying self-employment options and taking steps to move gradually toward realizing that goal. The more you can do for your future independence while pulling down a salary, the easier that eventual transition will be.

Enlightened Self-Interest

When a company dispenses with your services, they say it's nothing personal and it isn't to the company: It is doing what it must do to survive and satisfy the shareholders. It is only personal to you, because your life has just been turned upside down. A company doesn't care about you, they put their own needs first.

You need to do the same thing: Take control of your life; rethink the pathways for your economic survival and success by acting with the same forethought, objectivity, and self-interest as a corporation—something we discuss throughout the *Knock 'em Dead* books.

Yes, look for that job working for someone else, as you have probably always done, but do not ignore the financial opportunity and security that comes from building your own business—and if you are suffering from age and wage discrimination, you almost certainly have much of the experience necessary to do so, and make a success of your chosen path.

CHAPTER 23
THE STEALTH JOB SEARCH

IT IS FAR EASIER to find a new job when you already have one. When you are employed, it is proof that you are a desirable commodity. It makes managers think that other employers might want you too; this creates desire and urgency. When you don't have a job, none of these are working in your favor—in fact the opposite holds true.

It is always best for your cash flow and your career to plan and execute strategic career moves while you are employed. However, there are some traps to conducting a job search while you're working, and caution is critical.

Take Control of Your Career

You live in a different professional world than your parents, who were born into a world in which hard work, dedication, and sacrifice led to long-term job security and a steady, predictable climb up the ladder of success. You were almost certainly raised by, and have lived your life with, these admirable ethics. The only problem is that while you have been using these standards, American employers have changed. They still expect hard work, dedication, and sacrifice, but you are expendable. You hold the job you have just as long as it takes that employer to automate it out of existence, find someone younger and cheaper, outsource it locally, or export it overseas where the labor is cheaper.

If you are ready to become the architect of your own success, this new digitally dominated world is a place of enormous opportunity. But if you *aren't* prepared to take responsibility for the success of your professional life, a first job turns into another identical one a year or two down the road, and then another, and after seven to ten years all you'll see are the backs of people who were your peers at the start of your career.

Then, in your forties, you will realize your so-called "career" has just been an ongoing series of very similar jobs that are taking you nowhere, and by fifty, when wage and age discrimination begin to kick in, you'll be lost and depressed because a successful career and the skills that make it possible have all passed you by. You can avoid this fate by developing the career management skills that give you greater control over the quality of your life.

Don't exchange your current situation for another just like it, except with a different address and wall colors. Instead, make a strategic career move based on thinking through your long-term goals and the next steps you need to take that will help you progress toward those goals. Once you know where you want be years down the road, you can work backward through the steps that you will need to take to reach your destination. Bring it all back, first to this job and then to the next job and the opportunities it should offer you.

Be Realistic

Many people think job change is about getting promotions; unfortunately this is usually magical thinking. People get hired based on their credentials, not their potential.

Let's put ourselves on the interviewer's side of the desk for a moment. You and I are about to hire a new manager for one of our departments, and we've narrowed it down to two candidates: one who has been doing the job for five years, and one who has never done the job but would like to "have a go at it." As managers, our jobs and future success depend on making good hires. With that in mind, to whom are we going to offer that job? No-brainer, right? So yes, go after that job in management you've always wanted, but know that if you get interviews you will be up against candidates who have been doing that very management job for years.

This Is the Way Job Change and Promotions Work

You will pursue and land a job very similar to the one you have now, but perhaps with a better company and more opportunity. Once there you will dedicate yourself to making that job secure and pursuing the promotion you want (see *Knock 'em Dead Secrets & Strategies for Success in an Uncertain World*), developing the skills that will qualify you for the opportunity and gaining entrance into the inner circle where all the best opportunities and raises lie.

Of course there are exceptions. A company such as General Motors is so huge that it is said a department manager at GM is a VP at almost any other company, because most other companies are smaller.

We can turn this into career management rules of thumb:

1. Given the skills, you can get a title promotion when you change jobs, if you work at a larger company and move to a smaller company. So if you are a department manager at GM you might well qualify skill- and responsibility-wise for a director or VP position at a smaller company.
2. Given the right positioning with your resume, if you have the skills and experience of a higher title, and you are in fact doing that higher-level job but for some reason have not been given the title, then given the right positioning with your resume, you can usually get interviews. With adequate interview preparation you have reasonable odds of scoring the job.

Otherwise most people change for a similar job to the one they hold now, but with greater professional opportunity if they choose to pursue it strategically.

Keep It Private, Stupid!

When you make the decision that it is time to move, it takes up all your thinking and you are just itching to share your new horizons with others. Looking for a great way to get fired? Tell a friend about your plans or leave a copy of your resume on your desktop or in the office copier; this will often save you the awkwardness of resigning, because you'll likely get fired instead:

• You are announcing that the company is no longer good enough for you and that you intend to leave.
• You are using—some would say stealing—company time, materials, and equipment.

Look at your situation from your manager's point of view. His or her prime responsibility is to get work done through others. That means, amongst other things, hiring and firing employees on the company's timetable. Having people quit unexpectedly ruins your month and is bad for your reputation.

If you were that manager, whom would you terminate: the employee who is working hard or the one whose resume or computer usage has demonstrated the intent to quit unexpectedly?

As a manager in this situation, maybe you can't terminate this person immediately, but you will strongly consider replacing him with the first qualified person who comes along.

None of our jobs are safe, and no one is irreplaceable, so when you have work and are looking to progress in your career, don't screw it up by getting fired before you find that next step on your career path. Your responsibility is to protect what you've already got.

Never Job Search at Work

You must use your own computer, phone, printer, ISP, email, etc. Any use of company tools has a fair chance of biting you in the back of the neck and possibly costing you a job. That's a setback no one needs if it can be avoided—and in this case it can. Never, ever, use company time or equipment; it can and will be used against you. Did you know that for $300 a year a company as small as ten people can silently track computer usage of every employee, with automatic alerts of connections to questionable sites?

Always use your home rather than the office for job search activities of any kind. At work, your online activities are tracked, and at home, you can work with maximum privacy and productivity.

Your Current Job Is Still Important

No matter how bad the workday seems, you know that it is much harder to find a job when you don't have one. Without a job money is tight, you feel worse about yourself, and this all affects interview performance.

Don't quit the job you have but might hate until you have a firm offer for a job you believe will help your career progress; it is one of the foundations of the *Knock 'em Dead* career management canon that every short-term action should play into carefully considered long-term goals. This means your first commitment is to protect the job you have and avoid career disruption at all costs, while very quietly looking for the right new opportunity at the same time. You will do whatever is necessary to protect the job you have until you find the job you want. Especially:

- Don't let anyone in the office know that you're looking for another job. Even if you only tell your best friend, you've told one coworker too many. Gossip has a way of getting around, and if management finds out, you could be out on the street.

- Recommit yourself to the job and to the company. This might seem crazy at first but it does make sense. By approaching your work with a new fervor and commitment, you'll throw everyone off the scent of you conducting a stealth job search.

  You'll benefit in other ways too: You will do more, learn more, create more achievements for your resume, and because you are more engaged with your work, you'll find the time will go more quickly as well.

- Dress the way you've always dressed for work, contribute to meetings with equal or greater enthusiasm, and help others work for the common good at least as much as or more than you have in the recent past—even though your motivation has been steadily declining.

  We spend more of our waking hours with work colleagues than with loved ones—they know us and they notice the smallest things, so a change in your behavior is something that almost certainly has been observed. By upping your game, you reassure management and throw everyone off the scent.

- Keep the same hours; don't be late for work; don't take longer lunch hours, take off early, or call in sick unexpectedly.

- Keep office items at the office. Don't gradually start packing up your belongings, even if they're personal things such as photographs, until you're ready to leave.

In short, don't do anything that could be interpreted as a loss of interest in your job. Everything should go on as before, when you were fully committed to this job.

Make Your Boss an Ally

Do the best job that you can, and seek your manager's advice on how you can improve. Then take that advice to heart and implement the suggestions. It's not hard to make your boss an ally and a fan; you just have to deliver results and not headaches. Let your boss know you are committed to your job and to making a difference with your presence in the department. Your conversations need to make three points:

- I want to make a place for myself here, and to do that I need to be the best I can be.
- I'd like to hear any suggestions you have on skills that would make me more valuable to the team.
- These are skill sets I see as important in doing a stellar job, and I'd like to develop them by doing _____ (itemize the assignments that would develop these areas).

Your manager will make suggestions, and you should react positively to them. Lay out a plan of action, with realizable, step-by-step goals. Here are some smart ways to do this, which will also help you during the upcoming interviews for your next professional step along the road to success:

- Understand what your boss wants by way of results with every aspect of your job, then deliver it on time and in the way your boss prefers.
- Make your work accurate and deliver what is requested rather than what you can get away with.
- Seek advice and accept constructive criticism gracefully.
- Share the credit you receive for work well done.
- Communicate clearly, professionally, honestly, and as often as your boss wants.
- Be a reliable team member in thought, word, and deed.
- Become the most reliable team member in thought, word, and deed.
- Don't be passive-aggressive, looking for ways to misunderstand and avoid responsibilities so that you can squeak by with the least effort possible.

Implement this advice, and follow up informally with management every six to eight weeks to communicate both your commitment and your progress. This establishes credibility and visibility where it counts. Do this and, apart from improving your professional competencies, you will have marked yourself out as someone who thinks, cares, and makes things happen.

Professional Skill Development

You can't rely on hard work and loyalty to deliver a successful career, because behind the scenes your employer, and every employer, is constantly looking to contain costs by automating and outsourcing work.

To keep yourself maximally employable, stay in tune with the skills that employers are seeking when they hire people like you. Every day, technology changes the skills needed to compete in your particular professional workplace, so if you are not consistently developing new skills, you are being paid for abilities that are rapidly becoming obsolete. Hone the *technical skills* of your job to perfection, until you are not only competent but better than you ever thought you could be.

Before you start your stealth job search, collect half a dozen job postings for the job you will be pursuing, and then review them to discover what skills employers are seeking. (Review Target Job Deconstruction [TJD] in Chapter 3 for details of how to do this.)

Bring all these skills up to speed and develop them just as far as you can. You should consider adding any skill you do not have to your skill development program; if the skill is relevant to your work, often your employer will support you in acquiring it.

(Note: Because technology is changing all jobs at such a rapid pace, the TJD process mentioned previously should play a strategic twice-yearly role in your ongoing career management activities, allowing you to identify emerging skill sets and maintain employability with cutting-edge skills.)

When you are seen to be hard working, loyal, and striving to become better, you are securing your current job while learning behaviors that will help you get ahead in the next one.

You will feel better about your job, and at interviews you will be able to talk about who you are and what you do in far more positive and believable ways. You will become a much more credible and visible professional (which speaks to branding). Oh and BTW, this advice has on more than one occasion led to a sought-after promotion and negated the need to make a strategic career move outside the company after all. So following this advice has nothing but an upside for your professional succcess.

Job Search Strategy

The great advantage of job hunting while employed is the relative lack of urgency. You have time to rebuild your resume, craft *Knock 'em Dead* job search letters, create a more professionally relevant social network, build a comprehensive job search plan of attack, research companies and target jobs, and become one with the resume you create. A properly executed strategic career move will help you realign your *professional persona* with the professional goals you strive to achieve. The result will be a more focused and informed professional who is also more career buoyant. A successful job search strategy always starts with a resume.

Rebuild Your Resume

Show me a stalled job search and I'll show you an ill-conceived and badly executed resume. The technology that delivered the Internet continues to change our jobs in unforeseeable ways, and you cannot just add your current job onto an old resume and hope it will perform for you—it won't. Today a resume has to be written to surmount three challenges:

1. It has to be discoverable in resume databases that have millions of competitive resumes. This dramatically changes the way it is written and increases the need for the data density that makes it discoverable.
2. It has been proven in studies that recruiters spend an average of six seconds on the first scan of a resume; if the right information doesn't jump out, they move right on to the next one. This makes both visual accessibility and data density priorities, though conflicting ones.
3. Resumes that attempt to be all things to all people have been supplanted by resumes that focus on a single target job and meet the previous two criteria for data density and visual accessibility. When such a resume is discovered and passed on to a hiring manager, it must then speak succinctly to the deliverables of that specific job.

A productive resume in the new digital era is built in specific ways to help it successfully surmount all these challenges. The first step is to understand what your customers want to buy and then package your professional experience appropriately. This, you'll recall, echoes the first rule of business: "Find out what your customers want and then sell it to them."

The Target Job Deconstruction process that we discussed a couple of pages back (and in detail in Chapter 3) will not only help you create a powerful and productive resume, it will help prepare you for the questions you will face at job interviews.

Your resume is the single most financially important document you will ever own, and as such you must learn how to put one together. I suggest you either get a copy of *Knock 'em Dead Resume Templates*, or have us write a resume for you at *www.knockemdead.com*.

Create a Sanitized Resume to Protect Your Job

When you are employed and involved in a job search, discretion is paramount. To protect your job you must sanitize your resume by removing all "traceable-to-you" contact information (name, specific address, email, phone, etc.), and replace:

- Name with job title
- Specific address with city and zip code
- Regular email with a career email address (see the email section in Chapter 6)
- Known phone for confidential phone number (see phone section in Chapter 6)

Employer Identity

You can protect your identity by removing a current employer's name and replacing it with a generalized description of the company and location. For example, if you work for PepsiCo in Chicago, you could describe this as a "Leading Beverage Company." All recruiters and employers understand the need for this sanitization.

It usually isn't necessary to sanitize prior employer names. However, if you have a senior title associated with a particularly visible company, it could be a clue as to who you are. In this case, replace it with a more generic but recognizable job title.

Networking and Confidential Job Search

I have been coaching professionals for more than thirty years, and the single most common concern is that "I know networking is the best way to find a job, but I have always been so busy doing my job I didn't have time to build a network, and quite honestly I never thought I'd need one."

With everyone being somewhere in the midst of a half-century work life, without the reliability of long-term employment in return for competency, dedication, and sacrifice, this is exactly the time to build a network, because professional colleagues are going to be important in navigating the twists and turns of a long career.

Make the time to start building relevant professional networks now. Make contacts now but don't ask for anything. Rather, find ways to contribute to your professional community.

Social networking has become an essential tool for career management and for maintaining success over the arc of a long career. In modern professional life, with job security a myth, you must learn to anticipate and manage change, rather than being sideswiped by it. The people you meet through intelligently built social networks share many of your concerns, and so they are motivated to help you navigate the ups and downs of a long work life unlike employers, who have little concern for how your life plays out once they have used you up and thrown you out.

Making a success of your life is a long-term and complex challenge, and connectivity with others who understand and are likewise involved in your professional world is an important part of achieving success. The people in your professional world are more motivated to help you, because they realize, like you do, that *we need to know and help each other when the opportunities arise so that we can get help when we need it.* Social networking is foundational to establishing a more businesslike approach to managing the trajectory of your career.

Focused Social Messaging

The profiles you build for your social media platforms (your LinkedIn profile, etc.) always have a twofold purpose:

1. As a home base from which to build relevant networks peopled with professionals related to your profession and occupation.
2. To become visible to headhunters and recruiters.

In building a social media profile (see the earlier chapters in this book and read *Knock 'em Dead Social Networking*), it is important that your messaging reflect a brand that employers want. If you have followed *Knock 'em Dead* advice for writing your resume, or had us write one for you, you already have a carefully crafted showcase of your *professional persona*, and it will be easy to transfer this to your LinkedIn profile.

Never announce on a social media profile that you are looking for a job—especially when you are conducting a stealth job search. It makes you look needy to headhunters and recruiters, and no one needs to be told that you're open to new opportunities: Everyone is. More important, given that you already have a job, an announcement of this sort reveals your intentions to your current employer. Besides, recruiters search for job titles, not people looking for "new opportunities."

Build Relevant Professional Connections

Your networking activities should be focused on getting to know and be known by the most committed and best-connected people in your profession and the target location of your job search.

The best people to connect with are those holding your title (with both more and less experience), the people who hold the titles one, two, and three levels above you, and those who hold titles with which you interact in the course of your working week.

Why these titles? Because a job search should always focus on getting into conversations with the people who can hire you as quickly and as frequently as you can. These titleholders are the people who either have the authority to hire you or who are most likely to know the people who do.

As you search for professionals with whom to make contact, remember that titles vary from company to company. For those high-priority potential hiring titles (the titles one to three levels above you), you want to target at least three different titles at each of the three levels above you.

You need to make connections now and continue making them on an ongoing basis throughout your career. Earlier generations found to their detriment that they had sacrificed networking contacts for hard work and loyalty, thinking they'd never need them. You must commit to giving some of your time each week to becoming involved and making connections within your professional community; your ongoing employability and success depend very much on whom you know and can get to know.

Make connections now and build a relationship over time, because the people you meet now may well be prepared to help you a little, but three or four years from now, when you might be looking again, they are more likely to be prepared to help you a lot.

Online networking is an enormous boon to a confidential job search, as productive networking activites can be squeezed into just a few seconds, for example by "liking" comments of current and future connections on group discussions.

Professional Associations

Becoming more connected to the most committed and best-connected professionals in your area—getting to know them to the extent of being able to recognize one another in a grocery store—takes more time but is of inestimable value. All you have to do is join a professional association relevant to your work and go to the monthly meetings. All it takes is a couple of hours a month, but active involvement, by way of joining one of the many committees that allow associations to function, is the smartest career strategy you can initiate to achieve wide professional connectivity in your immediate location (see Chapter 5 for more details).

Attending monthly meetings puts you face-to-face with the best in your business and gives you the opportunity to get to know them in a professional but also quasi-social setting. Don't mention that you are looking for new opportunities on first meeting, just that you think it sensible to become more involved with your professional community.

Networking Conversations

I've discussed when and how to ask for networking leads in some detail in earlier chapters, so we won't cover that same ground again. However, when you are building your networks, and especially when you are doing a confidential search, you can engage in activities and ask questions that will be useful to your search and your career but are less likely to raise suspicions in an employer.

You can use the early weeks of network building to reach out to your online and bricks-and-mortar groups with questions about your industry. Take some time to ask questions and catch up on everything that is happening on the cutting edge of your profession. Ask who people think are the current dominant players and what the coming products, approaches, and companies will be; which companies are prospering, coming to town, and leaving town. Reconnect with old colleagues, and find out who's been promoted and congratulate them. Renew your focus on making friendly connections throughout your industry.

Job Sites and Resume Databases

There are thousands of job sites, and you can never hope to visit them all, so plan intelligently. Start by identifying which sites are relevant to your search. The easiest way to short-list sites is to do Google searches for variations on your target job title, visit the sites that mention an opening, and see what other similar jobs they have. A few considerations when evaluating a site's relevance to your job search:

- Does the site have job postings that are suitable for you? If it doesn't, you can move on to the next site. If it does, you will want to register with the site and receive email job alerts when new jobs matching your criteria get posted.
- When you are asked to define the jobs that interest you, set your sights wide. You may get too many responses initially, but you can gradually narrow the parameters. It's better to plow through a little junk than miss a great opportunity.
- When you find sites that have appropriate job postings, it means recruiters are also cruising their resume database, so you will want to upload your sanitized resume into that database.

Remember, those jobs you hear about that aren't quite right for you are not a waste of your time. They are worth saving in a trading file to share with network contacts for whom those jobs might be a perfect fit.

Visit job aggregator sites such as *www.Indeed.com* and *www.SimplyHired.com*, whose search engines scan thousands of sites looking for your search terms. Again, you can search by your target job title, then your professional or industry sector, your city, county, state, the variety of zip codes that cover your target market, and other database search term variations, as we have discussed throughout the book.

Search LinkedIn, Google+, Facebook, Twitter, and your professional and alumni networks using the same variety of search terms. Each of these sites now has job search apps specially configured for their platforms.

Make a folder for each relevant site you visit, and as postings come in, store them in the appropriate folder. You'll quickly see which sites are most productive. You can learn more about job sites and resume databases in the job search section earlier in the book.

Headhunters and Corporate Recruiters

Quick definition: Headhunters or executive recruiters are third-party recruiters who find candidates for hard-to-fill positions for client companies. Corporate recruiters, on the other hand, are employees of a corporation who work to fill internal vacancies and additionally are often the corporate point of contact for headhunters. Neither is involved or interested in finding you a job—they are both interested in filling specific positions they have open.

Consequently, making contact with both is a numbers game. The more you connect with them, the more opportunities you will learn about. You can learn more about working with headhunters and corporate recruiters in the job search chapters earlier in the book.

Direct Research

You will never identify all the employers and all the jobs that are suitable for you and located within commuting distance by networking, visiting job/resume sites, and connecting with headhunters and recruiters, effective though all of these strategies can be.

However, there is a way to find 99 percent of suitable opportunities within the geographic scope of your job search, and that is by doing direct research. This is exactly what the headhunters do to find companies with openings.

The geographic scope of your job search means deciding how far and how long you are willing to commute. Where I live, you can travel twenty miles in thirty minutes by car or cover the same distance by public transport in sixty minutes.

So first of all, you decide how much time you are willing to invest in a commute and how far you can travel in that time; for example, you might be prepared to commute for forty-five minutes or thirty miles. Now you can use sites such as Google Maps or MapQuest to judge times from your home to the prospective job location—this works for some people. However, neither of these tools allows you to draw a radius (circle) around a central point. Looking at a map that includes everything within thirty miles of your house enables you to quickly and memorably visualize everywhere that is within reach of your commute parameters. The website *www.mapbusinessonline.com* allows you to do this, and it has a one-month free trial, so you can do a number of radius maps (ten, twenty, thirty miles, etc.) in an hour one evening while watching TV. Such maps will allow you to quickly identify centers of employment within your reach and identify the time/distance to specific companies. Then all you have to do is find the companies within this target geography that might have suitable employment opportunities for you.

Direct research and approach is especially effective when you are conducting a confidential job search, because by identifying and then contacting companies directly, your job search maintains a lower profile. Once the physical radius of your search is defined, you can then start looking for companies within your target area with these resources:

1. Use the S&P (Standard & Poor's) Directories at your library or access them online at *www.standardandpoors.com.*
    This reference tool identifies every publicly traded company in the world by location and a couple of dozen other criteria. Checking the print editions at your library is free but takes time; the online database is fast but charges a monthly access fee.
2. Dun & Bradstreet through its Zapdata database tracks 240 million public and private businesses worldwide, some 17 million in the United States alone.

Together, no matter where you live or where you are looking, these two reference resources will enable you to find the vast majority of potential employers in your target profession and location. Visit the appropriate company websites (*www.standardandpoors.com/*; *www.dnb.com/*), check for jobs, and upload your resume, whether or not there are suitable jobs posted.

Then cross-reference each company with networking contacts across all your social networks (LinkedIn, Google+, Facebook, Twitter, plus professional and alumni networks), looking for contacts that work or have worked there. You'll especially look for the three ranks of high-value titles, those people most likely to be in a position to hire you or refer you to someone who can.

Develop a Plan of Attack and Stick to It

Decide what your job search plan of attack will be and what your work-at-home hours will be, whether it's thirty minutes before dinner or two hours before bedtime each night. Once you've established a plan of attack for your job search, stick to it.

Since your job search will be a low-profile affair by design, you'll need to keep yourself motivated. Reward yourself for your progress (for example, completing your resume or deciding on a resume writer). Go see a movie or eat a nice meal at a restaurant, etc.

You have to stay motivated and remain persistent. A friend of mine used to have a sign on the back of his office door, so that when he left in the evening, the last thing he saw was a message that read, "Keep Writing." It was a reminder for him to switch gears and get focused on his job search activities for the evening. When the going gets tough, remember your goal—a more interesting job, better pay, increased job security, etc.—and don't let anything deter you!

The key to stretching your job search hours is to make the most of every moment you have available instead of lamenting about the time you don't have. Use lunch hours, weekends, holidays, personal days, and any other off-the-clock time you have available to conduct research. When you go to lunch, you might not have your computer, but you almost certainly have a smartphone with which you can achieve almost as much as with a high-powered laptop. For example, it might be a good thing to use your lunch breaks one week to catch up with old college and corporate alumni and find those who are working in your industry and who have worked with companies that have operations in your target job search geography.

Ready to Launch

If you've built a good resume, or had me build one for you, interviews are going to start coming your way once you launch your job search and begin approaching companies. But how can you account for the time you need for job interviews? This is an area of enormous confusion for many employed professionals.

You'll discover that employers are very sensitive to your employed status, and that they will usually be happy to arrange interviews outside of normal business hours. In fact, this is not only convenient, it is also great positioning, because it encourages potential employers to see you as an in-demand professional.

However, that isn't always possible, and some people have problems with creating fictitious doctor and dentist appointments, as they feel that lying to an employer is unacceptable. Personally, I think this is being conned into living by a corporate double standard. Companies and managers lie to their staff every day of the week and justify it based on company priorities. Just think of the times employers have lied to you and your friends over the years. When caught, they justify it by saying, "It's nothing personal; it's just business."

Well, you are a company too; you are a company called MeInc., and you have to survive financially just as any *Fortune* 500 company does, so therefore you have the same right to dissemble as any employer. For example, employers usually know six to nine months ahead of time that layoffs are coming. Do they tell you, when they know your life is going to be turned upside down? No, they very often tell you at the last possible moment. So I suggest that you have more loyalty to MeInc. than you do to an employer who will throw you on the scrapheap just as soon as they can find someone cheaper or automate your job out of existence.

The problem with those doctor and dentist appointments, however, is that done haphazardly, they begin to look suspicious. So I suggest that you identify an irritating, very personal, but nonthreatening malady that will require a few visits; maybe you have a skin condition (how embarrassing) and you need to have some tests and then some treatments. Letting your employer know this in advance, and then being seen to conscientiously catch up on everything on your return, can work surprisingly well. You may not like this idea, but it does work. Yes, I agree it is deceptive but you are only operating on the same principles as your employer.

Organization and Time Management in a Confidential Job Search

A successful job search should always be focused on getting into conversations with the people who hold the authority to hire you, and to do so as quickly and frequently as you can.

With a stealth job search, you only have nights and weekends with hours of uninterrupted time, but you still need to have a life, so managing your time and the activities in which you invest that time becomes a priority.

In looking at job search strategy, we recognize that there is no single proven "best way," but we know that direct research, headhunters, job banks, and resume databases, all integrated with social networking (as we talked about in Chapters 4, 5, and 6) are collectively the most productive approach for working professionals.

You have five evenings during the week, and five consistently productive job search tactics. The research parts of four out of five of these job search activities aren't exactly brain surgery and can be done while watching TV; if you are not sure about this, you can always steal an hour from TV watching every night and invest it in the advancement of your career.

Invest your time in one or two of the five job search tactics each night of the week. For example, you can look at job postings for an hour, or alternatively you can look at job postings for thirty minutes and invest the other thirty in cross-referencing what you find with your professional network across all your social media platforms.

A stealth job search takes time, but stick with it and the job offers will come. You'll accept one of them and once you have it in writing, it will be time to resign.

How to Resign

Once you've accepted a job offer and you're ready to resign, do it graciously. Now is not the time to pay back your employer for years of grief. Save the bridge burning for your fantasies and go about the business of severing relations professionally. You never know when you'll run into your former employer or when you'll need the old so-and-so again.

Although employees who are terminated are usually expected to clean out their desks and leave immediately, resigning workers are generally required to give proper notice. Helping make a smooth transition for your remaining colleagues builds bridges for the future. You can even offer to hire and train a replacement—and you can promise to be available to answer questions even after you leave. Be sure to follow through if you make such a promise.

An important tip: It's okay to be happy, but keep your mirth under control while you're in the office. Save the rip-roaring celebration for family and friends. Even your closest colleagues can resent your good fortune, so don't do anything that encourages them to believe you might be gloating. Remember, those you offend on the way up could very well show you the way down sometime in the future.

CHAPTER 24
OUT OF SIGHT CAN MEAN OUT OF MIND

YOU LEAVE YOUR interviewers with a strong, positive image and don't want that memory to slip with the passage of time and a busy schedule. But out of sight means out of mind, and out of mind means out of the job offer race; the longer the decision-making period, the less distinct candidates become from each other in the hiring manager's memory. Following up with your interviewers shows that you pay attention to detail and are enthusiastic about the job.

The first thing you do on leaving the interview is breathe a sigh of relief. The second is make sure that "out of sight, out of mind" will not apply to you. You do this by starting a follow-up procedure immediately after the interview: Sitting in your car, on the bus, train, or plane, write a recap of the interview while it's still fresh in your mind.

This information will help with your follow-up with this company, and reviewing all your follow-up notes after two or three interviews may alert you to a weakness you hadn't noticed. Make notes on these categories:

- Who did you meet? What were their titles and email addresses?
- What did you find out about the job?
- What are its first projects/challenges?
- Why can you do the job? What are the problems?
- What did the interviewer say on any topic related to the job, company, competition, industry, or profession that might give you a unique follow-up were you to Google something interesting?
- What aspects of the interview went well? Why?
- What aspects of the interview went poorly? Why?
- What did the interviewer say was the next step?
- Are there other candidates in contention?
- When will a decision be made?
- What did the interviewer say in concluding the interview?

KNOCK 'EM DEAD TIP

Identify aspects of your interview that went poorly. A person does not get offered a job based solely on strengths; those questions will be easy enough for you to answer. On the other hand, you may get that job offer based on your lack of negatives compared to the other candidates. It is important to identify any negatives from your performance so that you can overcome them in your follow-up and during subsequent interviews.

Using the information gathered from this exercise, you can begin a follow-up campaign. Knowing if there is another round of interviews or if the decision is going to be made tomorrow afternoon or next week has a significant impact on how and when you will follow up.

Follow-Up Steps and Pacing

Knowing where you are in the selection cycle will help you execute a well-paced follow-up campaign. We'll start with a follow-up after the first interview in a series.

After the First Interview in a Series
Informal First Follow-Up Within Twenty-Four Hours

If you can find something interesting related to the job, company, competition, industry, or profession, your first follow-up will be professional-casual, reinforcing the tone of an ongoing conversation between two professionals with a common interest. You'll send an email that opens with a salutation: "Hi John/Jane" if you are close enough in years and experience to use first names. If you are younger and have been encouraged to use first names, that's okay too, but reverting to the formalities of Mr./Ms. in written communication (until after the second meeting), will usually be received as respectful and flattering. If use of first names hasn't been encouraged, don't presume: It won't win you points, while showing professional courtesies always does.

Note the short, punchy, conversational tone of this sample follow-up email; it is considerably more casual and direct than traditional follow-up letters:

"It was great to meet you this afternoon. I really enjoyed talking about the _____ position. Your comments/our conversation on _____ [*the topic of your attachment, or what you paste into the body copy*] has been buzzing in the back of my mind all day. I just ran across this and knew you'd enjoy it. On a deadline, so I'll follow up properly as soon as my schedule permits."

Send the email between 7 P.M. and 10 P.M. that evening or early the next morning when you first get up, whichever is closer to the limits of the twenty-four-hour mark. Do not send an email during business hours.

Your first meeting will have tagged you as someone different. This initial follow-up aims to continue the differentiation. The tone is respectful, and shows a committed professional working late (you can't write fully because you are working on a deadline) and being *intelligently enthusiastic* (you are actively engaged in thinking about this job and your profession outside of business hours).

Formal First Follow-Up

Your formal first follow-up should arrive two to no later than three days after the first interview OR after your first *informal* follow-up, adjusting your timing to the needs of each separate selection cycle. This formal follow-up letter should make the following points:

- The date and time you met with the interviewer and the title of the target job
- You paid attention to what was said in the interview
- Why you can do the job
- You are excited about the job and want it
- You have the experience to contribute to those first major projects as discussed in the interview

Here are some ideas and phrases you'll find useful:

- Appreciation: "I enjoyed meeting you to discuss . . ." Professional etiquette requires you express appreciation for the interview; remember to identify the date and time you met and the job you interviewed for.
- Recognition: "I recognize the importance of . . ."
- Observation: "Listening to the points you made . . ."
- Motivation: "I am excited about the job . . ." Let the interviewer catch your enthusiasm and see that you are motivated by the opportunity. This is very effective, especially as your communication may well arrive while other, less prepared applicants are stumbling their way through the interview.
- Enthusiasm: "I was impressed . . ." Let the interviewer know that you were impressed with the people/product/service/facility/market/position. "It was energizing to meet a group of people who really cared about their work."
- Confidence: Draw attention to one of the topics that was of special interest: "I feel confident I can handle the challenge of . . ." There is a job to be done and a challenge to be met; let the interviewer know you are confident of doing both well.
- Interest: "I want this job, and you can rely on me to do a good job for you." If you want the job (or next interview), say so. At this stage, the company is buying and you are selling. Ask for the job in a positive and enthusiastic manner.
- If interview nerves caused you to forget something, you can introduce it with "On reflection . . ."; "Interview nerves got the better of me . . ."; "When we were talking about . . ."; "I should have mentioned my work with . . ."; "Having thought about our meeting, I thought I'd mention . . ."; or "I should have mentioned that . . ."

Keep the note short (less than one page) and address it to the hiring manager or main interviewer if you haven't met your new boss yet. If you interviewed with other people and the meeting was more than cursory, you can send separate emails to each. Remember:

1. Whenever possible and appropriate, mention the names of the people you met at the interview.
2. Address the follow-up email/letter to the main interviewer. You can send separate emails/letters to others in the selection cycle. Each makes a positive impression and shows extra effort and attention to detail.
3. Don't write too much. Keep it short—less than one page—and don't make claims that will not withstand scrutiny.
4. Depending on the time constraints, send an email within forty-eight hours and a letter within twenty-four hours; this gives you time to write, edit, and polish. If the decision is going to be made in the next couple of days, email and/or hand deliver a traditional letter. This way your follow-up will refresh your image in the mind of the interviewer just when it would normally be starting to dim.

Email is the way almost all business communication is done today; the average executive gets 90 percent less traditional mail than she did ten years ago, but this doesn't mean you should ignore traditional mail. Incoming mail used to provide a pleasant short break from the affairs of the day. With so little mail arriving, the break it offers is even more appreciated; a large and neatly hand-addressed envelope will always get opened, something you can no longer say about an email. Sending letters by traditional mail is contrarian thinking and the more effective because of it.

5. When a hiring decision is imminent, follow up with an email, then a telephone call as the decision timeline dictates. A phone call might begin, "Mr. Massie? Martin Yate. We met for an interview on Wednesday afternoon at 2 p.m. about the _____ position. I know you are making a decision by close of business tomorrow and I wanted to catch up with you personally to say . . ."

Cover the following points in this phone conversation:

- Thanks for your time
- I can do the job and this is why
- I am excited about the job and this is why
- I will make a good hire and this is why
- I want this job; will you make me a fair offer?

If you are making a call, it is best not to write everything out in full sentences, as you'll sound like one of those telemarketers; instead, write down the bullet points you want to make. You'll sound more natural.

Additional Interviews

If the selection cycle is normal, three interviews for each of a handful of short-list candidates can take three or four weeks, so with the second and subsequent interviews (excepting the final interview), your follow-up pattern should replicate that of the initial interview.

1. An informal follow-up within twenty-four hours, essentially saying: "Good to see you again, Jack, and to meet the guys. Thanks for your time. Preparing for a client meeting. I'll get back to your properly in the next couple of days."

You might replace this with an equally brief phone call, when there is something to warrant a brief conversation. If the manager doesn't pick up, leave a complete but brief message. You don't need to call back.

2. A formal follow-up, following the same principles and timing as before. As the inter-view cycle progresses, you want to maintain awareness of your candidacy, but you don't want to be seen as doing anything by rote.

Although the bulk of business correspondence these days is done via email, remember that a traditional letter can make you stand out.

Extended Interview Cycles

You don't want to make a pest of yourself by calling or emailing every day, but neither do you want to drop out of sight. If the process stretches out into a month or months, make contact every couple of weeks, but keep it very low volume. You don't want to seem overly anxious, just interested. Google.com has a nice feature that allows you to track news on any topic you choose. Taking advantage of this allows you to keep up to speed on your profession and factors affecting it, and this knowledge gathering can be put to additional good use.

As you did before, you might send profession-relevant information:

"Harry, being so busy you may not have seen the article I've attached. It's about new legislation that's bound to affect us.

Regards,

Martin

P.S. I'm still determined to be your next _____."

You can do this in an email and/or by traditional mail.

Funny Emails

Getting a funny email always brightens the day, and giving the interviewer a smile is a great way to be remembered, but this requires judgment. Don't send anything of a sexual, political, or religious nature, as it constitutes a breach of *professional values*.

The same considerations apply when sending a cartoon via traditional mail. This works because it's a different delivery medium and the cartoon causes a smile; plus, if you're lucky, it gets stuck on the wall or passed on.

KNOCK 'EM DEAD TIP

Check out the *follow-up letter templates* at *www.knockemdead.com*. Here you'll find four different categories of cover letters, plus advice on networking, follow-up (telephone and face-to-face), candidacy resurrection, negotiation, rejection, acceptance, resignation, and after-hire thank-you letters.

Reposted Jobs

Sometimes jobs remain open for a long time, or they may be frozen because of budgetary constraints and reposted under a different job title. Here's what you do:

1. Match the needs of the new job description with your resume and what was addressed at the interviews. Refocus a customized copy of the resume using as many keywords from the job posting as you reasonably can.
2. If you are out of touch with the decision makers, apply again in the requested manner.
3. If you are in touch with the decision makers, approach them again with the newly customized resume, reiterating your continued interest and qualifications.
4. Make a follow-up call to the recruiter and the hiring manager.
5. After a couple of follow-up letters to decision makers, you need to change the tone and might try the article approach mentioned earlier; something that is of relevance to your profession and therefore by extension to your target decision makers.

Not sure this will work? As I was updating *Knock 'em Dead*, I heard from Michael, who wrote to me through the website; he said, in part, "I have been tracking jobs since last spring that are now reappearing and I'm wondering what to do."

Not long after I sent him the previous ideas I heard from him again. "Thanks Martin, I spoke with the recruiter a couple of times, then last Thursday, called the hiring manager directly. We spoke for almost ten minutes, so it was a well-received call. *She admired my guts in calling her directly because she had recently been out of work herself, and hated making those calls*" (my italics). It is this kind of extra effort that pays off in job offers.

> **KNOCK 'EM DEAD TIP**
> The longer the hiring process drags on, the less likely it is that you will get the offer. It can happen, but the odds get longer as time goes by. Don't let your job search stand still while you're waiting for a response from one company. Remember: *You don't have the job until you have a written offer in hand.*

When the Hiring Decision Is Imminent

Based on many years' experience, I can tell you that a decision next Friday means that an offer will be extended on that date, while the actual decision will be made *at least* seventy-two hours to five days prior (allowing HR the time to shepherd the paperwork through the authorization process). Of course this isn't the case if you are interviewing for a job today and they tell you the decision will be made at the end of the week. As always, you adapt the follow-up strategy to reflect the demands of the hiring cycle.

If you know in advance that a decision is coming, say Friday of the following week, you can aim to get an email on the hiring manager's desk this Friday/Monday; a slight variation of that message might arrive via traditional mail on the same or following day; and you can make a telephone call no later than Wednesday morning. This leaves seventy-two hours before decision time.

Final Written Communications

The content of these communications should cover:

- "We last met on _____ and have been talking about _____ job."
- "I can do the job and this is why: [talk about the *technical skills* you bring]."
- "I am excited about the job and this is why: [talk about how you can contribute to first projects and your desire to join a great group of people]."
- "I will make a good hire and this is why: [talk about the *transferable skills and professional values* you bring to the job]."
- "I want the job. What do I have to do to get it?"

Making That Final Call

If a hiring decision is imminent, succinctly following up on your emails and letters within seventy-two hours of decision time might help seal the deal. Work out what you want to say, write it down in bullet points, and make practice calls to friends, keeping it brief and to the point. Then, when you are ready, make the call; you have nothing to lose and a job offer to gain.

CHAPTER 25
NEGOTIATING THE JOB OFFER

THE JOB OFFERS finally begin to arrive and you're never going to have this much leverage with this employer again. In this chapter you will learn the essentials of salary and benefits negotiations: handling good job offers and poor job offers, negotiating future salary, and how to evaluate the salary and the offer.

When you negotiate salary, you shouldn't be thinking of a magic number that you'd love to make, but a reasonable and acceptable range. All jobs have salary ranges attached to them. Your approach is to come up with a salary range that *puts you in the running, but doesn't nail you down to a specific figure*. You need to come up with three different figures:

1. First, given your skills, experience, and location, determine the least you would accept for a suitable job with a stable company.
2. Second, given the same considerations, what would constitute a fair offer for a suitable job with a stable company? There are three ways to figure out what would constitute a fair offer:

- A salary calculator, such as the one at *www.salary.com*.
- Job postings
- Headhunters with whom you have a relationship

3. Third, given the same considerations of skills, experience, and location, come up with the figure that would make you drop dead and go to heaven on the spot.

At the end of this process, you've got three figures: a minimum, a midpoint, and a dream salary. Kick out the lowest because you can always negotiate downward. This leaves you with a salary range—your midpoint to your high point—that you can give with confidence.

When to Bring Up Salary

Why do you go to job interviews? You go to a job interview because you need more money, of course. But raising the issue too soon sends the wrong message. Headhunters and hiring managers say that many candidates imagine interviews are about deciding whether they want the job, and that often the only questions asked are about salary, vacation, and benefits. The fact is, you don't go to a job interview to decide if you want the job, you go to get an offer. You have nothing to decide until an offer is put on the table. Nothing else matters: Pay, benefits, vacation—they are all irrelevant until an offer is on the table.

Turn Weakness Into Strength

Of all the professional skills you need to survive over a long a career, perhaps the most critical—and almost certainly your weakest because of your lack of experience—is your ability to turn job interviews unto job offers.

Get smart and go to job interviews with one goal in mind: to turn it into a job offer. In the process, you will transform your greatest professional weakness—turning interviews into offers—into a professional strength.

You don't have to accept the job any more than a company is obliged to offer you one. Your loyalty is to the survival of MeInc., so you go to every job interview to improve your ability to get job offers, and treat each one as an opportunity to build this critical professional skill.

The Hiring Secret Nobody Knows

It's common sense that how you answer an interviewer's questions is of primary importance, but there is something else: We all make judgments about others based on both the statements they make (answers to our questions), and on the questions they ask, because their questions tell us what they know and how they think.

It's the same with job interviews: Your questions demonstrate the depth of your interest in and understanding of the job, so the quality of your questions also speaks to your understanding of the job. Furthermore, asking intelligent questions gets answers that give you insight into how you should frame your answers during the rest of the interview.

Ask Job-Related Questions

Ask questions that give you insight into the day-to-day challenges of the job and show your engagement with the work. Such questions also help you advance your candidacy, because you now know that judgments about you will be based, in part, on the questions you ask. Ask questions that show your professional engagement and values, like:

"What's the most challenging aspect of the job?"

"What problems do successful new employees experience most often?"

"What type of person succeeds in this job?"

"What type of person fails in this job?"

There's More To It

You know the responsibilities of the job, and you should know that *at its very core your job is about problem identification, prevention, and solution within your areas of responsibility.* Consequently you can ask about specific duties and their deliverables, for example:

"What are the biggest challenges your people face with accounts receivable?"

"How do you prefer these problems handled?"

"How do your best people execute their responsibilities in ways that minimize these problems?"

"Would it be of value if I talked about how I do my job in ways that help prevent these problems from arising?"

"Would it be of value if I told you how I handle them when they do?"

Stay Away from These Questions

Obviously stay away from the money question, and in the early rounds of interviewing, stay away from questions about professional growth and where the job can lead.

It's Still All about the Money

Of course it's still all about the money, but MeInc., the company you will always work for, demands that you focus on strategies and tactics that will move you toward the extension of a job offer.

You don't need to accept the offer, but until it's made you have no opportunity to consider or decision to make. Learn how to turn interviews into offers, and you develop a skill that results in a more fulfilled and successful life.

You Want Each Other, but Are Both Being Coy

They want you, but they don't have you. This is the first time you really have decisions to make: Do you want this job, and on what terms? The issues for your consideration are the job and its potential, the company and its stability, the money and the benefits. *This is probably the only time in your relationship with your new employer when you'll have even a slim negotiating edge*. If you under-negotiate your salary, that has an impact, not only today, but on your future earnings, because all raises will be based on a lower salary. Employers are also more inclined to respect and honor a person who has a clear understanding of her worth in the marketplace—they want a savvy and businesslike professional. Armed with this knowledge, you can move the conversation forward.

The interviewer will generally initiate salary discussions with one or more of the following questions. His goal is to make you name a figure; your goal is to avoid naming a figure: Otherwise, you'll be trapped.

Why should I hire you?

Keep your answer short and to the point. Demonstrate your grasp of the job's responsibilities, the problems typically occurring in each area, the *transferable skills* that allow you to consistently deliver on them, and then a brief review of what you are like as a professional colleague, personalizing the behavioral profile for success you identified in your TJD.

What are you earning currently? Or, What were you making on your last job?

Ideally the offer you negotiate should be based on salary norms and on the value you bring to the job, not your salary history. However, it can be difficult to make that statement clear to the interviewer without appearing objectionable. A short answer might include: "I am earning $xx,000, but I want you to know that a major reason for making a job change right now is to significantly increase my salary. I am currently underpaid for my skills, experience, and contributions, and my capabilities are under-utilized."

Education and salary are factors that very often get checked, and untruths in either of these areas are grounds for termination with cause. The interviewer could ask to see a payroll stub or W2 form at the time you start work, or could make the offer dependent on verification of salary. A new employer may request verbal or written confirmation from previous employers or might use an outside verification agency.

In any instance where an employer checks references, credit, or other matters of verification, he is obliged by law to get your written permission. The impossibly small print on the bottom of the job application form—followed by a request for your signature—usually authorizes him to do just that.

It is important to understand the "areas of allowable fudge." For instance, if you are considerably underpaid, you may want to weigh the dollar value of such perks as medical and dental plans, pay in lieu of vacation, profit sharing and pension plans, bonuses, stock options, and other incentives. For many people, those can add between 20 to 35 percent to their base salary—you might honestly be able to mention a higher figure than you at first thought possible. Also, if you are due for a raise imminently, you are justified in adding it in.

What is an adequate reward for your efforts?

A glaring manageability question and money probe all in one. The interviewer probably already has a typist on staff who expects a Nobel Prize each time he gets out a faultless letter. Your answer should be honest and cover all bases. "My primary satisfaction and reward come from a job well done and completed on time. The occasional good word from my boss is always welcome. Last but not least, I think everyone looks forward to a salary review."

What is your salary history? Or, What was your salary progress on your last job?

The interviewer is looking for a couple of things. First, he is looking for the frequency, percentage, and dollar value of your raises, which in turn tell him about your performance and the relative value of the offer that is about to be made. What you want to avoid is tying the potential offer to your salary history—the offer you negotiate should be based solely on the value of the job in hand.

Your answer needs to be specifically vague. Perhaps: "My salary history has followed a steady upward path, and I have never failed to receive merit increases. I would be glad to give you the specific numbers if needed, but I'll have to sit down with my records and give it some thought." The odds are that the interviewer will not ask you to do that; if he does, nod in agreement and say you'll get right to it when you get home. Don't begin the task until you are requested a second time, which is unlikely.

If for any reason you do get your back against the wall with this one, be sure to include in the specifics of your answer that "one of the reasons I am leaving my current job is that raises were standard for all levels of employees, so that despite my superior contributions, I got the same percentage raise as the tardy employee. I want to work in an environment where I will be recognized and rewarded for my contributions." Then end with a question: "Is this the sort of company where I can expect that?"

Have you ever been refused a salary increase?

This implies that you asked for one. An example of your justifiable request might parallel the following true story. An accountant in a tire distributorship made changes to an accounting system that saved $65,000 a year, plus thirty staff hours a week. Six months after the methods were obviously working smoothly, he requested a salary review; he was refused but was told he would receive a year-end bonus. He did: $75. If you can tell a story like that, by all means tell how you were turned down for a raise. If not, it is best to explain that your work and salary history showed a steady and marked improvement over the years.

How much do you need to support your family?

This question is sometimes asked of people who will be working in a sales job, where remuneration is based upon a draw against forthcoming commissions. If this scenario describes your income patterns, be sure you have a firm handle on your basic needs before you accept the position.

For salaried positions, this question is of dubious relevance. It implies the employer will try to get you at a subsistence salary, which is not why you are there. In this instance, give a range from your desired high-end salary down to your desired midpoint salary.

How much will it take to get you? Or, How much are you looking for? Or, What are your salary expectations? Or, What are your salary requirements?

Oh hallelujah, money is coming to the table. This is negotiation time, and you are there to make a deal. Here's the dilemma:

- Ask for too much and you might rule yourself out.
- Ask for too little and you could be kicking yourself for years.

What's your best option for maximizing the chances of getting what you want? To do this, think through your response in a businesslike and professional way before you ever set foot inside an interviewer's office.

ThemInc. and MeInc.

All jobs have painstakingly approved salary ranges. To avoid giving an answer that is too high or too low, you need to come up with a salary range for MeInc., just like ThemInc. does. This is serious: It's your job *and* life we're talking about because you spend the majority of your waking hours at work.

Some companies (and some career advisers) will tell you that to get and keep a job you must align your interests with those of the company you work for. The more closely you do this, they say, the better your chance for promotion and long-term employment.

I say this is nonsense.

You work for MeInc., but as an employee you also lease out a percentage of your time to work for ThemInc. It's true that your goals may often run parallel—it's in neither of your interests, for example, for the organization to perform poorly, since that may lead to layoffs or even the end of the company. But never forget that ThemInc.'s main goal is to make a profit and return value to shareholders. Helping ThemInc. maintain profitability is a goal of your employment with them, but your mission in life is geared toward the success of MeInc. and its dependents. As someone once said, "I have a hard time motivating myself to go to work in order to make someone else rich." This is not an issue for you, because while you are giving to that employer you are also investing yourself in learning from that employer, all the ways you can make MeInc. more profitable as time goes by.

Once you recognize the true relationship between the goals of MeInc. and ThemInc., you'll be well on your way to figuring out how to structure not only your job search, including salary negotiations, but the entire arc of your career management going forward.

Get What You Want

Learning how to turn job interviews into job offers is one small part of this self-guided professional education you give yourself. You have worked hard to educate yourself about what it takes to succeed in your profession and professional life. But face it: You are statistically likely to change jobs ten or fifteen times over your work life (and the number could easily be 20 percent higher than that). This makes *turning interviews into offers* a vitally important professional skill for you.

You may or may not want the job, but you do want to get an offer on the table so that there is a choice to be made and evidence that your control over your professional destiny is growing:

- Learning how to turn job interviews into job offers is a critical survival and success skill that you must change from a weakness into a strength.
- So you always want to get a job offer with a firm dollar amount attached on the table.
- Because you not only want experience turning interviews into offers, you also need to develop your negotiation skills. Until an offer is on the table and you have hammered out the best deal possible, your skill development is still in play and you have no decision to make. With this businesslike approach you build a critical career survival skill and act in the best interests of MeInc.

If at the end of the negotiation process you have an offer you don't want, you simply turn it down in a courteous and professional manner—it's nothing personal, it's just business.

Do this and you are building critical skill sets. As well, in a few pages I'm going to show you how to turn offers from companies you don't want to work for into offers from companies you would like to join.

What you need, once "How much money do you want?" is asked, is a salary range that puts you in the running, but one that doesn't nail you down to a specific dollar amount that you might later regret.

Competitive Salary Research

There are innumerable factors that can affect salary ranges, leading to wide variations for the same job. Geographic location is especially important, given that cost of living has an impact on salary range—it costs more to live and work in Manhattan than it does in Jacksonville, Florida.

Here are some great resources for competitive salary research:

- Salary calculators such as *www.salary.com* or *www.bls.gov.*
- Google "salary calculator" and "salary report" and include terms such as your job title, profession, and industry in separate searches and on different search engines.
- Job postings with salary ranges are steadily increasing.
- Headhunters you speak with usually know the salary range for your position.

Get Smart—Define Your Own Salary Range

Using the previous resources to define a broad salary range, you next assess your MeInc. salary range. It's an easy three-step process.

Step One. Given your skills, experience, and location, what is the least you would accept for a suitable job with a stable company? The *least* means what it will take to keep food on the table and a roof over your head. You will rarely ever mention this number to anyone; it is normally used just to establish a baseline.

However, sometimes, a strategic career can require taking a step sideways or even backward to take you forward on the path you want to pursue. In fact, the most important job change of my life involved a shift in career direction that required I take a 50 percent pay cut, but as I expected it changed my life completely and forever.

Step Two. Given the same considerations of skills, experience, and location, what would you consider a fair offer?

Step Three. Given the same considerations of skills, experience, and location, what would be the figure that would make you smile, drop dead, and go to heaven on the spot?

At the end of this process, you've got three dollar amounts:

- A minimum
- A midpoint
- A dream salary

Having come up with these three dollar figures, kick out the lowest, because you can always negotiate downward.

This leaves you with a MeInc. salary range—your midpoint to your high point—that you can give with confidence.

What do you hope to be earning two to five years from now?

A difficult question. The interviewer is probing your desired career and earning path and is trying to see whether you have your sights set high enough—or too high. A jocular tone might not hurt here: "I'd like to be earning just about as much as I can work out with my boss!" Then, throw the ball back with your own question: "How much is it possible to make here?"

If you give a specific figure, the interviewer is going to want justification. If you come up with a salary range, you are advised also to have a justified career path to go along with it.

You could also say, "In two years, I will have finished my CPA requirements, so with that plus my additional experience, industry norms say I should be earning between *$xx,000* and *$yyy,000*. I would hope to be earning at least within that range, but hopefully with a proven track record of contributions, I would be making above the norm." The trick is to use industry statistics as the backbone of your argument, express confidence in doing better than the norm, and, whenever possible, stay away from specific job titles unless pressed.

Do you think people in your occupation should be paid more?

This one can be used prior to serious salary negotiation to probe your awareness of how your job really contributes to the bottom line. Or it can occur in the middle of salary negotiations to throw you off balance. The safe and correct answer is to straddle the fence. "Most jobs have salary ranges that reflect the job's relative importance and contribution to a company. Those salary ranges reflect the norm for the great majority of people within that profession. That does not mean, however, that the extraordinary people in such a group are not recognized for their extra performance and skills. There are always exceptions to the rule."

Once an Offer Is on the Table

You don't have to accept or reject the first offer, whatever it is. In most instances you can improve the initial offer in a number of ways, but you have to know something about the existing market conditions for people in your line of work. If you are female, bear in mind that simply settling for a few points above your current rate of pay is bad advice for anyone and downright crazy for you.

The Women's Bureau of the U.S. Department of Labor tells us that men out-earn women in nearly every field. (For what it's worth, my research could not turn up a single industry in which this was not the case.) Even if a woman's responsibilities, background, and accomplishments are exactly the same as those of her male colleague, she is statistically unlikely to take home a paycheck equal to his. According to the Women's Bureau, male engineers make 14.3 percent more than their female counterparts. Male mathematicians make 16.3 percent more. Male advertising and public relations professionals make 28 percent more. Male lawyers and judges make 28 percent more. And male editors and reporters make a whopping 43 percent more than women performing the same or comparable work. No offense intended, but I think that this salary-parity gap will only be closed when every professional woman knows her true worth and has the ability to succinctly communicate what she brings to the table, plus the knowledge and willingness to use negotiating skills and determination to her own benefit.

Man or woman, there is no guarantee you are being paid what you are worth. The simple facts are these: If you don't get it while they want you and don't have you, you sure can't count on getting it once they do have you. When a thirty-year-old under-negotiates his salary by just $4,000 on a new job, it will cost him a minimum of $140,000 over the course of a career. Remember, every subsequent raise will come from a proportionately lower base; factor in inflation, and real dollars lost over an entire career span could actually be double this figure.

Salaries are fairly standardized, so the majority of offers will come within your negotiating range. But even if the offer is fair or even exceptional, you can still negotiate.

The state of the job market can impact negotiations, too: When supply exceeds demand negotiating upward is harder. Nevertheless, with an offer on the table, the hiring manager has made the decision that he can hire you and get back to work; he and everyone else wants to be done with this project. Negotiate in good faith and your negotiations will be accepted in the same way.

The formal offer can fall into one of two categories:

- It sounds fair and equitable: In this case, you still want to negotiate for a little more—employers almost expect it of you, so don't disappoint them. Mention a salary range again, the low end of which comes at about the level of their offer and the high end somewhat above it. You can say, "Well it certainly seems that we are close. I was hoping for something more in the range of *$xx,000* to *$yyy,000*. How much room do we have for negotiation here?"

  No one will withdraw an offer because you say you feel you are worth more. After all, the interviewer thinks you are the best person for the job and has extended a formal offer, and the last thing he needs now is to start from square one again. The employer has a vested interest in bringing the negotiation to a satisfactory conclusion. At worst, he can stick to the original offer.

- It isn't quite what you expected: Even if the offer isn't what you thought it would be, you still have options other than accepting or rejecting the offer as it stands. Your strategy for now is to run the money topic as far as you can in a calm and businesslike way. Once you have gone that far, you can back off and examine the other potential benefits of the job. That way you will leave yourself with an opening, if you need it, to hit the money topic once more at the close of negotiations.

If you feel the salary could do with a boost, say so. "I like the job, and I know I have what it takes to be successful in it. I would also be prepared to give you a start date of [e.g.] March 1 to show my sincerity. But quite honestly, I couldn't justify it with your initial salary offer. I hope we have some room for negotiation here."

Or you can say, "I could start on March 1, and I do feel I could make a contribution here and become an integral part of the team. The only thing standing in the way is my inability to make ends meet based on your initial offer. I am very interested in the opportunity and flattered by your interest in me. If we could just solve this money problem, I'm sure we could come to terms. What do you think can be done about it?"

The interviewer will probably come back with a question asking how much you want. "What is the minimum you would be prepared to work for?" he might ask. You can reply, "I'd really like to make at least [now respond with your midpoint]. Is something in this range going to be a stumbling block?"

Depending on the interviewer's response, this is the time to be noncommittal but encouraging and move on to the benefits included with the position: "Well, yes, that is a little better. Perhaps we should talk about the benefits."

Alternatively, the interviewer may come back with another question: "That's beyond our salary range for this job title. How far can you reduce your salary needs to fit our range?"

This question shows good faith and a desire to close the deal, but don't give in too easily—the interviewer is never going to want you as much as he does now. Your first response might be: "I appreciate that, but if it is the job title and its accompanying range that is causing the problem, couldn't we upgrade the title, thereby putting me near the bottom of the next range?" Try it—sometimes it works. If it doesn't, it is probably time to move to other negotiable aspects of the job offer.

Evaluating Non-Salary Factors

Money is important, but your career trajectory more so. New jobs are pivotal points in your life that affect not just this job and the next couple of years, but your whole life going forward. They shouldn't represent decisions made without thought or purely on salary.

If you have plans for your life, this isn't just another job: It's a step along your chosen path, so you want to land in an outfit that will help move you toward your goals. To find out if this is the job for you, ask a few questions relevant to your situation:

The Job and Its Potential

- How long has the job been open?
- Why is it open? Who held the job last?
- What is she doing now? Promoted, fired, or quit?
- How long was she in that job?
- How many people have held this job in the last three years? Where are they now?
- How often have people been promoted from this position—and how many, and where to?
- Who in the company was in this position the shortest length of time? Why? Who has remained in this position the longest? Why?

Other questions that might follow include:

- What does it take to succeed in this job?
- Who fails in this job and why?
- What personality traits do you consider critical to success in this job?
- What kind of training does the company provide/encourage/support?
- How long have you held this position?
- Why did you choose to work here?
- Tell me about your management style.
- How often will we meet?
- How frequent are performance and salary reviews? Are they weighted toward merit and performance, and if so, how?
- How does the performance appraisal and reward system work? Exactly how are outstanding employees recognized, judged, and rewarded?
- To what extent are the functions of the department recognized as important and worthy of review by upper management?
- Where and how does my department fit into the food chain?
- What does the department hope to achieve in the next two to three years? How will that help the company?
- What do you see as the strengths of the department? What do you see as weaknesses?
- What role do you see me playing in the department?
- What informal and formal benchmarks will you use to measure my effectiveness and contributions?
- Based on my effectiveness, how long would you anticipate me holding this position? When my position and responsibilities change, what are the possible titles and responsibilities I might grow into?
- What is the official corporate policy on internal promotion? How many people in this department have been promoted from their original positions since joining the company?
- How do I pursue promotion and how do you determine my suitability?
- What training and professional development programs are available?
- How does the company support independent skill development initiatives?
- Does the company sponsor all or part of any costs?
- What are the potential career paths within the company for someone with my job title?
- To what jobs have people with my title risen in the company?

Corporate Culture

All companies have their own way of doing things—that's corporate culture. Not every corporate culture is for you:

- What is the company's mission? What are the company's goals?
- What approach does this company take to its marketplace?
- What is unique about the way this company operates?
- What is the best thing you know about this company? What is the worst thing you know about this company?
- How does the reporting structure work? What are the accepted channels of communication and how do they work?
- What kinds of checks and balances, reports, or other work-measurement tools are used in the department and company?
- What advice would you give me about fitting into the corporate culture—about understanding the way you do things here?
- Will I be encouraged or discouraged from learning about the company beyond my own department?

Company Growth and Direction

For those concerned about employment stability and career growth, a healthy company is mandatory:

- What expansion is planned for this department, division, or facility?
- What is your value proposition to prospective customers?
- When you lose a deal, to whom do you lose it?
- What markets does the company anticipate developing?
- Does the company have plans for mergers or acquisitions?
- Currently, what new endeavors is the company actively pursuing?
- How do market trends affect company growth and progress? What is being done about them?
- What production and employee layoffs and cutbacks have you experienced in the last three years?
- What production and employee layoffs and cutbacks do you anticipate? How are they likely to affect this department, division, or facility?
- When was the last corporate reorganization? How did it affect this department? When will the next corporate reorganization occur? How will it affect this department?
- Is this department a profit center? How does that affect remuneration?

Benefits

Following is a listing of commonly available benefits. Although many of these benefits are available to all employees at some companies, you should know that, as a rule of thumb, the higher up the ladder you climb, the more benefits you can expect. Because the corporate world and its methods of creating a motivated and committed workforce are constantly in flux, never assume that a particular benefit will be available to you.

The basic rule is to ask—if you don't ask, there is no way you will get it. A few years ago, it would have been unthinkable that anyone but an executive could expect something as glamorous as an athletic club membership in a benefits package. Today, however, more companies have a membership as a standard benefit, and an increasing number are even building their own health club facilities. Benefits that may be available to you, if you ask, include:

- 401(k) and other investment matching programs
- "Cafeteria" insurance plans—you pick the insurance benefits you want
- A signing bonus
- A performance review after a specified number of days (90/120), followed by a raise
- A title promotion after a specified period
- A year-end bonus
- Car or car allowance
- Car insurance, maintenance, and/or gas
- Compensation days—for unpaid overtime/business travel time
- Country club or health club membership
- Accidental death insurance
- Deferred compensation
- Dental insurance—note deductibles and the percentage that is employer paid
- Employment contract and/or termination contract
- Expense account
- Financial planning and tax assistance
- Life insurance
- Medical insurance—note deductibles and percentage that is employer paid
- Optical insurance—note deductibles and percentage that is employer paid
- Paid sick leave
- Pension plans
- Personal days off
- Profit sharing
- Short- or long-term disability compensation plans
- Stock options
- Vacation

You can ask these questions over the phone, or request another meeting to review these points. I prefer the latter because you get to meet everyone as the new member of the team and the boss is buoyant because he can at last get back to work. These factors encourage agreement with reasonable requests, as might a *tiny* worry that you might walk and leave them back at square one.

You may get nothing more than the standard package, but you have nothing to lose by asking and everything to gain. Once the package is straightened out, *come back to the base salary one last time*: "I want the job, Charlie. I'm excited by the opportunity of working for you and joining the company, but is there anything we can do about the starting salary?" *The answer to this question is going to determine what the final offer will be.*

Negotiating Stock Options

Stock options, while typically handled in a separate document, will be offered at the same time as your other benefits. It is usually best to address the stock issue once all the others have been settled.

In good economic times, employers turn to stock options as an effective recruitment and retention incentive. Options give you the right to purchase a set amount of stock in the company at a predetermined price (usually attractive) and over a fixed period of time. In exercising your options (buying the stock), you need to remember that stocks can and do decrease in value, sometimes dramatically.

There are several types of stock options, each with its own specific tax ramifications. However, as an employee, you are most likely to be offered "incentive stock options." Fortunately, with this type of option, you only have to pay taxes on your gains when you sell the stock; if you keep the stock for at least a year after purchase, you will not have to pay capital gains tax.

When negotiating stock options, always bear in mind that they are a gamble. The employer is going to talk about the offered stock options as if they were money in the bank, but they are not. Don't get bamboozled by rosy descriptions of the company's future; stay focused instead on the current market value of the stock. This is especially important if you are being asked to accept options as part of your overall compensation package. In some instances, you can be asked to accept options in lieu of cash. If the options you are offered are in any way meant to replace salary, think carefully, as you can't eat stock options.

If you are accepting a job with a publicly traded company, learn the value and performance of that stock by obtaining public records. On the other hand, if the company is privately held, you'll have to rely on the information that is provided to you by the employer. In this instance, consider market segment, business strategy, operations, liquidity, and senior management track record. In effect, you are evaluating your faith in the company, the imminence of their going public, and whether or not the company is a start-up or a well-established entity.

Of course, if the stock options do not impact your take-home pay, it can't hurt to get as many as you can. There is a big difference between getting the options and actually exercising your right to buy and sell them. Your considerations will include: what the purchase price will be, when you can exercise your options, and the restrictions on when you can buy the stock and when you can sell it. These matters will all be laid out in the separate options agreement furnished by the employer at the same time as the employment agreement, so read it carefully before you start negotiations in this area.

Everything to do with stock is negotiable, so you don't have to accept whatever you are offered without question and negotiation. Naturally, you will ask for more options than you are initially offered. You may not exercise those options, but having them available is in your best interests.

Your stock options will have a vesting period—the length of time you must work for the company before you can exercise your options. The employer, who is using the options as a retention tool, wants the vesting period to be as long as possible, thus tying you to the company with the lure of the stock. You, on the other hand, want to shorten the vesting period and, if possible, get an "incremental vesting schedule."

An incremental vesting schedule allows you to buy a few shares every month or quarter, probably getting you fully vested in the same period of time, but in smaller, more frequent steps along the way. Another reasonable request is to ask for "accelerated vesting" in the event of the employer merging or being bought by another company. This way, you become fully vested at the time of the acquisition.

Your agreement will also limit the time period in which you can exercise your options—not only when you can first exercise them, but also the point at which your option ends. For your financial flexibility, you will want to negotiate to extend this period as far as you can, even after you leave the company. For example, if you have a noncompete clause, you are essentially still tied to the company for a specific period of time, so it is reasonable to ask if you can exercise your options through the same period of time covered by your noncompete and nondisclosure clauses.

If you are not offered a "cashless exercise provision" you should certainly negotiate for it. A cashless exercise provision allows you to buy stock without spending any of your hard-earned money. The way it works is that when you buy a block of stock, you are simultaneously allowed to sell as many shares as are required to cover the costs of buying the stock; hence it becomes a cashless exercise, leaving you with the stock but not out of pocket.

Getting the stock options is one thing. Exercising them is another step, which you will not want to take without professional financial counsel.

Raises, Bonuses, Promotions, and Other Goodies

Here are a few arrangements corporate headhunters frequently negotiate for their recruits:

- A single, lump-sum signing bonus—nice to have, but it is money here today and gone tomorrow. Don't make the mistake of adding it onto the base. If you get a $2,500 signing bonus, that money won't be figured in for your year-end review—your raise will be based on your actual salary, so the bonus is less meaningful than it appears.
- A 60-, 90-, or 120-day performance review with raise attached. You can frequently negotiate a minimum percentage increase here if you have confidence in your abilities.
- A title promotion and raise after two, three, or four months.

- A year-end bonus. When you hear talk about a year-end bonus, don't rely on "what it's going to be this year" or "what it was last year," because the actual bonus will never bear any resemblance to either figure. Base your estimate of any bonus on a five-year performance history.
- Things other than cash. Also in the realm of real disposable income are things like a company car, gas, maintenance, and insurance. They represent hard dollars you would not have to spend. It's not unusual to hear of employers paying car and/or insurance allowances, picking up servicing bills for your personal automobile, or paying gas up to a certain amount each month. But if you don't ask, you can never expect an employer to offer. What have you got to lose? The worst that can happen is that the employer declines. Remember to get any of those unusual goodies in writing—even respectable managers in respected companies can suffer amnesia.

Employment Obligations and Restrictions

Any verbal offer you accept is dependent on the offer being in writing and you being comfortable with what's in the employment agreement. Pay careful attention to what the company will ask of you in signing the agreement. Employment contracts are legal documents designed to obfuscate and intimidate the neophyte. You can and should take the time to have it explained and then take it home and see if you agree with that interpretation; if in doubt, take it to any employment lawyer.

Your employment contract may include:

Assignment of Inventions

If you create anything during the period of your employment, the company may require you to turn it over. This may include work you do on your own time if it relates to your duties at the company.

Nondisclosure Clauses

Companies will likely require that you not discuss company business with any outside source to prevent the competition from learning company secrets. The language is likely to be general and thus unfavorable to you. If you're concerned about this, try to get the language more specific.

Noncompete Clauses

The company may want to restrict you from working for competitors after you leave the company. This can have a negative impact on your future career, since it restricts your employability. Try to make the language more specific.

Severance

Negotiate for as extensive a severance package as you can—say, a month's salary for every year of employment or every $10,000 of salary, with outplacement/job search assistance. Since outplacement is only as good as the person giving it, it is preferable to negotiate a dollar amount so that you can spend the money in the way you think most suitable to your needs and with the consultant of your choice.

If you sign a noncompete clause, request that your severance extend through the entire period of your noncompete restrictions. This is a perfectly reasonable request that should be accommodated without trouble.

Relocation

When job-related relocation comes around, we all find ourselves in an ocean of unexpected expenses. So once the overall offer is acceptable to you, key in on relocation issues. Many companies expect to pay all or part of your relocation costs unless you live within fifty miles of your new workplace, in which case you are usually on your own. Since the employer regularly addresses these issues, you should not be reticent about negotiating them.

Relocation packages vary enormously from person to person and company to company. However, if they want you badly enough, employers will usually try to accommodate reasonable requests.

The higher up the corporate ladder you climb, the more relocation services you are likely to receive. On the low end, you may get offered reimbursement for a moving truck and a few hundred dollars for incidental expenses. While the employer expects to bear the cost of your relocation, every dollar spent affects the bottom line of the HR department. So no matter where you stand on the corporate ladder, getting above and beyond the standard offer will require your asking for it.

For example, companies know your relocation costs will be treated as taxable income, but they won't say anything about it unless you do. Explain that the taxes you expect to pay can amount to 30 percent of the monies spent, and that this would place a heavy burden on you financially. With a typical executive relocation running around $50,000, the tax implications of relocating to accept a new job could come as a nasty shock. Ask that the company pick up the personal income tax burdens you incur as a result of your move.

Only some aspects of your relocation are tax deductible. For example, the costs of moving your personal belongings and one trip to the new location are deductible, but house-hunting trips and the costs of temporary accommodation are not.

Other things you can ask the company to help or reimburse you for include:

- House-hunting trips before you start. After all, it is in the best interests of the company to have you settled as quickly as possible.
- Temporary housing costs while you find a suitable permanent residence. Again, most companies will comply with at least thirty days, sometimes as many as 90 to 120 days.

- Shipping of autos, boats, and so on.
- Costs of a professional moving company packing, shipping, and delivering your household goods.
- Costs of selling and buying a house if you are a homeowner.
- Job search assistance for a working spouse. Try to get a dollar amount so that you can choose your service provider. Come to *www.knockemdead.com* for advice on coaching services.
- Help in finding schools for the kids.
- Orientation programs for the new community.

It will help your negotiating position to estimate these costs in advance. You can pick up the phone and request estimates, or you can visit websites like *www.homefair.com* which have electronic calculation tools and cost-of-living comparisons. The latter will help you evaluate how far a dollar will go in the new town in comparison with where you live today.

When it comes to offer letters and employment agreements, the employer naturally hopes that you will accept them as they are presented, but you are under no obligation to do so. Every aspect of the offer is negotiable, and as these are largely issues that have not arisen in the interview cycle, the employer will expect a savvy professional to address them. Remember: *This is probably the only time in your relationship with your new employer when you'll have even a slim negotiating edge.*

Handling References When a Job Offer Arrives

A few words here on handling your references when an offer is imminent. When references get checked, employment dates and leaving salary are always verified; don't think of fudging, as it is cause for a dismissal that could dog your footsteps for years. Beyond that, your immediate past manager is the one most likely to be checked. Depending on the company and your level, coworkers and other past managers can also be contacted.

Call potential references, describe the job you have been (or are about to be) offered, explain why you think it is a good opportunity and why you believe you can be successful (omit these details when talking to exact peers unless the offer is already in the bag). Ask if they think it would be a good fit, and why.

You can then, if it's appropriate and time allows, tell the reference some of the questions he might be asked. These might include the time you have known each other; your relationship to each other; the title you worked under (be sure to remind your reference of promotions and title changes); your five or six most important duties; the key projects you worked on; your greatest strengths; your greatest weaknesses; your attitudes toward your job, your peers, and management; the timeliness, quality, and quantity of your work; your willingness to achieve above and beyond the call of duty (remind him of all those weekends you worked); whether he would rehire you (if company policy forbids rehiring, make sure your reference will mention this); your earnings; and any additional comments the reference would like to make. This whole list may be an overwhelming amount of information to unload on a colleague, so pass on questions tailored to your situation.

If you have any doubt about the quality of a pivotal reference, take the precaution of having a friend do a dummy check on all references just to confirm what they will say when the occasion arises. Of course, this only works if that friend is a consummate professional capable of carrying it off! This way you can distinguish the excellent references from the merely good.

Better yet, go to *www.allisontaylor.com*, the leader in the reference-checking business. For a modest fee (about $80 for a basic reference check), they verify references on your behalf. That way you'll know in advance just who will be your best spokespeople.

Offer Letters and Employment Agreements

Never resign an existing job until you have an acceptable written offer in hand. The rule is: if you don't have an offer in writing, you don't have an offer. When that offer letter or employment agreement does arrive, you are in the final stages of negotiation. This is the time when you'll see if the written offer reflects your understanding of previous conversations, and you'll see if there are some things still to negotiate.

An offer letter should include specifics about your compensation package, start date, benefits, policies and procedures, and relocation issues; an employee handbook detailing everything you are entitled to as an employee may well accompany the offer letter.

Employment agreements become more common the higher up the corporate ladder you climb and the more critical your work becomes to the success of the corporation. An employment agreement is a more restrictive document that goes into greater detail about what you can and cannot do as a result of employment with the company.

In the employment agreement, you'll find everything you would in an offer letter, plus issues such as assignment of inventions, nondisclosure, noncompete, severance, and relocation, all of which are all likely to be addressed in detail. Any stock option agreement will probably be in a separate document but presented to you at the same time as the formal offer. As these contracts can be extremely limiting and even affect your employability after you leave the company, you may wish to consult with counsel. An employment lawyer can review and advise you on the specific implications of each clause and help you with revised and less restrictive wording. As you will have a solid understanding of the issues, you will be able to phrase your questions succinctly and control the costs of any such legal consultation.

Once you have a clear understanding of the complete offer, review it with the employer: "I understand the offer is . . ." and after itemizing the components of the offer, finish by asking, "Is this your best and final offer?" With this question, you must look the interviewer directly in the eye, and maintain eye contact. Remember that the *tone* in which such a question is delivered is important: With the wrong intonation this can be interpreted as combative.

Evaluating the Offer

Once the offer has been negotiated to the best of your ability, you need to evaluate it—and that doesn't have to be done on the spot. Some of your requests and questions will take time to get answered, and very often the final parts of negotiation—"Yes, Mr. Jones, we can give you the extra $10,000 and six months of vacation you requested"—will take place over the telephone. Regardless of where the final negotiations are completed, *never accept or reject the offer on the spot.*

Be positive, say how excited you are about the prospect and that you would like a little time (overnight, a day, two days) to think it over, discuss it with your spouse, whatever. Not only is this delay standard practice, but it will also give you the opportunity to leverage other offers, as discussed in Chapter 27.

Use the time you gain to speak to your mentors or advisers. First, a word of caution: In asking advice from those close to you, be sure you know exactly where that advice is coming from—you need clear-headed objectivity at this time.

Once the advice is in, and not before, weigh it along with your own observations—no one knows your needs and aspirations better than you do. While there are many ways of doing that, a simple line down the middle of a sheet of paper, with the reasons to take the job written on one side and the reasons to turn it down on the other, is about as straightforward and objective as you can get.

You will weigh salary, future earnings and career prospects, benefits, commute, lifestyle, and stability of the company, along with all those intangibles that are summed up in the term *gut feelings.* Make sure you answer these questions for yourself:

- Do you like the work?
- Can you be trained in a reasonable period of time, thus having a realistic chance of success on the job?
- Are the title and responsibilities likely to provide you with a challenge?
- Is the opportunity for growth in the job compatible with your needs and desires?
- Are the company's location, stability, and reputation in line with your needs?
- Is the atmosphere/culture of the company conducive to your enjoying working at the company?
- Can you get along with your new manager and immediate work group?
- Is the money offer and total compensation package the best you can get?

Notice that money is but one aspect of the evaluation process. There are many other factors to take into account as well. Even a high-paying job can be less advantageous than you think.

For instance, you should be careful not to be foxed by the gross figure. It really is important that you get a firm handle on those actual, spendable, after-tax dollars—the ones with which you pay the rent. Always look at an offer in the light of how many more spendable dollars a week it will put in your pocket.

Accepting New Jobs, Resigning from Others

Once your decision is made, you should accept the job verbally. Spell out exactly what you are accepting: "Mr. Smith, I'd like to accept the position of engineer at a starting salary of $82,000. I will be able to start work on March 1. And I understand my package will include life, health, and dental insurance, a 401(k) plan, and a company car." Then you finish with: "I will be glad to start on the above date pending a written offer received in time to give my present employer adequate notice of my departure. I'm sure that's acceptable to you."

Notify your current employer in the same fashion. Quitting is difficult for almost everyone, so you can write a pleasant resignation letter, walk into your boss's office, hand it to her, then discuss things calmly and pleasantly once she has read it. A career spans upward of half a century, so you don't want to burn bridges today that you may need to cross again tomorrow. Take the time to craft professional documents. One of the companion volumes to this work, *Knock 'em Dead Cover Letters*, will help you create powerful, professional letters for all occasions. The book is full of examples and has specific sections on acceptance, rejection, and resignation letters.

Notify any other companies that have been in negotiation with you that you are no longer on the market but that you were most impressed with meeting them and would like to keep communications open for the future. (See Chapter 27, "Multiple Job Interviews, Multiple Job Offers" for more on this topic.)

It bears repeating that your resignation is not the time to air your grievances; you have simply been presented with a great opportunity and are thankful for the skills this job gave you. This same person may be checked for a reference down the line, and you want the recollections to be positive.

CHAPTER 26
SNATCHING VICTORY FROM THE JAWS OF DEFEAT

REJECTION? IMPOSSIBLE! THEN again, you won't be right for every job. Here are some techniques that help you to create opportunities in the face of rejection.

During the interviewing process, there are bound to be interviewers who come to the erroneous conclusion that you are not the right person for the job they need to fill. When that happens, you will be turned down. Such an absurd travesty of justice can occur in different ways:

- At the interview
- In a letter of rejection
- During your follow-up telephone call

Whenever the turndown comes, you must be emotionally and intellectually prepared to take advantage of the opportunity being offered to you.

When you get turned down for the only prospect you have going, the rejection can be devastating to your ego. That is why I have stressed the wisdom of having at least a few interviews in process at the same time.

You will get turned down. No one can be right for every job. The right person for a job doesn't always get it; however, the best prepared and most determined often does. While you may be responsible in part for the initial rejection, you still have the power to correct the situation and win the job offer. What you do with the claimed victory is a different matter—you will then be in a seller's market with choice and control of your situation.

Almost every job you desire is obtainable once you understand the hiring process from the interviewer's side of the desk. Your initial—and temporary—rejection is attributable to one of these reasons:

- The interviewer does not feel you can do the job.
- The interviewer feels you lack a successful profile.
- The interviewer did not feel your personality would contribute to the smooth functioning of the department—perhaps you didn't portray yourself as either a *team player* or as someone willing to take the extra step.

With belief in yourself, you can still succeed. Repeat to yourself constantly through the interview cycle: "I will get this job, because no one else can give as much to this company as I can!" Do that and implement the following plan immediately when you hear of rejection, whether in person, via mail, or over the telephone:

- **Step One:** Thank the interviewer for the time and consideration. Then ask politely: "To help my future job search, why wasn't I chosen for the position?" Assure the interviewer that you would truly appreciate an honest, objective analysis. Listen to the reply and do not interrupt. Use your time constructively and take notes. When the company representative finishes speaking, show that you understood the comments. (Remember, understanding and agreeing are different animals.)

  "Thank you, Mr. Smith, now I can understand the way you feel. Because I don't interview that often I'm afraid my nerves got in the way. I'm very interested in working for your company [*use an enthusiastic tone*] and am determined to get the job. Let me meet with you once again. This time, when I'm not so nervous, I am confident you will see I really do have the skills you require [*then provide an example of a skill you have in the questionable area*]. You name the time and the place, and I will be there. What's best for you, Mr. Smith?"

  End with a question, of course, and note here that you're asking *when* you can meet again, and not *if*. An enthusiastic request like that is very difficult to refuse and will usually get you another interview—an interview, of course, at which you must shine.

- **Step Two:** Check your notes and accept the company representative's concerns. Their validity is irrelevant; the important point is that the negative points represent the problem areas in the interviewer's perception of you. List the negative perceptions, and using the techniques, exercises, and value keys discussed throughout the book, develop different ways to overcome or compensate for every negative perception.
- **Step Three:** Reread Part III of this book.
- **Step Four:** Practice aloud the statements and responses you will use at the interview. If you can practice with someone who plays the part of the interviewer, that's even better. This will create a real interview atmosphere and increase your chances of success. Lacking a role-play partner, you can create that live answer by putting the anticipated objections and questions on a tape and responding to them.
- **Step Five:** Study all available information on the company.
- **Step Six:** Congratulate yourself continually for getting another interview after initial rejection. This is proof of your self-worth, ability, and tenacity. You have nothing to lose and everything to gain, having already risen phoenix-like from the ashes of defeat.
- **Step Seven:** During the interview, ask for the job in a positive and enthusiastic manner. Your drive and staying power will impress the interviewer. All you must do to win the job is overcome the perceived negatives, and you have been given the time and information to prepare. Go for it.
- **Step Eight:** Even when all has failed at the subsequent interview, do not leave without a final request for the job. Play your trump card: "Mr. Smith, I respect the fact that you allowed me the opportunity to prove myself here today. I am convinced I am the best person for the job. I want you to give me a trial, and I will prove on the job that I am the best hiring decision you have made this year. Will you give us both the opportunity?"

A reader once wrote to me as I was revising *Knock 'em Dead*, "I read the chapter entitled 'Snatching Victory from the Jaws of Defeat' and did everything you said to salvage what appeared to be a losing interview. My efforts did make a very good impression on the interviewer, but as it was finally explained to me, I really did not have equal qualifications for the job, and finally came in a close second. I really want to work for this growing company, and they say they have another position coming up in six months. What should I do?"

I also know of someone who wanted a job working for a major airline. He had been recently laid off and had high hopes for a successful interview. As it happened, he too came in second for the position. He was told that the firm would speak to him again in the near future. So he waited—for eight months. Finally, he realized that waiting for the job would only leave him unemployed. The moral of the story is that you must be brutally objective when you come out second best, and, whatever the interviewer says, you must sometimes assume that you are getting the polite brush-off.

With that in mind, let's see what can be done on the positive side. First of all, send a thank-you note to the interviewer, acknowledging your understanding of the state of affairs and reaffirming your desire to work for the company. Conclude with a polite request to bear you in mind for the future.

Keep an eye out for any news item about the company in the press. Whenever you see something, cut it out and mail it to the interviewer with a very brief note that says something like: "I came across this in *Forbes* and thought you might find it interesting. I am still determined to be your next account manager, so please keep me in mind when the next opening occurs."

You can also call the interviewer once every couple of months, just to check in. Remember, of course, to keep the phone call brief and polite—you simply want to keep your name at the top of the interviewer's mind.

And maybe something will come of it. Ultimately, however, your only choice is to move on. There is nothing to gain waiting on an interviewer's word. Go out and keep looking, because chances are that you will come up with an even better job. Then, if you still want to work for that company that gave you the brush-off, you will have some leverage.

Most people fail in their endeavors by quitting just before the dawn of success. Follow these directions and you can win the job. You have proven yourself to be a fighter, and that is universally admired. The company representative will want you to succeed because you are made of stuff that is rarely seen today. You are a person of guts, drive, and endurance—the hallmarks of a winner. Job turndowns are opportunities to exercise and build on your strengths, and, by persisting, you may well add to your growing number of job offers, now and in the future.

CHAPTER 27
MULTIPLE JOB INTERVIEWS, MULTIPLE JOB OFFERS

RELYING ON ONE interview at a time can only lead to anxiety, so you must create and foster an ever-growing network of interviews and, consequently, job offers.

False optimism and laziness lead many job hunters to be content with only one interview in process at any given time. That severely reduces the odds of landing the best job in town within your chosen time frame. Complacency guarantees that you will continue to operate in a buyer's market.

The recommended approach is to generate as many interviews as possible in a two- to three-week period. Interviewing skills are learned and consequently improve with practice. With the improved skills comes a greater confidence, and those natural interview nerves disperse. Your confidence shows through to potential employers, and you are perceived in a positive light. Because other companies are interested in you, everyone will move more quickly to secure your services. This is especially important if you are unfortunate enough to be unemployed. Being out of work is when you need money the most and is the time when the salary you can command on the open market is substantially reduced. The interview activity you generate will help offset this.

By generating multiple interviews, you bring the time of the first job offer closer and closer. That one job offer can be quickly parlayed into a number of others. And with a single job offer, your unemployed status has, to all intents and purposes, passed.

Immediately, you can call every company with whom you've met, and explain the situation. "Mr. Johnson, I'm calling because while still under consideration with your company I have received a job offer from one of your competitors. I would hate to make a decision without the chance of speaking with you again. I was very impressed by my meeting with you. Can we get together in the next couple of days?" End, of course, with a question that carries the conversation forward.

If you were in the running at all, your call will usually generate another interview; Mr. Johnson does not want to miss out on a suddenly prized commodity. Remember: It is human nature to want the very things one is about to lose. Your simple offer can be multiplied almost by the number of interviews you have in process at the time.

A single job offer can also be used to generate interviews with new firms. It is as simple as making your usual telephone networking presentation, but it ends differently. You would be very interested in meeting with them because of your knowledge of the company/product/service, but also because you have just received a job offer—would it be possible to get together in the next couple of days?

Relying on one interview at a time can only lead to prolonged anxiety, disappointment, and, possibly, unemployment. That reliance is due to the combination of false optimism, laziness, and fear of rejection. Those are traits that cannot be tolerated except by confirmed defeatists, for defeat is the inevitable result of those traits. As Heraclitus said, "A man's character is his fate." Headhunters say, "The job offer that cannot fail will."

Self-esteem, on the other hand, is vital to your success, and happiness is found with it. With it you will awake each day with previously unknown vitality. Your vigor will increase, your enthusiasm will rise, and a desire to achieve will burn within. The more you do today, the better you will feel tomorrow.

Even when you follow this plan to the letter, not every interview will result in an offer. But with many irons in the fire, an occasional firm "no" should not affect your morale. It won't be the first or last time you face rejection. Be persistent and, above all, close your mind to all negative influences. The success you experience from implementing this plan will increase your store of willpower and determination, affect the successful outcome of your job search, and enrich your whole life. Start today.

The key to your success is preparation. Failing is easy—it requires no effort. It is the achievement of success that requires effort, and that means effort today, not tomorrow, for tomorrow never comes. So start building that well-stocked briefcase today.

CHAPTER 28
CLOUDS ON THE HORIZON

YOU HAVE GUARANTEED employment, in exchange for total dedication and an endless workweek for just as long as it takes ThemInc. to automate your job out of existence or export it to Mumbai.

Even with a recovering economy layoffs are happening to professionals at every level and everyday, as technology continually empowers employers to do a little more with a little less manpower and with cheaper employees. This means that competition in job search is stiffer than it was a decade ago. So you have to ask yourself: Where would a layoff leave me? What would I do? Am I prepared?

Why Those Who Expect It Least Get Sideswiped

Longer-term employees are the most likely to feel fireproof. Having avoided prior restructuring and layoffs, you can make the mistake of ignoring what is going on right under your nose.

The higher you climb and the longer you are with a company, your experience and seniority cost more, your insurance costs more, your perks cost more, and you are considered more likely to coast on your experience and current skills set. If you aren't adding new skill sets every year, you are rapidly becoming obsolete.

Together these considerations make loyal longer-term employees especially vulnerable to unexpected layoffs.

Watch ThemInc. Like a Hungry Hawk

But with your eyes and ears open, you can know as much as the CEO and the board. An accountant can see that revenues are not meeting expenditures. A salesperson knows when quotas aren't being met. More lawyers, consultants, and strangers in suits being lunched by senior management are all signs of change. So are cost-cutting measures (no lights in parking lots, for example), outsourcing, and bonus reductions or elimination. You suddenly feel out of the knowledge loop, you are suddenly reassigned, or surprisingly you start to get bad reviews. These are all signs of a coming doom.

So are new projects being put on hold, a forthcoming merger or acquisition, and the slamming shut of the normal open-door culture of your company. There is an increase in senior management's meetings and no information about their content is available.

By thinking carefully about the events that affect your department or position and those other departments with whom you interact (discreetly, of course), you can monitor the health and business activities of your employer through third parties.

Subscribe to industry news websites. You'll benefit in many ways from this, apart from staying abreast of breaking news about mergers and layoffs. Google mergers, acquisitions, and layoffs regularly as separate search terms. You should also check out these sites that offer warning of forthcoming mergers and layoffs and advice on how to protect yourself:

- *www.thetruthaboutmortgage.com/a-list-of-recent-mortgage-closures-mergers-and-layoffs/*
- *http://employee-benefits.lawyers.com/employee-benefits/protect-yourself-in-a-merger.html*

When you catch the smell of mergers and layoffs on the wind, don't swallow the official company propaganda, because the last thing you want is to be caught in an unexpected job search with 500 or more of your closest friends. For example: Read Intel Says Layoff of 5000 is Not

Firing. Rumors of any restructuring are a clear signal that people will lose their jobs no matter what the company says.

Why ThemInc. Lies

Technology has changed the nature of employment forever. Today's employers and markets are ultracompetitive, geared toward sudden technological shifts, and increasingly global in nature. All companies—even those showing record profits—are streamlining their organizations. When there are mergers and acquisitions, the elimination of duplicate employees becomes the first order of business, so if you are an employee of the "merge," your head could well be on the chopping block.

No matter what fairy tales ThemInc. feeds you, they will lie because they have to. It is their responsibility to get maximum profitability out of the workforce, and telling you the truth isn't always in their best interests.

MeInc. and the New Career Management

Most people don't think about the unthinkable until it has happened, but you live in an uncertain world that demands a more pragmatic approach to your career management strategies. It's businesslike and plain common sense in a world without security, to find ways to treat the financial stability of you and yours in a more businesslike way.

As the CEO of MeInc., you are required to manage the company's strategic planning initiatives. You have to create options to fall back on in the event of potential setbacks. This strategic planning orientation is something MeInc. needs to learn from ThemInc. It's something you can easily do; just get to know people in strategic planning jobs, show an interest in their work, and learn what they think, how they think, and what their research resources are.

When You See Clouds on the Horizon

You take a number of simultaneous courses of action, geared to insure current employment as much as possible while creating a firm foundation from which to launch a job search:

- Collect job postings for what will be your replacement job. Look for skill sets you are missing and immediately start developing these skills. This makes you more marketable and makes your current job more secure.
- Establish a LinkedIn profile, join groups relevant to your profession, and start expanding your professional networks by connecting with everyone who:

- Is in your profession
- Is in your geography
- Holds the same job title
- (Even better) holds job titles two to three levels above you

Don't state anywhere on this profile that you are looking for a job. It won't attract a recruiter (who is only attracted by skills) and it could jeopardize your current employment.

Rethink Your Resume

This document is central to your success; it isn't something to leave until the last moment or do in a half-arsed way. When your resume works, you work; when it doesn't, you don't. This is the document that opens the doors of opportunity. It needs to be brought up-to-date in order to perform in a modern job. Looking forward, always keep it current in the event of clouds appearing on your horizon, or God forbid, a headhunter calling because you were smart enough to create a compelling LI profile.

When Opportunities Arise

All MeInc. corporations have two operating procedures in common:

1. Whenever a job opportunity comes along, you take it because you need the experience. Your ability to turn interviews into job offers is critical to MeInc.'s long-term success and, placed in context of a long career, is probably the weakest of all your professional skills.
2. Because of this, you go to a job interview to get the job offer. Nothing else matters. You don't have to accept the job (no thanks, nothing personal), but you do need to build the skills that generate job offers.

It may be sunny today, but you know the deluge will come and your survival and success depend on your being prepared.

GET A FREE RESUME REVIEW FROM MARTIN YATE!
Go to the website of the store where you bought the book, write an honest review,
and send the link with your resume to *MartinYate@KnockEmDead.com*.

General Index

INDEX OF INTERVIEW QUESTIONS